Teaching Models
in Education of the Gifted

Teaching Models in Education of the Gifted

THIRD EDITION

C. June Maker
Shirley W. Schiever

pro·ed
An International Publisher
8700 Shoal Creek Boulevard
Austin, Texas 78757-6897
800/987-3202   Fax 800/397-7633
www.proedinc.com

An International Publisher

© 1982, 1995, 2005 by PRO-ED, Inc.
8700 Shoal Creek Boulevard
Austin, Texas 78757-6897
800/897-3202   Fax 800/397-7633
www.proedinc.com

Library of Congress Cataloging-in-Publication Data

Maker, C. June.
    Teaching models in education of the gifted / C. June Maker, Shirley W. Shiever.—3rd ed.
        p. cm.
    Includes bibliographical references and index.
    ISBN 0-89079-999-7 (hc : alk. paper)
    1. Gifted children—Education.   I. Shiever, Shirley W.   II. Title.

LC3993.M293 2004
371.95—dc22

2004053444

Art Director: Jason Crosier
Designer: Nancy McKinney-Point
This book is designed in Minion and Gill Sans.

Printed in the United States of America

1 2 3 4 5 6 7 8 9 10   09 08 07 06 05

Contents

Preface ■ **vii**

Chapter 1
The Role of Teaching–Learning Models
in Curriculum Development
for the Gifted ■ **1**

Chapter 2
George T. Betts and Jolene K. Kercher:
The Autonomous Learner Model ■ **27**

Chapter 3
Benjamin Bloom and David Krathwohl:
The Cognitive and Affective
Taxonomies ■ **83**

Chapter 4
Jerome Bruner:
The Basic Structure of a Discipline ■ **129**

Chapter 5
C. June Maker and Shirley W. Schiever:
The DISCOVER Curriculum Model ■ **165**

Chapter 6
Sidney Parnes:
Creative Problem Solving ■ **195**

Chapter 7
Problem Based Learning ■ **231**

Chapter 8
Joseph S. Renzulli: The Enrichment Triad Model ▪ **257**
Joseph S. Renzulli and Sally M. Reis:
The Schoolwide Enrichment Model ▪ **259**

Chapter 9
Shlomo and Yael Sharan: Group Investigations Model ▪ **293**

Chapter 10
Hilda Taba Teaching Strategies ▪ **327**

Chapter 11
Belle Wallace and Harvey B. Adams:
Thinking Actively in a Social Context ▪ **375**

Chapter 12
Other Models ▪ **409**
Lawrence Kohlberg: Discussions of Moral Dilemmas ▪ **409**
Frank E. Williams: Teaching Strategies
for Thinking and Feeling ▪ **423**
A Promising New Model: Prism of Learning ▪ **435**

Chapter 13
Developing a Comprehensive Curriculum ▪ **449**

References ▪ **511**
Author Index ▪ **529**
Subject Index ▪ **533**

Preface

PURPOSE OF THE BOOK

About 10 years have passed since publication of the second edition of this review of teaching–learning models appropriate for the education of gifted students. Our purpose has not varied, but many changes have occurred in the field of general education, and particularly in the field of education for gifted students. New program models have been developed specifically for gifted students, more research has been done, and new materials have been published. In many areas, special programs are in jeopardy or have been eliminated. Greater emphasis has been placed on the development of programs to serve diverse populations, and the "mainstreaming" of all children into heterogeneous classrooms is practiced widely. The value of including some of the thinking process models in the education of all students has been recognized as well. Some of the models reviewed are recommended to all teachers who want to create a more effective learning environment in their classrooms. This book provides a comprehensive review of teaching–learning models that can be used in the development and implementation of a curriculum for gifted students. In providing this review, we hope to supply enough information to teachers, prospective teachers, program coordinators, and curriculum development specialists to enable them to (a) assess critically the match of the assumptions underlying a model with their own philosophies; (b) evaluate the validity of a model for their intended purposes; (c) apply the model appropriately in any situation; and, most important, (d) implement the model with gifted students. Because of its focus on implementation, the book provides many examples of the use of different models with gifted students of all ages.

This book also serves as a companion volume to *Curriculum Development and Teaching Strategies for Gifted Learners* (Maker, 1982a; Maker & Nielson, 1996). That volume includes modifications of the regular curriculum content, processes, products, and learning environment to make them more appropriate for gifted students. It also provides suggestions for curriculum development, along with examples of appropriate curricula. To implement such a curriculum, however, teachers need more specific teaching strategies, more examples, and more in-depth discussions of the variety of approaches available for teaching gifted students. In effect, this current book provides a variety of alternatives for implementing the general principles described in *Curriculum Development and Teaching Strategies for Gifted Learners.* No single model or way of teaching gifted learners can provide the comprehensive curriculum needed by the students. Therefore, the focus of this book is to help the reader understand a variety of approaches. Comprehension of these approaches assists teachers in designing curricula, taking into consideration the following important factors: (a) the philosophies of the teacher, school, and community that underlie the program goals; (b) the underlying assumptions of the theoretical and practical approaches and how these assumptions mesh with the philosophies of everyone concerned; (c) the varied characteristics and interests of the children; (d) parental concerns; (e) the teaching styles, strengths, and preferences of the teachers; and (f) the physical setting of the school. The product—a functional curriculum for gifted students—may have an emphasis on the use of one main model, one model as a framework with supplementary models, or the integration of several models into a framework constructed by those who develop curricula.

The models we describe were chosen for several reasons. First, each model must have demonstrated or potential success with gifted children. Each principle described in *Curriculum Development and Teaching Strategies for Gifted Learners* (Maker, 1982a; Maker & Nielson, 1996) was considered in this selection process. Second, these models were selected because of their widespread use in programs for the gifted or the integration of most of the modifications recommended in our companion volume into their structure. A third and final reason was variety and ease of combining each model with complementary models. No one model can encompass all the content, process, product, and learning environment changes necessary to develop a comprehensive curriculum; no one model will be attractive to all teachers; and no one model will fit every situation. For these and related reasons, the models chosen can be combined in a variety of ways to enhance their effectiveness and increase the chances that teachers will find a combination to fit their preferred styles of teaching and their students' preferred styles of learning.

ORGANIZATION OF THE BOOK

The first chapter provides an introduction to teaching–learning models and their role in programs for gifted students. The main body of the book consists of separate chapters about each model. Due to the variations of some models, not every chapter includes the same sections; however, the chapters follow a fairly consistent outline containing a discussion of the model, examples of learning activities that fit within the structure of the model, a brief history of how the model was developed, pertinent research, and a listing of additional resources. The approximate outline for most chapters is as follows:

A. Overview of the Model

B. Assumptions Underlying the Model
  1. About Learning
  2. About Teaching
  3. About Characteristics and Teaching of the Gifted
  4. Other

C. Elements/Parts

D. Modifications of the Basic Curriculum
  1. Content
  2. Process
  3. Product
  4. Learning Environment
  5. Examples of Teaching Activities/Strategies

E. Modifying the Approach

F. Development
  1. How
  2. By Whom

G. Research on Effectiveness
  1. With Nongifted
  2. With Gifted

H. Judgments

   1. Advantages

   2. Disadvantages

I. Conclusion

J. Resources

   1. Background Information

   2. Instructional Materials and Ideas

The final chapter is a discussion of how a comprehensive curriculum can be developed by combining and integrating more than one of the models described. The chapter includes information on assessing and selecting models, curriculum development, and an example of an integrated approach.

CHAPTER I

The Role of Teaching–Learning Models in Curriculum Development for the Gifted

THE NATURE OF TEACHING–LEARNING MODELS

A teaching–learning model is a structural framework that serves as a guide for developing specific educational activities and environments. A model can be highly theoretical and abstract, or it can be a more practical structural framework. Regardless of how theoretical or practical, the distinguishing features common to teaching–learning models are (a) an identified purpose or area of concentration, (b) underlying explicit and implicit assumptions about the characteristics of learners and about the teaching–learning processes, (c) guidelines for developing specific day-to-day learning experiences, (d) definite patterns and requirements for these learning activities, and (e) a body of research surrounding their development or an evaluation of their effectiveness.

Joyce and Weil (1986) identified more than 80 models of teaching and divided them into four families based on common viewpoints about teaching and learning:

1. *Social interaction models* have an emphasis on the relationship of the individual to society and to other groups and are focused on the individual's ability to relate to others, engage in democracy, and work productively within society.
2. *Information-processing models* focus on the ways people handle information, organize data, sense problems, and generate solutions to problems.

3. *Personal models* share an orientation toward the development of self-concept.
4. *Behavior modification and cybernetic models* focus on changing observable behaviors based on efficient sequencing of learning tasks along with manipulation of antecedents and consequences.

Most of the models presented in this volume fall into the first and second categories, although some could be considered personal models.

The area of concentration or focus in a teaching–learning model can be very broad or quite narrow. Renzulli's Enrichment Triad Model (discussed in Chapter 8) for example, was developed as a total enrichment program for gifted learners, integrating content knowledge, a wide range of intellectual skills, and the development of an investigative attitude. The Creative Problem Solving model (Chapter 6), on the other hand, was developed to enhance problem solving and creativity, a more narrow range of intellectual and affective skills.

Although the various models have different purposes or areas of concentration, they are not focused exclusively on one aspect of learning. For example, the information-processing models, such as Creative Problem Solving (Chapter 6) and the Hilda Taba Teaching Strategies (Chapter 10), also have an emphasis on the development of social relationships and an integrated, well-functioning self. The social interaction models, such as the Autonomous Learner Model (Chapter 2), the DISCOVER Curriculum Model (Chapter 5), Problem Based Learning (Chapter 7), Group Investigations (Chapter 9), and Thinking Actively in a Social Context (Chapter 11), also have an emphasis on the development of information-processing skills.

In each model some theoretical assumptions must be made regarding the nature of the learner (e.g., learning, motivational, intellectual, and emotional characteristics) and the nature or effectiveness of certain teaching methods. These assumptions range from relatively simplistic to complex and abstract. Hierarchical models such as Bloom's and Krathwohl's (Chapter 3) and Kohlberg's (Chapter 12) are based on the assumption that learning is an unvarying sequential process that occurs in steps and all learners experience each step. In contrast, the DISCOVER Curriculum Model (Chapter 5) includes assumptions about multiple intelligences, types of problem-solving tasks, and diverse learning styles. The "proof" of these assumptions also varies from model to model, and the models also differ in how clearly the assumptions are stated. Some authors clearly reveal the assumptions they reject and state the ones they accept, whereas others describe some assumptions and omit other critical ones. Still other authors say nothing about either their implicit or explicit assumptions, and teachers must search for the underlying ideas.

Furthermore, the models have varied guidelines for the development of specific learning experiences. The guidelines implicitly provide requirements or standards by which models may be judged. The Bloom and Krathwohl Taxonomies (Chapter 3), for example, provide definitions of cognitive and affective behaviors at each level in the hierarchies. One requirement or standard associated with the implementation of hierarchic models is that each lower level behavior is necessary before the higher level behavior can be executed effectively. The Hilda Taba Teaching Strategies (Chapter 10) entail a broad range of teacher attitudes and competencies that involve much more than simply knowing what sequences of questions to ask students.

All teaching–learning models have some basis in research, either as a background for their development or as a justification for use because of their effectiveness. Extensive research has been done on the elements included in DISCOVER (Chapter 5), Creative Problem Solving (Chapter 6), the Enrichment Triad Model (Chapter 8), the Schoolwide Enrichment Model (Chapter 8), and the Hilda Taba Teaching Strategies (Chapter 10), as well as on their effectiveness with various groups. The Taba strategies were developed and evaluated over a period of approximately 10 years. The DISCOVER model is based on research begun in 1987 and continuing for the foreseeable future. On the other hand, little research has been done on the effectiveness of the Autonomous Learner Model (Chapter 2) in achieving the stated purposes. The Enrichment Triad Model was developed based on Renzulli's experience in evaluating programs for the gifted and on reviews of research on the characteristics of gifted individuals; ongoing research is being conducted to determine the model's effectiveness on creative and affective outcomes.

CURRICULA FOR GIFTED STUDENTS

Qualitative Differences

The phrase most frequently used to describe the appropriate school curriculum for gifted students is "qualitatively different from the program for all students." This phrase implies that the basic curriculum must be examined, and changes or modifications must be made so that the most appropriate curriculum is provided for gifted students. Modifications must be qualitative changes rather than changes in the quantity of tasks assigned, and they must build upon and extend the characteristics (both present and future) that make these students different from other students. To make the basic curriculum more appropriate for gifted students (J. J. Gallagher, 1975), an educator can modify the *content* (what is learned), the *process* (the methods used and the thinking processes students are expected to use), and the *learning environment* (the psychological and physical environment in which the learning is to occur). Renzulli (1977) added *product* (the end products expected of students as a result of the processes used) as a dimension that must be modified.

Content Modifications

The content of the curriculum consists of the ideas, concepts, descriptive information, and facts that are made available to students in school settings. Curriculum may be structured in a variety of forms that can differ, for example, in degree of abstractness, complexity, organization, and subject areas covered. To meet the needs of gifted students, curriculum also must include a wide variety of topics and processes, efficient organization of learning experiences, the study of people, and the study of methods of study in various disciplines.

ABSTRACTNESS. The major focus of discussions, presentations, reading materials, and lectures in a program for gifted students should be on abstract concepts, themes, and theories—ideas that have a wide range of applicability or potential for transfer both within and across disciplines or fields of study. Concrete information and factual data are intended as illustrations or examples of the abstract ideas rather than as the major focus.

COMPLEXITY. Abstract ideas usually are complex as well but vary in the degree of complexity or richness. For gifted students, these ideas need to be as complex as possible so that students work at their challenge level rather than at or below comfort level. The complexity of an abstract idea can be determined by examining the number and complexity of concepts related to or contained within the idea or generalization, the number and complexity of the disciplines or traditional content areas that must be understood or integrated to comprehend the idea, and the variety of possibilities for student exploration.

VARIETY. In past years variety has been provided students in programs for the gifted through enrichment experiences and activities. Unfortunately, in many programs, variety is the only content modification made for gifted students. The concept of variety suggests that ideas and content areas not taught in the regular curriculum should be taught in a gifted program. A related suggestion is that gifted students work on different aspects of a broad theme and that the curriculum includes ideas of interest to students with varied gifts and abilities.

ORGANIZATION FOR LEARNING VALUE. Because knowledge in most areas increases and changes at an alarming rate and because gifted students have a limited amount of time to spend in the educational program, every learning experience must be the most valuable that can be offered. To achieve economy, content must be organized to facilitate transfer of learning, memory, and understanding of abstract concepts and generalizations. According to Bruner (1960), these results can be achieved if the content is organized around the key concepts or abstract ideas to be learned, rather than arranged in some other fashion.

STUDY OF PEOPLE. Gifted students are likely to become scholars, leaders, and creative, productive individuals in the future. Many of these students also enjoy reading biographies and autobiographies. For these reasons and their need to learn how to deal with their own talents and possible success, gifted students should study creative and productive individuals. An analysis of problems that these individuals faced, the way they handled their problems, their personal traits, their career or professional characteristics, and their social interactions can stimulate social and psychological development of gifted students.

STUDY OF METHODS. Gifted students should study the methods of inquiry—the investigative techniques—used by scholars in different disciplines. They need practice in using these methods, and they should learn a variety of techniques. Such studies can contribute to a better understanding of the content area and enhance the independence of the students.

Process Modifications
The process dimension of the curriculum is related to the ways in which new material is presented, the activities in which the students engage, and the questions that are asked. Process includes teaching methods and the

thinking skills or processes developed by the students. It also includes the use of technology as a way to gather and process pertinent information.

HIGHER LEVELS OF THINKING. The methods used in programs for the gifted should stress the use rather than the acquisition of information. Because gifted students can acquire information rapidly and almost effortlessly in their areas of strength, they should apply the information in new situations, use it to develop new ideas, evaluate its appropriateness, and use it to develop new products.

OPEN-ENDEDNESS. Questions and activities for gifted students should include many more open-ended than closed questions and learning activities. The principle of open-endedness indicates that no predetermined right answer exists. The questions or activities are provocative in that they stimulate further thinking and investigation about a topic. Openness stimulates more thought, permits and encourages divergent thinking, encourages responses from more children, and contributes to the development of an interaction pattern in which learning, not the teacher, is the most important focus.

DISCOVERY. The activities designed for gifted students should include a great many situations in which students use inductive reasoning processes to discover patterns, ideas, and underlying principles. Such guided discovery has several advantages for gifted children: (a) increased interest through being involved in learning; (b) use of their natural curiosity—that is, their desire to figure out how things work (Renzulli, Smith, White, Callahan, & Hartman, 1976); (c) their desire to organize and bring structure to their knowledge; and (d) increased self-confidence and independence in learning. All of these result from allowing and encouraging the students to figure things out for themselves.

EVIDENCE OF REASONING. Another important process modification for gifted learners is that they be required to express not only their conclusions but also the reasoning that led to these conclusions. This aspect of teaching is especially important when using a discovery approach, developing higher levels of thinking, and asking open-ended questions. Using this strategy, students learn different reasoning processes from each other, and they are encouraged to evaluate both the process and the products of others' thinking. Listening to students' reasons and evidence also is an effective way for teachers to assess the students' levels of thinking.

FREEDOM OF CHOICE. Whenever possible, gifted students should be given the freedom to choose learning experiences and topics. Their interest, motivation, and excitement in learning will be increased by such techniques. Not all gifted students, however, are independent learners; some students may need assistance in making and executing their choices, gradually leading them to become more autonomous.

GROUP INTERACTION. Structured activities and simulations, as well as unstructured opportunities to interact, should be a regular part of the curriculum for gifted students, to enable them to develop social and leadership skills. These activities should include rule-structured games and open-ended group investigations among a small group of students, peer evaluation, and self-analysis or critique. Both peer evaluation and self-analysis will be more effective if the activity has been video- or audio-taped for students to review.

PACING AND VARIETY. The final two process modifications serve mainly as facilitators for the success of other changes. *Pacing* refers to how rapidly new material is presented to the students. Research (George, 1976) and experience have indicated that rapid pacing often is important to maintain students' interest and provide a challenge. Rapid pacing, however, does not refer to the amount of teacher wait-time needed during discussions or following any open-ended questions. *Variety* simply suggests that the teacher use various methods to maintain the interest of the children and to accommodate the different learning styles of the students.

Product Modifications

Products are the "ends" of instruction. They can be tangible or intangible, sophisticated or unsophisticated. Sophisticated products result from detailed, original work, whereas unsophisticated ones contain paraphrasing or copying. Products can include reports, stories, plays, dances, ideas, speeches, pictures, and illustrations. The products expected from gifted students should resemble the products developed by professionals in the discipline being studied (Renzulli, 1977). These professional products will differ from typical student products in the following ways:

• *Result from real problems.* The products developed by gifted students should address problems that are real to them. Students can be encouraged to choose a specific area of concern within a certain field of study and design an investigation around that area.

- *Addressed to real audiences.* To the extent possible, the products developed by gifted students should be addressed to real audiences, such as the scientific community, the city council, or a government agency. At other times, the real audience consists of classmates or other students in the school. The gifted students should not develop products that are seen or heard only by the teacher.

- *Transformation.* Gifted students' products should represent transformations of existing information or data rather than mere summaries of others' conclusions. Original research, original artwork, and other such products should include the collection and analysis of raw data. If students use higher levels of thinking, their products must demonstrate true transformations of information.

- *Variety.* Gifted students should be encouraged to learn about and create a variety of types of products and to consider carefully the most appropriate representation of their content to the proposed audience. Variety in products allows students with different intellectual and creative strengths to demonstrate their competence with appropriate media. They also need practice using varied product options to meet the same goal.

- *Self-selected format.* Gifted students must be allowed to decide which formats to use in presenting their solutions to problems real to them. A student's interests, strengths, and prior experiences all may influence these choices. Certainly teachers can provide assistance in the selection of a format and may encourage students, at times, to try a format new to them; however, students should be allowed to make the final choices.

- *Appropriate evaluation.* Often, student products are directed toward and evaluated by the teacher only. The products of professionals are evaluated by the audiences for whom they were intended. Products of gifted students should be evaluated by appropriate audiences, including audiences of peers. Students also should be required to complete a comprehensive self-evaluation of their products.

Learning Environment Modifications

The learning environment is the setting in which learning occurs and includes both the physical setting and the psychological climate of the school and classroom. Many dimensions of learning environments are important; different individuals have different preferences for certain aspects (e.g., amount of sound and light or presence of color). The learning environments appropriate for gifted students resemble the environments appropriate for all children but differ in degree. All environment modifications presented in this section were chosen because they meet the following three conditions: (a) they are preferred by most gifted students; (b) they are necessary for implementing the content, process, and product modifications advocated; and (c) they build on characteristics of gifted students.

LEARNER CENTERED VERSUS TEACHER CENTERED. Environments for gifted students should include a focus on the students' ideas and interests rather than those of the teacher. Student discussions rather than teacher talk should be emphasized, and patterns of interaction seldom should have the teacher as the central figure or focus.

INDEPENDENCE VERSUS DEPENDENCE. Environments for gifted students should provide a sense of student independence. The degree of tolerance for and encouragement of student initiative is the main idea in this dimension of the environment. The focus is having students work to solve their own problems, including those related to classroom management, and make their own decisions instead of depending on the teacher.

OPEN VERSUS CLOSED. The physical environment should be open to permit new people, materials, and artifacts to enter. The same is true of the psychological environment. New ideas, diverse values, exploratory discussions, intellectual risk-taking, and the freedom to change direction to meet new situations must be encouraged.

ACCEPTANCE VERSUS JUDGMENT. The three major elements of an accepting learning environment are (a) attempts to understand students' ideas, (b) the timing of value judgments, and (c) evaluation rather than judgment. Before teachers can assess student ideas, they must accept and understand those ideas; that is, they must attend to or listen actively, accept the ideas, and then request clarification, elaboration, and extensions of the ideas before approving or challenging them. Timing refers to the stage of creative production or problem solving when evaluations occur. Idea production, for example, is one of the most inappropriate times for judgment to occur. Judgment implies rightness or wrongness, whereas evaluation implies an assessment of both the strengths and limitations of a product or person. Evaluation should be emphasized rather than judgment, and students also should be taught to respond to each other in nonjudgmental ways.

COMPLEX VERSUS SIMPLE. As a dimension of classroom climate, complexity versus simplicity refers to both physical and psychological environments. A complex physical environment, necessary for gifted students, includes a variety of materials; sophisticated and varied "tools," references, and books; a representation of varied cultures and intelligences; and a variety of databases and electronic resources. A complex psychological environment, also necessary for gifted students, includes diversity—human, cultural, and idealogical diversity, challenging tasks, complex concepts, and sophisticated methods.

VARIED VERSUS SIMILAR GROUPINGS. Grouping arrangements in programs and classes for the gifted should be varied and fluid rather than identical and static. The types of tasks and the purposes of learning experiences will be varied; therefore, the groupings needed to accomplish these purposes also must be different. Groupings should approximate real-life situations, and students need to be allowed to make choices about how the groups are set up.

FLEXIBILITY VERSUS RIGIDITY. One of the most important elements of both physical and psychological environments is flexibility. Flexibility is needed in scheduling, in requirements to be met, in criteria for evaluation, and in some teacher values. Learners often need extended periods of time to become engaged in complex projects or activities of interest; they also need to work on these projects long enough to achieve a sense of personal satisfaction. In addition, some events outside the school environment (e.g., death of a friend, outstanding achievement of an individual or the group) may be of such paramount importance to students that class time must be used for discussion of the event. If student time is rigidly and tightly scheduled and students always are expected to follow the teacher's predetermined schedule, student autonomy and internal motivation are not allowed to develop. Extreme frustration may be the result in highly motivated or sensitive students.

HIGH MOBILITY VERSUS LOW MOBILITY. The amount of movement allowed and encouraged is the most important aspect of this dimension of the environment. If gifted students are to develop professional products, have freedom of choice, and be allowed to develop the autonomy necessary for exploration and investigation, the environment must allow movement within and outside of the classroom and access to different environments, materials, and equipment.

Summary

The changes advocated in this section have been chosen to meet, collectively and individually, two basic criteria that are different in quality from the regular curriculum and based on the unique characteristics of gifted students. The chosen elements were based on the group traits of gifted students; not all children will possess every characteristic. Thus, the curriculum must be tailored to fit the needs of each child based on an assessment of that child's characteristics, needs, and interests.

ADAPTING AND SELECTING MODELS

The construction of a curriculum that incorporates the content, process, product, and learning environment modifications recommended for gifted students requires an approach in which educators provide specific strategies for accomplishing these changes. Several factors must be considered before selecting an approach: the setting (the school, the school district, and the community), the students, the teachers, and the teaching model(s) to be emphasized. In other words, a match must exist between what a model can offer and what is needed in a specific program for gifted students.

Assessing the Situation

The first step in adapting or selecting models is to assess factors related to the setting, teacher, and students. One of the situational factors, for example, is the kind of grouping arrangement used for the program, such as a regular classroom with a consulting teacher, resource rooms in each building, resource centers across the district, or a self-contained classroom. Another factor is the attitude of regular classroom teachers toward the program. If a particular approach requires the cooperation of teachers who will not cooperate, a different choice must be made. Factors related to the students include their common characteristics, as well as the range of those characteristics (differences), their ages, areas of giftedness, achievement levels, interests, background experiences, and learning styles.

The teacher is the single most important variable in determining the success of an educational approach. If the teacher does not have the skills necessary to implement the approach and does not believe in its value, the program cannot be effective. Teacher factors to consider can be separated into three groups: philosophical, personal, and professional. Philosophical characteristics include those pertinent to education, as well as the purpose and implementation of education. Personal traits include a love of learning, creativity, intelligence, motivation, and self-confidence. Professional characteristics include teaching skills, educational background, and past experiences. Factors related to the model include all items discussed at the beginning of this chapter. All these factors must be considered carefully when selecting or adapting a teaching–learning model (or models).

Assessing the Model

The next step in choosing an approach is to assess the model's appropriateness to the situation. We have selected five general criteria for evaluating a model: (a) appropriateness to the situation, (b) comprehensiveness as a framework for curriculum development for the gifted, (c) flexibility or adaptability, (d) practicality, and (e) validity. Other criteria could be added. The following specific questions can be asked during this assessment:

Appropriateness to the Situation
- To what extent do the model's purposes match the needs of the students, the school philosophy, parental values, and teacher characteristics?
- To what extent do the underlying assumptions made in the model fit the situational reality? (For example, if assumptions are made about the characteristics of gifted students, are these characteristics true of students in the program?)

Comprehensiveness
- What content modifications are provided by the model?
- What process modifications are provided by the model?
- What product modifications are provided by the model?

- What learning environment modifications are provided by the model?
- Which of the modifications actually not provided by the model could be generated by extension or integrated into the approach?

Flexibility or Adaptability
- How easily can the model be adapted to all content areas or subjects covered in the program?
- How easily can the model be adapted to the present administrative structure of the school and program?
- How easily can the model be combined with other models to provide a comprehensive program?
- How easily can the model be used with the age levels of children served by the program?
- How easily can the model be adapted to individual differences among gifted children?

Practicality
- What materials or services are available to implement the model?
- What is the cost of these materials or services?
- How much training is needed for the special teacher or regular classroom teacher to implement the model effectively?
- How easily could the approach be implemented in the present situation?

Validity
- Was the model developed using appropriate methods?
- What research is available to show the model's effectiveness as an educational approach?
- What research is available to show the model's effectiveness as an approach for use with gifted students?
- What evidence is available to indicate that the model is structurally sound?
- Is the approach defensible as a qualitatively different program for gifted students?

Two worksheets have been designed to facilitate the process of assessing models. On the Worksheet for Assessing Models' Appropriateness, the criteria and questions are listed on the left side, and the models are listed across the top (see Figure 1.1). Note that in Figure 1.1, acronyms are used

(*text continues on p. 20*)

WORKSHEET FOR ASSESSING MODELS' APPROPRIATENESS

Assign a rating to each model on each criterion using the following code: 1 = Poor, 2 = Average, 3 = Excellent.

Criteria and Questions	Affective Taxonomy (3)	ALM (2)	BSD (4)	Cognitive Taxonomy (3)	CPS (6)	DISCOVER (5)	DMD (12)	ETM and SEM (8)	Group Investigations (9)	HTTS (10)	PBL (7)	Prism (12)	TASC (11)	TSTF (12)	Comments
Appropriateness to the Situation															
To what extent do the model's purposes match needs of students, school philosophy, parental values, and teacher characteristics?															
To what extent do underlying assumptions of the model fit the situational reality?															

(continues)

FIGURE 1.1. Worksheet for Assessing Models' Appropriateness. *Note.* Numbers in parentheses refer to chapters in this book. ALM = Autonomous Learner Model; BSD = Basic Structure of a Discipline; CPS = Creative Problem Solving; DISCOVER = Discovering Intellectual Strengths and Capabilities while Observing Varied Ethnic Responses; DMD = Discussions of Moral Dilemmas; ETM = Enrichment Triad Model; SEM = Schoolwide Enrichment Model; HTTS = Hilda Taba Teaching Strategies; PBL = Problem Based Learning; Prism = Prism of Learning; TASC = Thinking Actively in a Social Context; TSTF = Teaching Strategies for Thinking and Feeling. Adapted from *Teaching Models in Education of the Gifted* (2nd ed., p. 14), by C. J. Maker and A. B. Nielson, 1995, Austin, TX: PRO-ED. Copyright 1995 by PRO-ED, Inc. Adapted with permission.

Assign a rating to each model on each criterion using the following code: 1 = Poor, 2 = Average, 3 = Excellent.

Criteria and Questions	Affective Taxonomy (3)	ALM (2)	BSD (4)	Cognitive Taxonomy (3)	CPS (6)	DISCOVER (5)	DMD (12)	ETM and SEM (8)	Group Investigations (9)	HTTS (10)	PBL (7)	Prism (12)	TASC (11)	TSTF (12)	Comments
Comprehensiveness															
What content modifications are provided by the model?															
What process modifications are provided by the model?															
What product modifications are provided by the model?															
What learning environment modifications are provided by the model?															

(continues)

FIGURE 1.1. Continued.

Assign a rating to each model on each criterion using the following code: 1 = Poor, 2 = Average, 3 = Excellent.

Criteria and Questions	Affective Taxonomy (3)	ALM (2)	BSD (4)	Cognitive Taxonomy (3)	CPS (6)	DISCOVER (5)	DMD (12)	ETM and SEM (8)	Group Investigations (9)	HTTS (10)	PBL (7)	Prism (12)	TASC (11)	TSTF (12)	Comments
Comprehensiveness (*continued*)															
Which of the modifications not provided by the model could be generated by extension or integrated into the approach?															
Flexibility or Adaptability															
How easily can the model be adapted to all content areas or subjects covered in the program?															
How easily can the model be adapted to present administrative structure of school and program?															

(continues)

FIGURE 1.1. *Continued.*

Assign a rating to each model on each criterion using the following code: 1 = Poor, 2 = Average, 3 = Excellent.

Criteria and Questions	Affective Taxonomy (3)	ALM (2)	BSD (4)	Cognitive Taxonomy (3)	CPS (6)	DISCOVER (5)	DMD (12)	ETM and SEM (8)	Group Investigations (9)	HTTS (10)	PBL (7)	Prism (12)	TASC (11)	TSTF (12)	Comments
Flexibility or Adaptability (continued)															
How easily can the model be combined with other models to provide a comprehensive program?															
How easily can the model be used with the age levels of students served by the program?															
How easily can the model be adapted to individual differences among students?															
Practicality															
What materials and services are available to implement the model?															

(continues)

FIGURE 1.1. *Continued.*

Assign a rating to each model on each criterion using the following code: 1 = Poor, 2 = Average, 3 = Excellent.

Criteria and Questions	Affective Taxonomy (3)	ALM (2)	BSD (4)	Cognitive Taxonomy (3)	CPS (6)	DISCOVER (5)	DMD (12)	ETM and SEM (8)	Group Investigations (9)	HTTS (10)	PBL (7)	Prism (12)	TASC (11)	TSTF (12)	Comments
Practicality (*continued*)															
What is the cost of these materials or services?															
How much training is needed for the special teacher or regular classroom teacher to implement the model effectively?															
How easily could the model be implemented in the present situation?															
Validity															
Was the model developed using appropriate methods?															

(continues)

FIGURE 1.1. *Continued.*

Assign a rating to each model on each criterion using the following code: 1 = Poor, 2 = Average, 3 = Excellent.

Criteria and Questions	Affective Taxonomy (3)	ALM (2)	BSD (4)	Cognitive Taxonomy (3)	CPS (6)	DISCOVER (5)	DMD (12)	ETM and SEM (8)	Group Investigations (9)	HTTS (10)	PBL (7)	Prism (12)	TASC (11)	TSTF (12)	Comments
Validity (*continued*)															
What research is available to show the model's effectiveness as an educational approach?															
What research is available to show the model's effectiveness as an approach for use with gifted students?															
What evidence is available to indicate that the model is structurally sound?															
Is the approach defensible as a qualitatively different program for gifted students?															
Totals															

FIGURE 1.1. *Continued.*

for models with long names (e.g., ALM for Autonomous Learner Model). Using the system of 1 = *poor,* 2 = *average,* and 3 = *excellent,* a rating should be assigned to each model on each criterion. Next, the ratings for each model (columns) should be totaled to indicate the model's overall appropriateness.

On the Worksheet for Assessing Models' Comprehensiveness (see Figure 1.2), the curricular modifications presented earlier are listed as criteria, and the models are listed across the top. A check mark is placed in the box if the modification is made by a model and left blank if not. The totals for each column can be used to indicate the comprehensiveness of each model. Information from this worksheet also can be used to examine the different models and determine how they complement each other.

Combining the Models

The final step in the process of adapting or selecting models is to decide whether one approach can serve as the only model used or whether the models should be combined, used together, or used in different situations. The models presented in this book are different in their purposes, as well as in the ways content, process, product, and learning environment modifications are provided. For example, Bruner's approach (Chapter 4) modifies content by suggesting that it be organized around basic concepts. His approach also addresses the process of discovery, although its major modifications are in the area of content. The Cognitive and Affective Taxonomies (Chapter 3), on the other hand, provide modifications only in the process area and only in one aspect of process, the development of higher levels of thinking and feeling.

The Enrichment Triad Model (Chapter 8) provides a unifying structure for changes in content, process, and product as dimensions of a learning task. Although it can provide a comprehensive framework for an overall approach, other process models need to be added, such as the Cognitive Taxonomy (Chapter 3), the Taba strategies (Chapter 10), Kohlberg's Discussions of Moral Dilemmas (Chapter 10), and the Affective Taxonomy (Chapter 3), to guide the development of Type II activities. The Autonomous Learner Model (Chapter 2), the problem continuum (Chapter 5), Problem Based Learning (Chapter 7), or Thinking Actively in a Social Context (Chapter 11) can provide the teacher with methods for moving students toward the development of their Type III investigations.

(*text continues on p. 26*)

WORKSHEET FOR ASSESSING MODELS' COMPREHENSIVENESS

Rate each model on each criterion by placing a ✓ in the column if the modification is made in the model. If modification is not made, leave the space blank.

Curricular Modifications	Affective Taxonomy (3)	ALM (2)	BSD (4)	Cognitive Taxonomy (3)	CPS (6)	DISCOVER (5)	DMD (12)	ETM and SEM (8)	Group Investigations (9)	HTTS (10)	PBL (7)	Prism (12)	TASC (11)	TSTF (12)	Comments
Content															
1. Abstractness															
2. Complexity															
3. Variety															
4. Organization for Learning Value															

(continues)

FIGURE 1.2. Worksheet for Assessing Models' Comprehensiveness. *Note.* Numbers in parentheses refer to chapters in this book. ALM = Autonomous Learner Model; BSD = Basic Structure of a Discipline; CPS = Creative Problem Solving; DISCOVER = Discovering Intellectual Strengths and Capabilities while Observing Varied Ethnic Responses; DMD = Discussions of Moral Dilemmas; ETM = Enrichment Triad Model; SEM = Schoolwide Enrichment Model; HTTS = Hilda Taba Teaching Strategies; PBL = Problem Based Learning; Prism = Prism of Learning; TASC = Thinking Actively in a Social Context; TSTF = Teaching Strategies for Thinking and Feeling. Adapted from *Teaching Models in Education of the Gifted* (2nd ed., p. 14), by C. J. Maker and A. B. Nielson, 1995, Austin, TX: PRO-ED. Copyright 1995 by PRO-ED, Inc. Adapted with permission.

Rate each model on each criterion by placing a ✓ in the column if the modification is made in the model. If modification is not made, leave the space blank.

Curricular Modifications	Affective Taxonomy (3)	ALM (2)	BSD (4)	Cognitive Taxonomy (3)	CPS (6)	DISCOVER (5)	DMD (12)	ETM and SEM (8)	Group Investigations (9)	HTTS (10)	PBL (7)	Prism (12)	TASC (11)	TSTF (12)	Comments
Content (*continued*)															
5. Study of People															
6. Study of Methods															
Process															
7. Higher Level Thinking															
8. Open-endedness															
9. Discovery															
10. Evidence of Reasoning															
11. Freedom of Choice															

(continues)

FIGURE 1.2. *Continued.*

Rate each model on each criterion by placing a ✓ in the column if the modification is made in the model. If modification is not made, leave the space blank.

Curricular Modifications	Affective Taxonomy (3)	ALM (2)	BSD (4)	Cognitive Taxonomy (3)	CPS (6)	DISCOVER (5)	DMD (12)	ETM and SEM (8)	Group Investigations (9)	HTTS (10)	PBL (7)	Prism (12)	TASC (11)	TSTF (12)	Comments
Process (*continued*)															
12. Group Interaction															
13. Pacing															
14. Variety															
Product															
15. Result from Real Problems															
16. Addressed to Real Audiences															
17. Transformation															
18. Variety															

(continues)

FIGURE 1.2. *Continued.*

Rate each model on each criterion by placing a ✓ in the column if the modification is made in the model. If modification is not made, leave the space blank.

Curricular Modifications	Affective Taxonomy (3)	ALM (2)	BSD (4)	Cognitive Taxonomy (3)	CPS (6)	DISCOVER (5)	DMD (12)	ETM and SEM (8)	Group Investigations (9)	HTTS (10)	PBL (7)	Prism (12)	TASC (11)	TSTF (12)	Comments
Product (*continued*)															
19. Self-Selected Format															
20. Appropriate Evaluation															
Learning Environment															
21. Learner Centered															
22. Encourages Independence															
23. Openness															
24. Accepting															
25. Complexity															

(continues)

FIGURE 1.2. *Continued.*

Rate each model on each criterion by placing a ✓ in the column if the modification is made in the model. If modification is not made, leave the space blank.

Curricular Modifications	Affective Taxonomy (3)	ALM (2)	BSD (4)	Cognitive Taxonomy (3)	CPS (6)	DISCOVER (5)	DMD (12)	ETM and SEM (8)	Group Investigations (9)	HTTS (10)	PBL (7)	Prism (12)	TASC (11)	TSTF (12)	Comments
Learning Environment (*continued*)															
26. Varied Groupings															
27. Flexibility															
28. High Mobility															
Totals															

FIGURE 1.2. *Continued.*

Some similarities also should be noted. Most of the models modify process, and few consider content changes at all. In fact, many models make similar process changes because of their emphasis on higher levels of thinking and on development of creative or divergent thought processes. Most also emphasize evaluation skills (e.g., the Cognitive and Affective Taxonomies and Creative Problem Solving) or decision making (e.g., the Autonomous Learner Model).

If these models are combined or used separately, their similarities and differences must be considered. In other words, they must be combined so that the total curriculum is comprehensive, but the degree of overlap also should be considered. Placing undue emphasis on process skills would not be desirable simply because more methods and materials are available for use.

CHAPTER 2

George T. Betts and Jolene K. Kercher: The Autonomous Learner Model

Programs for highly able students in secondary schools, when they do exist, frequently consist of advanced placement classes, acceleration in a specific content area, or concurrent enrollment in college classes. Although these options have a place in the education of gifted students, they offer few opportunities for young people to develop creative potential. Nor do they, due to their primary focus on content learning, foster independent learning abilities, creativity, or self-awareness.

Renzulli and Gable (1976) found that independent study or self-directed learning is highly successful with gifted students; however, not all gifted students have the self-regulatory strategies essential for independent study (Zimmerman & Martinez-Pons, 1990). Goal setting, planning strategies to reach the goal, and self-evaluation of progress and quality of work are essential to the success of self-directed learning, but few gifted students reported using those strategies. When gifted students are taught how to use strategies, however, they learn to use the strategies more efficiently and also are able to transfer them to new tasks (Scruggs & Mastropieri, 1988). The implication, from a review of research on self-regulatory strategies and metacognitive development, is that designing activities that help gifted students develop self-regulatory learning strategies is an effective and productive way to help highly able students. Teaching self-regulatory strategies may be particularly important to "underachieving gifted" students who are not living up to their potential (Risemberg & Zimmerman, 1992).

One major goal of differentiated education for gifted learners is to help highly able students realize their potential and experience a sense of personal fulfillment or self-actualization (Feldhusen & Treffinger, 1980). Another goal is to help these students understand their uniqueness (develop intrapersonal awareness) and cultivate the interpersonal skills needed to work effectively with others. The Autonomous Learner Model (ALM) was designed to meet the diverse social–emotional and cognitive needs of potentially gifted students and to help them to develop strategies and attitudes necessary for independent learning. Autonomous learners are those individuals who have the ability to be responsible for the development, implementation, and evaluation of their own learning (Betts, 1985). Becoming an autonomous learner is not an easy task; self-direction requires a new orientation to learning, development of cognitive and interpersonal skills, self-awareness, and formative experience in designing and conducting independent projects. As students develop needed skills, concepts, and attitudes through class activities, they also explore topics, information sources, careers, and other resources that might stimulate ideas for further research. Changing orientation and attitudes to move away from highly structured, traditional classes toward autonomous learning is an incremental process that takes time, energy, goals, patience, and support.

Betts and Knapp (1981) define an autonomous learner as one who solves problems or develops new ideas through a combination of divergent and convergent thinking and who functions with minimal external guidance in selected areas of endeavor. With that definition as a guide, the ALM was originally designed to help gifted students meet eight emotional, social, and cognitive goals (Betts, 1985). As the model was implemented widely, the original goals were modified and are now referred to as standards (Betts & Kercher, 1999). Additionally, each dimension and area has a set of standards and key components. For the information presented in this chapter, the primary reference is Betts and Kercher (1999) unless otherwise noted.

ASSUMPTIONS UNDERLYING THE MODEL

The ALM was first developed for gifted and talented learners at the secondary level. Over time, and with modifications, it has been used successfully with all learners, from kindergarten through 12th grade, in the United States and around the world. Betts and Kercher (1999) define "the gifted" as three different types of learners who have the potential of becoming autonomous: the intellectually gifted, the creatively gifted, and the talented. Individuals may have characteristics of one, two, or all three of these types of giftedness; some learners have multipotentiality.

Programs for gifted students must be multifaceted, encompassing elements to meet the needs of a variety of gifted learners. The five dimensions of the ALM—Orientation, Individual Development, Enrichment, Seminars, and In-depth Study—address these learning needs and are essential for the development of autonomous learners. The ALM is designed explicitly to integrate the emotional, social, and cognitive aspects of learning; its goal is "to facilitate the growth of students as independent, self-directed learners, with the development of skills, concepts and positive attitudes within the cognitive, emotional and social domains" (Betts & Kercher, 1999, p. 63).

One underlying assumption of the model is that as the needs of the total learner are met, gifted students gradually will become autonomous. They will become learners who are able to plan, implement, and evaluate their own learning. They become able to continue into the unknown, for their security comes from within. A related assumption is that a high level of support needs to be available in the early stages of the developmental process. Becoming an autonomous learner takes time, relevant experiences, effort, and support.

About Teaching

The teacher–facilitator must be dedicated to the goal of helping students become autonomous learners. Additionally, the person must be willing to acquire any professional skills needed and to empower students so they become independent rather than looking toward the teacher as the source of all knowledge. As students move from being "just students," with the teacher in charge of their learning, they progress from student–learner to learner–student to learner. As the student's role changes, so does that of the teacher, who must move from being the center of knowledge and focus to being a facilitator—that is, one who monitors progress and growth rather than prescribing content. "A facilitator guides, questions, and supports, but does not direct, specify, or restrict" (Betts & Kercher, 1999, p. 64). Teachers must be comfortable with empowering students to take charge of their own learning and they must understand that as the learner becomes autonomous, their role is to be on the sidelines, not front and center.

As many activities in this model are designed to help students develop self-understanding and interpersonal skills, it is assumed that the teacher–facilitator will need at least some counselor-type skills, a repertoire of team-building strategies, and skills in leading directed but open-ended group discussions. The teacher–facilitator must provide activities to help students develop skills and attitudes needed to work effectively in small groups. In addition, the successful teacher–facilitator will need to have or acquire organizational and interpersonal skills, a broad knowledge of community resources, and the ability to recruit appropriate guest speakers and mentors. Mentors are essential to the pursuit of in-depth studies.

Finally, the teacher also must be a lifelong autonomous learner. A passion for learning ignites such passions in others; demonstrating excitement about the ideas of others and new knowledge provides a powerful role model for potential autonomous learners. To model is infinitely more powerful than to tell, demonstrate, or lecture.

About Learning

With any teaching model or strategy, learner characteristics must match model or strategy elements; this "fit" helps ensure the success of programs and curricula. To this end in the ALM, parents, teachers, and students are led through a process to identify learner needs and school and community resources. Interviews with prospective students are conducted, with the purpose of finding unusual responses, creative answers, empathetic answers, vocabulary usage, examples of critical thinking, or other actions that might indicate giftedness. A variety of standardized test scores may be used—not for the purpose of exclusion, but to find strengths and levels of knowledge that might be indicative of a potentially successful candidate for an ALM program.

The Final Recommendation for Programming Options Form is used to assign ratings from 1 (*low*) to 5 (*high*) to find those students whose learning needs are not being met in the regular classroom and whose characteristics and interests will be a good fit with the ALM. A total score is not computed on students' forms, but rather the information is used to support decisions about the type of learners that will be served best within the ALM program. Once a student has been placed in an ALM program, further assumptions guide the processes and sequence of learning experiences.

Betts (1985) emphasizes the importance of experience as a catalyst for learning, that process of discovering what is important, what is available, and what can be created. Furthermore, he describes learning as a transformation of information and experience, as opposed to the acquisition of prescribed information. Learners incorporate the process and the materials into new and unique products.

Learners need opportunities to explore new ideas and gain awareness of the broad scope of possibilities for investigations and creative production. Even though a vast majority of a learner's time may be spent on in-depth pursuit of a passion, the remaining time needs to be used for the development of new areas of exploration, new skills, concepts and attitudes, and the development of activities that further develop the autonomy of the individual (Betts, 1985).

If a student is to become productive or self-actualizing, however, social and emotional skills also must be learned. Processes to enhance reflective thinking, self-awareness, metacognition, and interpersonal skills are a part of an autonomous learner's repertoire of skills. The ability to work as a member of a group is essential. Students need to learn coping skills, for they cannot control how the world handles them, but they can learn to control how they handle their world (Betts, 1985).

The skills learned in guided, open-ended learning experiences prior to initiating an in-depth independent study are necessary for student success. Teacher–facilitators must model the attitudes and skills needed for independent study and teach explicit strategies such as planning, decision making, organization, analysis, and synthesis. The structures and approaches learned through guided learning experiences and modeled by the teacher or another adult will provide the framework for the learner to become a successful autonomous learner.

Learners need to be able to investigate real-world problems and work toward real solutions. These investigations carry learners beyond the boundaries of ordinary schooling and prescribed curriculum, and lead to the development of products suitable for and interesting and informative to real audiences.

About Characteristics and Teaching of Gifted Students

The natural curiosity of gifted, creative, and talented children is a powerful motivational factor. Gifted students want to know, explore, and become active learners. Learning experiences should be interactive, challenging, and real. Potentially gifted and creative individuals need interactive experiences to learn essential self-regulation strategies such as self-monitoring, goal setting, and decision making. Emphasis must be placed on the development of the skills, concepts, and attitudes that will enable gifted students to become lifelong learners.

Curriculum must be based on the interests and learning needs of students. Although the school, district, or state-mandated curriculum must be addressed, in general the prescribed content is needlessly limiting to gifted students who possess different skills and strategies for learning compared with those of average students. Many highly able children are frustrated by a surface approach to knowledge and need the freedom and support to go in-depth in their learning. Student participation in planning and evaluating learning experiences and curriculum is important to the success of a program for gifted students. Input from these students helps the teacher plan learning activities that meet their cognitive, emotional, and learning needs. Learning and interacting with highly able peers facilitate social, emotional, and cognitive development; interacting with intellectual peers is a powerful stimulus to personal and intellectual growth.

ELEMENTS/PARTS

Broad standards have been designed for the ALM to optimize ability and develop lifelong autonomous learners. These standards underlie the basic principles of the ALM.

The model has five dimensions—Orientation, Individual Development, Enrichment, Seminars, and In-depth Study—that contribute to emotional, social, and cognitive development and guide a student toward autonomous learning (see Figure 2.1). These dimensions have changed somewhat since the model was first developed in 1981; as the ALM has been used in more and more schools and school districts, additions, modifications, and adaptations have evolved. Although the emphasis remains on meeting the individual needs of gifted and talented learners, ALM users have realized that the activities designed and used in implementing the model can help students who are not identified as gifted take the responsibility for their learning and make the transition from student to learner.

The dimensions of the model rest on the original underlying principles. These basic principles were developed through consultation with nationally recognized leaders, reviews of the literature on teaching and learning, teacher training practices and beliefs, and the experiences of

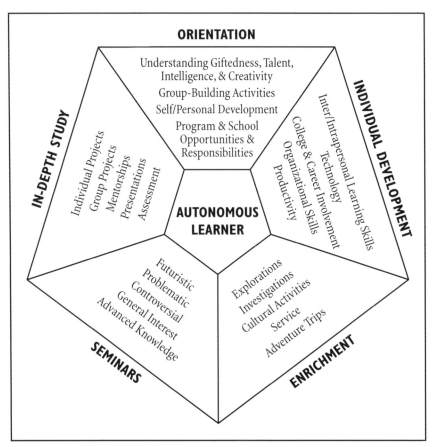

FIGURE 2.1. The Autonomous Learner Model. From *The Autonomous Learner Model: Optimizing Ability,* by G. Betts and J. Kercher, 1999, Greeley, CO: Autonomous Learning Publications and Specialists. Copyright 1999 by Autonomous Learning Publications and Specialists. Reprinted with permission.

learners, teachers, administrators, and parents. Working together, these groups of people built a new model to meet the needs of learners.

Orientation

The Orientation dimension is designed to provide a foundation for learners, teachers, parents, administrators, and community members. The areas of development in this dimension are understanding giftedness, talent, intelligence, and creativity; group-building activities; self/personal development; and program and school opportunities and responsibilities. By the end of orientation, all people concerned with the program should be able to define intelligence, talent, giftedness, and creativity. They also should be able to understand how these terms relate to the learners selected for the program, the selection process, expectations for the learners, and opportunities that will be available to these learners.

Understanding Giftedness, Talent, Intelligence, and Creativity

Few students have had opportunities to develop understanding of the concepts of giftedness, talent, intelligence, or creativity. Individual and group activities, readings, discussions, and interviews with gifted and creative individuals are a major part of this component of the Orientation dimension. The standard and sample learning activities for orientation follow.

Standard

Comprehend own abilities in relationship to self and society. (Betts & Kercher, 1999, p. 78)

To implement the key components of this standard, learning activities might include having students, individually or in small groups, identify a person they consider to be gifted or outstanding in any way. Depending on the person chosen, students could read about or interview the person or his or her associates, or use technology to learn as much as possible about the person. Next, they could develop a list of their subject's characteristics. At this point, an entire class could share characteristics, using Hilda Taba's Concept Development strategy (Chapter 10). Following this, the small groups or individuals could clarify their lists of characteristics and identify the characteristics that they believe they possess. At this time, students should consider individually their educational experiences and how they perceive gifted individuals are treated in school and in the outside world. Furthermore, students should reflect on how they have responded to these experiences. A culmination activity could be a "Me" poem, an autobiography, a dance, a mime presentation, a painting, a sculpture, a musical composition, or whatever product conveys the essence of what students feel they have learned.

Group-Building Activities

Students explore the dynamics of group process, apply group processes in their environments, and participate in group-building activities to learn more about themselves and others. The functions of groups, roles necessary for successful group interaction, and the importance of learning to work together are taught through classroom activities and special projects. The standards and sample learning activities for group-building follow.

Standards

Comprehend own abilities in relationship to self and society.

Develop skills appropriate to interact effectively with peers, siblings, parents, and other adults.

Integrate activities that facilitate the emotional, cognitive, social, and physical development of the individual. (Betts & Kercher, 1999, p. 95)

If students are to become empowered and therefore more able to be autonomous learners, they must learn the dynamics of group processes and how to apply these dynamics for their own purposes. Role playing in simulations, "inside–outside" circles, and class discussions where half the class observes (with specific behaviors to be aware of) are ways to develop understanding of individual roles and interactions within groups. Debriefing after such activities is critical to maximize learning.

Self/Personal Development

Students explore their interests and aptitudes, and have group experiences exploring who they are as individuals and how they may be similar to or different from others in the group. The standards and sample learning activities for self/personal development follow.

Standards

Develop more positive self-concepts and self-esteem.

Comprehend own abilities in relationship to self and society.

Develop appropriate skills to interact effectively with peers, siblings, parents, and other adults. (Betts & Kercher, 1999, p. 109)

Mastery of skills is one way in which positive self-concept and self-esteem can be developed. Therefore, as students conduct investigations, interact with others, and produce tangible proof of their learning, teachers can spot special capabilities, note them to individual students, and assist them in mastery. Risk-taking also builds self-confidence. By creating a safe environment and encouraging risk-taking, teachers set the stage for timid or cautious students to take intellectual, social, and academic risks.

One-on-one debriefing helps students to clarify and realize what they have accomplished, and to begin to understand who they are.

Program and School Opportunities and Responsibilities

Students learn about the goals, objectives, dimensions, and activities of the ALM. They are exposed to the concept of lifelong learning, and they brainstorm key features of such learning. The standards and sample learning activities for this area follow.

Standards

Comprehend own abilities in relationship to self and society.

Develop decision-making and problem-solving skills.

Demonstrate responsibility for own learning in and out of the school
    setting. (Betts & Kercher, 1999, p. 124)

Eminent guest speakers help students see how people with high ability or high potential function within their profession, how they relate to their community, and how they can make a difference to society. Reflection and written introspective pieces help students bring the knowledge to the personal or application level.

Working within a small group on an academic pursuit of high interest allows students to see themselves and to see how they change their role(s) in the group. The decisions that must be made, the compromises, the problems that must be solved, and the intellectual interaction contribute to the students' understanding of their opportunities and their responsibilities for their own learning.

Individual Development

The second dimension of the ALM, Individual Development, is designed to provide learners with opportunities to develop the cognitive, emotional, social, and physical skills, concepts, and attitudes needed to become lifelong learners. Six basic areas of development are included in this dimension: inter/intrapersonal, learning skills, technology, college and career involvement, organizational skills, and productivity.

Inter/Intrapersonal

The inter/intrapersonal area provides a transition from the Orientation dimension by building on and expanding the concepts and attitudes developed during orientation, and sets the stage for their incorporation into a Personal Educational Plan (PEP). The PEP is a road map or plan for students to assist them in achieving their objectives for personal and academic growth, as outlined in the ALM. They develop these plans during a weeklong series of individual and group discussions, personal reflection, and conferences with their teachers. At the end of the week, they present their completed PEP to their peers and teachers. As learners progress through dimensions of the ALM, they and their teachers review the plan and modify, extend, or clarify as necessary. The standards and sample learning activities for the inter/intrapersonal area follow.

Standards

Develop more positive self-concepts and self-esteem.

Comprehend own abilities in relationship to self and society.

Develop appropriate skills to interact effectively with peers, siblings, parents, and other adults. (Betts & Kercher, 1999, p. 138)

The Individual Development dimension builds on concepts and skills taught and practiced in the Orientation dimension. The same types of activities, such as small-group work, interacting with eminent adults, and unique productions, continue. Two differences are noticeable at this level, however: (a) All of the pursuits go to a greater depth (self-analysis, reflection on interactions with others, etc.) and (b) the teacher needs to be more vigilant in assessing or perceiving student progress and growth, or the lack thereof. Group and individual debriefing need to probe deeper, and the teacher needs to monitor progress carefully and perceptively.

Learning Skills

The student who is to become an autonomous learner needs a variety of cognitive skills that include the following: creative thinking, critical thinking, problem solving, decision making, and futures thinking. The standards and sample activities for the learning skills area follow.

Standards

Comprehend own abilities in relationship to self and society.

Develop critical and creative thinking skills.

Develop decision-making and problem-solving skills. (Betts & Kercher, 1999, p. 225)

The themes or threads of learning become apparent as the reader progresses through the standards of the ALM. The standards and key components build on those that precede them, expanding and pursuing in greater depth those qualities and habits that will create the lifelong autonomous learner. The learning skills dimension makes this obvious: Students will continue to pursue topics of interest, but to a greater depth; they will develop critical and creative thinking skills as they engage in individual tasks and in group discussions; and they will develop decision-making and problem-solving skills as they engage in group projects.

Technology

Lifelong autonomous learners must acquire and become comfortable with and proficient in using computers, software, the Internet, CD-ROMs, DVDs, digital cameras, modes of multimedia, and long-distance learning. The standards and sample activities for the technology area follow.

Standards

Comprehend own abilities in relationship to self and society.

Develop critical and creative thinking skills.

Increase knowledge in a variety of areas.

Demonstrate responsibility for own learning in and out of the school
  setting. (Betts & Kercher, 1999, p. 215)

Many students have easy access to technological information and considerable expertise in finding the information they seek. Teachers, however, need to ensure that (a) *all* students have access to and acquire expertise, and that (b) time spent in a computer lab or using classroom computers is time used for academic purposes. Teachers need to monitor closely the use of technology, especially with very proficient students.

College and Career Involvement

Students must understand the importance of personal college and career choices, explore college and career options, and complete college and career projects. They need to explore questions such as "What do I want to do with my life?" and "How should I prepare for what I want to do as my life work?" The standards and suggested activities for this area follow.

Standards

Comprehend own abilities in relationship to self and society.

Develop critical and creative thinking skills.

Develop decision-making and problem-solving skills. (Betts & Kercher,
1999, p. 225)

Guest speakers, shadowing experiences, and internships offer students
ways to learn about careers in which they might be interested. In conjunction with these experiences, they need guidance and ways to assess their
own skills and abilities, to know how best to prepare for a specific career.
Equally important is the opportunity of discovering that a particular career field may not be as appealing as it first seemed.

Organizational Skills
Organizational skills are included because of their importance in the immediate, interim, and distant future. The activities in this area of Individual Development serve as a starting place for developing the necessary
skills, and include an investigation of life management concepts, practice
in goal setting, and time management enhancement. The standards and
sample activities for the organizational skills area follow.

Standards
Comprehend own abilities in relationship to self and society.

Develop critical and creative thinking skills.

Develop decision-making and problem-solving skills. (Betts & Kercher,
1999, p. 241)

Developing timelines for projects, assisting with the allocation of class
time to various activities, and keeping a personal daily log assist students to
become aware of time management. The log might be considered by individual students and the teacher together to see where the strengths and
weaknesses lie and how time use might be altered. This could lead into setting priorities and deciding the amounts of time and order of activities to
be undertaken. Efficient time management is an important component of
overall organizational skills, and can be used as a starting point for organizational strategies in other areas of life.

Productivity
The productivity area provides opportunities for students to learn techniques for developing products. Students need to explore those areas of
learning about which they are passionate, create appropriate products, and

evaluate their products. The standards and suggested activities for the development of productivity follow.

Standards

Comprehend own abilities in relationship to self and society.

Develop critical and creative thinking skills.

Develop decision-making and problem-solving skills. (Betts & Kercher, 1999, p. 241)

As student strengths and preferences become apparent, teachers can make suggestions of ways these might be incorporated into a future product. Additionally, teachers should include a variety of objects and displays that are not of the usual school type (i.e., sculptures, paintings, mechanical objects or inventions) to demonstrate that ideas can be communicated in many ways. A wide variety of materials also need to be available for experimentation and perhaps incorporation into students' products. As always, the environment must be supportive of risk-taking and daring to do something out of the ordinary.

Enrichment

The purpose of the Enrichment dimension is to introduce learners to the concept of learner-based content, wherein they have opportunities to decide what to study. This dimension includes explorations, investigations, cultural activities, service, and adventure trips.

Explorations

The exploration level provides opportunities for students to learn what is out there and what is unknown but available to them. The standards and suggested activities follow.

Standards

Develop the appropriate skills to interact effectively with peers, parents, and other adults.

Increase knowledge in a variety of subject areas. (Betts & Kercher, 1999, p. 268)

As students experience a variety of people, media, topics, and learning activities, they may find a topic that becomes a passion. The teacher needs to encourage their desire to pursue this topic and provide guidance and assistance with content sources (people, books, online resources, etc.). A number of students will be interested in an area that allows them both to follow their individual passions and to contribute to the efforts of the entire group when they meet to report and strategize. The product of such a collaboration necessarily will be complex, and the presentation will include a variety of components as each student in the group will contribute information and a preferred method of sharing the learning.

Investigations

An investigation is a mini in-depth study about a topic selected by the student–learner. Its purpose is to provide learners with opportunities to experience a longer term commitment to a topic. The standards and possibilities for the investigations follow.

Standards

Increase knowledge in a variety of content areas.

Develop thinking, decision-making, and problem-solving skills.

Demonstrate responsibility for learning in and out of the school setting. (Betts & Kercher, 1999, p. 277)

The long-term commitment to selecting a topic, planning an investigation, completing the research, and presenting what was learned is the end result toward which the previous experiences and activities have aimed. More than ever, the teacher is the facilitator, guide, supporter, and resource person as student needs surface. Success in this endeavor empowers and validates students as competent (probably lifelong) learners.

Cultural Activities

Cultural activities enable individuals to become more aware of the variety of such opportunities available to them in the community. Any event that involves a worthwhile new experience for a student may qualify as a cultural activity. The standards and some sample cultural activities follow.

Standards

Demonstrate responsibility for learning in and out of the school setting.

Complete experiences that facilitate understanding other people and other communities. (Betts & Kercher, 1999, p. 281)

Most cities and many urban communities contain increasingly diverse populations, which means that students in most schools and classrooms represent a rich mixture of diversity. This variety can be tapped into in many ways. For example, students may gather information about their culture from interviewing family and friends, prepare a way to share this with the class, and be featured speakers or part of a featured cultural group, to share their culture. As a culmination or as an introduction to diverse cultures, families can be invited to bring a cultural food to a potluck. After eating, the students and families can share one of their favorite cultural traditions or practices.

In a neighborhood school where the population is primarily of one ethnicity, students can research the history of the neighborhood in a variety of ways, including interviews of the inhabitants, especially the older people. This information and old and recent photographs of landmarks and artifacts can be crafted into a book that becomes part of the school library, or perhaps copies can be sold to interested persons.

Service

Participation in an activity that benefits the community is intrinsic to developing an understanding of oneself as a contributing member of a larger society. Each learner in the program completes a service unit every year. The standard and sample activities follow.

Standard

Develop the appropriate skills to interact effectively with peers, siblings, and other adults. (Betts & Kercher, 1999, p. 283)

Giving back to the community or making a difference is a critical part of personal growth and maturity. The specific requirement of this experience is possibly unique among teaching–learning models, and it makes a valuable statement about the philosophy of those who developed the model. Because opportunities to make a difference are abundant, one need not work hard to search out opportunities. Students may assist in collecting nonperishable food items, clothing, blankets, diapers, toiletries, or a multitude of other items distributed by various agencies. They may choose to engage in more hands-on experiences, such as working at a food distribution center; working on a community garden project; cleaning up yards of elderly or disabled people; or working as a volunteer for a hospital, the Red Cross, the Salvation Army, or other agencies. With the help of the school nurse, counselors, or school social workers, students can set up a giving tree during the winter holidays. Paper ornaments with the age, gender, and gift wish are hung on the tree, and students and school personnel make or purchase, wrap, and return the gifts by an appointed date. These are distributed to the intended persons, giving all participants a warm glow for the holidays.

Adventure Trips

Students may elect to participate in a yearlong project to plan, organize, finance, and implement trips that promote growth in cognitive, emotional, social, or physical skills. The standards and some possibilities for adventure trips follow.

Standards
Develop knowledge in a variety of subject areas.

Demonstrate responsibility for learning in and out of the school environment. (Betts & Kercher, 1999, p. 284)

Planning an adventure trip, though time-consuming and difficult, is extremely motivational for students. They choose a city, an area, a national park, or a wilderness area that interests them. Then they plan the visit and assume responsibility for logistics, expenses, activities, and the evaluation of the trip. This is one of those learning experiences in which the students become so engrossed and have so much fun that they may have no idea how much they are learning.

Seminars

The fourth dimension of ALM, Seminars, emphasizes the production of new knowledge. Individuals are evolving into self-directed learners with greater opportunities and greater responsibilities. In small groups, learners select and research a topic from one of five areas: futuristic, problematic, controversial, of general interest, or containing advanced knowledge. The standards and some possibilities for such seminars follow.

Standards
Increase knowledge in a variety of subject areas.

Develop thinking, decision-making, and problem-solving skills.

Participate in activities selected to facilitate and integrate the cognitive, emotional, social, and physical development of the individual.

Demonstrate responsibility for own learning in and out of the school setting.

Ultimately become responsible, creative, independent learners. (Betts & Kercher, 1999, p. 290)

The seminars must include three phases: (a) presentation of factual information, (b) group discussion or activity, and (c) closure. Students must participate in self-evaluation, discuss the concept of a seminar, evaluate the effectiveness of the presentation, and discuss ways to improve future seminars. At this point, students are in charge of their learning and have learned the concepts and skills that empower them to continue to control their learning experiences when the opportunities are available. The criteria for evaluating an ALM seminar appear in Table 2.1.

In-Depth Study

The fifth ALM dimension, In-depth Study, is the most challenging in that it requires the highest level of thinking and learning. Through their participation in the previous ALM activities, learners have attained the skills and knowledge to select a topic, develop a learning plan, execute the in-depth study, create a product, and evaluate the process and the product.

An in-depth study ranges in length from 2 months to 2½ years, and learners are more than 90% responsible for their own studies. Support from teacher–facilitators and mentors is still important, however. Some of the forms used for In-depth Study are included in Appendix 2.A (i.e., a study proposal, personal evaluation, project rubric). The standards and a description of the In-depth Studies dimension follow.

Standards

Develop more positive self-concepts.

Comprehend own abilities in relationship to self and society.

Develop the appropriate skills to interact effectively with peers, siblings, parents, and other adults.

Increase knowledge in a variety of areas.

Develop critical and creative thinking skills.

Develop decision-making and problem-solving skills.

(*text continues on p. 49*)

TABLE 2.1

Autonomous Learner Seminar Criteria

	Excellent		Proficient		Basic		In Progress	
	8	7	6	5	4	3	2	1
Content								
30%	Uses a variety of forms of evidence and support; recognizes bias of sources; balances between "hard data" and "stories." Thinking is logically consistent. Uses imagination and materials in unusual ways.		Uses at least a limited variety of support and examples. Sources are cited correctly; evidence is suitable for the purpose. Thinking is characterized by using factually reliable materials, by distinguishing facts from opinion and by fluency, flexibility, originality, and elaboration.		Little or inappropriate evidence is used; sources not cited or limitations ignored. Demonstrates less than adequate knowledge or preparation. Little or no evidence of original thinking is evident. Students unaware that opinions are not facts; focuses on trivial for support.		Evidence limited to generalizations or personal opinion; resource material not used. Unwilling or unable to exhibit logical and consistent thinking skills. Unable or unwilling to exhibit creative thinking skills.	
Audio/Visuals								
15%	Audio/visual forms are professional, appropriate to and enhancing of the presentation. Show important, not trivial, information.		Group uses a variety of audio/visual forms, which are visually and aesthetically pleasing and neat.		Few audio/visual aids are used, or those used are hastily assembled and presented.		No attempt made to use aids.	

(continues)

TABLE 2.1 *Continued.*
Autonomous Learner Seminar Criteria

	Excellent		Proficient		Basic		In Progress	
	8	7	6	5	4	3	2	1
Delivery								
5%	Body language projects poise. Effective use of materials and technologies. Sounds enthusiastic, assertive. Articulation and pronunciation are clear. Adjusts to audience reactions.		Erect posture, relaxed and natural expressions and gestures. Eye contact and energy are appropriate. Poised. Uses conversational tone; controls vocal pauses, pitch, loudness. Articulation and pronunciation are acceptable. Evidence of practice and effort. Grammar is correct.		Appearance or gestures inappropriate, at times. Minimal eye contact; refers often to notes. Pace of speech is distracting; pronunciation interferes with message. Word choice is characterized by inappropriate language.		Appearance or gestures not appropriate; lacks eye contact. Vocal behaviors interfere. Unwilling to use appropriate language.	
Organization								
Introduction 5%	Group uses humor, dramatic tension, or analogy without detracting from the integrity of the content.		Group uses introductory attention device; clearly states thesis; previews main points.		Group lacks attention-getting device, unclear or missing thesis statement.		None evident.	

(continues)

TABLE 2.1 *Continued.*
Autonomous Learner Seminar Criteria

	Excellent		Proficient		Basic		In Progress	
	8	7	6	5	4	3	2	1
Organization (continued)								
Body 10%		Each presenter demonstrates a body of knowledge that is well-organized and demonstrates expertise in the subject.		Each presenter demonstrates a central body of knowledge. Evidence of practice and effort.		Body of knowledge is loosely organized by the presenter and/or does not flow logically.		The presenter shows little or no organization.	
Conclusion 5%		Group uses concluding techniques that are summative or reinforcing or demonstrate application.		Group uses concluding technique (i.e., repetition for effect).		Group uses loose or inappropriate conclusion.		Presentation ends without appropriate conclusion.	
Handout								
10%		Uses creativity; pictures are clear; lettering is professional; neatness and professionalism are evident.		Supports and enhances the presentation; visually pleasing. Spelling and grammar are correct.		Little thought or preparation. Does not support topic.		None or inappropriate.	

(*continues*)

TABLE 2.1 *Continued.*
Autonomous Learner Seminar Criteria

	Excellent		Proficient		Basic		In Progress	
	8	7	6	5	4	3	2	1
Group Dynamics								
15%	Team atmosphere is obvious. Leadership is shared and cohesiveness and support [are] demonstrated by each member.		Group cooperation is evident as each member carries through with various team responsibilities.		Limited evidence of team work. Acceptance of responsibility is limited. Group interaction and group cohesiveness are limited.		No evidence of cooperation among group members. Members may act in detracting or destructive ways.	
Bibliography								
5%	Annotates the sources used. Wide variety of resources are referenced.		Follows an accepted form; spelling is correct. Variety of resources are noted.		Limited attempt at developing a list of resources. Incorrect use of correct form. Limited resources are noted.		Little or no resources are referenced. Incorrect form is used.	

Note. From *The Autonomous Learner Model* (p. 301), by G. Betts and J. Kercher, 1999, Greeley, CO: Autonomous Learning Publications and Specialists. Copyright 1999 by Autonomous Learning Publications and Specialists. Reprinted with permission.

Integrate activities which facilitate the cognitive, emotional, social, and physical development of the individual.

Develop individual passion area(s) of learning.

Demonstrate responsibility for own learning in and out of the school setting.

Ultimately become responsible, creative, independent learners. (Betts & Kercher, 1999, p. 306)

When students have had the experiences leading up to the final dimension of an in-depth study, they are expected to have discovered a passion area, understand how to plan and conduct an in-depth study, and be ready to design a learning contract for the study. They have been prepared ultimately to become professionals within their passion area and to make interim and final presentations. Students expect to evaluate and assess the process, the product, and the study, and to receive appropriate feedback from others.

IMPLEMENTATION

The implementation of the Autonomous Learner Model is guided by an extensive list of basic principles. These principles demonstrate that the ALM is designed to develop a well-rounded, knowledgeable, socially apt, motivated, self-confident student. (For the entire list of basic principles, see Betts & Kercher, 1999, p. 6.)

The ALM is designed to be implemented as a one-period-per-day elective class in secondary schools; a 3-year commitment from gifted students is recommended. During the first year of implementation, students continue to take regular content and elective classes for the balance of the day. In subsequent years, a learner, with the cooperation of a teacher–facilitator, a content-area teacher, and community resource persons or mentors, may develop in-depth study expansions for one or more content areas. If an elective class is not feasible, ALM may be integrated into a content course (e.g., language arts, science, social studies); the regular curriculum is compacted into 2 or 3 days per week, and curriculum for the autonomous learners is implemented during the other days. When the teacher–facilitator and individual student believe the necessary level of thinking, learning, and intrapersonal skills have been developed, an individual Personal Growth Plan is prepared by the learner with the cooperation of teacher–facilitators, content teachers, counselor (if available), and parents. The Personal Growth Plan provides direction for learning growth in the next 2 or 3 years and identifies what activities and investigations in the school and community are planned, how the student will be involved, and where the activities and investigations will take place. Figure 2.2 illustrates the suggested timeline for implementation of the Autonomous Learner Model.

At the elementary level, the ALM can be implemented in a resource room program in which students are involved for a minimum of 2 half-days per week. Students participate in curriculum decisions and evaluate

Dimensions	Year One Months 0 3 6 9	Year Two Months 0 3 6 9	Year Three Months 0 3 6 9
Orientation	▬	▬	▬
Individual Development	▬▬▬ ▬▬	▬ ▬▬ ▬	
Enrichment Activities	▬	▬	▬
Seminars	▬▬	▬▬▬	▬▬
In-depth Study*[1]	▬▬▬▬▬▬▬▬▬▬▬▬▬▬▬▬▬▬▬▬▬▬		

*Some students may begin in-depth study immediately.
[1]After the third year, the majority of time would be concentrated on in-depth study expansion and out-of-school experiences.

FIGURE 2.2. Suggested timeline for implementing the model. From *The Autonomous Learner Model for the Gifted and Talented,* by G. Betts, 1985, Greeley, CO: Autonomous Learning Publications and Specialists. Copyright 1985 by Autonomous Learning Publications and Specialists. Reprinted with permission.

the effectiveness of the model. Student ownership is an important element of the program. The suggested scope and sequence emphasizes the first three dimensions in elementary schools. Students in Grades 4 and 5 also are introduced to the last two dimensions, but few students are ready to develop seminars and in-depth study prior to Grade 6. Betts does recommend, however, that if students are ready (intellectually, socially, and emotionally) for an in-depth study, they should not be restricted by expectations of what is age appropriate or "best" for most gifted students (Betts, 1981, cited in Betts & Kercher, 1999).

Betts suggests areas of emphasis in each dimension. Appendix 2.B illustrates a sample 4-year approach for implementation of the ALM, and Table 2.2 provides examples of possible activities within each component of the ALM.

MODIFYING THE MODEL

The Autonomous Learner Model provides a comprehensive framework for curriculum modification appropriate for gifted students in all areas. As with the Enrichment Triad Model (Chapter 8), the content, process, product, and learning environment modifications suggested by Maker (1982b) and Maker and Nielson (1995) are incorporated within the framework.

Content Modifications

The content modifications of abstractness, complexity, variety, and study of people are incorporated into recommended activities and principles. The modification of organization for learning value is suggested in the principle that content topics are broadbased with emphasis on major themes, problems, issues, and ideas. One recommendation to strengthen this component is to organize guided investigations and enrichment activities around abstract concepts and generalizations, as recommended by Bruner (see Chapter 4), to facilitate transfer of learning and cognitive development. Recommended student activities also include numerous opportunities to

(*text continues on p. 62*)

TABLE 2.2
Summary of Student and Teacher Activities and Roles in the Autonomous Learner Model

Step, Type, or Level of Thinking	Student		Teacher	
	Role	Sample Activities	Role	Sample Activities
Orientation				
Understanding giftedness, talent, intelligence, and creativity	Active participant Observer Inquirer Synthesizer	Do biographical research on a gifted individual. Role-play the gifted individual at a news conference or open house. Read and discuss books and selected articles about gifted people. Brainstorm questions for guests. Interview gifted people in the community. Do an informal survey on attitudes about giftedness or creativity. Participate in discussions. Develop own definition of giftedness.	Resource Facilitator	Plan experiences to put students in contact with gifted individuals. Encourage students to visit the library and use a variety of resources to research aspects of giftedness. Arrange visits, field trips, guests. Model interviewing skills and provide a resource list of at least 25 gifted persons in the community that students can interview. Plan group and individual exercises to develop survey questions and skills.
Group building	Active participant Friend Interviewer Planner	Conduct a personal interview with a fellow student. Nurture a "secret" friend. Participate in a "Starve your vulture" campaign to build self-esteem.	Resource Facilitator Planner	Demonstrate and help students to analyze varied group process skills. Model esteem-building behaviors. Plan individual and group activities to develop thinking/feeling processes students can use for varied purposes.

(continues)

Orientation (*continued*)

Group building (*continued*)		Use Taba conflict resolution strategy to resolve interpersonal problems. Participate in group discussions about your own and others' feelings and perceptions about being part of the group. Use Creative Problem Solving to design and implement a project to benefit the group, school, or community.	Plan process experiences to meet both individual and group needs. Ask thought-provoking questions. Model active listening and communication skills. Assist students in the development of plans and acquisition of resources for special projects.
Self/personal development	Active participant Self-analyzer Synthesizer	Review identification information and procedures for selection to the program for the gifted. Analyze and discuss "nourishing" and "toxic" behaviors and how they affect oneself and other people. Do a learning style inventory. Brainstorm differences between role of a student and role of a learner. Keep a journal of personal thoughts. Design and implement a project to synthesize new self-understandings.	Facilitator Resource Discussion leader Plan and implement activities to assist students in understanding identification procedures. Plan group and individual exercises to increase student's awareness of behavior patterns and effects. Provide resources for inventories of learning styles and interests. Share results of inventories with individual students. Facilitate a discussion of autonomous learner characteristics.

(*continues*)

TABLE 2.2 *Continued.*
Summary of Student and Teacher Activities and Roles in the Autonomous Learner Model

Step, Type, or Level of Thinking	Student		Teacher	
	Role	**Sample Activities**	**Role**	**Sample Activities**
Orientation *(continued)*				
Program and school opportunities and responsibilities	Active participant Observer Inquirer Presenter Planner	Learn the dimensions, structure, and goals of the ALM. Analyze presentations of various speakers and own abilities to discover topics of interest for seminars and/or in-depth studies. Individually or in small groups, explore libraries and community resources for possible seminar and in-depth study topics. Prepare and present an oral report to classmates on possible topics. Develop a "personal growth plan" that includes activities, resource people, in-school participation, and out-of-school participation. Include skills, concepts, and attitudes necessary to become a lifelong learner.	Researcher Planner Presenter Facilitator Resource	Do a "program search" to identify all activities available for gifted students in the school and community. Identify potential advisors, resource people, and possible mentors. Develop a presentation on *Autonomous Learner Model* for students and all interested persons. Implement individual and group activities to assist students in development of skills and attitudes needed for lifelong learning. Plan guest speakers, discussions, and exploratory experiences to put students in contact with topics of interest and possible mentors. Provide information and a format to assist students in the development of individual Student Growth Plans.

(continues)

Individual Development

Inter/intra-personal skills	Active participant Reflective thinker Inquirer	Periodically complete open-ended questions from *Journeys Into Self* (Betts & Kercher, 1999, pp. 165–194) exercises in self-exploration. Participate in role-playing simulations and subsequent discussions of behaviors. Explore creative lifestyles and the advantages and disadvantages of varied occupations. Synthesize all information/ideas developed in these activities. Participate in activities designed to develop skills in communication, interviewing, discussion, leadership, group processes, and coping. Participate in a "coping group," if desired, to discuss issues and problems of concern. As a group, plan and implement a closure activity for this unit.	Facilitator Resource Trainer	Provide structured self-exploration exercises to students three or four times yearly. Confer with students to discuss similarities and differences in responses to the same questions. Plan and implement activities in which students role-play appropriate and inappropriate behaviors; facilitate discussion of experiences. Assist students to acquire background to develop a Personalized Learning Plan. Plan and implement activities to assist students in the development of skills in each of the target areas (e.g., reflective listening and congruent sending in communications). Plan and implement role-playing simulations in which students develop interview skills. Provide expertise and support for coping group meetings.

(continues)

TABLE 2.2 *Continued.*

Summary of Student and Teacher Activities and Roles in the Autonomous Learner Model

Step, Type, or Level of Thinking	Student		Teacher	
	Role	Sample Activities	Role	Sample Activities
Individual Development (*continued*)				
Learning skills	Active participant	Participate in thinking skill activities. Do research skill activities. Develop goal setting and organizational skills. Develop skills in computer use. Develop skills in photography and/or multimedia production. Do activities designed to improve writing and communication skills.	Facilitator Trainer Resource	Guide varied problem-solving, creativity, and thinking activities to develop skills students can use in investigations. Provide activities to develop goal-setting, decision-making, research, and organization skills. Facilitate activities to help students develop skills in writing, the use of computers, photography, and media production.
Technology	Inquirer, active participant	Determine what technology will be useful now and in the future to reach educational and personal goals.	Facilitator Resource Trainer	Provide speakers and experiences regarding recent technology. Encourage students to master necessary skills, allow time for them to practice.
College and career involvement	Inquirer/ researcher Intern	Participate in activities designed to develop awareness of a broad range of careers. Investigate career(s) of choice in depth.	Facilitator Resource Coordinator	Plan and implement activities to encourage students to learn about many diverse colleges and careers.

(continues)

Individual Development (*continued*)

College and career involvement (*continued*)	Synthesizer	Participate in an internship in a career of choice.	Invite guest speakers to discuss specific careers and to provide information on specific college programs.
		Plan a closure activity to synthesize new career knowledge.	With students, identify individuals and/or businesses for student internships.
		Investigate colleges based on strengths and interests.	Provide support as needed in research skills and internship behaviors.
			Provide information or contacts.
Organizational skills	Active participant	Self-determine level of organizational skills possessed.	Facilitator
	Self-analyzer	Self-determine skills that need to be learned or developed to a greater degree.	Guide
			Lead students to set class goals, then individual goals in academic, personal, and community areas.
			Instruct and lead in practice of time management and life management strategies.
			Use Life Management Wheel (Betts & Kercher, 1999, pp. 244–245) to help students assess areas of strength and need.
Productivity	Active participant	Brainstorm types of products (ways to share information).	Facilitator
	Self-analyzer	Determine what skills need to be learned to create a variety of products.	Guide
			Resource
			Keep brainstormed list of possible products posted.
			Encourage students to expand their methods and techniques of production.
			Arrange for guest speakers to instruct students in necessary skills and techniques.

(*continues*)

TABLE 2.2 *Continued.*

Summary of Student and Teacher Activities and Roles in the Autonomous Learner Model

Step, Type, or Level of Thinking	Student		Teacher	
	Role	Sample Activities	Role	Sample Activities
Enrichment				
Explorations	Active participant	Individually, or in small groups, brainstorm topics of possible interest.	Facilitator	Plan and implement a group exploration activity to review research skills/strategies and help students develop the concept of information retrieval from multiple resources.
	Inquirer/researcher	Individually identify "passion areas" for possible in-depth study.	Resource	Provide assistance to small groups and individuals, as needed, during explorations.
	Synthesizer	In small groups, plan and conduct an exploration of different facets of a chosen topic.		Provide a structure for the sharing of information learned.
		Individually, plan and conduct three to five explorations of chosen topics using multiple resources.		Encourage students to "branch out" to topics about which they know little but that are of interest to them.
		Select a format and share information about the topic with the group.		Assist students in assessing presentations to determine areas for growth.
Investigations	Active participant	Individually, select a topic and prepare a proposal for an investigation.	Facilitator	Plan and implement activities designed to help students develop an investigation proposal.
	Investigator	Conduct the proposed investigation.	Resource	Review proposal with each student.
	Presenter		Adviser	

(continues)

Enrichment (*continued*)

	Student role	Student activities	Facilitator role	Facilitator activities
Investigations (*continued*)	Reflective thinker	Evaluate the investigation. Synthesize the results and prepare a presentation for an appropriate audience. Compare/contrast an exploration, an investigation, and an in-depth study.		Meet with individual students weekly during the investigation to discuss progress. As needed, review specific skills and provide support to investigators. Provide appropriate audiences for presentations.
Cultural activities	Observer Participant	In small or large groups, prepare a proposal for participation in after-school, evening, or weekend cultural events (e.g., visits to museums, plays, concerts, speeches, historical events) and go "behind the scenes" to see how events are set up. Synthesize the experience in a summary paper after each event.	Facilitator Resource	Review proposals. Assist students in making "behind the scenes" arrangements. Facilitate discussions of appropriate behaviors for attendance at cultural activities.
Service	Active participant	Plan and conduct research on an individual humanitarian. Share research with group. Brainstorm common characteristics of humanitarians. Plan and complete a service project in the community.	Facilitator Proposal evaluator Resource	Guide a discussion on the concept of humanitarianism. Compile a list of agencies or organizations that provide humanitarian services in the community. Confer with individual students to review proposals prior to approval.

(*continues*)

TABLE 2.2 *Continued.*

Summary of Student and Teacher Activities and Roles in the Autonomous Learner Model

Step, Type, or Level of Thinking	Student		Teacher	
	Role	Sample Activities	Role	Sample Activities
Enrichment (*continued*)				
Adventure trips	Decision maker and planner Active participant Evaluator	Participate in decision making to decide destination, purpose, goals, and the focus area of the study. Participate in planning all aspects. Participate in trip activities. Participate in evaluation focused on both academic and group process aspects of the adventure trip.	Facilitator Resource	Plan a meeting for interested members of the group, parents, and other teachers to explore possibilities and make decisions. Advise student planners. Coordinate student efforts in fund-raising, travel arrangements, and administrative requirements. Conduct "debriefing" for evaluation.
Seminars	Active participant Planner Researcher Presenter Evaluator	In small groups, develop a seminar on some aspect of a broad topic such as futuristics, controversial issues, social problems, or advanced knowledge in a field. Prepare contract for seminar. Conduct research.	Facilitator Resource	Plan activities to help students understand the purpose and structure of seminars. Negotiate seminar contract with each group. Guide students to focus on topics that are futuristic, controversial, or of general interest, or that contain advanced knowledge.

(*continues*)

Seminars (*continued*)

		Prepare and present factual information about topic. Conduct discussion or involvement activity.	Provide appropriate audiences for the seminars. Guide an evaluation discussion.

In-depth study

Student roles	Student tasks	Teacher roles	Teacher responsibilities
Active participant Inquirer Producer Presenter Evaluator	Select a topic for in-depth study. Design a learning plan; select a mentor. Conduct the in-depth study. Make progress presentations. Develop the product(s). Evaluate the experience.	Facilitator Resource Advisor	Confer with individuals on in-depth study proposals. Approve proposals when complete. Arrange mentorships. Assist students as needed to develop criteria for assessment and evaluation. Help mentors define role and responsibilities. Answer questions or provide support as needed. Monitor student progress. Provide appropriate audiences for presentations. Guide evaluation discussions.

Note. Adapted from *The Autonomous Learner Model*, by G. Betts and J. Kercher, 1999, Greeley, CO: Autonomous Learning Publications and Specialists. Copyright 1999 by Autonomous Learning Publications and Specialists. Reprinted with permission.

develop general methods of inquiry—that is, the study of methods. A comparison of methods of inquiry used in various disciplines would complement the enrichment activities and better prepare learners for in-depth studies. When students are learning to conduct investigations and present seminars, the Group Investigations model (see Chapter 9) provides an excellent way to structure content and help students develop essential cognitive and social skills needed for group collaboration.

Process Modifications

Process modifications stressed in ALM include higher levels of thinking, open-endedness, discovery, freedom of choice, group interaction, pacing, and variety. Because evidence of reasoning is not explicitly stressed in ALM, inclusion of the Hilda Taba Teaching Strategies (Chapter 10) in learning skills, explorations, investigations, seminars, and in-depth study could be used to incorporate this important element into the model very easily. Teacher–facilitators also can ask individuals and discussion groups to state reasons and support for inferences or decisions.

Higher level thinking processes are included in the standards for each of the dimensions of ALM, but specific techniques for developing higher level thought and problem-solving skills are not identified. A recommended change is to use Bloom's Taxonomy (Chapter 3), Creative Problem Solving (Chapter 6), the DISCOVER Model's problem continuum (Chapter 5), and the Taba strategies (Chapter 10) as process models in enrichment activities. The value of guided discovery also is addressed implicitly in the investigations component of the Enrichment dimension, but teachers can enhance this component by encouraging learners to use Taba's Interpretation of Data strategy to discover patterns, ideas, and underlying principles as an integral part of synthesizing the results of investigations.

Product Modifications

One of the strengths of the ALM is that product modifications recommended for gifted students (Maker, 1982b; Maker & Nielson, 1995) are specifically identified in the basic principles and in most recommended activities. Students deal with real problems (e.g., community traffic patterns near the school that represent a danger to students), and solutions are presented to real audiences (e.g., a better traffic plan presented to the city council) using formats of their choice.

Transformation is assured by an emphasis on products that are new and unique to the learner, and self-evaluation is an integral part of all activities in the ALM. When students select their own topics for investigations, seminars, and in-depth study, the teacher–facilitator can encourage choice of a topic related to issues, problems, and areas of concern.

Learning Environment Modifications

The basic principles of the ALM assure that the program will be learner centered, promote independence, and involve students in decisions regarding curriculum, special activities, and evaluation. High mobility is required; many activities are planned that encourage students to leave the classroom to explore or investigate in other parts of the school and community. Complexity is assured through offering challenging tasks, teaching advanced strategies, and involving learners in the planning, implementation, and evaluation of such activities as field trips, service projects, seminars, and in-depth study. Obviously, a classroom in which students are carrying out these types of activities will display flexibility in its organization and structure.

Summary

The ALM provides a framework for long-term development of potentially gifted and creative students with the goal of developing gifted and creative lifelong learners. The modifications recommended for gifted students either are intrinsic to the model or can be made easily through the integration of specific process models and the organization of skill development activities or investigations around complex, abstract concepts and generalizations.

DEVELOPMENT

The ALM grew from a program designed by teachers at Arvada West High School in Jefferson County, Colorado, in the late 1970s. One of the first enrichment programs developed for secondary students, the program deliberately emphasizes emotional and social development in conjunction with cognitive development. George Betts, then teacher–facilitator of gifted and talented learning at Arvada West, was responsible for the design and implementation of the program. The present model has been developed, refined, and expanded based on the 1980 model and the input of professionals and learners. Betts, now a professor at the University of Northern Colorado, and professor and director of the Summer Enrichment Program at the university since 1978, does not cite the theoretical foundations of the model, and no large-scale, empirical research has been conducted to assess the overall effectiveness of the model.

Jolene K. Kercher is the coordinator of gifted and talented programs and teacher of advanced placement mathematics at Arvada West High School. She has worked closely with Betts in developing the model as it is now presented.

Originally developed as an elective class for gifted and creative students in secondary schools, the model has been expanded to include a framework for a comprehensive, resource room–based program for elementary-age students as well. A scope and sequence of elements in each dimension suggests appropriate grade levels for awareness, introduction, development, and application of each element. The elementary school program has a focus on the first three dimensions—Orientation, Individual Development, and Enrichment; because of their complexity, Seminars and In-depth Study dimensions generally are limited to gifted students in secondary schools.

RESEARCH ON EFFECTIVENESS

No empirical research on the effectiveness of the model is available. Although formative program evaluations have been conducted at several sites, results are not available. Traditional measures of student growth, in which content knowledge is emphasized, are not appropriate for assessing the effectiveness of this model. Substantial research, however, is needed to support the belief that the program is effective. Are all five dimensions of the model essential for the development of autonomous learners? What are graduates of the program doing now? What effect did participation in the program have on their career decisions? How did it affect their lives? A well-designed longitudinal follow-up study of program participants, at periodic intervals following graduation from high school, might be the most valid research for this complex model. The multitude of interaction variables among participants, teachers, community resource persons, mentors, and sites for investigations may make comprehensive empirical research impossible; however, participants can be compared with nonparticipants at several sites to obtain needed information about possible effects of the model.

JUDGMENTS

Advantages

One outstanding advantage of the Autonomous Learner Model is that it was designed by teachers specifically for gifted, creative students in secondary schools. The downward extension of the scope and sequence of the model to kindergarten is an added plus. Unlike Renzulli's Enrichment Triad Model (Chapter 8), task commitment is not assumed, and specific activities and experiences are designed to help potentially gifted learners develop the social, emotional, and cognitive strategies that will enable them to become autonomous learners. Another advantage is the emphasis on student independence and choice. Not only do learners choose their own topics for investigations, seminars, and in-depth study, but they also make decisions about culminating activities and plan, implement, and evaluate those activities. Another advantage is that the model can be incorporated into the framework of secondary schools and includes procedures for cooperative planning with content teachers and community resource persons to allow in-depth study expansions in subject matter classes. As the suggested timeline (see Figure 2.2) illustrates, the model is flexible. Some students may spend more time in developmental activities; others may begin in-depth study almost immediately. A suggested scope and sequence, from awareness through introduction, development, and application of each component in all five dimensions, is provided for Grades K–1, 2–3, 4–5, 6–8, and 9–12.

Learners who have developed the essential cognitive, emotional, social, and organizational skills through participation in ALM in earlier grades may pursue in-depth studies throughout the majority of their high school experience.

Another advantage is that the model can be adapted to the needs of the school, the characteristics and needs of gifted students, the talents and gifts of teacher–facilitators, and the resources of the community. The skills emphasized in the Individual Development dimension are appropriate to all students and could be included in heterogeneous classes. With the availability of a mentor or facilitator, the model also could be used as a guide for assisting highly able students in smaller schools or communities to develop the skills and attitudes for participation in seminars and in-depth study investigations.

Disadvantages

One obvious disadvantage of the model is the lack of research on the effectiveness of the approach. The complexity of interactions among participants, along with the variations among content areas, study sites, mentors involved, and activities selected for Personal Educational Plans, makes empirical research difficult and may preclude comparative effectiveness studies with other approaches for gifted individuals. Research has been conducted, however, on the importance of developing strategic self-management (or metacognitive) skills and on the effectiveness of self-directed study with gifted students. Other research (e.g., Schneider, 1987) also has validated the importance of facilitating the development of social competence by gifted children. Unfortunately, Betts has not identified the philosophical, theoretical, or research bases of the ALM, and no information is available about the demographic or personal characteristics of students who successfully make the transition to autonomous learner. Many questions remain to be answered. What are the characteristics of students selected for participation in the model? What are the effects of the program on special populations of gifted students? What has happened to program participants in the years following high school graduation? What is the "durability" of the program (e.g., How long do adopting school districts maintain the implementation)? What cognitive, social, and emotional characteristics and skills are essential for successful teacher–facilitators?

Another disadvantage of the program is the complexity of the instructional, management, and interpersonal skills required of teacher–facilitators. The flexibility of the model, which may be an advantage for some dedicated teachers who also are autonomous learners, may not provide the support tools necessary for a less assured teacher–facilitator. The scope of skills to be developed in the Individual Development dimension alone requires an extensive knowledge of learning skills, group processes, and counseling skills to facilitate students' personal understanding and career exploration. Comprehensive staff development, including strategies for involving community resource persons and mentors, is essential for implementing the model. Teachers–facilitators must have a variety of resources available, skill in the use of the resources, and time to locate both human and material resources.

CONCLUSION

The Autonomous Learner Model, with its five dimensions, is designed to provide comprehensive learning experiences that will enable students dependent on teacher direction to become autonomous learners capable of self-directed, lifelong learning. The goals, assumptions, and basic principles in the model are based on needs of gifted students identified by leaders in the field (e.g., Clark, 1983; Feldhusen & Treffinger, 1980; Renzulli, 1977; Treffinger, 1978). Educators who wish to adopt or adapt this approach may need intensive staff development to acquire the process, management, and interpersonal skills necessary to implement the model. With these reservations, the model is recommended as appropriate for programs for gifted students.

RESOURCES

Background Information

Torrance, E. P. (1984). *Mentor relationships: How they aid creative achievement, endure, change, and die.* Buffalo, NY: Bearly Limited.

Instructional Materials and Ideas

Betts, G. T. (1985). *Journeys into self.* Greeley, CO: Autonomous Learning Publications and Specialists.

Betts, G. T., & Kercher, J. K. (1999). *The Autonomous Learner Model: Optimizing ability.* Greeley, CO: Autonomous Learning Publications and Specialists.

Dalton, J. (1992). *Creative thinking and cooperative talk in small groups.* Portsmouth, NH: Heinemann.

Featherstone, B., & Reilly, J. (n.d.) *College comes sooner than you think!* Scottsdale, AZ: Great Potential Press.

Fleisher, P. (1993). *Changing our world: A handbook for young activists.* Tucson, AZ: Zephyr Press.

Galbraith, J. (n.d.). *The gifted kids survival guide: A handbook for ages 10 and under.* Minneapolis: Free Spirit.

Galbraith, J. (n.d.). *The gifted kids survival guide: A teen handbook.* Minneapolis: Free Spirit.

Garvin, K. (1989). *Primary activities: A treasure chest of primary-level ALM exercises.* Greeley, CO: Autonomous Learning Publishers and Specialists.

Reilly, J. (1992) *Mentorship: The essential guide for schools and business.* Scottsdale, AZ: Great Potential Press.

Udall, A. J., & Daniels, M. A. (1991). *Creating the thoughtful classroom: Strategies to promote student thinking.* Tucson, AZ: Zephyr Press.

Autonomous Learning Publications and Specialists (ALPS) (P.O. Box 2264, Greeley, CO 80632; www.alpspublishing.com) also publishes a number of other books for use with ALM, including *Community Search, Future Studies, Images of Greatness, Discovering Who's Who in Our Community,* and *Research Skills for Beginners.* The ALPS catalog includes a number of other resources recommended for use in this model.

Useful Web sites:

http://www.awpeller.com

http://www.giftedbooks.com

http://www.zephyrpress.com

APPENDIX 2.A

Autonomous Learner In-depth Study Forms

IN-DEPTH STUDY PROPOSAL

I will study: (*Topic*)	Name:
More specifically: (*Description*)	My material resources:
	My human resources (mentor):
My content standards:	My final product:
The specific activities I will do as a part of my project:	My presentation:
	My date of presentation:
	I will present to appropriate audiences at:
I will show analysis by:	My grade will be based on: (*Criteria*)
I will show synthesis by:	

IN-DEPTH STUDY PERSONAL EVALUATION

In reflecting about your topic, its content, the process you followed and what you learned, please answer and summarize your experiences in the following:

1. Give a brief description of your project.

2. What insight did you gain about (a) your topic, (b) the process you designed and followed and (c) your self?

3. Did you **successfully** demonstrate your knowledge and what you learned as a result of your work? Is there evidence that you thought abstractly, made a "great leap" in the application and insight of your thought process?

4. Did you challenge yourself to think—about your topic, your result and/or findings, your process, and your **growth**—and how successfully did you reach your goal?

5. Was the production of your final product and the presentation of your findings of a **professional** quality that sets you apart from others or would favorably compare you to accepted standards in the field? Did you show a level of sophistication not commonly seen in your other classes or experiences?

6. What **skills** did you enhance and improve in your (a) research, (b) production, (c) presentation, (d) other?

7. Rate yourself on how well you **met the standards** cited in your contract proposal.

8. What are your **feelings** about (a) the research, (b) the product, (c) what you learned, and (d) what you experienced?

9. Anything else?

Turn your typewritten responses in with your project. Include your name and date submitted. This will be retained for the records.

Note. From *The Autonomous Learner Model Optimizing Ability*, by G. T. Betts and J. K. Kercher, 1999, Greeley, CO: Autonomous Learning Publications. Copyright 1999 by Autonomous Learning Publications. Reprinted with permission.

IN-DEPTH STUDY PROJECT RUBRIC

	Excellent		Proficient		Basic		In Progress	
	8	7	6	5	4	3	2	1
In-depth Research								
	Skillfully gathers and analyzes relevant written and nonwritten material. Independently finds answers to questions using a wide variety of sources.		Attempts to gather and analyze relevant written and nonwritten material. Uses several different sources to answer questions.		Attempts to gather a limited collection of written and non-written material that may or may not be relevant. Seeks information from a limited number of sources.		Gathers little or no written or nonwritten material. Uses very few sources.	
	Documents and supports research through notes, copies of pertinent articles, recordings, etc. References information.		Attempts to document and support research through some notes, copies, etc. Attempts to reference information.		Provides limited documentation and support of research. Information is incorrect or not referenced.		Gathers little or no support or documentation.	
	Supports and assists in completing the research project (outlines, notes, copies of pertinent articles, recordings).		Attempts to organize information and material in such a way as to assist in completing the research project.		Requires guidance to organize information and material needed to complete the research project.		Demonstrates little or no attempt at organizing information.	
	Organizes information, material, and final product.							

(continues)

IN-DEPTH STUDY PROJECT RUBRIC *Continued.*

	Excellent		Proficient		Basic		In Progress	
	8	7	6	5	4	3	2	1
Thinking and Production								
Higher level thinking	Independently applies analysis, synthesis, and evaluation to the learning process.		Applies analysis, synthesis, and evaluation in most situations.		Demonstrates knowledge, comprehension, and application with very little evidence of the use of analysis, synthesis, or evaluation.		Demonstrates knowledge and comprehension.	
Creative production	Independently applies fluency, flexibility, originality, and elaboration to create exemplary and original products. Elaborates and exceeds requirements of individual proposal.		Demonstrates productive thinking skills. Occasionally creates unique and original products. Meets requirements of individual proposal.		Demonstrates little or no evidence of original thinking or production. Makes vague attempts at exhibiting unique or original products or performances. Does not fulfill requirements of proposal.		Is unable or unwilling to exhibit creativity. Makes little attempt to fulfill proposal requirements.	
Mechanics								
Bibliography	Annotates sources. References wide variety of resources in acceptable form.		Follows an accepted form. Uses correct spelling. Notes variety of resources.		Makes limited attempt at developing a list of resources. Uses incorrect form.		References few resources. Uses incorrect form.	

(continues)

Mechanics (*continued*)

Spelling/grammar	Uses correct spelling and grammar. Employs vocabulary of the discipline.	Uses acceptable spelling and grammar. Makes few mistakes.	Makes several mistakes in spelling and grammar.	Makes many errors in spelling and grammar.
Delivery				
Visual presentation	Demonstrates nonverbal poise, controlled use of space, and effective use of audio/visual technologies.	Demonstrates erect posture, relaxed facial expression, natural use of gestures, effective use of visual aids when appropriate, and acceptable use of movement. Uses appropriate eye contact and energy. Is poised.	Demonstrates inappropriate appearance or gestures at times. Makes little eye contact or refers often to notes.	Demonstrates inappropriate appearance or gestures. Lacks eye contact or reads speech.
Vocal presentation	Sounds enthusiastic, assertive, and confident. Uses clear articulation and pronunciation. Shows evidence of practice and effort.	Includes conversational tone, control of vocal pauses, rate, pitch, and loudness. Uses acceptable articulation and pronunciation.	Uses vocal behaviors that may interfere with transfer of message, distracting pace of speech, and/or pronunciation that interferes with message.	Giggles, expounds, or uses other interfering vocal behaviors. Speaks too fast or slowly. Runs words together.
Word choice	Uses the language and vocabulary of the topic, and responds appropriately to audience.	Uses vocabulary specific to topic. Uses correct grammar. Demonstrates few instances of slang, "um,""uh," etc.	Uses inappropriate language, clichés, vernacular, double negatives, or sexist terms.	Is unwilling or unable to use appropriate language.

(*continues*)

IN-DEPTH STUDY PROJECT RUBRIC *Continued.*

	Excellent		Proficient		Basic		In Progress	
	8	7	6	5	4	3	2	1
Organization								
Introduction	Uses introductory attention device such as quotes, humor, dramatic tension, or analogy as a key element without detracting from the integrity of the content.		Clearly states thesis. Previews main points of presentation.		Lacks attention-getting device, unclear or missing thesis statement.		Has no clear introduction.	
Body	Presents a body of knowledge that is well organized, planned, and flows from topic to topic. Demonstrates effort and practice.		Presents a central body of knowledge.		Poorly organizes information.		Evidences no organization.	
Conclusion	Uses memorable concluding device that emphasizes major components or points of presentation.		Uses concluding technique (i.e., repetition for effect).		Presents loose or inappropriate conclusion.		Ends without appropriate conclusion.	

(continues)

Handout

Handout	Demonstrates creativity, including clear pictures, professional lettering, and neatness and professionalism.	Supports and enhances the presentation, is visually pleasing, and has limited originality. Uses correct spelling and grammar.	Demonstrates little thought or preparation. Does not support topic.	Provides no or inappropriate handout.

Content

Evidence	Uses a variety of forms of evidence and support, including application of research, analogies, or visual details; recognizes bias of source; balances between "hard data" and "stories."	Uses at least a limited variety of support and examples, which may include stating statistics, testimony or opinions of others. Cites suitable sources.	Uses little or inappropriate evidence; does not cite; ignores limitations of sources; misuses resource material.	Limits evidence to generalizations or personal opinion; does not use resource material.
Expertise	Demonstrates superior knowledge of topic; is expert.	Demonstrates adequate knowledge of topic.	Demonstrates less than adequate knowledge or preparation of topic.	Does not demonstrate knowledge or preparation of topic.
Critical thinking	Demonstrates logical and consistent thinking, characterized by judging, synthesizing, and speculating.	Uses factually reliable materials, distinguishes facts from opinion, and uses visual imagery.	Confuses opinions with facts. Confuses imagery with evidence. Focuses on trivial for support.	Does not exhibit logical and consistent thinking skills.

(continues)

IN-DEPTH STUDY PROJECT RUBRIC *Continued.*

	Excellent		Proficient		Basic		In Progress	
	8	7	6	5	4	3	2	1
Content (*continued*)								
Creative thinking	Presents product or knowledge in original and creative manner.		Occasionally uses originality and creativity to present knowledge or product.		Makes vague attempts at exhibiting unique or original products or performances.		Does not demonstrate creativity.	
Proposal specifications	Elaborates and exceeds requirements of individual proposal.		Meets requirements of individual proposal.		Does not fulfill requirements of individual proposal.		Makes little attempt to fulfill proposal requirements.	
Audio/Visuals	Independently applies analysis, synthesis, and evaluation to the learning process. Independently applies fluency, flexibility, originality, and elaboration to create exemplary and original products. Elaborates and exceeds requirements of individual proposal.		Uses a variety of audio and visual forms, which may include recordings, videos, posters, maps, etc., that are visually and aesthetically pleasing, are neat, and show important information. Demonstrates effort.		Uses few audio or visual aids or presents hastily assembled aids.		Makes no attempt to use aids.	

Note. Adapted from *The Autonomous Learner Model: Optimizing Ability*, by G. T. Betts and J. K. Kercher, 1999, Greeley, CO: Autonomous Learning Publications. Copyright 1999 by Autonomous Learning Publications. Adapted with permission.

APPENDIX 2.B

Sample 4-Year Approach for Implementation of the Autonomous Learner Model

AUTONOMOUS LEARNER I & II

	Semester I	Semester II	Semester III	Semester IV	Other
Orientation	Find Someone Who Intriguing Answers	Partner Interview Intriguing Answers	Twenty Questions Intriguing Answers	Coat of Arms Intriguing Answers	
Individual Development	Colla'ge Group Building Creativity (Skits—Loc, Char, Sit) (Envelopes)	Paper Puzzle Group Building Creativity (Skits—Borge) (Structures/murals)	Colla'ge Group Building Creativity (Skits—Loc, Char, Sit) (Envelopes)	Paper Puzzle Group Building Creativity (Skits—Borge) (Structures/murals)	
Seminar I	Creativity (45 min. presentations)	Multiple Intelligences (45 min. presentations)	Giftedness (45 min. presentations)	Learning Styles Personality Traits (45 min. presentations)	Bloom Myers/Briggs
Project I	College Explorations (10–15 min. presentations)	Intriguing People (10–15 min. presentations)	Journeys into Self (10–15 min. presentations)	Futures/Inventions (10–15 min. presentations)	Images of Greatness
Enrichment	Service Classmate Career Risk 2 Choice	Service Classmate Performing Arts In-depth 2 Choice	Service Classmate Interview Yellow Pages 2 Choice	Service Classmate Live Performance In-depth 2 Choice	Always Wondered
Seminar II	Choice (90 min. presentation)	Choice (90 min. presentation)	Choice (90 min. presentation)	Choice (90 min. presentation)	Themes
Project II	Choice (30 min. presentations) (25 hour minimum— increasing increments)	Choice (30 min. presentations) (25 hour minimum— increasing increments)	Choice (30 min. presentations) (25 hour minimum— increasing increments)	Choice (30 min. presentations) (25 hour minimum— increasing increments)	Field Trips

Note. Adapted from *The Autonomous Learner Model: Optimizing Ability*, by G. T. Betts and J. K. Kercher, 1999, Greeley, CO: Autonomous Learning Publications. Copyright 1999 by Autonomous Learning Publications. Adapted with permission.

AUTONOMOUS LEARNER I & II
SEMESTER I

Orientation and Individual Development

Personal Colla'ge	(40 points)
Creativity	
Envelope	(15 points)
Group Skit	(60 points)

Enrichment

Each activity will demonstrate curiosity, growth, and participation.

Evidence of participation is required. (Signatures are usually not acceptable.)

A **written reaction** describing the event, who attended, when and where the event occurred, what was learned, and possible extensions of the activity is required.

Two activities per six week grading period will be submitted, resulting in a total of six for the semester.

One activity must be **service** oriented, one demonstrating a **career** interest, one should be attended with **someone in the class that you don't know well,** and one should involve some element of **risk** (not physical).

(15 points each = 90 points)

Seminar

Preparation and participation in **two** self-directed seminars. One series of seminars will address the topic of **creativity;** the other series' topics will be determined by individual groups.

Standards will be set by the class, and participation will be evaluated.

(100 points each; 45 points participation)

Individual Projects

Preparation and participation in two self-directed independent studies, one based on a **A College Study** (200 points) and the other based on individual student interests in a **"passion area"** (350 points). Both will demonstrate growth, research, use of a variety of sources, organization, and creativity.

Reference to Content Standards.

Organized and creative **presentation** to the class of knowledge learned, using a variety of presentation aids.

Standards will be set individually by negotiating a plan of action that includes grading criteria that refer to meeting, exceeding, or not meeting different benchmarks.

(550 points)

Total Possible Points = 1,000 Points

Note. Adapted from *The Autonomous Learner Model: Optimizing Ability,* by G. T. Betts and J. K. Kercher, 1999, Greeley, CO: Autonomous Learning Publications. Copyright 1999 by Autonomous Learning Publications. Adapted with permission.

AUTONOMOUS LEARNER III & IV

	Semester I	Semester II	Semester III	Semester IV	Other
Orientation	Find Someone Who Intriguing Answers "I Am" Poems	Group Builders	Twenty Questions Intriguing Answers "I Am" Poems	Group Builders	
Individual Development	Colla'ge Group Building Creativity (Skits—Loc, Char, Sit) (Envelopes)	Paper Puzzle	Colla'ge Group Building Creativity (Skits—Loc, Char, Sit) (Envelopes)	Paper Puzzle	
Seminars I and II	Theme (90 min. presentations) Choice (180 min. presentations)	Choice (180 min. presentations) Choice (180 min. presentations)	Theme (90 min. presentations) Choice (180 min. presentations)	Choice (180 min. presentations) Choice (180 min. presentations)	
In-depth Project	Choice (10 min. updates) (45 min. presentation) (65 hour [minimum]—increasing increments)	Choice (10 min. updates) (45 min. presentation) (85 hour [minimum]—increasing increments)	Choice (10 min. updates) (45 min. presentation) (65 hour [minimum]—increasing increments)	Choice (10 min. updates) (45 min. presentation) (85 hour [minimum]—increasing increments)	
Enrichment	Service Classmate Career Risk 2 Choice	Service Classmate Performing Arts In-depth 2 Choice	Service Classmate Interview Yellow Pages 2 Choice	Service Classmate Live Performance In-depth 2 Choice	Always Wondered

Note. Adapted from The Autonomous Learner Model: Optimizing Ability, by G. T. Betts and J. K. Kercher, 1999, Greeley, CO: Autonomous Learning Publications. Copyright 1999 by Autonomous Learning Publications. Adapted with permission.

AUTONOMOUS LEARNER III & IV
SEMESTER I

Orientation and Individual Development

"I Am" Poem	(50 points)
Personal Colla'ge	(50 points)
Creativity	
Envelope	(25 points)
Group Skit	(75 points)

Enrichment

Each activity will demonstrate curiosity, growth, and participation.

Evidence of participation is required. (Signatures are usually not acceptable.)

A **written reaction** describing the event, who attended, when and where the event occurred, what was learned, and possible extensions of the activity is required.

Two activities per six week grading period will be submitted, resulting in a total of six for the semester.

One activity must be **service** oriented; one should demonstrate an element of **risk**; one should be attended with **someone in the class that you don't know well;** and one should be attendance at a **professional lecture.** These requirements can be combined (e.g., doing a service activity with someone in the class you don't know well). The remaining activities can be personal choice.

(50 points each = 300 points)

Seminar

Preparation and participation in **TWO self-directed seminars.** One seminar will be presented within a 90-minute block period. The second seminar will be presented over two 90-minute block periods. Standards will be set by the class and/or the group.

(Seminar I = 200 points)
(Seminar II = 300 points)

Individual Project

Preparation and participation in a self-directed **independent study** which shows growth, research, use of a variety of sources, organization, and creativity.

Reference to and assessment by **Content Standards.**

Organized and creative **presentation** to the class of knowledge learned, using a variety of presentation aids.

Standards will be set individually by negotiating a **plan of action** that includes **grading criteria** that refer to meeting, exceeding, or not meeting different benchmarks.

(800 points)

Total Possible Points = 1,800 Points

Note. Adapted from *The Autonomous Learner Model: Optimizing Ability,* by G. T. Betts and J. K. Kercher, 1999, Greeley, CO: Autonomous Learning Publications. Copyright 1999 by Autonomous Learning Publications. Adapted with permission.

CHAPTER 3

Benjamin Bloom and David Krathwohl: The Cognitive and Affective Taxonomies

One model frequently used for the development of higher level thinking skills is the Taxonomy of Educational Objectives. This model is an integral part of many programs for the gifted and of many thinking skills programs. Although both the Cognitive and Affective Taxonomies were developed by essentially the same group of educators and psychologists, the Cognitive usually is referred to as Bloom's Taxonomy and the Affective as Krathwohl's Taxonomy. In this chapter they are referred to as the Cognitive Taxonomy (Bloom) and Affective Taxonomy (Krathwohl).

The purpose of the taxonomies is to provide a set of criteria that can be used to classify educational objectives according to the level of complexity of the thinking required. They are generic in that they apply to any academic subject area and any level of instruction from kindergarten through adult education (including graduate school). The two taxonomies have a different focus; one is on cognitive, or intellectual, behaviors, whereas the other is on affective, or emotional, behaviors. Although their focuses and levels differ, most of the taxonomies' underlying assumptions, their development, and their uses are similar. The basic references are Bloom (1956) for the Cognitive Taxonomy and Krathwohl, Bloom, and Masia (1964) for the Affective Taxonomy. Because these are the only references used in descriptions of the taxonomies, they are not cited each time. Whenever the taxonomies' general development, use, and essential elements are described, the sources are the basic ones unless otherwise specified. In discussions of their use or applicability in programs for the gifted, the information and perceptions have come from the authors' experiences in education of the gifted.

The taxonomies were developed to facilitate communication between psychologists and educators in such areas as test construction, research, and curriculum development. At the time of their development, probably no one anticipated the widespread use of the classifications to develop teaching activities. However, they provide a simple, easy-to-learn structure for developing teaching–learning activities that take students through a sequential process in the development of a concept or the learning of relationships. The cognitive taxonomy has been criticized for the emphasis on microlevel skills (French & Rhoder, 1992), the vagueness of its concepts, and the lack of criteria for evaluating performance in the use of the skills (Ennis, 1985). A major concern is that the assumption of a one-way hierarchy of thinking skills disregards the complexity of interrelationships in thinking processes (Paul, 1985). Another criticism is that the focus on basic, discrete skills may draw attention away from the complex process strategies, such as reflective thinking, problem solving, and decision making (French & Rhoder, 1992). With the caveat that discrete thinking skills should be taught in the context of their use, the Cognitive Taxonomy is "the best available inventory of micro-thinking skills we should be teaching" (Beyer, 1984, p. 556).

ASSUMPTIONS UNDERLYING THE MODEL

About Learning

The most basic assumption made by the developers of the taxonomies is that they are hierarchical. Each higher level depends on all the levels below it. Thus, application, the third level in the Cognitive Taxonomy, cannot be achieved without knowledge and comprehension. If students are to be able to solve a problem they have never seen before, they must know and understand whatever principles or computational methods are necessary for its solution. The fourth level, analysis, which often is required of students on exams (e.g., "Compare and contrast the following ideas …"), cannot be reached adequately unless the student has applied the ideas to a situation never before encountered. Students cannot be expected to develop a system of values unless they have first considered whether they value certain things, as well as how two or more of their values might compare. In short, the implications of this assumption are important to the instructional process. Teachers must make certain that their students are able to perform the behaviors at the lower levels before expecting them to function at the higher levels.

Related to this assumption is the implication that all learners are capable of the thinking and feeling processes described at each level of the taxonomies. In other words, if given enough time, all children are capable of the thinking processes of analysis, synthesis, and evaluation, as well as the feeling processes of valuing, organizing values, and internalizing values. If students are provided with proper teaching conditions and allowed enough time, most can master any learning task. Teachers must have a view of the final level to be attained and concentrate on movement toward that goal in a fashion that helps students achieve mastery.

Another underlying principle of the taxonomies is that thinking or feeling processes or teaching objectives can be defined behaviorally and, when defined, can fit into one of the classifications of the taxonomies. In other words, certain types of thinking can be observed and classified. Implicit in this assumption and the methods used to develop the taxonomies is the belief that educators and psychologists working together can develop a logical classification that approximates reality.

About Teaching

Basic to the use of the taxonomies as a teaching tool, but not proposed by their developers, is the view that by designing activities that evoke the types of thinking at each level of the hierarchies, thinking and feeling processes can be improved. Through systematic emphasis on each level from the lowest to the highest, students ultimately will be better thinkers at the higher levels. Therefore, teaching activities can be developed that evoke certain types of thinking, and teachers can be reasonably accurate about the underlying processes that go into a particular activity. For example, in designing a factual or knowledge question (the lowest level of the Cognitive Taxonomy), the teacher assumes that a child has had prior contact with the information being requested. If the child has not, the question requires a higher level of thinking than knowledge. To answer the question, the student may have to think about some related information, put it together in a new fashion, and develop a possible answer. Similarly, when teachers design questions to evoke a higher level of thinking, such as evaluation, which requires students to make a judgment, they must assume that when the students give their answers, they are giving their own judgments rather than simply recalling judgments made by someone else (i.e., knowledge level). Often, a teacher asks questions of the appropriate form calling for higher levels, such as evaluation (e.g., "What do you think are the advantages and disadvantages of this approach?"); however, the teacher actually expects the students to list the pros and cons previously presented by the teacher. In these cases, the students must operate at the lowest level rather than the highest.

A related idea is that any learning task can and should be broken down into smaller units or steps. The step-by-step approach assumes a skills-based model of learning. An underlying assumption is that all people learn in the same way and, as a result, an appropriate sequence can be developed for all learners. This idea is directly opposed to the belief that each individual thinks differently and comes to learning encounters with different experiences and the related view that people often learn through a process of intuitive leaps rather than sequential steps.

About Characteristics and Teaching of Gifted Students

The authors of the taxonomies do not make statements directly related to use of the taxonomies with gifted children. They believe that all children are capable of the various processes. Educators of gifted students, however, assume that more time should be spent at the higher levels with these children because they are already capable of high-quality thinking and feeling at the lower levels. Although this observation usually is valid due to the wide range of information the children possess, the need for knowledge and comprehension often goes unrecognized, and these important steps are neglected. When attempting to concentrate on the higher levels, educators often forget to check the children's knowledge and understanding of the concepts involved. A related assumption is that gifted students should spend more time at the higher levels because this type of thinking is more challenging for them.

ELEMENTS/PARTS

The Cognitive Taxonomy consists of six levels: knowledge, comprehension, application, analysis, synthesis, and evaluation. The Affective Taxonomy consists of five levels: receiving or attending, responding, valuing, organization, and characterization by a value or a value complex. Although the two taxonomies usually are viewed as parts of two different domains, human behavior, especially at the higher levels, is impossible to separate into two different components. Affective processes, particularly those related to the value placed on learning, will affect greatly children's motivation to develop the thinking processes required of them. Affective behaviors, then, can be viewed as one of the necessary means for attaining cognitive objectives. On the other hand, cognitive objectives can be seen as one of the necessary means for attaining affective objectives. For an individual to develop a value complex, for example, the person must be able to evaluate available choices (including, by implication, prior knowledge, comprehension, analysis, and synthesis related to these choices). More will be said about the relationships between the taxonomies after each is explained separately, and examples of thinking levels will be provided.

The Cognitive Taxonomy

Knowledge

The first cognitive level, knowledge, requires no transformation of the information an individual receives. This level might be more properly labeled "rote recall" (Paul, 1985). Students must remember what has been read, heard, or observed. The knowledge level consists of remembering the following: (a) specifics, including terminology and specific facts; (b) ways and means of dealing with specifics, including conventions (e.g., characteristic ways of treating or presenting phenomena), trends and sequences, classifications and categories, criteria, and methodology; and (c) universals and abstractions in a field, consisting of principles, generalizations, theories, and structures.

Comprehension

At the second cognitive level, comprehension, an individual is at a fairly low level of understanding a concept or process. The person is able to make use of information that has been acquired and restate ideas in his or her own words. Comprehension might be compared to Piaget's (1963) definition of assimilation; information can be incorporated into existing conceptual structures with little change in information or conceptual frames. Comprehension consists of three related skills: translation, interpretation, and extrapolation. *Translation* involves paraphrasing or restating an idea without changing its meaning. *Interpretation* is explaining or summarizing a communication and can involve reordering or rearranging its parts. *Extrapolation,* the highest level of comprehension, involves the extension of trends or tendencies beyond the given data. Immediate implications or effects are predicted on the basis of known facts.

Application

Putting abstractions or general principles to use in new, concrete situations involves the third level of cognitive behavior, application. Principles or abstractions can be in the form of general ideas, rules of procedure, technical procedures, or theories. Application, like comprehension, requires that students use previously learned ideas, procedures, or theories. Unlike comprehension, however, rules or procedures are not used in the context in which they were learned. At the application level, students are neither told which rule is the proper one nor shown how to use a principle or rule. Instead, they must draw on past experience to select relevant principles or procedures that apply to new problems or situations. Application may require students to accommodate or modify conceptual schemes to cope with new information or problems.

Analysis

The fourth level, analysis, involves the breaking down of a complex whole into its elements or parts so that the nature of the components is made clear and the interrelationships between the parts are made explicit. Analysis has as its purpose a greater understanding of the underlying structure, effect, or theoretical basis of ideas or systems. Included in this level are such behaviors as recognizing unstated assumptions (i.e., analysis of elements), checking the consistency of hypotheses with existing information (i.e., analysis of relationships), and recognizing the use of propaganda techniques (i.e., analysis of organizational principles).

Synthesis

Synthesis is, in many ways, the opposite of analysis. It involves the putting together of parts to form a whole. These pieces or elements are rearranged or combined so they make a pattern or structure not present before. In other words, the products of synthesis are new and unique, as distinguished from the comprehension-level skill of interpretation, which simply involves reordering or rearranging the parts to demonstrate an understanding of the idea. The products of interpretation are not really new. Synthesis, however, includes the following elements: (a) producing a unique communication; (b) producing a plan or proposed set of operations (e.g., a proposal, a unit of instruction, a blueprint for a building); and (c) derivation of a set of abstract relations, including classification schemes, hypotheses, and inductive discovery of mathematical principles or abstract generalizations. One justification for the use of discovery learning is that the intellectual skills involved in discovery are at the synthesis level, whereas in a deductive approach, in which principles are given and then applied, the intellectual skills involved are at only the application level.

Evaluation

The highest skill in the Cognitive Taxonomy is evaluation, or making judgments about the value of something (e.g., materials, methods, ideas, theories) for a given purpose. These judgments can be based on criteria chosen by students or criteria given to them, and can be either quantitative or qualitative. Also included in evaluation are judgments based on either internal or external evidence.

Internal evidence consists of criteria such as logical accuracy or consistency, whereas external evidence consists of comparing a work with other recognized works of high quality or with standards of excellence established in a particular field, or assessing the worth of an idea in terms of a particular theory. Most of the critical thinking skills discussed by Ennis (1985) involve evaluation. These judgments can be made through application of internal criteria, as in judging whether a statement follows from the premises.

External evidence is important in judging whether an observation statement is reliable by using a set of principles from the fields of law, history, or science (i.e., a statement is more reliable if the observer is unemotional and alert, is skilled at observing the sort of thing observed, and uses precise techniques).

Table 3.1 gives a summary of teacher and student roles and activities at each level in the model.

The Affective Taxonomy

Receiving or Attending

At the receiving level of the Affective Taxonomy, the learner is simply sensitive to the fact that certain things exist. Awareness and sensitivity also include a willingness to attend, although they do not imply a judgment. Each student has had experiences that will influence this willingness either positively or negatively.

(*text continues on p. 94*)

TABLE 3.1
Summary of Student and Teacher Activities and Roles in the Taxonomy of Cognitive Objectives

Step, Type, or Level of Thinking	Student		Teacher	
	Role	Sample Activities	Role	Sample Activities
Knowledge	Passive recipient Memorizer Active recipient	Pay attention to information read or heard. Answer questions almost verbatim about specific facts. Answer questions requiring recall or memory.	Provider of information and resources Questioner Organizer of learning activities Evaluator	Present information about a subject. Provide students with resources on a topic. Ask questions to check whether students know the information presented to them. Assist students in finding information identified as necessary or desirable.
Comprehension	Active participant	Answer questions or engage in activities that require • translation of information (e.g., explain a metaphor); • interpretation of information (e.g., "After you read the paragraph, what did you think the meaning was?"); and • extrapolation of existing information (e.g., "What do you think will happen next in space exploration?").	Provider of information and resources Organizer of learning activities Evaluator	Check to see if students have the knowledge required for the task. Ask questions to see whether students can paraphrase, extend, and/or make inferences based on the information. Provide sequential activities that first require the student to translate, then interpret, then extrapolate meanings from the given information.

(continues)

Application	Active participant	Use some previously learned rule or method in a new situation. Decide which method to use or which principle to apply to a new task. Based on an understanding of a task and its requirements, select an appropriate procedure to complete the task.	Provider of information and resources Assigner of tasks Questioner Evaluator	Check to see if students have the knowledge and comprehension necessary for the task. Provide students with a new problem or situation in which they can apply principle(s) or method(s) previously learned. Ask questions to determine student understanding of requirements of the task. Provide feedback to students on their performances (e.g., "You chose a good method to solve that problem" or "You used the right method but need to do this step differently" or "This method would be better for solving that problem").
Analysis	Active participant	Break down a whole (e.g., plan, communication, proposal, system) into its parts (e.g., "What are the unstated assumptions in the planned goals?"). Identify the relationships between parts of a whole (e.g., "In what ways is the hypothesis consistent with the assumptions given?"). Identify the arrangement or structure of a complex whole (e.g., "Chart the patterns of meaning in a literary work").	Provider of information and resources Questioner Organizer of learning activities Evaluator	Ask questions to determine whether and how students have analyzed elements, relationships, and organizational principles. Provide feedback to students (e.g., "That is a clear analysis that contains all the necessary steps" or "You may have overlooked an element you need for a complete analysis" or "In your hypothesis, you seem to have incorrectly identified the underlying principles").

(continues)

TABLE 3.1 *Continued.*
Summary of Student and Teacher Activities and Roles in the Taxonomy of Cognitive Objectives

Step, Type, or Level of Thinking	Student		Teacher	
	Role	Sample Activities	Role	Sample Activities
Synthesis	Active participant	Combine elements in a new way so that a different pattern or product is developed. Organize and write original statements or narratives. Develop a plan, research proposal, or new product. Formulate or modify a theory.	Provider of information and resources Questioner Organizer of learning activities Evaluator	Check to see whether students have the necessary knowledge, comprehension, and application skills. Design sequential learning activities to develop the component skills of identifying the elements of a whole, analyzing the relationships among elements, and recognizing the organizational principles involved. Provide feedback to students on their products (e.g., "You've arranged your essay effectively so that others can understand your ideas" or "Check the steps in your plan carefully; you may have left something out" or "Show me how your theory is consistent with the general principles of this discipline").

(continues)

| Evaluation | Active participant | Make judgments about the value of information, materials, or methods for a given purpose.

Select or develop appropriate criteria for making a judgment for a given purpose.

Use internal and external criteria as a basis for judgment.

Use quantitative and qualitative data in making judgments. | Provider of information and resources

Questioner

Organizer of learning activities

Evaluator | Check to see whether students have the necessary knowledge, comprehension, application, analysis, and synthesis skills to do the task.

Structure situations in which students must evaluate products based on different kinds of evidence (logical, internal, external, qualitative, quantitative).

Provide criteria for evaluation of some activities or products; invite students to develop criteria for evaluation of some activities or products.

Devise learning activities to help students select or develop criteria for evaluation (e.g. logical principles for evaluating arguments).

Give students specific feedback on their performances (e.g., strengths demonstrated, suggestions for improvement, and mini-lessons on a specific skill, technique, or principle needed). |

Receiving is divided into three subcategories on a continuum from a passive role on the part of learners to the point at which they direct their own attention. *Awareness,* the lowest sublevel, includes being conscious of something and taking it into account. This level does not imply that the individual can verbalize what has caused the awareness. The second sublevel, *willingness to receive,* requires a neutrality or suspended judgment toward the phenomenon, but the student is inclined to notice it. An individual will not necessarily seek out something but is not actively seeking to avoid it. The highest sublevel of receiving is *controlled or selective attention,* in which the student selects a favored stimulus and attends to it despite competing or distracting stimuli.

Responding
The second level, responding, includes most "interest" objectives. At this level, students are so involved in or committed to a subject or activity that they will seek it out and gain satisfaction from participation. Responding also includes three subcategories: (a) acquiescense in responding, (b) willingness to respond, and (c) satisfaction in response. *Acquiescence in responding* can be described as obedience or compliance. Students are passive in the sense that they do not initiate the behavior, but they do not resist or yield unwillingly. *Willingness to respond* implies that students will do something "on their own" and that they choose to do an activity or participate in the learning process. At the next higher sublevel, *satisfaction in response,* the element of enjoyment is included. Students have a feeling of satisfaction, pleasure, or zest when participating in an activity.

Valuing
Of all the levels in the Affective Taxonomy, valuing has received the most attention in educational practice. It includes three levels or subcategories: ascribing worth, demonstrating preference, and making a commitment. Valuing simply means deciding that a person, thing, phenomenon, or idea has worth or importance. Behavior at this level is consistent and stable and has taken on the characteristics of a belief or an attitude. Actions resulting from values are motivated by a commitment to the underlying value rather than by the desire to comply or obey.

Ascribing worth, the first subcategory, includes a consistency of behavior enabling the underlying value to be identified but is at the lowest level of commitment. Individuals have a tendency to behave in a certain way but would probably be more willing to reevaluate their position than at the higher levels. The second sublevel of valuing, *demonstrating preference for a value,* includes not only a willingness to be identified with a value but also an intent to seek out or want that value. *Commitment,* the third subcategory, implies beliefs that are certain beyond a shadow of a doubt. Individuals who are committed will act in ways that further the particular value, will try to convince others, and will try to deepen their own involvement with it.

Organization

As values are internalized, situations that involve more than one value arise. People then must organize these values, determine the relationships among them, and establish the pervasive ones. Two subcategories are included in this level. The first, *conceptualization of a value,* is developing a view that enables an individual to see how a particular value relates to other values already held or to new ones being developed. At the next sublevel, *organization of a value system,* students bring together a set of attitudes, beliefs, and values into an ordered relationship with each other. Some of these values may be quite different or in opposition to one another in certain situations. The individual must synthesize these into a value complex that, if not harmonious and internally consistent, is at least in dynamic equilibrium.

Characterization by a Value or a Value Complex

At the final level of the Affective Taxonomy, values already have been internalized and organized into a hierarchy and have controlled behavior long enough that individuals behave in ways consistent with the value complex. The subcategories, (a) developing a generalized set of values and (b) characterization, represent two aspects of the individual's behavior. A *generalized set of values* is a basic orientation, a persistent and undeviating reaction to a family of related situations or things. This usually unconscious set guides action without individuals deliberately considering alternatives beforehand and can be thought of as an attitude cluster. At the *characterization* sublevel, behavior results from a philosophy of life, a broad range of behaviors constituting a world-view. Objectives included in this subcategory are broader or more inclusive than those considered a part of the generalized set, and emphasis is placed on internal consistency.

Table 3.2 gives a summary of teacher and student roles and activities in the implementation of the Affective Taxonomy.

(*text continues on p. 98*)

TABLE 3.2
Summary of Student and Teacher Activities and Roles in the Taxonomy of Affective Objectives

Step, Type, or Level of Thinking	Student		Teacher	
	Role	Sample Activities	Role	Sample Activities
Attention	Passive recipient to active recipient	Attend to what is being presented. Be aware. Be willing to take notice. Choose one stimulus over others.	Provider of stimuli Organizer Presenter Covert evaluator	Present learning activities or information to capture the attention of the learner. Check to see if learner is aware of the stimuli. Plan sequential activities that will lead the student through the levels of awareness, willingness to receive, and selected attending.
Responding	Passive respondent to active, pleased respondent	Comply with suggestions. Voluntarily seek out activities of interest. Enjoy activities chosen.	Provider of stimuli Organizer Presenter Covert evaluator	Check to see if students have attended to relevant stimuli. Plan activities designed to stimulate interest (pleasure in responding). Ask questions regarding student response (feelings) toward activities, ideas, people, and objects.
Valuing	Chooser	Accept a value; be willing to be identified with that value. Act consistently so that others can identify perferences as values.	Provider of stimuli Organizer Questioner	Check student's response to a phenomenon, idea, or other people. Organize activities in which students can make value choices.

(continues)

Valuing (*continued*)		Choose a position and seek it out. Attempt to convince others that your value choices are important.	Presenter	Provide situations in which students can exhibit and discuss their value choices. Assist students in clarification of their values with provocative questions.
Organization	Chooser Believer Organizer of beliefs	Identify the essential characteristics of values held. Determine the relationships between values. Synthesize parts of values into a new value complex.	Provider of stimuli Organizer Questioner Presenter	Check what values students hold. Arrange situations in which students must choose between competing values they already hold. Assist students in the examination of relationships between their values by asking questions. Help students to develop equilibrium in their value systems.
Characterization by a value or values complex	Internalizer of values	Act consistently in accordance with internalized values. Act consistently in accordance with a total world-view. Develop a consistent philosophy of life.	Provider of stimuli Organizer Questioner Observer	Check to see that students have organized and examined their values. Arrange situations in which students can demonstrate internalized values. Assist students in the identification of the values they have internalized.

Examples of Thinking Levels

To illustrate the differences among the types of thinking generated in specific levels, consider the lessons described in Tables 3.3 and 3.4, which are based on the Cognitive and Affective Taxonomies.

In any activity, complete separation of the cognitive and affective domains is impossible and, based on brain research, undesirable. Four basic kinds of relationships between the cognitive and affective workings of the brain seem to exist. First, explicitly or implicitly, a cognitive component can be found in every affective objective and an affective component in every cognitive objective. At every level of the Cognitive Taxonomy, the affective behavior of receiving or attending is a prerequisite. Responding is required if a student is to answer a question or participate in an activity. At every level of the Affective Taxonomy, with the possible exception of receiving, the cognitive behavior of knowledge is prerequisite to responding, and comprehension is prerequisite to valuing and organizing values.

A second relationship between the domains is that educators often use one of the domains to achieve objectives in the other. Usually, cognitive objectives are used as a way to achieve affective objectives. Students are given new information with the hope that an attitude change will result. For example, students can be given information about other societies and people's reactions to them as a way to help them examine their own feelings and values. The relationship can go the other way, however. Affective goals can be used to achieve cognitive goals. Educators can develop students' interest in something as a way to increase their knowledge of a phenomenon. Krathwohl et al. (1964) suggested that guided discovery methods provide a way to use an individual's drive for competency (an affective behavior probably at the valuing level) to enhance the possibility that children will discover or develop necessary cognitive abilities.

The third relationship is only slightly different; affective and cognitive goals can be achieved simultaneously. Again, Krathwohl et al. (1964) referred to discovery learning as an example. In Suchman's (1965) inquiry training, children are presented with a puzzling event. They ask questions of the teacher, who acts only as a data giver, in a manner similar to the 20-questions activity. Teachers observe the pattern of the students' strategies and offer suggestions for improving them. In this way, the cognitive goal of improving the child's inquiry skill is achieved in a situation that engages the child's interest. By providing a critique of the strategy, the teacher also builds motivation to use the skill in other situations.

(*text continues on p. 104*)

TABLE 3.3

Examples of Thinking Levels: Cognitive Domain

To illustrate the differences between the levels of thinking in the Cognitive Taxonomy, consider this sample lesson.

The purpose of the lesson is to work toward the development of the following generalization:

Every society has rules, written or unwritten, through which social control over individual conduct is maintained.

Level of Cognitive Taxonomy	Activity	Questions
Knowledge	Information about three civilizations——Roman, Cherokee, and Industrial American——is presented to students in print and audiovisual formats. Students view, listen to, and read data about the social and political structures of the three civilizations.	What were some of the written rules in Roman civilization? in Cherokee communities? in industrial America? How were these laws used to control behavior? [Each of these questions can be answered directly from presented information.]
Comprehension	Students present a sociodrama depicting their interpretation of an event about which they have read. The class is divided into three groups so that one sociodrama is presented for each civilization. A discussion follows each sociodrama.	What were some of the written rules governing each situation presented in the sociodrama? What were some of the facts that contributed to individuals' reactions to these laws or rules? What do you think will happen next? Why do you think so?
Application	Students view a videotape or film about a trial in a different society (e.g., American frontier, Japan, South Africa, Egypt). Discussion follows. Students draw a diagram to illustrate the relationship between social characteristics of a society and its criminal laws.	Based on what you know about other societies and cultures, what might be some characteristics of this society? What reasoning led you to make that conclusion? Draw a diagram to illustrate how the social characteristics of this society may have affected the development of its criminal laws.

(continues)

TABLE 3.3 *Continued.*

Examples of Thinking Levels: Cognitive Domain

To illustrate the differences between the levels of thinking in the Cognitive Taxonomy, consider this sample lesson.
The purpose of the lesson is to work toward the development of the following generalization:
Every society has rules, written or unwritten, through which social control over individual conduct is maintained.

Level of Cognitive Taxonomy	Activity	Questions
Analysis	Students reflect, in writing, on unwritten codes of conduct that governed the three civilizations. Discussion follows.	What were some unwritten codes of conduct, mores, and values in the [Roman/Cherokee/Industrial American] civilization? In your opinion, why were these unwritten codes? How did the unwritten codes differ from written laws? Why do you think that is so? How did unwritten codes differ among the three civilizations? What factors might have contributed to the differences? How were the unwritten codes among the three civilizations similar? In your opinion, why were these codes similar in that way?
Synthesis	Students are grouped in two teams; each team develops laws and codes for its own hypothetical civilization. Students in each team then devise a way (e.g., skit, visual representation) to present the legal structure of the civilization to the other team without actually specifying the laws and social codes.	How might you represent the social codes of our civilization through a skit? Why would that be a good way? What is another way to present your ideas? What important data do you want your audience to understand?

(continues)

Evaluation	Following a team presentation, the audience is asked to assess the consistency of the presentation with the legal structure the team has created for the hypothetical civilization.	What evidence did you see in the presentation that helped you to identify [written/unwritten] laws in this civilization? In what ways was the presentation [consistent/inconsistent] with the identified structure of the civilization?
		What items/actions in the presentation led you to believe the team [identified/failed to identify] some important codes of conduct or values?
	Teacher presents the lesson generalization following the evaluations of both team presentations. Discussion follows.	Think about the validity of this statement: *Every society has rules, written or unwritten, through which social control over individual conduct is maintained.*
		Why do you [agree/disagree] with it?
		What would you change about the statement to increase your agreement?
		Why would this change make the statement more agreeable to you?

TABLE 3.4

Examples of Thinking Levels: Affective Domain

To illustrate the differences between the levels of thinking in the Affective Taxonomy, consider this sample lesson.
The purpose of the lesson is to work toward the development of the following generalization:
Every society has rules, written or unwritten, through which social control over individual conduct is maintained.

Level of Affective Taxonomy	Activity	Questions
Receiving	Information about three civilizations—Roman, Cherokee, and Industrial American—is presented to students in print and audiovisual formats. Students view, listen to, and read data about the social and political structures of the three civilizations.	What were some of the [events/acts] you saw happen in the film? What were some of the reactions of the people when their leader spoke to them? What did you see that led you to say that?
Responding	Students and teacher continue to discuss the information presented about the three civilizations.	What were your feelings when you [watched the film/read the story]? When [you/someone you know] [were/was] involved in a similar situation, what are some of the things that happened? How did you feel about that situation? What did you [read/see] that helped you understand how an individual of the [Roman/Cherokee/Industrial American] civilization might feel about its laws? How did it make you feel? As you participated in the sociodrama, what were some of your feelings? What are some social controls that you have experienced? What were your reactions?

(continues)

Responding (continued)		Why do you think you reacted [positively/negatively] to that control?
Valuing	The teacher presents an attitude/value continuum to the students: no control ←——————→ strict rules and enforcement Students are asked to indicate their judgment about how much social control a society needs by placing an X at some point on the line.	Where on this continuum would you stand? Why do you feel that way? What are some things that have happened to make you feel that way? In the sociodramas, what were some of the values of the characters involved? What led you to think that [specify value] was valued by that person?
Organization	Students brainstorm and list all the means of social control currently in effect in their own society and those they learned about in the three civilizations studied. By group consensus, students select five of the most important means of social control in each society; then each student individually ranks those five according to (a) desirability and (b) effectiveness.	In what ways are your values (as expressed in the social continuum activity) different from those you discovered in the three civilizations we studied? In what ways are the values similar? Why do you think your values are [different from/similar to] those of citizens in the other civilizations (i.e., What experiences have you had that contribute to the formation of values [similar to/different from] citizens in the other societies)?
Organization by a value complex	After a discussion of the team presentations in the cognitive evaluation activity, each student individually develops an ideal set of social controls for the society.	How would you describe your ideal society? What social controls are absolutely necessary to the operation of the society? What social controls are just desirable? What do you believe about the necessity for social controls? Why do you believe that?

The fourth relationship is the most exciting and includes the most data regarding what learning experiences need to include for students to learn information or to achieve curriculum goals. Contrary to traditional educational practices, brain research has provided information that emotional components are not only desirable in learning, but critical. Emotions are the entities that generate and drive the execution of a person's goals and plans (Freeman, 1995). When students are asked to record and share reasons why reaching their goals is important to them, the reasons are the emotions that underlie the goals and the source of the energy to accomplish them. Jensen (1998) described experiences as the catalysts that generate emotions, such as fear, anger, surprise, disgust, sadness, and joy. These emotions generate thoughts, opinions, and decisions. The emotions also generate responses such as anticipation, cynicism, optimism, confidence, frustration, and confusion, and they strongly influence whether or not students will be motivated to take action (p. 78).

Emotions mediate meaning and are the framework of our social interactions, our learning, and in fact our lives. Everything we experience has an emotional aspect, and "we remember those events that are most emotionally laden, because all emotional events receive preferential processing" (Christianson, 1992, as cited in Jensen, 1998, p. 79). "Emotions give us a more activated and chemically stimulated brain, which helps us recall things better" (Jensen, 1998, p. 79). Furthermore, "good learning does not avoid emotions, it embraces them" (Jensen, 1998, p. 79).

In fact, Wolfe (2001) recommended adding an "emotional hook" to learning through the use of simulations, role playing, and the solving of real-life problems. If teachers choose, for example, to use the structure of the taxonomies but to allow the students to choose a real-life, substantive problem as the focus for their learning experiences, the roles of students and teachers as noted in Tables 3.1 and 3.2 change quite dramatically. Students are virtually never "passive recipients" or "passive responders," but rather are active throughout the process. Teachers, of course, must shift from providers of knowledge and organizers of activities to facilitators and resources for active learners. (See Table 3.5.)

The relationships between levels of the taxonomies are more clear at some levels than at others. At the lowest levels, the relationship is clear: Learners must attend before they will know, and they can develop knowledge only if they have a willingness to pay attention. Thus, in the examples of thinking levels in Tables 3.3 and 3.4, students must attend affectively to information in a film or videotape to develop cognitive knowledge about

(*text continues on p. 109*)

TABLE 3.5

Summary of Student and Teacher Roles When the Cognitive and Affective Taxonomies
Are Used as a Structure for Solving Real-Life Problem Situations

Step, Type, or Level of Thinking (Cognitive, Affective)	Student		Teacher	
	Role	Sample Activities	Role	Sample Activities
Knowledge, Receiving	Active participant in selecting problem situation and determining what is known and needs to be known	Create personal- and small-group lists of problem situations. Participate in brainstorming. Begin log of this project.	Guide Resource Instructor	Brainstorm problem situations. Require students to begin a log (or journal) of their work on the project and their thoughts as they proceed.
Comprehension, Responding	Active participant in seeking needed information	Interview a variety of people to determine what problem situations exist in the school and community. Determine which students complement their own learning and working styles. Keep log entries current.	Guide	Instruct students on developing criteria for selection of a problem situation on which to focus. Provide instruction and guidelines as needed. Suggest possible interviewees. Assist students in narrowing the field of possible problem situations.

(continues)

TABLE 3.5 *Continued.*
Summary of Student and Teacher Roles When the Cognitive and Affective Taxonomies
Are Used as a Structure for Solving Real-Life Problem Situations

Step, Type, or Level of Thinking (Cognitive, Affective)	Student		Teacher	
	Role	Sample Activities	Role	Sample Activities
Responding *(continued)*				With student input, determine composition of small groups.
				Be sure students are aware of issues—societal, economic, environmental, moral, legal, and ethical—related to the problem situation.
				Allow time for log entries.
Application, Valuing	Active participant	Conduct research using appropriate and varied sources—documents, people, Internet, books, periodicals, etc.	Resource Instructor	Meet regularly with small groups. Assist students with focus, timeline for study, skills for working within a group, and other skills and strategies as needed.
		Include questions related to societal, economic, environmental, moral, legal, and ethical issues as appropriate.		
		Include views and factual information related to considerations of these issues.		
		Screen information and sources for relevancy.		

(continues)

Application, Valuing (continued)		Check for validity and accuracy of information gathered. Develop criteria for evaluating the product. Record criteria and thoughts in log.		
Analysis	Active participant	Examine data, looking for information that might lend itself to comparison or contrast. Examine opinions and perceptions of interviewees for those differences that may be significant in a final proposed resolution. Keep log current with group and individual ideas.	Observer Facilitator Guide	Provide instruction or strategies for analyzing data efficiently. Stay in close touch with groups, should they need extra support or instruction. Allow time for students to make log entries.
Synthesis, Organization	Active participant	Synthesize (transform) the information gathered, including the emotional, societal, and moral issues attached to the topic. Decide how the information can best be presented to the appropriate audience (i.e., those people most likely to be able to bring about change). Address each pertinent issue in the presentation. Use a variety of formats in the final presentation. Record thoughts and progress in log.	Resource Instructor	Teach mini-lessons on organization of data. Ask thought-provoking questions about conclusions reached. Require evidence of reasoning for conclusions and decisions. Assist students to find an appropriate audience. Allow time for students to make entries in their logs.

(continues)

TABLE 3.5 *Continued.*

Summary of Student and Teacher Roles When the Cognitive and Affective Taxonomies
Are Used as a Structure for Solving Real-Life Problem Situations

Step, Type, or Level of Thinking (Cognitive, Affective)	Student		Teacher	
	Role	Sample Activities	Role	Sample Activities
Evaluation, Characterization by a value or values complex	Active participant	Note the variety of value systems present among the key people in the problem situation. Engage in self- and group evaluation, based on predetermined criteria. Write a journal or log entry about what was learned and what might be done differently next time. If a session is scheduled, share interesting thoughts and learning experiences from logs.	Facilitator Organizer Devil's advocate	Schedule time for thoughtful reflection prior to evaluation. Schedule time after the evaluation for students to record their thoughts in their logs or journals. If it seems appropriate and productive, ask students to share thoughts or ideas from their logs—how their thinking changed, things they learned, thoughts they recorded, or other insightful or interesting entries. Ask how student ideas changed about moral or ethical issues related to their study. Follow with evidence-of-reasoning questions.

the reactions of people in each of the three societies. At the higher levels of analysis and synthesis and the related affective levels of conceptualization, the cognitive ability of analysis is needed as students "break down" the common elements of values or situations in which they are involved and put the elements back together (synthesis) into a value that is important to them. In the example, students must analyze the presentations of other teams, as well as their own, and then relate their own behaviors to the presentations.

The cognitive skill of evaluation clearly is involved in both the organization category of a value system and in the highest affective level, characterization by a value complex. To develop a total philosophy of life and to weigh one value or way of behaving against situational considerations requires that an individual be able to make defensible judgments. The criteria for making these judgments become internalized to the extent that the individual behaves almost automatically in some situations. In the example, students are asked to develop their ideal society, which requires them to evaluate the other societies on the basis of some criteria and to put into their ideal those aspects that are consistent with their own philosophy.

As is apparent from the information in this chapter and Tables 3.1 through 3.4, the two domains can be combined easily. Further support for combining these taxonomies can be found by examining teacher and student roles, which correspond roughly as the higher levels of both taxonomies are reached. The student moves from the role of a passive recipient who remembers to an active learner who makes judgments. The teacher provides the information and develops the experiences and then moves to a more facilitative role as the student takes an increasingly active part in the learning situation.

As is apparent in Table 3.5, the taxonomies also can be used within a problem-based curriculum. This combination is appealing for all students, but especially for gifted students, who may resist the "drill and kill" memorization of information they do not see as relevant. Ultimately, these two taxonomies, which appear to be rather rigid in their hierarchical structure, are found to be more adaptable than first glance would indicate.

MODIFICATIONS
OF THE BASIC CURRICULUM

In programs for gifted students, the Cognitive and Affective Taxonomies have been used mainly as systems for making one process modification:

development of higher levels of thinking. Although they were developed as schemes for classifying objectives or specified outcomes of instruction, what is described or classified is student behavior, either thinking (cognitive) behavior or feeling (affective) behavior. As such, the taxonomies provide ways to classify the thinking and feeling processes that children use as they participate in a learning activity or answer a teacher's question.

The taxonomies, however, have other valuable uses in making certain curriculum modifications for gifted students. They can be used as structures for evaluating the sophistication of products and as systems for classifying content according to its complexity and abstractness.

Although seldom used for this purpose, the knowledge level of the Cognitive Taxonomy contains a scheme for classifying content according to its type, as well as its abstractness and complexity. Three types of knowledge are described: (a) specifics, (b) ways and means of dealing with specifics, and (c) universals and abstractions in a field. These categories can be used in a variety of ways to make the recommended content changes for gifted students.

The knowledge of specifics category is considered to be the lowest level of complexity and abstraction. It includes the facts or specific information about a field of study. These specifics, the basic elements the learner must know to become acquainted with a field, include knowledge of terminology and knowledge of specific facts. Each field contains a set of terms that serves as the basic language of that field and both verbal and nonverbal symbols that have particular referents. Some examples are terms associated with work in science, definitions of geometric figures, and important accounting terms. Each field also has a large number of dates, events, people, places, and research results that are known by specialists in the field and used in thinking about specific topics and defining certain problems. Examples include significant names, places, and events in the news; knowledge of the reputation of a particular author; and recall of facts about a certain culture.

The second category of knowledge, knowledge of ways and means of dealing with specifics, includes ways of organizing, studying, judging, and critiquing ideas, events, and phenomena in a field. Methods of inquiry, patterns of organization, and standards of judgment within disciplines are included in this category. These are different from specifics in that they are the operations necessary for dealing with specifics. Included in this section are five subcategories: (a) conventions, (b) trends and sequences, (c) classifications and categories, (d) criteria, and (e) methodology.

Knowledge of conventions includes the characteristic ways of treating and presenting ideas and phenomena that scholars or workers in a field use because they suit their purpose or fit the phenomena. Examples include rules of etiquette, correct form and usage of English in speaking and writing, and standard symbols used on maps and charts.

Knowledge of trends and sequences includes trends involving time sequences as well as cause–effect relationships that are emphasized by scholars and workers in a field. Some examples are the following: (a) the evolutionary development of humans, (b) effects of industrialization on the culture of a nation, and (c) trends of government in this country during the last 50 years.

The third group, knowledge of classifications and categories, includes the classes, sets, or divisions that are considered fundamental or useful in a particular field. These classification systems are used to help structure and systematize the phenomena being studied. Objectives in this group include types of literature, the classification of elements in chemistry, and the classification of living things in biology.

Knowledge of criteria includes the standards by which facts, principles, opinions, and behaviors are tested or judged. This includes standards such as those used to judge the nutritive value of a meal, the aesthetic value of a work of art, or the validity of sources of information.

Knowledge of methodology includes methods of inquiry, techniques, and procedures that characterize a particular field and those usually employed in investigating certain problems. Examples include the steps in a scientific method, attitude surveys, and procedures for conducting health and medical research.

The most abstract and complex of the groups is the category of knowledge that includes the major ideas, schemes, and patterns that dominate a field and serve as organizing themes for the other information available. Universals and abstractions bring together a large number of facts and events and describe the relationships among them. The category includes two subgroups: (a) principles and generalizations and (b) theories and structures. Knowledge of principles and generalizations includes abstractions that summarize observations of phenomena and are valuable in explaining, describing, or predicting. These include such items as fundamental principles of logic, generalizations about cultures, biological laws of reproduction and heredity, and principles of learning.

Theoretical knowledge is the result of a body of principles and generalizations interrelated into a structure that has broad explanatory and predictive power. Knowledge of theories and structures corresponds to the "thought systems" described by Taba (1962) as the characteristic modes of thinking employed by scholars in a particular field. Some examples include the theories of relativity, evolution, social learning, and philosophic bases for judgment.

For example, chemistry is not simply a study of elements and compounds, with their characteristics and interactions. Rather, a "language" or body of knowledge common to practitioners in the field embodies specific facts, classifications, inquiry methods, symbol systems, and conventions for reporting research and communicating findings to others.

Content Modifications

Abstractness and Complexity

The Cognitive Taxonomy's classification system may be used to guide curriculum modifications by placing the major emphasis or focus at each level of the taxonomy on the third category, principles and abstractions. Although knowledge and understanding of specifics are important to understanding abstract ideas, the focus should be on the principles and abstractions. At the knowledge level, specifics would perhaps be as important as the generalizations and abstractions, but as an individual moves up the levels of the taxonomy, specifics assume much less importance.

Variety

The Cognitive Taxonomy's scheme for classifying knowledge can be used to allow gifted students to sample systematically from a variety of types of knowledge, making certain that they have been exposed to a range of ideas in a particular field or across several fields (Maker, 1982b; Maker & Nielson, 1995). The Cognitive Taxonomy also can be used as a scheme for viewing the knowledge in each field of study and for making certain that gifted students have received exposure to all types of knowledge available in each field—that is, the specifics, the methods, and the theories.

Methods of Inquiry

The classification scheme proposed by Bloom (1956) brings attention to the fact that within each field of study, certain conventions, techniques, and strategies are unique. When teaching gifted students methods of inquiry, this system can be used to suggest methods that might otherwise have been forgotten.

THE AFFECTIVE TAXONOMY

Because of its concentration on aspects of behavior that are traditionally considered only a small part of the educational process, the Affective Taxonomy also can be considered a vehicle for making content changes by deliberately including affective components in the curriculum. This idea relates especially to the content change of variety. However, no system of classification of affective content exists in the Affective Taxonomy.

Process Modifications

One critical point needs to be made clear. Even though the taxonomies have enjoyed widespread use as schemes for making process modifications for gifted students and, to a lesser degree, in the regular curriculum, the developers did not intend them to be used in this way. As they developed the systems, they were attempting to make each description neutral. They did not suggest, for example, that everyone should develop activities at all levels of the taxonomies or that specified amounts of time be spent at the various levels. The developers did not even suggest that learning objectives or activities be arranged sequentially according to the levels of the taxonomies. All knowledge is not at a lower level than all analysis, for example. Knowledge of specifics, strategies, and generalizations in theoretical physics may require a higher level of thinking than analyzing the components of a chemical solution. The authors implied a sequential arrangement with their statement that the Cognitive Taxonomy is arranged from the simplest to the most complex intellectual behavior. The most common uses and implications of the taxonomies have been added by those who subsequently have used them as structures for developing curriculum or programs for gifted students.

The Cognitive Taxonomy provides a useful way for educators of gifted students to develop learning activities that require higher levels of thinking or more complex intellectual activity, one of the most basic goals of curriculum modification for the gifted. The implication that follows is that more time is spent at the higher levels with the gifted, whereas equal amounts of time may be spent at all levels with most students.

The Affective Taxonomy, although not particularly intended for this purpose, can be used as a means for making process changes emphasizing greater complexity or higher levels. Because intellectual activity cannot be separated entirely from its affective components, this taxonomy can be incorporated into the methodology as a way to develop higher levels of feeling. Although the concept of complexity was not used as an explicit organizing principle in this taxonomy as it was in the cognitive one, the behaviors are arranged in a developmental order (e.g., a person must be aware of something before developing a preference for it or before it can become a part of a total world-view). Because the behaviors are arranged in this way, the taxonomy can provide a framework for devising learning activities that systematically develop affective processes, for designing learning center tasks to lead students to more complex thinking, or for creating games for the same purpose. The taxonomies also are useful in preparing auto-instructional programs or as the basic structure in learning contracts.

Product Modifications

Because of the arrangement of thinking behaviors from simple to complex, the Cognitive Taxonomy can be used to evaluate the complexity of student products, particularly in assessing whether they involve a mere summary of prior information (comprehension level) or reflect a higher level involving reordering, reinterpreting, and recombining information (synthesis level). Students can be taught to use the taxonomy in evaluating their own products.

Learning Environment Modifications

Neither of the taxonomies provides specific guidelines for the development of appropriate learning environments. The Affective Taxonomy, however, provides the teacher with some suggestions for developing an effective psychological climate, particularly in the dimensions of learner centeredness and independence. Teachers can structure their own behaviors in such a way that the students can reach the higher levels; teachers must respect each learner's prior level of feeling about a situation and build upon these feelings in the learning process.

MODIFYING THE MODELS

In addition to the curricular changes directly suggested by the taxonomies, other modifications important in programs for gifted students can be made by combining the taxonomies with other models or by using them in ways other than those intended by their authors.

Content Modifications

Abstractness, Complexity, and Organization for Learning Value

Both taxonomies can be combined easily with Bruner's ideas about teaching the structure of a discipline (Chapter 4). To combine the models, the first step is to identify or develop the abstract themes that will be used to unify the content. These ideas and the key concepts contained in them will serve as the content organizers. Then specific information and facts to be taught are selected as examples of the concepts. Learning activities at the lowest level of the taxonomies use data or specific facts, whereas the concepts and themes become more important at the higher levels.

In the examples presented earlier in this chapter (see Tables 3.3 and 3.4), a general statement was used as the content organizer. At the knowledge and receiving levels, students were presented with data about three different civilizations. They were asked questions designed to check their memory of this information—that is, to check whether they had attended and received the information they would need to use later.

At the comprehension level in the Cognitive Taxonomy and at the responding level in the Affective Taxonomy, the data continue to be important, but concepts enter into the process. For example, at the comprehension level, when students present the sociodrama, they demonstrate their understanding of some underlying concepts, such as written rules and people's reactions to rules, and they predict what might happen next based on this understanding. At the responding level, students indicate their responses to some of the concepts and describe personal experiences with these aspects of social control. At the valuing level of the Affective Taxonomy, the value placed on the concepts also is important.

At the application level of the Cognitive Taxonomy, general statements and themes assume importance as the students apply a rule or principle in a new situation. The rule or principle can be a concept (category) or a statement of relationships between certain concepts. Analysis might include examining different aspects of concepts or examining several concepts to learn how they relate to each other to form a generalization. Although students are dealing with information, they use it as examples or proof for ideas. Synthesis involves developing new generalizations or new products through combining encountered ideas in a new way. At the evaluation level, all types of content are important. Students judge the accuracy or appropriateness of information and the validity of concepts and general statements. In the two highest levels of the Affective Taxonomy, the major emphasis is on generalizations, with some focus on concepts and how they are related.

In the examples presented in this chapter (Tables 3.3 and 3.4), the element of complexity is included in that both the affective and cognitive processes are used. Complex ideas or thought systems, as described by Taba (1962), consist not only of facts, principles, and concepts, but also of methods and characteristic ways of thinking about ideas, objects, or phenomena, including value systems. To aid in fully understanding others' feelings about an idea, method, or phenomenon, students can be led through a process of examining their own affective behavior related to the same idea, method, or phenomenon.

To achieve maximum learning value, in addition to organizing content around key concepts and themes, educators can begin the learning process at the application level as a way of discovering what is not known and thus needs to be taught. In this way, previous learning is not repeated. The same process can be used with the Affective Taxonomy by beginning at the valuing level.

Variety

Because of its emphasis on affective content, Krathwohl's Taxonomy suggests the incorporation of content usually not taught in the regular curriculum. To achieve variety of content with the Affective Taxonomy, the suggested procedure and worksheet presented in the discussion of Bruner's approach is appropriate (see Figure 4.4 in Chapter 4).

Study of People

The taxonomies can be used as structures for studying the lives and accomplishments of eminent individuals. A teaching approach that uses the taxonomies concurrently is especially appropriate in this context. Students can be led through a process of examining the individuals and their characteristics, and also study the reactions of other people. The gifted students can then examine their own lives, including value systems, and compare themselves with the individuals studied.

Methods of Inquiry

The taxonomies can be used easily as structures for studying different methods of inquiry. The structure of the taxonomies can be used as an outline of methods and, as such, can be taught to the students. The taxonomies are classification systems to facilitate communication between professionals in the behavioral sciences. Students can use them in the same way that professionals do.

Process Modifications

Open-Endedness and Evidence of Reasoning

The process modifications of open-endedness and evidence of reasoning are incorporated easily into teaching strategies that use the taxonomies as a basis. To achieve open-endedness, an educator can simply design all questions and learning activities to encourage varied perceptions, be provocative, and have multiple answers. Stimulating, divergent activities and questions can be designed easily at the higher levels of the taxonomies but may be more difficult at the lower ones, unless another model or approach is combined with them. Asking students to explain their reasoning or to cite examples as evidence to support their conclusions is incorporated easily by asking for these explanations when answers are given at the higher levels of the taxonomies or when students are gathering the data and information at the lower levels. Asking for evidence of reasoning also may be appropriate at the responding and comprehension levels depending on the content and activities.

In the examples presented in Tables 3.3 and 3.4, all questions were designed to be open-ended and to stimulate further activity or thought. The examples also included questions calling for explanations of reasoning or logic when appropriate. For instance, two questions at the responding level were "What are some social controls you have experienced? What were your reactions?" After this second question, a question calling for support is appropriate: "Why do you think you reacted that way?"

Discovery

Incorporating discovery learning into the use of the taxonomies is difficult if they are used strictly as hierarchical models. If the assumption is accepted that activities must be presented at each level of a taxonomy, beginning with knowledge and receiving and then progressing to comprehension and responding, the learning sequence would be deductive rather than inductive. With the Cognitive Taxonomy, for example, students are given the information needed to solve a problem (i.e., the rule or principle) at the knowledge level, learn how to use the principle at the comprehension level, and are given a new problem and expected to apply the rule or principle in solving the problem at the application level. Following this, they analyze or break down the problem or solution, create something new, and then evaluate. This is essentially a deductive learning sequence. As illustrated in Table 3.5, however, when the taxonomies are combined with a problem-solving approach, discovery learning will occur.

To incorporate an inductive or discovery approach, one must reject the assumption that activities must be presented sequentially at each level of the taxonomies and make a major adaptation of the approach. Because research data are not adequate to indicate that sequential presentation is necessary, and support is available for the idea that inductive approaches work well with gifted students, such an adaptation seems justified.

One way in which the taxonomies can be adapted for the gifted is by presenting the first activities at the application level rather than beginning at the knowledge level. An obvious advantage of this approach is that the teacher does not reteach what the students already know. A new problem or situation is presented to the students, and they attempt to solve it. If they do solve the problem, the teacher asks them to explain how they arrived at the solution. If they can explain the principle involved, as well as the process, further activities can be presented at higher levels of the taxonomy. When students are unable to solve the problem, teachers have several options. They can change to a deductive approach and present some applicable rules and principles, show how they are used, and then present more new problems. Teachers also can continue with an inductive approach and present several new problems that illustrate the rules or principles to be learned and, through questioning, lead the students to discover the underlying principles.

Freedom of Choice

The Cognitive and Affective Taxonomies can be used effectively to incorporate the element of freedom of choice into learning activities and topics. The teacher can design a variety of learning activities at each level and allow the students to choose those that are of the most interest. The taxonomies can be presented to the students and used as a structure for designing their own learning activities. Students may choose their own topics of study and structure their learning about a topic so that mastery of each level of the taxonomy is demonstrated.

Group Interaction and Variety

Educators can design activities for small groups using the taxonomies as the structure, thus providing group interaction. Activities can be designed at the higher levels that will challenge students. Analysis activities are suited to the examination of tapes or other observational data, whereas synthesis activities are appropriate for designing plans to improve a group's interaction patterns. Evaluation is particularly appropriate for assessing individual and group participation and guiding plans for improvement.

The Affective Taxonomy is helpful as a procedure for examining each individual's participation in group activities. Observers can, for example, examine and discuss the differing values of the individuals involved and how these values may have influenced their interaction in the group. In this same context, this taxonomy could be used as an observational tool. Observers can look for behaviors and statements that indicate the stage of development of certain values in the individuals being observed. In other words, does a person's behavior indicate that he or she has incorporated a particular belief to the extent that it has become a part of a philosophy of life? Also, does he or she always behave consistently with that belief (i.e., at the organization by a value complex level), or is the person simply willing to be identified with that belief (i.e., at the valuing level)?

Both taxonomies can be used to develop a variety of activities, which adds the element of variety to the curriculum. For example, a structured series of questions for use in a class discussion can lead students through the levels of thinking. They can be used to design learning center tasks that lead students to higher levels of thinking. The taxonomies can be used in designing games, as a part of contract learning, and as the basis for auto-instructional programs. Creative teachers can generate many more uses for these adaptable classification systems.

Pacing

The most important aspect of pacing with regard to the taxonomies is that movement through the lower levels must be as rapid as possible because gifted students can acquire the knowledge quickly and learn to put it to use rapidly. They must be allowed to move from one level to the next as soon as they have demonstrated competence.

Product Modifications

Neither taxonomy provides specific suggestions for product modifications, although the Cognitive Taxonomy provides a useful way of assessing whether a product is a transformation of existing information or merely a summary. Criteria for evaluating products should be developed early in the process, and the taxonomies readily lend themselves to this task. When products are ready to be evaluated, both classifications can be used by the students in self-evaluation and by other audiences in the evaluation process.

When using the taxonomies as evaluation schemes, the evaluator examines the product in two ways. First, the evaluator attempts to determine whether the student's product reflects the use of all levels of thinking in the development process, or only the lower levels. In other words, the product as a whole is evaluated to determine its level in the taxonomy scheme. Next, the evaluator attempts to determine the quality and accuracy of the product with regard to each level. For example, the evaluator asks these types of questions: "How accurate and complete is the information in the product?" (knowledge level), "How valid are the trends and implications that are presented?" (comprehension level), and "How consistent with the attitudes and behaviors are the values presented?" (characterization level). These questions provide a structure that can be used to determine the product's quality and accuracy.

Learning activities at the analysis level can be valuable in helping students decide on problems to investigate or to narrow an area of study so that a solvable problem or researchable question is posed. Teachers can assist in this process by helping students design their own activities, topics, or problems narrow enough to be manageable.

The evaluation level of the taxonomy can be used as a guide for developing criteria for real or simulated audiences to use in evaluating the product. Activities at this level also can be used to generate possible criteria that a real audience can use in product evaluation.

Learning Environment Modifications

The learning environment changes advocated for gifted students are important to the successful use of the (modified) taxonomies. If learners are to achieve the objectives of reaching the highest levels, the environment must be centered around their ideas and interests. They must be encouraged to be independent; the environment must be open and must include complex tasks and materials. If students are allowed the freedom to choose activities at all levels, they will need flexibility, varied grouping arrangements, and high physical mobility.

One aspect of the environment that is particularly critical in the development of higher levels of thinking is the accepting versus judging dimension. If students do not believe they are free to express their ideas, they will respond only at the lower levels by repeating what the teacher or someone else has said, rather than take a risk by generating their own ideas. Because expressing feelings is riskier than expressing ideas, this dimension of the environment is more important with the Affective Taxonomy than the Cognitive Taxonomy. The hierarchy of teacher behaviors presented by Maker (1982b; Maker & Nielson, 1995) that moves from attending through accepting, clarifying, and challenging is especially critical.

The authors of the taxonomies do not make suggestions about the kind of learning environment that should be established when the taxonomies are used. Their comments do not address the environmental dimensions important at different levels of the classification schemes.

Summary

By combining the Cognitive and Affective Taxonomies with Bruner's content suggestions (Chapter 4) or with a problem-solving approach (Chapters 5, 7, 11), and by using the taxonomies differently (e.g., not progressing rigidly through each level), teachers can make many of the content, process, and product modifications appropriate for gifted students. Two major adaptations of the models have been suggested: (a) teaching the taxonomies to gifted students so they can apply the ideas to their own investigations and (b) beginning learning sequences at the application level rather than at the knowledge level so that learning is not repeated and inductive learning is facilitated.

DEVELOPMENT

In 1948, at an informal meeting of college examiners attending the American Psychological Association (APA) convention (Bloom, 1956), the idea for developing a theoretical framework for classifying educational objectives was proposed. This meeting became the first of a series of informal annual meetings of college examiners. The members were not always the same, but a core group usually was present. Early in the process, the group decided that the major purpose of the taxonomy should be to facilitate communication between educators. To fulfill this purpose, it would need to have at least the following four characteristics:

1. It should be an educational taxonomy and, whenever possible, should be related closely to the decisions that educators must make.
2. The classification system should be logical; it should define terms as concisely as possible and should use them consistently.
3. It should be consistent with psychological theories and principles that are accepted widely and are relevant.
4. It should avoid value judgments, being neutral about principles and philosophies so that objectives from many different orientations could be classified.

The committee of approximately 30 people began its work by collecting a large list of educational objectives, dividing each objective into intended behavior and content of the behavior, and then attempting to group the behaviors according to their similarities. In an attempt to develop an order from simple to complex, the committee looked for a psychological theory that could be used as an overall framework. They found none, so they developed their own logical system. After developing the categories and definitions of the categories, the committee members classified objectives independently, using the system. They then compared their separate classifications to clarify ambiguities and further refine the system.

At the outset, the committee's intent was to develop taxonomies in three domains: (a) cognitive, (b) affective, and (c) psychomotor. Because the cognitive domain was most central to their work, it was the first to be developed and was the only taxonomy completed by the original committee. A subcommittee responsible for the affective domain finally completed its work and published that taxonomy without submitting it to the original committee for review (Krathwohl et al., 1964). Thus, the Cognitive Taxonomy has been subjected to more critical reviews, both by the committee and by other educators, than the Affective Taxonomy.

After the committee completed its work, a preliminary edition of 1,000 copies was published and sent to college and secondary teachers, administrators, and research specialists, who were asked to read and offer suggestions. Their critiques and ideas were incorporated into the final version of the Cognitive Taxonomy. The Affective Taxonomy, although read by a wide variety of educators, has not received the same depth of criticism.

RESEARCH ON EFFECTIVENESS

With Nongifted Students

Research on the use of the taxonomies, because of their nature as hierarchies, must concentrate on three related issues: (a) the validity of the hierarchical arrangement (Are they actually arranged from simple to complex? Do the higher levels actually include the lower levels?), (b) their clarity and comprehensiveness (If two or more independent observers classify an objective or a question, will they put it in the same category? Can every educational objective be classified according to the taxonomy?), and (c) the effectiveness of the taxonomy's use with students (By participating in learning activities designed according to the taxonomies, are students more capable of behaving competently at the higher levels?). Most research to date has concentrated on the first two issues, although some evidence is available on the third.

Whether the Cognitive Taxonomy's hierarchical arrangement is valid is a question that still has not been resolved. Some evidence exists (Ayers, 1966; Bloom, 1956; Chausow, 1955; Dressel & Mayhew, 1954; Stoker & Kropp, 1964) that the complex behaviors at the higher levels are more difficult than those at the lower levels. In other words, fewer students will perform as well on tests of the higher abilities. Each individual's performance will decrease as the tasks become more complex. The level that usually seems out of place, however, is evaluation, which does not appear to be the most difficult intellectual behavior (Solman & Rosen, 1986; Stoker & Kropp, 1964).

In general, the research supports the Cognitive Taxonomy's comprehensiveness and clarity when used by both practitioners and researchers (Bloom, 1956; Buros, 1959; Dressel & Nelson, 1956; Gabbert, Johnson, & Johnson, 1986; Lessinger, 1963; McGuire, 1963; Morris, 1961; Stanley & Bolton, 1957; Stoker & Kropp, 1964; Tyler, 1966). The first test of the taxonomy's clarity and comprehensiveness was made by its developers when they independently classified additional objectives using their system. They identified only a few objectives that could not be classified. In subsequent studies of its use, considerable agreement exists among raters attempting to classify objectives, as well as conclusive evidence that almost no objectives exist that do not fit into the system. Factor analytic studies of its structure (Milholland, 1966; Stoker & Kropp, 1964; Zinn, 1966), however, indicate that the categories are not mutually exclusive; a student's general ability and motivation appear to be the factors determining his or her achievement of objectives at all levels.

Relative to the use of the Cognitive Taxonomy as a basis for developing sequential learning activities, some empirical support can be found in studies of the effectiveness of asking higher level questions before, during, and after students read material. In most of these studies, subjects are given questions at some or all levels of the taxonomy to guide in their reading or recall of the information, and they are tested later to see how effective their learning has been. For example, when students study materials containing either knowledge-level or evaluation-level materials and then are given test questions at all levels of the taxonomy, students who receive evaluation questions during instruction do better on evaluation questions on the posttests.

Students who are given inferential questions do better overall and significantly better on the questions calling for new inferences about old groups than do those given only factual questions. In some studies using classifications of cognitive questions other than the taxonomy (Dapra & Felker, 1974; Felker & Dapra, 1975; Watts & Anderson, 1971), the results indicate that when students have practice at a certain level, they do better on posttests at that level. Practice at the lower levels does not seem to improve performance at the higher levels. Other studies (Andre, 1978; Holland, 1965) however, have not provided support for this finding.

In research of a different nature, results indicate that certain types of learning activities improve performance at the higher levels. Knowledge objectives may be learned equally well under both lecture and discussion conditions, but performance at the higher levels is facilitated by discussions and laboratory experiences in which students engage in problem solving and are helped to see how their skills can be improved. Gabbert et al. (1986) found that first-grade students ($N = 52$) who were randomly assigned to either cooperative or individual learning conditions on a series of 10 higher level Cognitive Taxonomy tasks, from comprehension through synthesis and analysis, showed improvement in higher level thinking, but the productivity of students in cooperative learning groups was significantly higher than that of students working alone. Because discussions, laboratory experiments, and cooperative learning projects usually require learning activities similar to those designed to develop the higher levels of thinking, whereas lectures do not really encourage their use, this research provides some indirect evidence supporting the use of the Cognitive Taxonomy in designing learning experiences.

Sultana (2001) used the Cognitive Taxonomy to examine lesson plans of 67 teacher interns over a 3-year period (1995–1998) to determine the extent to which their lesson objectives were designed to develop higher order thinking skills. The results indicate that 41.3% of the objectives were at the knowledge level and 3.2% at the highest level. Obviously, training in the taxonomy and its use is critical to student opportunities to think at higher levels.

Apparently, no studies of the Affective Taxonomy address any of the three issues identified at the beginning of this section. Perhaps this lack of research is due to a general lack of interest in affective outcomes. It also could be due to the ambiguity often found in affective objectives or the emotional aspects of dealing with values or value-laden subjects. Regardless of the causes for this lack of research, the widespread use of this taxonomy implies a need for some tests of its validity.

With Gifted Students

Roberts, Ingram, and Harris (1992) investigated the effect of special versus regular classroom programming on the higher cognitive processes of intermediate elementary-age gifted and average-ability students. In this study, gifted and average-ability students in a special treatment group were given thinking skill training based on Bloom's Taxonomy and Guilford's (1967) Structure of Intellect. Control groups of gifted and average-ability students studied the same content without the addition of thinking skills training. Gains from pretest to posttest favored the two treatment groups.

When searching for information about the possible effectiveness of curricula based on the Cognitive and Affective Taxonomies with gifted children, researchers discover that few such studies have been reported. Although programs with curricula based on the Cognitive Taxonomy have generally been effective, as evidenced by their evaluations, one cannot determine the role of the taxonomy in producing these results. Their effectiveness might simply be due to the fact that gifted students are identified, thus enhancing the students' perceptions of themselves as capable individuals. Similarly, programs based on or using the Affective Taxonomy have shown success, but the program evaluations have not shown that this success is attributable to the use of the taxonomy.

JUDGMENTS

Advantages

The most obvious advantage for use of the taxonomies is the ease of understanding them. The Cognitive Taxonomy, especially, enjoys widespread use and acceptance in educational circles, which is an additional advantage. The taxonomy project certainly has achieved its goal of facilitating communication through developing a useful system of classification. Because the system is known, understood, and used in numerous classrooms as a part of the regular curriculum, building on this regular curriculum by concentrating on a greater number of experiences at the higher levels is easy. Communication with parents, other teachers, and administrators is enhanced by having clear, nonambiguous terms with which to communicate. Also, due to widespread use of the Cognitive Taxonomy, many classroom materials based on the taxonomy are available.

Another advantage of the taxonomies is their relative simplicity and applicability. They are not difficult for teachers to learn and use, and they can be applied in all content areas and at all levels of instruction. The taxonomies are comprehensive enough to include most objectives that have been developed. Research shows that the hierarchy is valid except for the possible misplacement of the evaluation level.

In addition to their use as a way to develop learning activities that improve students' higher levels of thinking and feeling, the taxonomies have certain related uses (Limburg, 1979). First, they help teachers develop more precise, measurable objectives. If teachers have in mind a general objective, such as "understands concepts involved in...," the Cognitive Taxonomy can be used to suggest a more quantifiable statement of the objective. Second, the taxonomies can be used as guides for the development of better teacher-made tests that sample a variety of levels of thinking, feeling, or both. A related use is evaluating standardized tests for measuring the success of programs for the gifted. Often, even though the program is designed to facilitate the higher levels of thinking, achievement tests that assess recognition and recall are the only instruments used to evaluate their success. In construction of evaluation measures, the taxonomies provide a useful way of matching the instructional emphasis according to levels with the emphasis in evaluative procedures.

Important to the effective use of the taxonomies is the availability of a practical reference source for the teacher. Both systems have comprehensive handbooks available that describe the various categories, relationships among the categories, and numerous specific examples of items included in each category (Bloom, 1956; Krathwohl et al., 1964). The handbooks also include self-assessment sections to aid the reader in learning the system.

Disadvantages

On the negative side for use of the taxonomies, the most important considerations are the lack of research on effectiveness with learners, particularly gifted ones, and the limited scope in providing a structure for curricular modifications for the gifted. This review of research has not resulted in evidence that the use of the taxonomies will have the hypothesized effect of improving higher levels of thinking. No research even touches on the validity of the categories or the hierarchical arrangement of the Affective Taxonomy, and the research on one level of the Cognitive Taxonomy, evaluation, suggests that it may not be placed at the right level.

The assumption of a sequential approach to levels of thinking in the Cognitive Taxonomy can be misleading. Those who develop curricula or assessments find that constructing activities that focus on specific knowledge or recall of information is relatively easy. At all other levels of the taxonomy, an interplay of many types of thinking seems to occur. Comprehension, for example, is an interactive process that includes recall of information, analysis of the relationship of the information to one's existing knowledge base, and evaluation of its potential usefulness. Beyer (1987) characterized the elements in the Cognitive Taxonomy as microthinking skills or building blocks for more complex operations such as conceptualizing, problem solving, and decision making.

The third disadvantage, a limited scope, was discussed earlier, along with the description of curricular modifications suggested by the models. Curricular adaptations made possible through use of the taxonomies are mainly in the areas of process (e.g., the development of higher levels of thinking and feeling) and content (developing objectives that focus on the principles and abstractions in a particular discipline). Use of the Affective Taxonomy facilitates content changes by suggesting ways to integrate "feeling" content into academic areas and providing a structure for doing so. Some psychological environment modifications also are facilitated by the use of the Affective Taxonomy. To provide a framework for a total approach to curriculum development for gifted students, however, the taxonomies must be combined with other models or used differently.

CONCLUSION

The Taxonomies of Educational Objectives cannot be defended as a total approach to curriculum development for gifted learners and are sometimes difficult to justify at all, due to their widespread use in regular education. They can, however, be used as one aspect of a program for gifted students, particularly to show the relative emphasis on higher versus lower level thinking and feeling processes. Associated uses (i.e., evaluation, development of teacher-made tests, evaluation of standardized tests, construction of more quantifiable objectives) and modifications of the taxonomies can make them more defensible as models to be used in programs for the gifted.

RESOURCES

Background Information

Solman, R., & Rosen, G. (1986). Bloom's six cognitive levels represent two levels of performance. *Educational Psychology, 6,* 243–263.

Instructional Materials and Ideas

Swartz, R., Kiser, M. A., & Reagan, R. (1999). *Infusion lessons: Teaching critical and creative thinking in language arts.* Pacific Grove, CA: Critical Thinking Books & Software.

Udall, A. J., & Daniels, J. E. (1991). *Creating active thinkers: 9 strategies for a thoughtful classroom.* Tucson, AZ: Zephyr Press.

CHAPTER 4

Jerome Bruner: The Basic Structure of a Discipline

Of all the teaching–learning models discussed in this book, Jerome Bruner's Basic Structure of a Discipline (BSD) is the most philosophical. The BSD is not actually a framework but a way of approaching the development of a framework. Bruner's ideas have contributed to many of the other models presented in this book and to our own views of curricular modifications appropriate for gifted learners. The "basic concept" idea assumed great importance in several innovative curricula developed in the 1960s and 1970s that proved to be very effective with gifted students (e.g., *Man: A Course of Study* by the Education Development Center, 1970).

At the same time, many of these curricula were not enjoying the same degree of success with average students. One school district in Illinois, for example, attempted to implement a curriculum based on the BSD concept in all of its regular social studies classrooms because of the curriculum's success as an innovation in the program for the gifted. Much to the educators' disappointment, the curriculum had to be "watered down" so much that most of the original form was lost. As an aside, the educators also felt that to teach the curriculum effectively, the teacher needed to be gifted. J. J. Gallagher (1966), who was involved in the development of the Illinois program, also noted the value of Bruner's approach for gifted students.[1] Taba, in the development of both her theory of curriculum development (1962) and her Teaching Strategies program (1964, 1966), drew heavily on the concept of teaching the "basic structure" of a discipline as a

---

[1]Throughout this chapter, text cites mentioning Gallagher refer to J. J. Gallagher; however, initials are not repeated through the chapter.

way to organize and structure the content to be taught. Teaching the methodology and "thought systems" of the various disciplines, an associated idea attributed to Bruner, also influenced Taba (see Chapter 10), as it did Renzulli (1977) in the conception of his Type III Enrichment activities (see Chapter 8). Students acting as "real inquirers" is another Brunerian concept influencing curricular practices in education of the gifted.

Many ideas discussed in this chapter are actually a result of the now-famous Woods Hole Conference on education in science, sponsored by the National Academy of Sciences and directed by Jerome Bruner. In the report from the conference, *The Process of Education* (Bruner, 1960), five aspects of education are discussed: (a) the importance of structure, (b) readiness for learning, (c) intuitive and analytic thinking, (d) motives for learning, and (e) aids to teaching. Although the first four of these areas are discussed in this chapter, the importance of structure is of most interest in this book because of the influence these ideas have had on practices in the field of education of the gifted. The basic reference for the ideas is Bruner (1960), but the implications for curriculum development for the gifted are ours unless otherwise noted.

ASSUMPTIONS UNDERLYING THE MODEL

About Teaching and Learning

One assumption has formed the basis for most of Bruner's ideas: "Intellectual activity anywhere is the same, whether at the frontier of knowledge or in a third-grade classroom" (1960, p. 14). The difference is in degree, not in kind, and the best way to learn history is to do it by behaving like a historian. Thus, instead of focusing on the conclusions in a field of inquiry, the focus should be on the inquiry. Most of Bruner's ideas follow from this basic conviction. A person more nearly approximates an inquirer if the basic ideas of that discipline are understood and are of concern, if concepts are "revisited" as understanding increases, if a balance is established between intuition and analysis, and if a long-term commitment to intellectual activity and the pursuit of knowledge is clear.

The Importance of Structure

The theme underlying Bruner's approach is that the aim in education should be to teach the basic structure of academic disciplines in such a way that this structure can be understood by children. This basic structure consists of certain concepts (e.g., biological tropisms in science; revolution in social studies; supply and demand in economics; and commutation, distribution, and association in mathematics) and the important relationships between them. In addition to basic concepts, themes, and theories, each discipline has characteristic patterns of inquiry or strategies for research and information management. For example, Table 4.1 illustrates key generalizations from social science disciplines and Table 4.2 provides a look at the varied approaches taken by practitioners in the discipline toward the problems of world poverty and hunger.

A discipline's concepts and relationships, when understood, enable the learner to comprehend most of the phenomena in that discipline. Understanding the basic structure means that an individual not only has learned a specific thing but also has learned a model for understanding similar things that may be encountered. A phenomenon is recognized as a specific instance of a more general case. Carefully developed understanding also permits the student to recognize the limits of applicability of the generalizations.

When developing this theme, Bruner made several assumptions. These beliefs have varying degrees of acceptance or proof in the psychological and educational literature. The first assumption is that the primary objective of learning is service in the future; whatever people learn should allow them to go further more easily. Learning serves people in the future through both specific and general transfer. By definition, Bruner argues, basic concepts or ideas have wider applicability and thus greater transfer to future situations. By learning underlying ideas, the student can master more of the subject more quickly, and because educators have little time and much to cover, teaching these basic ideas makes good sense.

Related to this idea is the belief that memory is facilitated if a structure is learned. Bruner states that research on memory has shown that unless details (e.g., facts or data) are placed in a structured pattern, they are forgotten easily. Once the structure is learned, these facts or details can be remembered more easily or reconstructed if necessary. Another underlying assumption is that by teaching basic structure, a teacher can narrow the gap between basic and advanced knowledge. One difficulty faced by

TABLE 4.1

Example of the Importance of Structure: Key Social Science Generalizations

Discipline	Generalizations
History	Biologic, climatic, geologic, geographic, and cultural factors influence the development of communities and societies.
	History is recorded and interpreted through the lens of individual bias, knowledge, and culture.
	Conflict between individuals, groups, and nations is an ongoing part of human history.
Sociology	Human interaction is the basis for learning.
	Groups establish norms of behavior and exert pressure on individuals to meet these norms.
	Conflict can arise from differences between societies and cultures.
Anthropology	Individuals, communities, and nations learn from each other; cultural and language similarities result from this interaction.
	Cultural exchange may diminish or extinguish unique characteristics of cultures.
Geography	Environmental variables affect the development of societies.
	The distribution of resources varies significantly between areas and may give rise to conflicts.
	Individuals, communities, and cultures are influenced by the geographic characteristics of where they live.
Political science	Groups, societies, and institutions need governance (i.e., laws and a governing body with the power of enforcement).
	The purposes, values, and principles of groups or of those in power are reflected in the laws they create.
Economics	Individuals, groups, and societies have infinite wants and needs and finite resources.
	Communities and nations are interdependent; the rich must assist the poor for the good of all.
	Extreme differences in wealth between groups or nations may result in serious and costly conflict.

learners from elementary schools through universities is the necessity of "relearning" because traditional information-based curricula often lag far behind new developments in a field of study.

For the teaching of structure to be effective, the curriculum must be written and materials devised so that the most basic ideas are taught. This

TABLE 4.2
Example of the Importance of Structure:
Perspectives on Global Pollution, Hunger, and Poverty

Sociologist

Analyzes the effects of global pollution, hunger, and poverty; examines the human cost of these conditions. Provides explanation for human behavior as influenced by pollution, hunger, and poverty.

Anthropologist

Studies the effects of conditions on various peoples; compares and contrasts responses of populations to pollution, hunger, and poverty.
Notes that physical, geographic, and cultural factors affect how human beings respond to these serious problems.

Geographer

Analyzes data on human response to global pollution, hunger, and poverty by geographic region.
Pursues the concept of the effect of geographic location on response to adverse conditions, including environmental pollution.

Political Scientist

Is aware that large discrepancies of resources and wealth between groups and nations breed political unrest, terrorism, and perhaps war.
Attempts to influence the richer to assist the poverty stricken, including environmental cleanup.

Economist

Understands that the extreme imbalance of wealth and resources can doom the "haves" as well as the "have-nots."
Tries to persuade affluent nations that assisting underdeveloped countries is to their benefit in the long run.

Historian

Analyzes events and factors that result in global pollution, hunger, and poverty; presents findings and beliefs to the public.
Records own perception of events that may become part of a historical record.

can best be done by scholars and competent persons in their respective fields. Another requirement is that the materials and presentation must be matched to the abilities of students at different grade levels. This can be done only by those familiar with and experienced in sound educational practices.

Certainly problems are involved in these two assumptions. A major problem is difficulty in achieving agreement among scholars about what constitutes the structure or the most basic ideas that should be taught. Indeed, several attempts to define these basic ideas have resulted in the development of thousands of ideas due to the lack of agreement.

Readiness for Learning

Bruner states that "any subject can be taught effectively in some intellectually honest form to any child at any stage of development" (1960, p. 33). This statement implies that the form in which the basic structure is taught must be matched to the level of the child's intellectual development, and that the basic concepts involved should be revisited as time goes on and the child becomes capable of understanding more of the concept's complexities.

Underlying the ideas about readiness for learning is the basic assumption that Piaget (1963) and other developmentalists (Brief, 1983; Bruner, Goodnow, & Austin, 1956) are right in saying that at certain stages of development children have a characteristic way of viewing and explaining the world. A young child learns through direct sensory and motor experiences, whereas children in the next stage—concrete operations—no longer need direct trial-and-error experiences and can learn through mentally carrying out activities. At the concrete operational stage, internalized cognitive structures or "schema" are developed that guide the child's perception of reality; however, at this stage the child still must deal only with present reality or direct experiences from the past. Only after children have reached the stage of formal operations can they deal with hypothetical propositions.

The obvious implication of a developmental view of learning readiness is that in the stage of concrete operations, for example, understanding of a basic concept would need to be developed by providing the child with direct concrete experiences. Learning can be accomplished through exercises in manipulating, classifying, and ordering objects, but attempting a formal, logical explanation of the principles involved would be futile. After students have reached the formal operations stage, they are able to understand a formal logical proof or explanation and also develop logical explanations.

One assumption that Bruner makes, however, is somewhat different from Piaget's emphasis. Although Piaget recognizes the role of the environment in the learning process, he does not encourage manipulation of the environment. Instead, he suggests that the normal course of development be allowed to occur. Bruner, on the other hand, suggests that educators "tempt" children into the next stages of development by presenting them with challenging and usable opportunities to move ahead.

When educators think about what concepts to teach a child, in addition to the methods used and consideration of the act of learning, they also must contemplate whether, when fully developed, these concepts would be valuable for an adult to know. This requirement underlies the idea of a spiral curriculum. As time goes on, the learner returns to these basic concepts, building on them and making them more complex. The learner also relates them to more complex stimuli, so the concepts must be valuable to know.

In his discussion of readiness, Bruner also includes the assumption that learning a subject involves three almost simultaneous processes. First, the learner must acquire information. That information may replace, enhance, contradict, or refine present knowledge. Second, students transform the new information; that is, they manipulate new and existing knowledge to make it fit new tasks. Learners transform knowledge in a way that enables them to go beyond what they have taken in. A third process is evaluation, checking to see whether the manipulation or transformation of information was adequate. In each learning "episode," which may be brief or long and contain many or few ideas, all three processes are present. What is not known, and what Bruner makes no assumptions about, is the amount of emphasis that should be placed on each process in a learning episode, the length and intensity of an episode, the techniques used to increase motivation to learn in each episode, and ways to achieve a balance between intrinsic and extrinsic rewards to enhance learning in each episode.

Intuitive and Analytic Thinking

Although the nature of, predisposing conditions for, and techniques of measuring intuitive thinking are unknown or undeveloped, intuition is an important complement to analytic thinking and should be developed to the fullest extent possible. The two thinking processes are almost direct opposites. In contrast to analytic thinking, intuitive thinking does not proceed in a step-by-step order with full awareness of the information and operations needed. Rather, it involves maneuvers based on implicit perception of the total problem with little or no awareness of the process used. An individual who uses intuition appears to make seemingly careless, big leaps instead of smaller, measured steps.

According to scholars in various academic fields, the effectiveness of intuition lies in an individual's knowledge of a subject. Through familiarity with the subject, individuals feed their intuition or give it something with which to work. After making an "intuitive leap" and coming up with a solution or hypothesis, the individual can then check or prove its validity through more careful analytic means. The nature of intuitive thinking, ways of measurement, possible predisposing characteristics, and factors affecting the process are areas in which further study is needed.

Davidson and Sternberg (1984) developed a subtheory of insight as intellectual giftedness composed of three separate, but related, processes: selective encoding, or the process of sifting relevant from irrelevant information; selective combination, or blending pieces of relevant information into a unified whole; and selective comparison, or relating newly acquired information to knowledge acquired in the past. They devised varied tasks to assess the level of intuition among gifted and nongifted learners and also to discover whether an insight training program would be feasible for students of at least average ability. The results of their research indicated that gifted students appeared to solve insight problems more efficiently and with fewer cues than nongifted students. Additionally, gifted students profited little from the training program, whereas average students improved performance significantly after training. The results of the experiments were consistent with the information-processing theory of insight. Because selective encoding, selective combination, and selective comparison can exist in the absence of insight, however, additional research is needed with more consequential problems, to discover the nature of the processes that constitute insightful thinking.

Bruner makes some observations about the nature of these processes but does not assume he is correct. He believes, for example, that effective intuitive thinking requires self-confidence and courage on the student's part. Mistakes can be made easily by relying on intuition, so a certain willingness to take risks is important. When drawing a parallel with business and industry, where the increasing importance and novelty of a situation causes a decrease in the tendency to think intuitively, Bruner suggests that the present system of rewards and punishments (usually in the form of grades) actually may discourage intuitive thinking.

When considering the development of this process of thinking, educators also must recognize the problems involved. Teachers must be sensitive enough to differentiate between an ignorant answer and an answer from an interesting wrong leap. They must have a thorough knowledge of subject matter, and they must encourage students to venture into new areas and explore new thoughts.

Motives for Learning

Motivation, an important step toward a pursuit of excellence, must be a happy medium between frenzied activity and apathy. One of the important goals of education must be to arouse long-term interest, or a continuing commitment to learning and the world of ideas, rather than a commitment to capturing the short-term interest of children necessary for learning a lesson. Bruner believes that the pursuit of excellence should be emphasized through education and that one way to facilitate this pursuit of excellence is through a continuing interest in learning, along with a high regard for intellectual activity.

Students have varied and mixed motives for learning, including the approval of parents, teachers, and peers, as well as their own sense of mastery. To foster such motivation, educators can develop interesting curricula, improve teaching methods, and pursue relevant, exciting topics.

About Characteristics and Teaching of Gifted Students

In his book, Bruner makes several references to the gifted that are interesting in light of the subsequent application of his ideas to the education of gifted children. The first statement he makes is, "Good teaching which emphasizes the structure of a subject is probably even more valuable for the less able student than for the gifted one, for it is the former rather than the latter who is most easily thrown off the track by poor teaching" (1960, p. 9). By this statement he does not mean that the content or pace of courses should be the same, but means that if good teaching occurs, even the slowest students can achieve. What he does not take into account with this statement, however, is that not all students can handle or learn the basic concepts identified. Many concepts important to the understanding of a discipline are abstract and highly complex; reasoning and inferential powers sufficient for dealing with complex concepts may not have developed in some students.

From this statement, one assumption seems clear: The Woods Hole Conference participants, who were themselves scholars in academic disciplines, were assuming that all learners could profit from the kind of inquiry activities from which the scholars themselves profited. That is, what literary critics or students studying literature do in reading a literary work is the same if they are to achieve understanding. This assumption may be true for all learners, but perhaps it is true only of those who are able to achieve a complete understanding of the basic abstract concepts that form the structure of an academic discipline.

Bruner's requirement that each concept taught to students should be useful to them as adults raises some practical considerations and issues. Some students, for example, may not need a deep understanding of algebraic principles, the principles of logic, or even the idea of biological tropism. Only those who choose to pursue further study in a field will be interested in ideas such as these or use them as adults.

A second reference to the gifted is in Bruner's speculation that improvements in the teaching of science and mathematics may accentuate the gaps between children of differing ability levels. This possibility, though, should not deter educators from making modifications that will allow learners to develop their reasoning powers fully. Democracy and leadership will have a better chance of surviving if the top quarter of this nation's students are not neglected as they have been traditionally.

Bruner states that the pursuit of excellence should not be limited to gifted learners. On the other hand, teaching should not be aimed simply at the average student. The curriculum should contain something for everyone. The challenge is to develop materials that are difficult enough for the most able learners without destroying the confidence of those who are less able—an almost impossible task.

Although not made by Bruner, an assumption made by those who implement his ideas is expressed in the previous discussion related to which children need to learn (or will use as adults) the basic ideas or concepts in academic areas. Basic modes of inquiry, the thought systems, and certain abstract ideas necessary for complete understanding of a field of study will most likely be of use to potential scholars, who often are gifted learners.

ELEMENTS/PARTS

Rather than explaining how an individual can implement each of the five themes expressed by Bruner, which would require volumes, in this chapter we select and explain the parts of his approach appearing to have the most potential for success with gifted children. Selection of the ideas that we explain is based not only on our own experience but also on the recommendations of other educators of the gifted (e.g., Gallagher, 1985; Renzulli & Reis, 1985; Ward, 1961).

MODIFICATIONS OF THE BASIC CURRICULUM

Content Modifications

The most important curricular suggestions made by Bruner are changes in content, or what is taught. His major theme focuses on the basic structure of a discipline. Incorporated into his definition of basic structure are several of the recommended content modifications: abstractness, complexity, organization for learning value, and the teaching of methods of inquiry in each discipline. In fact, the only content modifications not addressed in his approach are variety and the study of people. The first three concepts (i.e., abstractness, complexity, and organization) are, from Bruner's point of view, implications resulting from the teaching of basic structure and necessary requirements for its successful implementation. All of these are discussed together because they are related. The recommendation for teaching methods of inquiry is discussed as a process or method modification, because Bruner suggests that students learn history the way a historian would or learn science like a scientist.

Bruner's first suggestion is related to the first task in curriculum development: What should be taught? In other words, what are those basic ideas that form the structure of a subject? Which ideas or concepts, when understood, will have the widest applicability to new situations? Which concepts will be needed by students as adults? The people qualified to make these decisions are the scholars in various disciplines. Only they have a complete enough understanding of their discipline to decide what is basic. Because the problem involves not only what concepts should be taught but also how they can be put into a form that children at different levels of development can understand, Bruner suggests that curriculum committees, made up of both scholars and child development specialists, can address both questions simultaneously.

A problem with this suggestion is the apparently erroneous assumption that scholars can agree on the basic concepts that should be taught. Some of the earlier curriculum development projects that grew out of this suggestion included lists of 3,500 generalizations in the social sciences. This phenomenon defeated the purpose of the project, because teachers still had to make the major decisions about what was most important. All of these general ideas could not be taught. One can, however, force the issue; ideas agreed upon by the majority can constitute the basic or required curriculum, whereas those ideas with lesser degrees of agreement can make up the optional or extended curriculum.

The idea of organization for learning value is significant in implementing a basic concept approach. In that children have only a limited amount of time in school and an almost unlimited number of things to learn, educators must make each learning experience a valuable one and each concept important. As a guiding principle for implementing this idea, Bruner suggests as criteria the following dual consideration: (a) When fully developed, is the concept worth being known by an adult? and (b) Having known it as a child, does a person become a better adult? According to Bruner, "If the answer to both is negative or ambiguous, then the material is cluttering the curriculum" (1960, p. 52).

A related principle, implicit in Bruner's discussions but not stated as such, is that of organizing the content so that it will facilitate the discovery or development of a basic idea. Using the methods of a scholar—that is, studying phenomena with the potential to increase the chances that a basic idea will be discovered—is at the heart of this approach. By structuring activities so that discovery is facilitated, teachers also develop the interests of learners and capitalize on their natural curiosity and excitement.

One example of the organization of content or learning experiences to facilitate discovery is Bruner's (1960, pp. 6–7) classic example of a basic concept in the area of biology. Presented as an example of a basic idea and how it can transfer to a new situation, it also illustrates how content can be organized. Students make and record a set of observations on an inchworm crossing a sheet of graph paper on a board. When the board is tilted so the inclined plane or upward grade is 30 degrees, the worm moves at an angle of 45 degrees from the line of maximum climb. With the board tilted to 60 degrees, the worm travels along a line 75 degrees off the straight-up line. Based on these two measures, the students may infer that inchworms "prefer" to travel uphill, if uphill they must go, along an incline of 15 degrees. The students have discovered a tropism, actually a geotropism. It is not an isolated fact. Further investigations may show that among simple organisms, such phenomena—regulation of locomotion according to a fixed or built-in standard—are the rule.

Once students grasp the basic concept of the relationship between external stimulation and locomotor action, they can be asked to make similar observations about animals' preferences for environmental conditions, such as illumination, level of salinity, and temperature. In this way, the teacher has organized the content or the specific facts and data to be used around a concept. By having experiences arranged within a definite time period, the teacher facilitates discovery of the underlying principle of tropism. Organization around basic ideas also facilitates selection of the data to be used. Economy is achieved at the same time, because fewer experiences will be needed if arranged closely together to facilitate more rapid transfer.

Process Modifications

Although mainly a theory suggesting content changes, Bruner's ideas include the three following process modifications appropriate for gifted students: (a) higher levels of thinking, (b) discovery, and (c) open-endedness. Underlying the development of the concept of teaching basic structure is the idea that all intellectual activity is the same regardless of the level and that the best way to learn is to act the way a scholar would act or "create" knowledge in the way that someone on the frontier of knowledge would create it. This underlying assumption contributed to the development of Bruner's basic structure theme, and it also suggests a method for the effective teaching of structure. The suggestion is an obvious one: Methods of teaching should put the learner in the role of a scholar or inquirer in each subject area being taught.

In the physical sciences, the child should behave as a physicist, chemist, or engineer; in the natural sciences, as a biologist, herpetologist, or geologist; and in literature, as a poet, a short-story writer, a literary critic, or a playwright. Teachers must be familiar with the data and basic ideas of a discipline and also know its characteristic methods of inquiry. Alternatively, teachers need to make arrangements for skilled mentors who can work with students in a disciplined inquiry and give them suggestions for improving methodological skills. When a child acting as a sociologist is conducting an attitude survey, for example, the teacher must be prepared to give specific suggestions for designing better questions, analyzing the data, conducting interviews, scaling, and using other data collection or evaluation methods.

Because of Bruner's emphasis on putting the learner in the role of a scholar or inquirer, three process modifications are made. When children behave as scholars, they will use, rather than simply acquire, information. Information gained will be applied in practical situations, evaluated, and used to form products new to the students. While using professional methods, the learners also are participating in open-ended activities that are provocative in nature. Discovery is an integral part of Bruner's approach, and he makes many suggestions for implementing it to allow the learner to behave as a scholar or professional. Aspects of open-endedness not included as part of Bruner's approach, however, relate to the questions asked of students while engaged in inquiry.

The following are three important aspects of implementing guided discovery: (a) organization and selection of data to be used in facilitating the child's discovery of some basic idea, (b) the use of questions or activities that will guide students in their process of inquiry, and (c) ways of teaching that will develop in the child an excitement about learning that will translate into an "inquiry attitude." Bruner does not give specific suggestions for implementing the approach, but he does provide general guidelines. First, a balance needs to be established between (a) an approach in which the basic idea is first stated by the teacher with students providing the proof (a deductive approach) and (b) an inductive or discovery approach. Presenting all of what a student needs to know through a discovery approach would be too time-consuming. With gifted learners, however, this process does not take nearly as much time as with other students. If an inductive approach were used exclusively, though, it no doubt would get boring, and learners would not get practice in deductive reasoning. In short, a balance is necessary between the two types of approaches, but just what constitutes balance is as yet unknown, and probably varies between learners and topics. Bruner makes no assumptions about the relative emphases of the approaches.

Discovery learning need not be limited to formal subjects such as mathematics. They can and should be used in social studies, language arts, the sciences, and the arts.

Related to the use of discovery is the theme of intuitive versus analytic thinking. Intuitive thinking, which is a series of "jumps" rather than an analytical step-by-step process, often is the scientist's or scholar's way of making an important new discovery. In mathematics, for example, individuals are said to think intuitively when they suddenly achieve a solution but still have not provided the formal proof. Another example of intuition in mathematics is the ability to make good, quick guesses about the best possible approaches for solving a problem. The phenomenon of intuition as described by Bruner is similar, if not identical, to the "Aha!" experience described by Parnes (see Chapter 6). In an "Aha!" experience, an individual suddenly understands or has a great idea. This experience usually comes after a period of incubation in which the person has been working on a problem subconsciously. Suddenly things click, and the person knows the answer but has no idea how the idea came.

According to Bruner, little is known about the nature of intuition and the factors affecting it. He speculates that solid knowledge of a subject helps a person become skilled at intuitive thinking, but that not all people who are familiar with their subject areas are good at intuitive thinking. Thus, a good background in the basic ideas of the subject may be necessary but not sufficient for intuition to occur. Other conditions that may be necessary, or at least increase the probability that intuitive thinking will be developed, include (a) intuitive teachers who can provide a model of effective intuition or a willingness to use intuition, (b) emphasis on the structure or connectedness of knowledge, (c) encouragement of guessing, and (d) a change in grading practices in certain situations so that less emphasis is placed on getting the right answer.

One way to increase the possibility that intuitive thinking will occur is to use a discovery approach. Discovery, if true to its definition, should more nearly approximate the inquiry process of a scholar. In their own fields in day-to-day work, scholars often make intuitive leaps. Thus, by using an approach that is more like the true inquiry process, educators increase the probability of intuitive thinking. In the day-to-day work of a scholar, intuitive thinking often is used to come up with a hypothesis that can be tested by analytical means. When using a discovery approach, this aspect of the inquiry process can be incorporated. Learners can be encouraged to use intuition to make guesses about underlying principles and then check their guesses through research. Constructive evaluation can be given on the student's use of intuition in forming the hypothesis, and assessment can be based on the methods of proof chosen to test the hypothesis.

Product and Learning Environment Modifications

Although Bruner does not specifically address curricular modifications in the areas of product and learning environment, modifications of products are implied (and, in fact, required) by his approach. Because students are acting as real inquirers and scholars, their products address real problems and involve transformations rather than summaries of existing ideas or information. Directing products toward real audiences and the realistic evaluation of products are ideas neither implied nor addressed by his approach.

With regard to the learning environment, Bruner makes no specific suggestions. Some of his comments imply that the environment would need to resemble the environments of professionals. This idea is related to the dimensions of centering on learning, encouraging independence, complexity, varying grouping options, flexibility, and high mobility. An open environment is implied by Bruner's basic beliefs and stated principles; however, because no mention is made of the environment, these modifications are not really addressed. Table 4.3 provides a way for the reader to integrate Bruner's underlying themes approach with the basic ideas relating to curriculum development for gifted students. In this table, student roles and activities and teacher roles and activities are related to each major theme.

Examples of Teaching Activities

A prime example of Brunerian activities and strategies is found in the Education Development Center's (1970) *Man: A Course of Study* (MACOS). Through this social studies curriculum, students learn a set of key concepts, acquire new information, and then are led to generalize from these newly assimilated facts and to evaluate their generalizations. Through a series of films that simulate field study and a set of 30 booklets, the students assimilate information about animal and human behavior arranged around a few basic themes. Much of the learning comes from the work of Irven DeVore, Jane Goodall, and Niko Tinbergen, all admired scientists and specialists in their fields who devoted their energies to long-term investigation. By studying the works of such people, students develop an understanding of and appreciation for ongoing scientific investigation. Through independent and small-group study and group discussion, students arrive at generalizations about the essence of being human.

The basic theme of MACOS is "What makes man human?" This conceptual question forms the basis for organizing the course, which is concerned with the nature of humans as a species and the forces (e.g., tool making, language, social organization, management of prolonged childhood, the urge to explain the world) that shape and have shaped humanity. Nine conceptual themes are explored through both primary and secondary data sources using the inquiry methods of scholars in the major fields that are associated with the themes: biologists, psychologists, sociologists, and

TABLE 4.3

Summary of Student and Teacher Activities and Roles in Bruner's Basic Structure of a Discipline

Step, Type, or Level of Thinking	Student		Teacher	
	Role	Sample Activities	Role	Sample Activities
Basic concepts	Inquirer Data gatherer Analyzer Synthesizer	Using primary sources, study some phenomenon by collecting "raw data." Using secondary sources, study the conclusions or ideas of others about some phenomenon. Acquire, transform, and evaluate new information.	Organizer Facilitator Methodological consultant Resource	Choose concepts or basic ideas identified as most important by scholars in a field. If those ideas are not already available in a discipline, form a committee made up of scholars and child development specialists to develop ideas and suggestions about how the ideas can best be learned by children. Subject each concept to be taught to the tests of usefulness to an adult. Select the data and plan learning experiences that are the "richest" and most economical in developing concepts and basic ideas.
Inquiry as a scholar	Inquirer Data gatherer Analyzer Synthesizer	Be a professional in a discipline (e.g., scientist, mathematician, social scientist, writer, playwright, artist, musician).	Organizer Facilitator Methodological consultant Resource	Provide students with constructive feedback on their inquiry skills. Provide students with feedback on the validity of their conclusions and logic in reaching them.

(continues)

TABLE 4.3 *Continued.*

Summary of Student and Teacher Activities and Roles in Bruner's Basic Structure of a Discipline

Step, Type, or Level of Thinking	Student		Teacher	
	Role	Sample Activities	Role	Sample Activities
Discovery	Inquirer	Try to figure things out, make sense of phenomena, observations, data. Make hypotheses and test them.	Organizer Facilitator Resource Stimulator	Organize content and plan learning experiences that will facilitate students' discovery of basic concepts. Provide a balance between discovery (inductive) and deductive approaches. Develop discovery techniques in all content areas.
Intuitive thinking	Hypothesizer Risk taker	Make guesses intuitively and then check hypotheses by analytical methods. Hypothesize (guess) about solutions as well as about the best approaches for investigation.	Supporter Facilitator	Help children develop good solid knowledge of a discipline to enable them to become good intuitive thinkers. Model the use of intuitive thinking by making hypotheses. Encourage the students to make hypotheses. Emphasize the structure and connectedness of knowledge. Change grading practices so that "wrong hunches" are not unnecessarily detrimental.

anthropologists. Table 4.4 gives a summary of conceptual themes, data sources, classroom techniques, and learning methods used in the MACOS curriculum. The example introductory lesson, shown in Table 4.5, demonstrates how students can act as anthropologists studying behavior.

MODIFYING THE MODEL

Bruner's model does not include curricular modifications appropriate for gifted students in the following areas: (a) content—variety and the study of people; (b) process—evidence of reasoning, freedom of choice, pacing, variety, and group interaction; (c) product—real audiences, appropriate evaluation, variety, and self-selected format; and (d) learning environment. Because his approach is so comprehensive, it can almost be used as a total curriculum; however, if the elements described in the following sections were added, his approach would be more appropriate for gifted learners.

Content Modifications

Variety

To add the element of variety, a person simply needs to assess the regular curriculum to determine what is being taught and make certain that the content in the program for the gifted is different. In so doing, however, the educator must continue the organization of content around key concepts, as Bruner suggests. To illustrate this process, Maker (1982b) developed a worksheet for assessing content plans (see Table 4.6). The generalization students are expected to discover is written at the top of the worksheet, and the concepts contained in the generalization are listed below it. Each concept is analyzed separately. On the left, the data and information pertaining to the concept that is taught in the regular curriculum are listed. On the right side, the teacher lists additional data that students need to be taught to achieve a full understanding of the concept. In the example, the generalization and concepts pertain to the scientific method and its use. Two concepts—observation and organization of data—are analyzed. The process should be continued until each concept contained in the generalization has been analyzed.

TABLE 4.4

Summary of Conceptual Themes, Data Sources, Classroom Techniques, and Learning Methods in *Man: A Course of Study*

Conceptual Themes	Data Sources	Classroom Techniques	Learning Methods
Life cycle (including reproduction)	1. *Primary Sources* Student experiences	*Examples* Individual and group research (e.g., direct observation or reading of texts)	Inquiry or investigation: problem defining, hypothesizing, experimentation, observation, literature searching, summarizing, and reporting
Adaptation	Behavior of family		
Learning	Behavior of young children in school		
Aggression			
Organization of groups (including group relationships, the family, the community, division of labor)	Behavior of animals	Large- and small-group discussions	
	2. *Secondary Sources* Films, slides, video tapes	Games	Sharing and evaluating interpretations
		Role play; simulations	Accumulating and organizing information for retention
Technology	Recordings	Large- and small-group projects such as art, construction, drama	
Communication and language	Anthropological field notes		Exchanging opinions, defending opinions
	Written data on humans, other animals, diverse environments	Writing songs, poems, stories, plays	
World-view			Exploring individual feelings
Values			Exposure to and experience with diverse aesthetic styles

Note. Adapted from *Man: A Course of Study,* by J. P. Hanley, D. K. Whitla, E. W. Moo, and A. S. Walter, 1970, Cambridge, MA: Education Development Center. Copyright 1970 by Education Development Center. Adapted with permission.

Study of People

The study of people is an interesting content modification to Bruner's model and is easy to incorporate. When considering each key concept to be developed, the teacher can, as a part of the process of deciding what data to teach, also choose a person or persons who have contributed significantly to the development and explanation of that concept. Learners can examine the ideas and methods of those individuals and attempt to trace the

(*text continues on p. 152*)

TABLE 4.5
Example of MACOS Lesson: The Study of Human Beings
from an Anthropological Perspective

Materials

A selection from:

lipstick	road map	notepad
aspirin	magazine	pencils or pens
address book	photographs	spoon
newspaper	calendar	eyeglasses
tissues or handkerchief		wallet with some contents
letter from a friend		candy bar or gum

I. Introducing the Task

Before class, fill a pocketbook, briefcase, or desk drawer with several of the items listed above and/or other common items. In a brief introduction to the class, explain that the students are to pretend that they have just discovered these items and do not know anything about the person to whom they belong or the place or time the person lived in. What can they learn about the person's way of life from these belongings? What can they guess about the society the person lives in? What does the person seem to care about? Which items seem necessary for survival? What questions would they like to ask this person?

After examining one item together, small groups can take other items and examine them in light of some of the questions raised. (You might reproduce the questions for each group; the class could then compile their guesses on a chart.)

II. Focusing on Ways of Studying Human Beings

After students have discussed what they think they know about the owner of the items and the society to which he/she belongs, you can explain that, in some ways, they have been acting as anthropologists, scientists who study human beings. They have been using available evidence to inquire into the nature of human beings and the societies in which they live. Students should think about some of these questions:

- What would you have to know about another group of people to understand their culture?
- How would you keep records of what you learn?
- Are some of the ways you study about human beings similar to the ways you study other animal species?
- How is the study different?

In response to the last question, it should be clear that we can observe human beings to try to see what is important to them, but we can also ask them questions and ask them to give their opinions. What can be learned through observations? What cannot be learned through observation alone? To focus on these questions, students can list their responses and develop a chart similar to the one that follows. The chart points

(continues)

Table 4.5 *Continued.*
Example of MACOS Lesson: The Study of Human Beings from an Anthropological Perspective

out the different kinds of things we can learn about human beings, based upon our ability to speak with each other.

Learned Through Observation	Learned Through Talking
What they look like	What they did yesterday and will do tomorrow
How they meet basic needs	How they like what they do
How they act toward one another	What their favorite color is
How they play	What they think or feel about an event in another part
How the young act with the old	of the world
How parents act with offspring	What they believe in
What they do not like to eat	What they think is funny

III. A Visit from an Anthropologist

Students may be interested in learning more about anthropology as a field of study and about what anthropologists do. The teacher might make a statement such as the following:

> Some anthropologists look mostly at the physical structure of human beings; others examine traces of human beings from the past. Still others are what we call cultural anthropologists; they look at what a group of people share in common: their beliefs, their tools, the ways they define their relationships with each other, their language, the way they raise their children, and so on. Anthropologists call all the things that people share their culture. Cultural anthropologists often study groups of people who share a culture, such as the Netsilik Eskimos, the people whose way of life is the focus of the course.

Students might think about what an anthropologist visiting their classroom would observe. How does an anthropologist decide what to record? Would every anthropologist record the same things? This question can lead to a discussion of the bias of different anthropologists. How might a woman's view differ from a man's? Suppose one anthropologist was an artist as well an anthropologist, and another was a school teacher as well as an anthropologist. How might this affect the way they look at a group of people? How would you feel about having your customs recorded by a person taking notes on your activities and talking with you? (Possible conflict over individual privacy versus scientific study could come out of a discussion of this question. How does a real anthropologist answer that question?)

Students will better understand anthropology as a professional field if they indeed meet and speak with an anthropologist. Frequently, colleges and universities have departments of anthropology with professors or graduate students who enjoy talking with young people about their field. You could probably locate such a person through a call or note to the head of a nearby anthropology department.

TABLE 4.6
Example of Worksheet for Curriculum Design

Generalization No _1_ : The growth of knowledge in science occurs through questioning, observation, experimentation, manipulation of materials, observation of results, and revision of original theories.

Key concepts to be developed:

Observation*	Organization of data*	Control groups
Prediction	Classification	Hypothesis
Environment	Inferences	Energy
Scientific method	Contamination	Variable
	Raw data	Brainstorming

Data taught in the regular curriculum	**Data needing to be taught in the special curriculum**
Observation	*Observation*
Ways to observe and record changes in temperature	Different kinds of observations that can be made: checklists, coding schemes, timed observation, use of microscope, changes in color from use of chemicals
The importance of careful observation	Types of measurement for observations: weight, length, color, density, temperature
	Experimental and control observations
	Examples of incorrect inferences resulting from careless observations
Organization of Data	*Organization of Data*
Keeping records of observations in notebooks	Types of graphs: bar, line
Grouping like observations together	Choosing units for graphs
	Separating experimental from control observations

---

*Concepts developed in this worksheet.

Note. From *Curriculum Development for the Gifted,* by J. Maker, 1982, Austin, TX: PRO-ED. Copyright 1982 by PRO-ED, Inc. Reprinted with permission.

evolution of their ideas. At the same time, they can examine how these individuals' methods differed and how the different methods may have contributed to the development of different theories or ideas.

As learners are using the methods of scholars and investigators, they can engage in discussions of the different investigative techniques and examine the lives of eminent individuals who developed and used these methods. In addition, they can discuss the creative or productive accomplishments of these individuals and others' reactions to these discoveries or accomplishments.

Process Modifications

The most effective way to modify Bruner's model is to combine it with the Hilda Taba Teaching Strategies (see Chapter 10), the Autonomous Learner Model (ALM; see Chapter 2), and the Enrichment Triad Model (see Chapter 8). The Taba strategies can be used to guide class discussions of key concepts and methods, and the ALM and Enrichment Triad Model can be used to help students structure and implement independent or group investigations. Another useful model to combine with Bruner's approach is Sharan and Sharan's Group Investigations (see Chapter 9).

Because many of Taba's ideas were influenced by Bruner, the two approaches are compatible. For example, in planning a Taba discussion, the teacher begins with a concept or generalization and plans a series of focusing questions to stimulate the students' interaction with each other, through which they will reach their own statement of a generalization or organization of information around a concept.

Bruner suggests that students use investigative techniques; however, in many cases, teachers tell them what techniques to use and what problems to study. With gifted students, an effective approach is to assess their level of self-direction and either guide their investigations or serve as a resource for their study of a problem of interest to them. The teacher can retain the organization of content around key concepts by encouraging investigations related to a particular concept. The teacher also can suggest that students attempt to use a variety of methods selected from the many investigative techniques available to them.

When teachers use the Taba strategies, they are ensuring the systematic development of higher levels of thinking, the use of open-ended questions, and the use of questions calling for explanations or support of reasoning and logic. An element of variety (class discussions) is added, and specific suggestions for pacing are included. If elements of the other process models are included, freedom of choice and other elements of variety become part of the curriculum.

Pacing

When using Bruner's ideas or the curricula developed from his ideas, teachers must realize that gifted learners need, in addition to faster pacing of discussions, only a few examples (or specific facts) to enable them to discover a principle or understand a concept. Thus, an important aspect of implementation is to select only a few examples and to move quickly from one concept to the next, depending on how quickly learners grasp the ideas.

Variety

In addition to the variety added by discussions based on the Taba strategies, as well as varied investigative techniques, learning experiences should include field trips to observe scientists, poets, visual artists, musicians, or other professionals at work. Methods of the disciplines also can be included in learning centers for investigations, lectures, demonstrations, and simulations.

Group Interaction

Adding simulations and other interactive activities to the basic methods suggested by Bruner increases interest and stimulates student participation. In fact, such additions do not represent a significant deviation from Bruner's suggestions. Many good simulations are available from vendors who include materials for gifted students in their products. These simulations include situations in which students take on roles such as those Bruner advocated: archaeologists, legal and judiciary professionals, medical personnel, anthropologists, political figures, and scientists and others involved in ecological situations.

Product Modifications

Although the problems studied when using Bruner's approach are "real," some may not be of interest to individual learners. The use of real problems is critical because they are relevant and motivating to the students. Using ALM (Chapter 2) or Group Investigations (Chapter 9) provides the structure for students to select problems to investigate. With the guidance of a teacher or other professional, the products can incorporate a variety of self-selected formats as well.

Real Audiences

Adding the element of real audiences to Bruner's approach is easy. As the emphasis in his method is on use of the techniques of professionals, the teacher can assist the students by asking questions such as the following: What do anthropologists do with the results of their research? What do creative writers do with their poems, short stories, novels, or plays? The answers to these questions suggest what the students should attempt to do with their products. This aspect of product development can mesh well with the study of people, as the students can use these people's products and audiences as a way to stimulate their own ideas (Renzulli, 1979).

Appropriate Evaluation

Building on the previous example, the teacher can ask the students, "How are the anthropologist's products judged? How do different audiences view these products?" A study of eminent individuals also can provide answers to these questions. The products and the reactions of different audiences to the products can be examined. An analysis of the reactions of eminent individuals to their varied audiences and critics adds interest and helps students gain a greater understanding of the assessment of products.

Learning Environment Modifications

Even though Bruner does not address directly the question of what kind of learning environment a teacher should establish, environments similar to those described for gifted learners are essential if Bruner's ideas are to be implemented effectively. For students to function as real inquirers, the focus must be on student ideas and learning activities; teacher talk must not dominate the classroom. The environment must permit a high degree of mobility to enable students to carry out their investigations, and this requires the element of openness. As students pursue investigations, others must accept, rather than judge, their ideas and beliefs along the way. The following sections provide suggestions of how teachers can make the learning environment more appropriate.

Learner Centered

If Bruner's approach is combined with the Taba strategies (Chapter 10), as suggested earlier, discussions will be learner centered. Teachers will talk very little, they will not be the center of discussions, and they will not serve as authority figures. The classroom can become even more learner centered if Betts's (Chapter 2), Sharan and Sharan's (Chapter 9), and Renzulli's (Chapter 8) suggestions are followed; student ideas and topics of investigation will be emphasized rather than those of the teacher.

Encouraging Independence

Ideally, the classroom climate should extend the emphasis on independence into the nonacademic realm as well as the academic one. Bruner's objectives of having students learn as professionals can be achieved simultaneously with student independence. If, for example, the teacher has been having difficulty with classroom management but does not want to impose solutions on the students (an important aspect of this dimension), the next topic of study could be government, wherein students could begin to learn how government works by establishing their own classroom government, electing their own officials, and developing and enforcing their own laws. Thus, they learn the system while solving their own problems.

Openness and Flexibility

The classroom environment must be open to allow learners to make "wrong" intuitive leaps during the discovery process, to make their own hypotheses, and to test them with experiments. The teacher must let them make their own mistakes and learn from them. Students must be allowed to pursue solutions without interruptions. Other people, including content experts, should be brought into the classroom. Teachers must make few restrictions on the areas of study, the methods used, and the timing of activities.

Accepting

During the discovery process, the teacher must be careful to avoid both negative and positive judgments of student ideas. If one student has developed a hypothesis that the teacher knows will "work," the teacher should avoid providing positive feedback to this student until after the hypothesis has been accepted by other students. This gives that learner opportunities to explore his or her own ideas and other students equal opportunities to develop and test their own ideas, rather than using the hypothesis "approved" by the teacher. Acceptance does not imply nonevaluation. In fact, evaluation is necessary to the process. Learners must be assisted in examining their hypotheses to determine both the accurate or valid aspects and the inaccurate ones. They also must examine the appropriateness of their methods.

Complexity

To enable gifted students to learn as a scholar does and facilitate their discovery of abstract, complex ideas, the classroom must include a variety of sophisticated references, equipment, technology, and milieus. These students need environments that simulate those used by professionals in as many ways as possible.

High Mobility and Varied Grouping Arrangements

A high degree of mobility also is necessary. If reference materials are not available in the classroom, students must have the independence to leave the class to find them. They also must be allowed to leave the classroom and school to conduct their investigations. They must learn to work individually, in small groups, and in flexible groupings during various activities. Such provisions are essential if Bruner's approach is to work.

Summary

The Basic Structure of a Discipline, while mainly a content model, emphasizes discovery and techniques and processes used by practicing professionals in each discipline. Bruner's ideas can be combined effectively with ALM (Chapter 2), Enrichment Triad Model (Chapter 8), Schoolwide Enrichment Model (Chapter 8), Group Investigations (Chapter 9), the Taba strategies (Chapter 10), DISCOVER (Chapter 5), or Prism (Chapter 12) to achieve a comprehensive curriculum. Bruner's approach also can be combined with other thinking–learning models, such as Bloom's Cognitive Taxonomy (Chapter 3), Krathwohl's Affective Taxonomy (Chapter 3), or Creative Problem Solving (Chapter 6).

DEVELOPMENT

After the Woods Hole Conference, Jerome Bruner began his massive task of synthesizing the major points made by the conferees after 10 days of discussion and debate. The conference members had been divided into five work groups and, as each of these groups had prepared a lengthy report to present to the rest of the participants for debate, the task of synthesizing the ideas was not easy. In an attempt to reflect as accurately as possible the major themes, conclusions, and disagreements, the conference chair prepared a draft report based on the conference papers and sent copies to all participants for their comments and critiques. The final draft, which incorporated as much of the flavor of the meetings and comments as possible, became a classic book in curricular reform.

Bruner's ideas have continued to develop along the lines suggested in the conference report. Subsequent writing and research have extended and refined many of them. In the massive social studies curriculum, *Man: A Course of Study* (Education Development Center, 1970), Bruner incorporated and extended his ideas into an exciting, effective learning program; however, the curriculum was sharply criticized by conservative groups and others who considered the materials too difficult or inappropriate for children. This superb curriculum may be difficult to find but is well worth the search.

RESEARCH ON EFFECTIVENESS

With Nongifted Students

In a comprehensive evaluation of MACOS, Hanley, Whitla, Moo, and Walter (1970) found the curriculum to be highly effective in achieving its goals with students in Grades 4 through 6 and in effecting desirable changes in the teachers who used it. In the teachers, a noticeable shift occurred from didactic to interpersonal modes of teaching and learning. After teaching the course, teachers talked less and were less dominating, allowed students to give longer responses, raised more issues for discussion, and engaged in more student-to-student interaction. In comparisons of control and experimental groups, several differences favored the classes using MACOS. Following are some of the outcomes for students:

- Students had increased desire and ability to work independently.
- The wide range of course materials seemed to modify students' views of traditional data sources.
- Students learned both content and methods of investigation. They began to understand the meaning of serious investigation.
- Students were personally involved in and reflective about the course ideas.

- Students began to fully understand the concept of interdependence of species members.

Evaluation of the course materials and relative effectiveness for achieving the goals of the course yielded the following results:

- The materials and methods were enjoyable, exciting, and interesting to the students.
- Students tended to become much more aware of the similarities rather than of the differences between humans and animals.
- Ability to master and use the concepts in the course correctly seemed to depend heavily on the quality and number of examples given.
- Students became impatient with obvious repetition in material but also were disturbed when ideas were not presented thoroughly.
- The Netsilik unit (the section on humans) was the favorite of the majority of the students.
- The hunting activities were highly successful teaching devices, but youngsters must reflect on the activity to learn much from it.

In addition to MACOS, many other curricula have been based on Bruner's approach. Most were developed and evaluated in the 1960s, some quite extensively. In a large-scale evaluation of the University of Illinois Committee on School Mathematics (UICSM) math program involving almost 2,000 students, Tatsuoka and Easley (1963) found significant gains in the experimental group over the control group on a traditional test of algebraic concepts. Others (Begle & Wilson, 1970; Grobman, 1962; W. L. Wallace, 1962) found that when progress was measured by traditional tests of achievement, which usually measure factual information, curricula built on Bruner's approach were not as successful as traditional curricula. On tests constructed by the developers of the curricula, however, the experimental groups were similar to control groups in performance. Most of these researchers say what a person would logically predict: Both the traditional and the new approaches are effective for achieving student learning objectives.

Bruner (1985) observed that developing a curriculum involves political decisions on the nature of learning and learners based not simply on data but also on ideals and cultural conditions in which the learning is to take place. The best approach is one that requires reflection and inquiry on whether the "script" imposed on learners is there for the stipulated reasons or whether the activities or curriculum serve other purposes.

We would do well to equip learners with a menu of their possibilities and, in the course of their education, to arm them with procedures and sensibilities that would make it possible for them to use the menu wisely.... The appreciation of that variety is what makes the practice of education something more than a scripted exercise in cultural rigidity. (Bruner, 1985, p. 8)

With Gifted Students

Some research has compared the achievement of students with different ability levels using Bruner-type curricula. Generally, however, these comparisons have been more or less afterthoughts, except for two well-designed studies. In an evaluation of the UICSM material stressing the discovery method, Lowman (1961) compared this method with a traditional algebra class. He found a significant difference favoring the UICSM materials for students in the top third in ability, but not for the middle and lower thirds. In a 3-year study of six curricular approaches with more than 1,500 gifted junior high students, Goldberg, Passow, Camm, and Neill (cited in Gallagher, 1975) found that the ranking of these programs was as follows: (a) School Mathematics Study Group (SMSG)—accelerated (4 years of SMSG in a 3-year period); (b) UICSM—normal; (c) UICSM—beginning earlier; (d) SMSG—normal; (e) traditional accelerated; and (f) traditional enriched. Thus, the new curricular approaches were superior to traditional ones, and the most superior was one of the new approaches taught in a more concentrated period of time.

In other evaluations, gifted and high-ability students seemed to profit more from learning abstract concepts and using a discovery approach. In evaluations of Biological Sciences Curriculum Study (BSCS) materials, W. L. Wallace (1962) and Grobman (1962) concluded that high ability was an important factor in the mastery of the concepts presented and that low intelligence was a negative factor. Others (Mayor, 1966; Proviss, 1960; Suppes, 1969) concluded that modern math students do as well as students in traditional programs in arithmetic fundamentals and do better at conceptualization.

For the gifted, the difference in conceptualization is even greater. The MACOS evaluation showed that IQs made no difference in the amount of learning from pretest to posttest in the animals unit but did make a difference in the Netsilik unit. Some of the important differences between the two units include the following: (a) The animal unit has much more repetition of the basic ideas and concepts through returning to them each time a new animal is studied; (b) more inferential skill and transfer of concepts is needed in the Netsilik unit because children compare humans with all the animals studied to "discover" important similarities and differences; and (c) the unit on humans requires the most speculation and reflection on how all the learned concepts contribute to and affect personal lives.

Throughout these evaluations, a consistent trend emerges. Gifted students enjoy dealing with abstract, complex ideas and can handle them more easily than other students. They need fewer examples to learn the concepts, and they need to revisit the ideas much less frequently in the learning process. In fact, when the curriculum includes too many examples and too many returns to the ideas, they get "turned off" and do not achieve as well as when the content is accelerated or economically chosen.

In addition to high ability, two other characteristics of gifted students support the logic for their success with Bruner-type curricula: Gifted and creative individuals prefer to use their intuition in searching for deeper meanings rather than using direct sensory data in forming impressions and making decisions, and they tend to learn in a series of intuitive leaps. Support for the idea that gifted persons prefer to use an intuitive mode for gathering information and making decisions comes from research with the *Myers–Briggs Type Indicator* (Myers & Briggs, 1976), a personality assessment tool based on Carl Jung's (1923) theory of psychological types. According to the theory, a major dimension of personality is an individual's preferred way of gathering information. The two opposite psychological types are called sensing and intuitive. A sensing person prefers to get information directly through the five senses and to stick with the verifiable facts. An intuitive person relies on the deeper meanings and possibilities obtained through intuition, based on hunches and perceptions rather than verifiable facts. Although the general population includes fewer intuitive than sensing types (i.e., approximately 75% are sensing and 25% are intuitive), an extremely high percentage of intellectually gifted and creative individuals can be classified as intuitive types (Myers & Briggs, 1980). In fact, in MacKinnon's (1965) studies of creative people, 90% of the creative writers, 92% of the mathematicians, 93% of the research scientists, and 100% of the architects were classified as intuitive types.

Studies of concept formation (Osler & Fivel, 1961; Osler & Troutman, 1961) have provided the basis for saying that the gifted tend to learn through a series of intuitive leaps. The learning curves of the higher ability subjects showed a series of dramatic increases interspersed with an almost flat progression. Lower ability subjects showed a steady progression over a series of trials. Osler and her associates interpreted the results to mean that the high-ability subjects were forming hypotheses and then testing them. When they hypothesized correctly, their performance increased dramatically. The periods when learning curves were flat occurred while subjects were operating on the basis of incorrect hypotheses. Another finding in the study was that the high-ability subjects were more distracted by certain kinds of irrelevant cues than were subjects of lower ability. The interpretation of this finding was that those of higher ability were attempting to use all of the situational cues in forming their hypotheses, whereas the trial-and-error learning of the other subjects did not require their use of these cues.

Educators and researchers have continued to be interested in thinking, problem-solving, and learning strategy differences between gifted and other children, searching for those "qualitative" differences that will justify special programs. Generally, however, most research has revealed that gifted students use strategies and demonstrate cognitive traits similar to nongifted, older individuals (Carter & Ormrod, 1982; Scruggs & Mastropieri, 1988; Scruggs, Mastropieri, Monson, & Jorgensen, 1985). Such results are not surprising because IQ tests are designed such that those who are "developmentally advanced" have higher scores. Shore and Dover (1987) suggested that gifted students possess and use more metacognitive strategies but that their process of assessment depends on the ability to explain (verbally) their strategies. Regardless of the reasons, gifted students usually learn differently from their same-age peers.

JUDGMENTS

Advantages

Bruner's approach has a number of important characteristics to recommend its use with gifted students. First, it is a total approach that provides a framework for most if not all the curricular modifications suggested in Chapter 1. The majority of the adaptations are addressed directly by the approach (e.g., content changes of abstractness, complexity, organization, methodology; process changes of varied methods, higher levels of thinking, discovery), whereas others are suggested indirectly (e.g., process modifications of pacing, open-endedness, expressing logic or reasoning; product changes related to real problems and the use of raw data; learning environment changes of available resources and equipment and free expression). Those not addressed, such as freedom of choice of topics, choice of method, real audiences, variety, self-selected format, and appropriate evaluation, can be incorporated easily into the approach and will enhance its effectiveness.

A second major advantage is that evaluations have shown that the approach is effective with gifted students, although its effectiveness with other students is less consistent. Typical students seem to be unable to handle the abstract concepts without numerous, frequently repeated examples. Therefore, in this case, educators can answer "no" to the tough question, "But isn't the approach good for all students?" Some of the other methods are good for all students to some degree, so the "no" answer given in other situations must be qualified endlessly.

Another practical advantage is that a variety of materials and comprehensive curricula are built on this approach. Although some have been revised so that nongifted learners can be successful in using them, some are still available in their original forms. Selective use of the material is possible. Usually, in using commercial materials with gifted learners, teachers must add to the materials by introducing higher level content, more challenging ideas, and so on; however, because the problem with some of the Bruner-based curricula is that often too many examples and activities are given for the abstract concepts, teachers have an easier task leaving out rather than making up activities. Another way for teachers to be selective is to revisit each concept less often or fewer times. This helps avoid the unnecessary repetition that causes boredom in gifted students.

Building on the unique characteristics of gifted students while preparing them for the roles they will be likely to assume in society is one final advantage of the basic structure approach. Gifted students will need the inquiry skills and the abstract concepts. Most important, the attitude toward discovery—a love of learning—can carry over into their lives as adults, regardless of whether they become scholars or leaders.

Disadvantages

The major disadvantage in using Bruner's approach is that teachers have a difficult role. They not only must keep up on the latest informational and theoretical developments in a field but also must be knowledgeable enough in the methods of inquiry to be able to give students assistance in their investigations. To teach these high-level concepts adequately, the teacher must understand them. Many, if not most, elementary teachers are not knowledgeable enough about the academic areas because child development and teaching methods (e.g., techniques for individualizing instruction) have been viewed as a more important part of teacher education than academic understanding. This emphasis is probably valid in most cases. Teachers of the gifted, however, must be special people. They may need to go back to school or in some way develop academic understanding before teaching in the way Bruner suggests. Because one person cannot be an expert in every academic area or even all the major ones, the teacher needs to have the will, ability, and time to find willing experts in various disciplines in order to implement Bruner's approach successfully.

Another problem is that even the scholars in a field have difficulty deciding what basic concepts should be learned. Certainly, if scholars disagree, others will have difficulty reaching consensus.

CONCLUSION

Based on the available research, the Basic Structure of a Discipline, combined with teaching methods emphasizing inquiry and discovery, can be highly successful with gifted students. Although the teaching of structure and abstract concepts is a difficult task for the teacher, materials and comprehensive curricula are available as aids. With Bruner's approach, the advantages greatly outweigh the disadvantages.

RESOURCES

Background Information

Banks, J. A. (1990). *Teaching strategies for the social studies: Inquiry, valuing, and decision-making* (4th ed.). White Plains, NY: Longman.

Instructional Materials and Resources

Aicken, F. (1991). *The nature of science* (2nd ed.). Portsmouth, NH: Heinemann.

Banks, J. A. (1990). *Teaching strategies for the social studies: Inquiry, valuing, and decision-making* (4th ed.). White Plains, NY: Longman.

Carin, A. A., & Sund, R. B. (1985). *Teaching science through discovery* (6th ed.). Columbus, OH: Merrill.

Hyde, A. A., & Hyde, P. R. (1991). *Mathwise: Teaching mathematical thinking and problem solving*. Portsmouth, NH: Heinemann.

Simulations

Numerous *Interact Simulations* in varied disciplines are available for elementary and secondary students from the following Web sites:

http://www.awpeller.com

http://www.zephyrpress.com

Other Sources

Professional societies of specific disciplines, such as the following, often have curriculum guidelines and materials.

National Council for the Social Studies
3501 Newark Street NW
Washington, DC 20016

National Council of Teachers of English
1111 Kenyon Road
Urbana, IL 61811

National Council of Teachers of Mathematics
1906 Association Drive
Reston, VA 22091-1593

National Science Teachers Association
1742 Connecticut Avenue NW
Washington, DC 20009

CHAPTER 5

C. June Maker and Shirley W. Schiever: The DISCOVER Curriculum Model

ISCOVER (Discovering Intellectual Strengths and Capabilities while Observing Varied Ethnic Responses) is an ongoing program of research and development that began in 1987. The primary goal of the research is to design and continue to polish better ways to assess and develop the problem-solving abilities of children and youth.

In the DISCOVER Projects, an educational framework has been developed in which students typically considered at risk are viewed as being "at promise" for success due to their problem-solving strengths in diverse cognitive domains. When students' strengths are identified and teaching approaches developed so that strengths are used as vehicles for developing academic and real-life skills, students from all groups, including those considered to be at risk, experience greater success in school (Maker, Rogers, Nielson, & Bauerle, 1996). Although DISCOVER is widely touted as effective with students who might conventionally be considered at risk, the curriculum also meets the criteria for curriculum for gifted students. The problem-solving element brings complexity as well as other recommended modifications to the curriculum. When academic skills are taught within the context of real-world problem solving and students make choices regarding what situation to focus on and how they tackle problems, school and academic skills are perceived as relevant, and motivation and learning soar. An understanding of the history of the DISCOVER Projects and the DISCOVER Assessment is necessary to an understanding of the curriculum model.

THE DISCOVER PROJECTS

In 1987 Maker and Schiever conducted research based on the theory of multiple intelligence (MI) (Gardner, 1983) and Getzels and Csikszentmihalyi's (1967, 1976) problem-solving continuum. The initial research focused on adults (a man and a woman) and children (a girl and a boy) who were considered highly competent in one of the intelligences. The participants were given a series of problem-solving tasks, ranging from highly structured to completely open-ended, in the intelligence in which they were highly competent. The participants were videotaped as well as observed as they completed the tasks. The findings supported the theories that (a) highly competent individuals preferred open-ended tasks in their area of strength and (b) motivation and interest increased dramatically as the individuals progressed from structured to open-ended tasks. Later research revealed that highly competent individuals used some of the problem-solving strategies from their area of strength in areas where they were less competent. Further research confirmed that the core capabilities of each intelligence are important, but that other problem-solving strategies also are valuable.

PROBLEM SOLVING:
A KEY CONCEPT

The traditional definition of *intelligence* as the score an individual makes on an IQ test does not adequately reflect human abilities. Gardner (1983) defines *intelligence* as "a set of skills of problem solving enabling the individual to resolve genuine problems or difficulties … and must also entail the potential for finding or creating problems—thereby laying the groundwork for the acquisition of new knowledge" (pp. 60–61). In this definition, Gardner includes both psychological ideas and practical ones, and goes beyond the traditional to view creativity as integral to intelligence. In other words, within each intellectual domain, people can merely adapt to the world around them and solve problems in ways they have learned, but they also can conduct research on the frontiers of knowledge, making new advances in knowledge and creating new and innovative products. In the DISCOVER Projects, these ideas are made practical and easily applicable by using a continuum of problem-solving situations derived from the work of researchers in creativity.

In the DISCOVER Curriculum Model, problem-solving situations are categorized according to whether the problem, method, and solution are known by the presenter, the solver, or both. Getzels and Csikszentmihalyi (1967, 1976) identified three problem types, which are now Types I, II, and VI of the problem continuum. Schiever and Maker (1991, 1997, 2003) added two to provide for the gap between the original Types II and III, and recently added another, making a total of six problem types (see Table 5.1). These six problem types are arranged on a continuum of decreasing structure. Because this *is* a continuum, some problems are "special case" problems and may not fit neatly with the definition of one type.

☞ **Type I.** The problem and the method of solution are clearly stated by the teacher to the student, the teacher knows the correct solution, and the student knows or has been taught the strategy for solving the problem. Type I problems include solving math problems by a known algorithm or method; following a formula in language, music, math, or science; and performing prescribed body movements, as in dance or sports.

☞ **Type II.** The problem is specified, but the method of solution and the solution are known only to the teacher. Type II is close to Type I in structure, except that the student does not know the method by which to arrive at a solution. Type II problems include mathematical word problems requiring the student to figure out and apply the

TABLE 5.1
The Problem Continuum

Problem Type	Problem		Method		Solution	
	Teacher	Student	Teacher	Student	Teacher	Student
I	Specified	K	K	K	K	U
II	Specified	K	K	U	K	U
III	Specified	K	R	U	K	U
IV	Specified	K	R	U	R	U
V	Specified	K	U	U	U	U
VI	U	U	U	U	U	U

Specified = Preestablished or clearly stated; K = Known; U = Unknown; R = Range.

appropriate method to find the solution; answering questions about factual material; scientific "experiments" with prescribed materials and variables; playing an instrument while sight reading the music; and creating a scale drawing.

☛ **Type III.** The problem is specified, but more than one method may be used to arrive at the correct solution, which the teacher knows. Type III problems require a specific solution, but many methods may be used to reach this solution. Examples of Type III tasks are finding the "key" to mathematical, word, or linguistic patterns; movement sequences created to meet specific requirements; and construction using specified materials and meeting given criteria.

☛ **Type IV.** The problem is specified, but it may be solved in more than one way and the teacher knows the range of solutions. Examples include problems that can be solved inductively but that have an accepted range of answers, such as geometry problems that may be solved using manipulatives; creating as many equations as possible using three (provided) numbers and the operations of addition and subtraction; writing Haiku; and creating music or movement sequences within defined parameters.

☛ **Type V.** The problem is specified, but the method and solution are unknown to both teacher and students. Questions such as, "In what ways might you share the results of your survey?" are Type V problems, as are constructions using specific materials and meeting preset goals (e.g., building a mousetrap vehicle). Other examples include creating prose or poetry; making a self-sustainable terrarium or aquarium; writing lyrics to an existing melody; writing a melody for existing lyrics; and finding new ways to apply existing formulas. Future Problem Solving (FPS) is a special case of Type V; the problem is known to the presenter and the solvers, and the solvers are taught the Creative Problem Solving process (see Chapter 6) to use in developing their solution, but the solution is unknown to all.

☛ **Type VI.** The problem is unknown or undefined, and the method and solution are unknown to both teacher and student. Type VI problems have the least structure; are the most complex; need to be defined and, possibly, redefined; and have numerous possible solutions. These are the problem situations found in real life that can be defined in more than one way and that may need redefining during the problem-solving process. Type VI problem situations include those such as environmental pollution; student behavior; ethical behavior and standards; global warming; urban problems; social issues, such as violence or declining literacy; and international border issues. Type VI problems not only are appropriate for gifted students to grapple with, but are a critical aspect of their education.

REVIEWS OF THE RESEARCH ON CREATIVITY ASSESSMENT

In Maker's (2001) review of the research on problem solving, she reported the following (pp. 234–235): Reviews of research on problem solving (Rogers, 1993) have revealed that very few studies have included Type IV or V (current continuum Types V and VI) problem situations. As a result, little has been learned about the abilities and skills actually needed in the structuring and solving of real-world problems. Extensive research on the prediction of adult accomplishments highlights the significance of the DISCOVER Assessment's inclusion of Type V (Type VI) problem-solving situations. In these situations, the individual must "raise new questions, new possibilities,… regard old problems from a new angle, [which] requires creative imagination and marks real advances in science" (Getzels & Csikszentmihalyi, 1967, p. 83). Scholars who have completed critical reviews of research (Baird, 1985; Hoyt, 1965; Nelson, 1975; O'Leary, 1980; Reilly & Chao, 1982; Wallach, 1976), including meta-analysis (Cohen, 1984; Samson, Grave, Weinstein, & Walberg, 1984), have reached surprisingly similar conclusions: Although achievement and ability test scores are related to academic success (e.g., grades and later achievement test scores), their relationship to adult success factors is minimal. O'Leary (1980), for example, reports that the average correlation between measures of academic success and indicators of adult career success is .17.

Research on the predictive validity of creativity tests yields a different picture. Only a few studies are available; the most notable is Torrance's 22-year follow-up of 211 individuals whose mean age was 27.5 years. All had been assessed with the *Torrance Tests of Creative Thinking* (TTCT) as elementary school students. Using a creativity index made up of scores on the TTCT over a 3-year period, and a variety of indicators of adult creative achievements, he found a correlation of .58 (<.001) between the creativity index and measures of adult success (Torrance, 1981). In a well-designed reanalysis of Torrance's data, Yamada and Tam (1996) found that four predictors—the creativity index, childhood future career image, IQ, and the presence of a mentor—explained 49% of the variance in adult creative achievement. The standardized regression coefficients were .44, .24, .20, and .16, respectively. The results of Torrance's research are more conclusive than other studies of creativity, but the trend can be seen in numerous studies (cf. Baird, 1985; Howieson, 1982).

Across these prediction studies, reviewers and authors have concluded that the more the predictor (e.g., test or behavior such as high school or college achievements) resembles the criterion to be predicted (e.g., another test, grades, behaviors such as adult achievement), the more successful the prediction. For example, measures of creative writing predicted later publications of fiction better than measures of general ability; the advanced knowledge sections of the GRE predicted productivity in physics, geology, engineering, and chemistry better than general verbal and quantitative sections; and student achievements in high school (e.g., publications, winning science fair competitions) predicted later achievements of the same nature better than grades, academic achievement, or ability tests.

To realize the vision articulated in new curriculum standards and prepare a generation capable of designing new approaches to new problems, educators must assess and develop a wide range of problem-solving abilities. Instead of measuring and developing knowledge or divergent thinking out of their real contexts, teachers must measure the production, flexible use, originality, and addition of richness and detail in the solving of complex, realistic problems in specific academic and intellectual domains. This is the intent and promise of the DISCOVER Assessment Model. Teachers also must develop those abilities in real-life problem-solving situations. This is the intent and promise of the DISCOVER Curriculum Model.

THE DISCOVER ASSESSMENT[1]

The DISCOVER Assessment (Maker, 2001) is typically administered to an entire classroom of students who are clustered at tables in groups of four or five. A trained observer is assigned to each table, and observers rotate after each task, to eliminate the "halo" effect (i.e., the effect of one set of ob-

---

[1]The information in this section is taken from Maker, Rogers, and Nielson (1994) and Rogers (1998), unless otherwise noted.

servations on another). The assessment is done differently at various grade levels (prekindergarten, K–2, 3–5, 6–8, 9–12). Approximately 3 hours of observation and problem solving are needed for each classroom, and most students need a break of some kind or movement between activities.

Specially designed forms include Behavior Checklists that list specific problem-solving behaviors and information on products for each of the following intelligences: linguistic, spatial, logical–mathematical, interpersonal and intrapersonal, bodily kinesthetic, and general. A Summary Sheet is attached to the front of the Behavior Checklists, and a comprehensive packet of information on each child is compiled, using the written observations, photographs, sketches, remembered instances, and team discussion.

Four problem sets are included: (a) Spatial Artistic, a series of activities with some optional verbal components; (b) Spatial Analytical, a nonverbal series of activities that forms the basis for quantitative reasoning; (c) Oral Linguistic, an oral verbal activity; and (d) Math, a logical–mathematical small-group activity for Grades K and 1, or a worksheet done individually by each student in Grades 2 through 8. A written linguistic assessment is given by the classroom teacher, preferably prior to the group assessment.

The trained observers at each table have a one-page sheet for recording behaviors observed during the problem-solving tasks. Pictures are taken of students' creations, and their precise comments are recorded. Additionally, observers are responsible for asking probing questions and encouraging students or giving specific hints at specific points if the student *wants* a hint. During the Spatial Analytical activity, the observers record the time each student requires for each task and the order (within their group) in which they complete tasks.

Normally the regular classroom teacher reads the instructions to the students, and translators or bilingual observers are provided for students whose first language is other than English. Teachers and observers are instructed that each student's response is accepted without judgment or show of favoritism; every contribution is valued equally.

Debriefing

Immediately following the assessment, the observers meet to complete the observation and debriefing tasks. Each observer is responsible for the following:

1. Completing observer notes on each student observed.

2. Transcribing the tape-recorded stories and completing the Oral Linguistic Behavior Checklist while or immediately after listening.
3. Completing the front page of the Behavior Checklists for each student observed during the Oral Linguistic tasks and noting the observer's name in the correct section.
4. With the team, discussing students' performance in general on the Oral Linguistic activity and making a group decision about criteria for distinguishing the ratings.
5. Recording ratings on the front cover of the Behavior Checklist and passing along checklists to those who observed the same children in the Spatial Artistic activity.
6. Completing the Spatial Artistic checklist for the students observed and recording observer's name.
7. With the team, discussing students' performance on the Spatial Artistic activity, sharing photographs and observations; making group decisions about the criteria for distinguishing ratings.
8. Recording ratings on the front cover of the Behavior Checklist and passing along the checklists to those who observed the same children in the Spatial Analytical activity.
9. Completing the Spatial Analytical checklist for students observed after first filling out the "amount of time taken" on the front cover of each child's Summary Sheet.
10. With the team, discussing students' performance on the Spatial Analytical activity; making a group decision about criteria for distinguishing ratings.
11. Discussing students who are outstanding in interpersonal interactions and recording the rating on the front cover of the Behavior Checklist.
12. Compiling all information for each student (Spatial Artistic pictures, transcribed stories, tapes of stories, Observer Notes, and Behavior Checklists). (Maker, 1997)

Scoring

Scores are determined in the context of the child's setting; that is, after the assessment, the team discusses the group's performance as a whole as well as those individuals who stand out as exceptionally competent in an activity. The ratings are as follow: *Redo, Unknown, Maybe, Probably, Definitely,* and *Wow!* These ratings are assigned to students within the context of competency within an activity, *as compared to their peer group.* One of the reasons that DISCOVER is so effective for children from other-than-mainstream backgrounds is that they are rated not only based on their problem-solving skills within a variety of domains, using performance-based assessment, but also based on how their performance compares with that of others in the group with which they are most closely identified. Obviously, *Wow!* is reserved for those who are outstanding in a particular area; less obviously, *Redo* means that the observer felt that the observation, for whatever reason, was not necessarily an accurate measurement of the child's competence in that activity.

THE DISCOVER
CURRICULUM MODEL

The DISCOVER Curriculum Model has evolved over time into a comprehensive approach that empowers students and makes teaching more rewarding. Based on what the authors and their colleagues learned from the assessments, their experience with students and problem solving, and the concept of multiple areas of human competence, the model has emerged as a strong and effective way for students to learn. Although it is appropriate for all students, it is essential for gifted learners; it is based on their learning needs, which are determined by their characteristics.

ASSUMPTIONS UNDERLYING
THE MODEL

The authors' fundamental belief in the equal distribution of abilities across diverse groups, the existence of multiple intelligences, and the efficacy of problem-solving strategies as indications of abilities led to the creation of the DISCOVER Assessment. The curriculum rests on these same fundamental beliefs, and the DISCOVER Assessment and Curriculum Model are designed to be interdependent; that is, information gained during the assessment can be used to construct learning experiences that will capitalize on strengths and build in weak areas, using prior knowledge, strengths, and interests to facilitate the learning process.

About Learning

As the following quotes demonstrate, a consistent message of school reform advocates is that students in U.S. schools must learn to think and solve problems rather than memorize facts and mindlessly apply algorithms: "Problem solving is an integral part of all mathematics learning" (National Council of Teachers of Mathematics [NCTM]), 2000, p. 11); "Inquiry into authentic questions generated from student experiences is the central strategy for teaching science" (National Academy of Sciences [NAS], 1996, p. 31); "Our children will thus need to be prepared not just with a larger set of facts or a larger repertoire of specific skills but with the capacity to readily acquire new knowledge, to solve new problems, and to employ creativity and critical thinking in the design of new approaches to existing problems" (President's Committee of Advisors on Science and Technology Panel on Educational Technology [PCAST-PET], 1997, p. 10).

The DISCOVER Curriculum Model is based on the belief that children learn best by constructing their own learning from guided but open-ended experiences, making significant choices about their own learning, and having access to a wide variety of materials. This is consistent with the school reform movement, which advocates a "constructivist" (rather than a "reductionist") approach as the most effective way to achieve the national standards. Certain key elements characterize this approach: (a) actively building new knowledge from experience and prior knowledge; (b) acquisition of higher order thinking and problem-solving skills; (c) basic skills learned in the course of undertaking higher level, "real-world" tasks whose execution requires the integration of a number of skills; (d) information resources available to be accessed by the student at that point in time when they actually become useful for executing the task at hand; (e) fewer topics covered and explored in greater depth; and (f) students as active "architects" rather than passive recipients of knowledge (NCTM, 2000; NAS, 1996; PCAST-PET, 1997).

Additionally, the DISCOVER Curriculum Model includes three elements that broaden its applicability to students with diverse backgrounds and personal traits, including types of abilities. These elements are (a) arts integration, especially visual arts, music, creative dance/movement, and theater arts; (b) development of a wide range of problem-solving abilities; and (c) integration of the cultures and languages of the children (Maker, 2001).

About Teaching

The teacher's role is that of guide to information and learning, rather than source of all knowledge. Teachers must consider student interests and strengths, as well as their knowledge and skill levels, to develop a curriculum that will teach the prescribed skills and concepts. The key idea about curriculum and teaching is that students use their dominant intelligences to stimulate learning in all subjects, especially weaker ones (Maker & Lane, 2001).

Effective teachers of the DISCOVER Curriculum implement the following principles in their classrooms: (a) opportunities for students to develop their multiple intelligences; (b) opportunities for students to solve problems ranging from highly structured to completely unstructured; (c) active, hands-on learning through consistently available learning centers containing the "tools" of the multiple intelligences; (d) integration of the culture of the students and of the community into the curriculum; and (e) curriculum planned around abstract themes (Maker et al., 1996). The integration of the arts enhances learning and motivation, and brings a richness to the entire learning experience.

About Characteristics and Teaching of Gifted Students

The DISCOVER Curriculum is designed to develop the production and flexible use of original ideas and to add richness and detail to student learning through the solving of complex real-life problems (Maker, 2001). This curriculum is constructivist and uses the principles of a good program for gifted students: (a) integrated, interdisciplinary content; (b) higher order thinking, appropriate pacing, self-directed learning, and complex problem-solving processes; (c) development of unique products for real audiences; (d) student interaction between and among themselves, as well as interaction with experts; and (e) learning environments with physical and psychological flexibility, openness, and safety. The environment is rich in resources, and the teacher is a guide as the students make choices based on interest and ability (Maker, 1981, 1982a; Maker & King, 1996; Maker & Nielson, 1995, 1996). These principles meet the learning needs of gifted students, who usually exhibit advanced comprehension, varied interests, and curiosity; an ability to generate original ideas and solutions; an ability to use and form conceptual frameworks; and a broad base of information on subjects that interest them.

The DISCOVER Curriculum is designed to teach more effectively students with a wide range of backgrounds, language skills, and learning abilities. This goal is accomplished through the incorporation of materials and methods appropriate to the populations being served. Use of the curriculum tends to level the playing field by allowing diverse student populations to reach educational standards, arriving there in different ways, through diverse and flexible teaching methodologies. Classrooms set up to use the DISCOVER Curriculum Model are designed to allow the same concepts to be taught in many different ways at the same time. All students are expected to learn the same core subject concepts and skills, but using methods they choose, as guided by their teacher(s) (Maker & Lane, 2001).

ELEMENTS/PARTS

The essential components of the DISCOVER Curriculum Model include solving varied problem types; the multiple intelligences; group activities and choice; active, hands-on learning; access to the tools of the multiple intelligences; interdisciplinary themes; integration of the arts; and integration of the cultures and languages of students.

Problem Solving

The problem-solving continuum (Schiever & Maker, 1991, 1997, 2003) is key to the development of the DISCOVER Curriculum (see Table 5.1). The curriculum for gifted students should consist primarily of Types III, IV, V, and VI, with Type VI being the most appropriate and motivating. Solving real-life problems raises the emotional and motivational stakes for the learner, and although these require significant amounts of time and resources, it is through struggling with the issues contained therein that students learn both content and critical thinking (Wolfe, 2001).

Multiple Intelligences

In 1983 Howard Gardner proposed the existence of seven separate human intelligences: linguistic, logical mathematical, musical, bodily–kinesthetic, spatial, and two forms of personal intelligence—intrapersonal and interpersonal. In 1999 he added naturalist intelligence and left the door open for the possible identification of additional intelligences in the future. As noted previously, the concept of multiple intelligences is key to the DISCOVER Curriculum Model; this concept emphasizes the importance of identifying individual strengths and validating those in curriculum and instruction. Additionally, the concept of multiple intelligences provides a structure for curriculum that is rich and varied, and that offers students experiences in their areas of strength as well as experiences that will strengthen their weaker domains. Using this concept, teachers are able to develop curriculum that is appropriate for the whole child and that enhances the development and growth of each student.

Group Activities and Choice

Allowing students to make significant choices about their learning empowers and motivates them. Choosing a problem to solve or a way in which to demonstrate learning and knowledge creates immediate ownership and buy-in; the students are engaged precisely because they have made a choice.

Choices may be offered in a variety of ways. Students can be free to choose (a) the format of a product, (b) the "tools" of particular intelligences to use while learning a concept or developing a product, and (c) the part to be contributed to a group production. They may choose to work alone or with one or more other students, and they can select the materials to illustrate a concept they are studying (Maker et al., 1996). At times teachers may create problem situations and allow students to choose the situation or to define a problem within the situation for which they want to develop a solution.

Real-world experiences include (a) individual observation and decision making, (b) small-group interactions, (c) large-group interactions, or (d) some combination of these elements. The structure of the DISCOVER Curriculum should include all of these possibilities on a regular basis. Individual decision making emphasizes the cause and effect of personal choice, small-group interactions build teamwork and group decision-making skills, and large-group interactions require both individual and small-group perspectives and agendas to be subordinate to the larger group perspective and context. The significant emphasis on individual choice and small-group decision making allows students to determine which learning styles work best for them and to experience the ways in which their abilities fit together with those of their peers (see http:// discover.arizona.edu).

Active, Hands-On Learning

Including all of the multiple intelligences in the structure of curriculum ensures some hands-on and bodily–kinesthetic activities; however, more than token inclusion of such experiences must be included in the DIS-COVER Curriculum. Students must be encouraged to experience factual and conceptual knowledge and to express what they have learned in a variety of ways. Students come to school having learned about their world through observing, manipulating, tasting, feeling, hearing, and smelling— in other words, by *sensing* their environment. The DISCOVER classroom experience incorporates a rich sensory environment and opportunities to move, manipulate, and experience fully so that students build from their strengths through their weaknesses as they master the concepts and skills of the mandated curriculum.

Access to the Tools of the Multiple Intelligences

One way to encourage individual student choice is by using "Exploratoriums," places where students explore various facets of learning and self-expression. Exploratoriums include centers such as music, art, science, social science, linguistic, technological, bodily–kinesthetic, and so on, depending on the school's resources. For example, a music center might contain various instruments and objects that can be used to make sounds, and an art center might include clay, brushes, paints, paper, palettes, scissors, fabrics, pipe cleaners, and other items (http://discover.arizona.edu). Students should have opportunities and be encouraged to spend extended periods of time in a center of their choosing, experimenting with the tools therein and constructing their own understanding of these tools of the intelligences.

Interdisciplinary Themes

To organize effectively and efficiently the components of learning, which include the state- or district-mandated core curriculum and the critical elements of the DISCOVER Curriculum Model, teachers organize content and problem-solving exercises using interdisciplinary themes. After selecting a theme based on student interest, teachers may use the problem-solving continuum (Table 5.1) and the standards they are expected to teach to ensure that the instructional unit has an orderly and thorough structure. Interdisciplinary themes include systems, patterns, change, relationships, cultures, structures, cycles, exploration, conflict, invention, or others that lend themselves to including the concepts and skills to be taught (Maker, 2001).

After the theme is selected, teachers develop learning activities that include problem solving of all problem types and experiences in each of the intelligences. For example, an elementary school teacher created a problem matrix based on the theme "patterns." Problems using linguistic intelligence included identifying rhyming schemes in poems (Type III), writing a poem with an ABAB rhyme pattern (Type IV), and creating a "word picture" using any rhyming scheme (Type V). Logical–mathematical problems included identifying patterns in nature (Type III) and analyzing the role of structure in poetic patterns and natural patterns (Type IV). Spatial intelligence was required to examine Navajo rugs and draw the recurring patterns (Type I) or to represent the patterns from poetry in some spatial form (Type V). Listening to several types of very different music and demonstrating the different rhythmic patterns using instruments from the music center exercised musical intelligence. Interpersonal intelligence was employed as the students discussed the behavior patterns that helped or hindered groups to work effectively together without conflict (Interpersonal, Type III). Journals to record and reflect on their habitual behavior patterns and reasons for these behaviors required intrapersonal skills (Type V). Bodily–kinesthetic experiences included creating a pattern of movement and body shape that represented an emotion such as fear, surprise, anger, or happiness (Type IV) and creating a mime or a dance to communicate the ideas and patterns from a poem they selected (Type V) (Maker, 2001). Had the teacher wanted to give students experience with a TYPE VI problem, she could have asked students, as a group, to brainstorm a list of societal patterns (bullying, family structure, crime, violence, political events, etc.). From this list students could select one that is of most interest to them. In small groups they could begin to research pertinent issues, engage in group discussions, and work toward defining and finding solutions for the problem they chose as most intriguing or closest to them.

Integration of the Arts

In his book *Arts with the Brain in Mind,* which is grounded in brain research, Eric Jensen (2001) presents the concept that the arts promote the development of valuable human neurobiological systems. He explains how the arts enhance the process of learning by providing learners with opportunities to develop and mature multiple brain systems simultaneously, and he makes a sound case for the arts as a major discipline. The arts are motivational—performing arts are a key factor in reducing school dropouts—and they foster task commitment and the development of social skills. Based on the DISCOVER research and pilot studies, Maker (2001) concluded that in addition to the general constructivist education principle underlying the DISCOVER Curriculum Model, the infusion of the arts is the most significant of the unique principles in the model.

Each of Gardner's intelligences is directly related to several types of art, and three of them are art forms by definition: musical, bodily–kinesthetic, and spatial–artistic; therefore, a curriculum model based on the multiple intelligences theory requires that the arts be an integral part of the curriculum. A commitment to providing learning experiences in all of the intelligences further dictates that the arts must be included. Bodily–kinesthetic intelligence can be honed and developed through the use of mime, dance, and theatre, and spatial intelligence through sculpture, painting, design, architectural forms and structure, and computer-enhanced imagery. Quiet, reflective, solitary art forms (and often indirect audiences) are appealing to those with high levels of intrapersonal intelligence, whereas those with high levels of interpersonal intelligence prefer interactive, social art forms and a live, visible audience (DISCOVER, 2002).

Integration of the Cultures and Languages of Students

Integrating students' languages and cultures into the curriculum sends a signal that the teacher values and respects these parts of the students' lives, and is motivating and empowering for the students. This important component of the DISCOVER Curriculum Model leads students to value their own cultures as they participate in activities of varied cultures of their community and learn about the origins and customs of various cultures, including their own (Maker et al., 1996). Learning about a wide variety of cultures creates a rich tapestry of knowledge and appreciation for students and a valuable context within which they can examine and appreciate their own culture.

The integration of varied cultures and languages can be accomplished in a variety of ways. To be effective, this integration must be ongoing, not tied to certain holidays or special events. Appealing and interesting books in many languages should be available, and students can be encouraged to teach others their native language. The art techniques and styles, songs, musical instruments, dances, foods, and folklore of the students' cultures should be shared, taught, and learned. Customs, traditions, and religious practices and beliefs should be discussed and, when students feel comfortable, shared (Maker, 2001).

Table 5.2 presents sample activities and roles of students and teachers within the DISCOVER Curriculum Model.

MODIFICATIONS OF THE BASIC CURRICULUM

The DISCOVER Curriculum Model provides a comprehensive structure for curriculum modification appropriate for students whose giftedness is in any of the multiple intelligences. The content, process, product, and learning environment modifications suggested by Maker (1982a) and Maker and Nielson (1996) are incorporated within the structure of the model, as well as those elements determined to be critical to or desirable for learning in the current educational research and literature.

Content Modifications

Using the problem continuum as a structure and developing curriculum that primarily includes Types III through VI ensures that curriculum content will be abstract and complex. Curriculum that is designed using

(*text continues on p. 185*)

TABLE 5.2
Summary of Student and Teacher Roles and Activities in the DISCOVER Curriculum Model

Problem, Type, or Critical Component	Student		Teacher	
	Role	Sample Activities	Role	Sample Activities
Problem Type III	Active participant in constructing own knowledge base and gaining problem-solving skills	Patterns theme: Invent a card game based on the value of a four-card hand.	Planner Resource Facilitator	Gather appropriate materials for student exploration. Ask proof of reasoning questions.
Problem Type IV	Active participant	Incorporate the use of one or more wild cards into the card game and predict the ways this could change the game's outcome.	Facilitator Resource	As students develop predictions, ask proof of reasoning questions. Hold small-group discussions when several students have made predictions. Emphasize the pattern aspect of predictions.
Type V	Active participant	Create a game based on manipulation of components.	Resource Facilitator	Ask proof of reasoning questions to related game rules and object.
Type VI, Interdisciplinary themes, Choice,	Active participant in finding an interesting problem situation and	Identify a natural, linguistic, social, or mathematical pattern. Explore the ways the pattern might be	Resource Guide Facilitator	Monitor progress of individuals or small groups as they identify a pattern and prepare presentation.

(continues)

Type VI (*continued*)

Group activities	developing a presentation within a small group	used to benefit mankind.		
Multiple Intelligences; access to the tools of the intelligences; active, hands-on learning	Active participant	Explore various centers. Find ways you might use strengths to learn and produce in areas of weakness.	Plan, gather materials for centers, contact community members who may demonstrate expertise in various intelligences	Monitor individuals, assist them in identifying strengths and ways to use strengths in areas of lesser strength.
Flexible pacing	Active participant	Work at own pace individually and within small groups, be accountable for time spent and progress made.	Facilitator	Monitor students to ensure appropriate material (challenge level) and appropriate learning pace and amount.
Integration of the arts	Active participant in exploring and learning ways to communicate through the arts	Assist in preparing small-group presentations that use a variety of media.	Resource Facilitator	Gather materials for artistic expression. Plan for guest speakers and experiences that examine patterns in the arts. Be sure students "see" patterns across disciplines.

(*continues*)

TABLE 5.2 *Continued.*
Summary of Student and Teacher Roles and Activities in the DISCOVER Curriculum Model

Problem, Type, or Critical Component	Student		Teacher	
	Role	Sample Activities	Role	Sample Activities
Integration of arts *(continued)*				
Integration of students' cultures and languages	Active participant in sharing own culture and language	Interview parents, grandparents, or neighbors to learn more about own culture.	Resource Facilitator	Instruct students in developing effective interview questions. Plan a "Meet Yourself" multicultural potluck and event. Invite parents and friends to bring a type of food characteristic of their culture. After meal, have presentations of cultural traditions and arts, by students or others.

interdisciplinary themes is organized for the learning value of the concepts contained within the units of instruction. Framing learning activities and experiences within the multiple intelligences and integrating fine arts provide the curricular variety that gifted learners need. The study of people is included naturally as students investigate topics of interest; learning about the trail-blazers in a field or eminent people therein has a natural appeal when the topic is self-chosen and may be a passion. Indeed, when students interview experts in their chosen area, they are learning a great deal, not only about the field, but about the interviewees as well.

Process Modifications

Maker (1982a, 1982b) and Maker and Nielson (1995, 1996) posit specific process modifications based on the characteristics of gifted learners. These modifications include higher level thinking, pacing, open-endedness, discovery, a variety of methods, freedom of choice, group interaction, and evidence of reasoning.

Gifted students need to spend significant amounts of classroom time engaged in the higher level thinking processes, such as creative thinking, problem solving, decision making, planning, forecasting, hypothesis generating, and inductive reasoning. Curriculum developed with the structure of the problem-solving continuum as a guide and an emphasis on Types III through VI provides opportunities for students to interact with information, to *process* the information rather than merely committing it to memory.

Instruction needs to be paced to match the speed of student thinking and learning. The open-ended structure of the DISCOVER classroom allows students to move forward in their thinking and develop a product when they are ready to do so; with guidance from the teacher and an appropriate classroom structure, self-pacing will meet the learners' needs.

Teachers need to use a variety of methods of instruction for gifted students. By designing curriculum based on the multiple intelligences, a variety of methods of instruction and student production will come about. As students wrestle with defining and solving real-life problems, they will need to use a variety of sources and means of acquiring information, as well as a variety of thinking strategies and processes.

Gifted students need to have opportunities to make significant choices regarding their learning. Choice is a critical element of the DISCOVER Curriculum; students are to be allowed choices in content studied, products, and mode of presentation of the product.

Interaction with intellectual peers is critical to cognitive development. Small-group problem finding and solving set the stage for high-quality intellectual interaction, and receiving information from experts may provide students with opportunities for interaction with a mature and expert intellectual peer. The DISCOVER Curriculum Model is designed so that even independent studies will contain opportunities for group interaction.

All students need to be required to provide evidence of reasoning to support conclusions or generalizations. For gifted students, the need is even greater; adept thinkers can benefit tremendously from hearing the thinking processes of others, which may be very different from one student to the next. Requiring evidence of reasoning is incorporated easily within the DISCOVER Curriculum; teachers can be trained to ask probing questions at critical points as students engage in problem solving and as they explore the arts and diverse languages and cultures.

Product Modifications

Student products are the end result of the interactions of the thinking and creating processes in which students engage as they pursue understanding of content. Products are used to evaluate learning and to determine student strengths and weaknesses. Gifted students in a DISCOVER classroom are expected to generate appropriate products: These products have a real purpose in the life of the individual, are aimed toward a particular (real) audience, and are a result of the individual's desire to investigate a phenomenon or to create new ideas or objects (Maker & Nielson, 1996).

Maker and Nielson (1996) stated that (gifted) students' products should approximate, as much as possible, those developed by professionals. They provided the following guidelines (pp. 136, 170):

- The proposed product addresses a real problem or concern.
- The product has a real rather than a contrived purpose.
- The intent of the producer is to please, inform, convince, impress, or otherwise have an impact on a real audience.
- The product is a transformation or synthesis rather than a recapitulation or summary of existing information.
- The product will be evaluated by someone other than the teacher, using criteria appropriate to the field.

- The format has been selected by the producer as appropriate to the proposed audience and to the talents of its creator.
- Products should include multiple ways of communicating and multiple ways of demonstrating proficiency.

The DISCOVER Curriculum Model includes all these modifications through the use of the problem-solving continuum (see Table 5.1). A DISCOVER classroom teacher offers students the opportunities they need to develop their capabilities appropriately and holds high expectations of excellence for what they will produce.

Learning Environment Modifications

Maker (1982a) and Maker and Nielson (1996) recommend the following principles for modifying learning environments for gifted children: learner centered; student independence; open to new ideas, acceptance; complexity; variety of grouping options; flexibility; and high mobility. A classroom set up to implement the DISCOVER Curriculum is learner centered, as evidenced by the offering of a variety of ways to learn and to express oneself, the choices available, and the emphasis on students' constructing their own learning and thinking. Independence is encouraged through the various choices available and through the option of pursuing personal interests. New ideas flow into the DISCOVER classroom through expert speakers, the students' research and problem solving, and the integration of the arts. Students venture out of the classroom in the exploration that is a necessary part of real-life problem solving, to explore and use new ideas, new resources, and new people as sources.

MODIFYING THE MODEL

Only a few of the modifications recommended by Maker (1982a) and Maker and Nielson (1996) for gifted students are *not* inherent in the structure of the DISCOVER Curriculum Model. Each of them, however, can be incorporated easily into the curriculum. Acceptance of student diversity of ideas, opinions, interests, and learning modes is compatible with the basic principles and tenets of DISCOVER, as is flexibility (i.e., of the teacher and the use of time). The study of people and methods of the disciplines can be encouraged and facilitated as students pursue their passions and explore their strengths and preferred modalities of expression. Furthermore, questioning techniques and strategies modeled by the teacher and adopted by the students require evidence of reasoning. These modifications all are a good fit with the personalities and teaching styles of teachers who are trained in and adopt the DISCOVER Curriculum Model.

DEVELOPMENT

As stated previously, the DISCOVER Curriculum Model is based on the DISCOVER Research Projects, which have been ongoing since 1987. The primary goal of the projects has been to design better ways to assess and develop the problem-solving abilities of children and youth. In her doctoral dissertation, June Maker (1978) identified problem solving as a key component in the achievements of successful scientists with disabilities. She explored further the concept of disabilities and problem solving in later works (Maker, 1981, 1993; Whitmore & Maker, 1985). Based on this research and the theory of multiple intelligences (Gardner, 1983, 1999), the DISCOVER Projects have investigated problem solving in varied domains, with diverse populations, in projects funded by the Javits Gifted and Talented Education Program and the Office of Bilingual Education and Minority Languages Affairs. Observations of thousands of students from diverse populations engaged in problem solving across multiple domains enabled researchers to identify effective and efficient problem-solving strategies.

The DISCOVER Curriculum Model is a result of combining the problem-solving strategies identified by observation as effective or efficient with expert knowledge of how children learn, sound curriculum principles, and effective teaching strategies. The findings and beliefs of school reform advocates, information from brain research, and the national curriculum standards also were included as the model was developed. The result is unique: a bottom–up curriculum model, developed directly from observational data and inclusive of recent educational developments and knowledge.

RESEARCH ON EFFECTIVENESS

From 1996 to 2000, the DISCOVER Projects used a total-school approach, involving all teachers and all students in four elementary schools. These schools were situated in impoverished or extremely remote areas, and all staff development opportunities were offered to all teachers in the schools. With a combination of teacher belief interviews and extensive classroom observations, teachers were characterized by level of implementation of the DISCOVER Curriculum Model. Five levels were established. Teachers who seldom or rarely used the DISCOVER Curriculum principles were Level 1 implementers, and those who often or always used them were Level 5 implementers, with other levels identified between these end points.

Results of a pilot study in Arizona indicated significant growth in spatial–artistic and logical–mathematical problem solving by students in a high implementer's classroom compared with those in a middle implementer's classroom. Additionally, a statistically significant difference was found between pre- and postimplementation assessment scores of problem-solving ability and storytelling (Maker et al., 1996).

Infusion of the arts is a critical part of the DISCOVER Curriculum, as previously noted. Interdisciplinary researchers have demonstrated the transfer effects from arts-based instruction to improvement in other cognitive domains. In New York City, Arts Connection sponsored arts-based instruction using student strengths to assist in their learning. Reading scores increased by 52% and 65% even though class, school, and school district reading scores decreased (Baum, Owen, & Oreck, 1996).

Significant gains in academic achievement were demonstrated at two school sites where the DISCOVER Model, including an arts-based curriculum, was implemented. Students at Pueblo Gardens Elementary School in Tucson, Arizona, who were assessed for 4 years beginning in 1993, showed significant increases in their *Stanford Achievement Test* (1989; standardized, norm-referenced achievement test) scores for each of the 4 years of the study. Mean scores from the Reading, Math, and Language assessments clustered around the 20th percentile when the study began and were near and above the 60th percentile at the end of the 4 years. More recently, the students have received, in addition to the DISCOVER Curriculum, many hours of arts and integrated arts instruction from Arts-Build, a program that also is based on the theory of multiple intelligences (Maker, 2001).

Students enrolled in classrooms where teachers implemented the DIS-COVER Curriculum at Byck Elementary School in Louisville, Kentucky, demonstrated significant increases on the state standardized assessments, the *Kentucky Instructional Results Information System* (KIRIS) and the *Commonwealth Accountability Testing System* (CATS). These gains were noted in classrooms of high implementers of the DISCOVER Curriculum Model, when compared to those of low implementers. On the KIRIS in 1998, the following assessments were analyzed: science open-ended response, science multiple-choice response, on-demand writing sample, and writing portfolio. Significant differences were found in favor of the high-implementer 4th-grade teacher as compared to the low-implementer 4th-grade teacher on both science assessments. On the on-demand writing sample, 41% of the high-implementer's students scored in the "apprentice" rather than "novice" range, compared with 14% of the middle-implementer's students and 13% of the low-implementer's students. The same four CATS assessments were analyzed, and again significant differences were found in favor of the high-implementer teacher's students compared with those of the low-implementer. For example, 30% of the high-implementer's students scored in the "apprentice" classification, compared with 4% of the low-implementer's students. In the low-implementer's class, 4% of the students also scored in the "proficient" range (Maker, 2001). Although not statistically significant, the Stanford 9 mean scores of the high-implementer teacher were higher than those of the low-implementer teacher. Both KIRIS and CATS include open-ended questions requiring a problem-solving focus, whereas the *Stanford Achievement Test* does not (Taetle & Maker, 2001, cited in Maker, 2001, p. 248).

Interdisciplinary research reveals transfer effects from arts-based curriculum to improvement in other cognitive domains. In New York City, Arts Connection, a DISCOVER Projects' collaborator, sponsored arts-based instruction using student strengths. They found that over 52% and 65% of participating students increased their achievement scores in reading even though class, school, and school district scores decreased (Baum et al., 1996). At-risk students seemed to benefit the most from arts integration; they were able to transfer artistic self-regulation behaviors into an academic setting (Baum, Owen, & Oreck, 1997). Caterall (1995, cited in Maker, 2001) found that an arts-based curriculum, Different Ways of Knowing, for 460 at-risk students resulted in significant improvement in achievement scores, motivation, and learning task engagement, compared with an equal number of at-risk students who did not have access to the arts-based curriculum.

A researcher at Harvard's Project Zero, Hetland (2000, cited in Maker, 2001), performed a meta-analysis of studies of over 700 children who participated in classroom music activities. He discovered that active, hands-on musical instruction lasting 2 years or less leads to significant improvement in spatial–temporal measures. Spatial ability is related to mathematical reasoning.

Additionally, the math scores of 95% of the over 3 million students taking the SAT from 1987 to 1993 were compared. The highest SAT math scores were those of students in music performance classes (College Entrance Examination Board, 1993, cited in Maker, 2001).

JUDGMENTS

Advantages

The most important advantage of the DISCOVER Curriculum Model is that it is research based and accommodates a variety of types of giftedness. Further advantages are that it was developed to include the national curriculum standards, learning theory, sound teaching strategies, and provisions to include and capitalize on the gifts of diverse populations. Additionally, it has been modified and polished through projects in various cities and rural areas throughout the United States and the world. It is inclusive, building on a few of a child's strengths to develop other talents, as well as strengthening areas of weakness. It increases student interest and involvement in learning, and empowers learners as they become more proficient and self-sufficient.

Students in general are happy in a DISCOVER classroom; many times they do not realize they are learning because they are so absorbed that they think they are just having fun. As they learn new skills and have new experiences, they become more self-confident and believe in their ability to do anything they set their minds to do. Learning the DISCOVER way is a joyous experience—for the students and for the teachers. Sharing their families' cultures and traditions reinforces students' belief that these are valuable parts of their personalities. The arts help them be more efficient learners and develop new skills. Mastering an academic concept, learning to play an instrument, knowing how to use various art media, and learning to move one's body more gracefully or more effectively bring a sense of accomplishment that may not come from any other part of a child's world.

Disadvantages

Because the DISCOVER Curriculum is best used in conjunction with the DISCOVER Assessment, which is labor intensive, the program is expensive. As educational budgets are frequently where legislators look first to cut funds, the assessment many times depends on special grants or other funding, which limits its availability. Additionally, the DISCOVER Assessment identifies *more* gifted students than traditional instruments used for identification. Additional students require enlarging programs, which, if administrators are committed to a pull-out program for these students, is more expensive. What is ideal, however, is to implement the DISCOVER Curriculum schoolwide, and *all* students will benefit. This is no empty claim; research results support the use of DISCOVER for all students by documenting increases in standardized and other assessment scores. Although the assessment provides a stronger base for delivering the curriculum, where administrators choose to provide training on the DISCOVER Curriculum for all teachers in their schools, all students receive a superior education and test scores rise.

To implement the DISCOVER Curriculum Model effectively, teachers must be open to learning new methods and teaching strategies, and some need to undergo a philosophical shift. Intensive and ongoing inservice training is necessary for teachers and administrators. Change is difficult for many people, and changing the way one has done something for years is a major chore. Many administrators also must change their image of what a well-run classroom looks like and what types of activities result in real learning. Support for implementation of DISCOVER must come from the top *and* the bottom of the educational hierarchy, with significant support at every level in between.

The instrument used to evaluate teacher performance also must be changed if teachers using the DISCOVER Curriculum are to be evaluated fairly. Traditional teacher evaluation instruments (and mind-sets) are typically antithetical to the principles of DISCOVER.

The inclusion of the arts can be seen as a disadvantage by those who consider the arts to be an educational "frill," not worth the expense. This attitude is shortsighted, but frequently those who hold the educational purse strings believe it to be true. The expense of student dropout and increased unemployment and crime rates are seen as inescapable and unrelated to a sound, student-friendly educational system.

A disadvantage not unique to DISCOVER is that *any* learning takes time; new strategies do not produce instant results. The amount of learning needed to show significant gains on assessment scores takes time. Unfortunately, the field of education is noted for implementing new models or theories and abandoning them before they really have the time necessary to show measurable gains. Some parents believe that their children should be taught using a "back to the basics" approach (i.e., in the same way *they* were taught). Seemingly, however, the only time some legislators and community members value the best education available is when they are shopping for a brain surgeon or other medical doctor.

CONCLUSION

Although the DISCOVER Curriculum Model is expensive to implement, especially when connected to the assessment and the necessary teacher training and support, the resulting educational benefits could turn around public education in the United States. Even if it were only implemented in classes for gifted learners, it could make a major impact on society. Shirley Schiever's experience in a middle school where the DISCOVER Assessment was administered to 6th-grade students was that during the assessment, the classroom teachers saw students in a new light. For instance, a student who was unsuccessful in most academic tasks, due to language difficulties or other hindrances, might be extremely successful in one or more of the DISCOVER tasks. Not only did the teacher see these students with new eyes, but other students suddenly had more respect for them because their abilities in an area of the assessment obviously were "over the top." A further spin-off was that the teachers' insights into a student's abilities made them willing to try new ways to teach this child and to give the child opportunities to use these areas of strength in class projects, making the child more valued by his or her peers. Furthermore, the structure of the assessment tasks gave some teachers ideas as to how they might structure learning activities in different ways so that more students could be successful. The next spin-off was to 7th- and 8th-grade teachers who heard students or 6th-grade teachers talking about the assessment and children's strengths, and then went to the teachers of the gifted and talented program, asking about their curriculum and teaching strategies. This is how systems can change—one step at a time.

RESOURCES

Background Information

Jensen, R. (2001). *Arts with the brain in mind.* Alexandria, VA: Association for Supervision and Curriculum Development.

Stefanakis, E. H. (2002). *Multiple intelligences and portfolios: A window into the learner's mind.* Portsmouth, NH: Heinemann.

Wolfe, P. (2001). *Brain matters: Translating research into classroom practice.* Alexandria, VA: Association for Supervision and Curriculum Development.

Instructional Materials and Ideas

Jones, R. S. (n.d.). *Tools for the geographer.* Waco, TX: Prufrock Press.

Kaufeldt, M. (1999). *Begin with the brain: Orchestrating the learner-centered classroom.* Tucson, AZ: Zephyr Press.

Maker, C. J., & King, M. (1996). *Nurturing giftedness in young children.* Reston, VA: Council for Exceptional Children.

Pirto, J. (n.d.). *Understanding those who create.* (2nd ed.). Scottsdale, AZ: Great Potential Press.

Selwyn, D. (n.d.). *Living history in the classroom: Integrative arts activities for making social studies meaningful.* Waco, TX: Prufrock Press.

Simulation Series, (n.d.). Waco, TX: Prufrock Press.

Udall, A. J., & Daniels, J. E. (1991). *Creating active thinkers: 9 strategies for a thoughtful classroom.* Tucson, AZ: Zephyr Press.

You decide. (n.d.). Waco, TX: Prufrock Press.

Useful Web sites:

http://www.awpeller.com

http://www.prufrock.com

http:// www.zephyrpress.com

CHAPTER 6

Sidney Parnes: Creative Problem Solving

One model that has been used widely in programs for the gifted is the Creative Problem Solving (CPS) model developed by Sidney J. Parnes, long-time director of the Creative Problem Solving Institute (CPSI). Parnes, influenced greatly by the work of Alex Osborn (1963) in applying imagination to the practical problems encountered in the business and professional worlds, attempted to develop the most comprehensive process possible for stimulating the use of imagination in practical situations. He used his own applied research on the development of creative thinking in the program at the State University of New York (SUNY), along with the applied and theoretical research of others, to come up with a process that would be comprehensive, theoretically sound, and above all, effective. He and others are involved continually in the modification of this process as new information becomes available. CPSI sponsors the world's premier creativity events, held in Buffalo, New York, every June and in San Diego, California, every January or February. Many participants return repeatedly to refine their working knowledge of CPS, learn new facilitation tools and techniques, and attend work sessions covering a wide variety of topics.

The CPS model provides a structured method for approaching problems in an imaginative way. It differs from the usual problem-solving methods in its emphasis on generating a variety of alternatives before selecting or implementing a solution. In each step of the process, the problem solver defers judgment during ideation or generation of alternatives to avoid inhibiting even the wildest possibilities, which may turn out to be the best ideas. Judgment then is exercised at a more appropriate time.

The purpose of the model is twofold: (a) to provide a sequential process that will enable an individual to work from a "mess" to arrive at a creative, innovative, or effective solution and (b) to enhance an individual's overall creative behavior. Creative behavior, according to Parnes, is "a response, responses, or pattern of responses which operate upon internal or external discriminative stimuli, usually called things, words, symbols, etc., and result in at least one unique combination that reinforces the response or pattern of responses" (1966, p. 2). Creative behavior is a function of knowledge, imagination, and evaluation and results in a product that has both uniqueness and value to an individual or group. In other words, through participation in a process, such as that developed by Parnes, individuals apply their own knowledge, imagination, and evaluation to both internal and external "stimuli" and as a result develop a product (e.g., a plan, idea, performance, or report) that is both unique and valuable. These definitions of creative behavior, although precise and rather dry, provide clear and measurable guidelines for program development and evaluation.

The need for creativity training in all phases of education can no longer be ignored. The current state of the educational process, with its emphasis on standardized achievement tests and "the right way," together with the necessity of dealing with massive amounts of information, a constantly and rapidly changing world, and pressing social concerns, makes the development of creative problem-solving skills imperative. Parnes cites Maslow's (1970) "need for self-actualization" as a goal that can be met through education for creativity. Thus, the kind of education developed from a creative problem-solving perspective meets both individual and societal needs.

Of the many teaching–learning models currently used in programs for the gifted, the CPS model provides the most hard data showing its effectiveness. It also demonstrates the most versatility based on successful practical application in business, government, health care professions, and education. The process is taught to university students, teachers, young children, adolescents, parents, artists, managers, scientists, city planners, architects—anyone who is interested—through the CPSI. Participants are almost unanimous in their response to these institutes: "It was the most valuable personal and professional experience I've ever had. It's fun and it also works!"

⚜ ⚜ ⚜ ⚜ ⚜ ⚜

ASSUMPTIONS UNDERLYING THE MODEL

About Learning

A major assumption made by Parnes is that creativity is a behavior or set of behaviors that can be learned. Creativity is not an inborn, fixed characteristic but is present to varying degrees in all individuals. It can be manipulated and cultivated deliberately. Because creativity is learned, a related assumption is that examples and practice will strengthen it and that the methods used in a creative problem-solving course are generalizable to new situations. In other words, all persons can become more creative, and they can apply this creativity in all facets of their lives.

Another assumption is that creativity is related positively to other characteristics of individuals, such as ability to learn, achievement, self-concept, and intelligence. These characteristics, when combined, contribute to a "wholeness" of objective (factual–logical) and subjective (sensing–feeling) aspects of an individual. Inherent in this assumption is Parnes's belief that knowledge is important in creative productivity. Although factual information must be manipulated and transformed into usable ideas, a person cannot be creative without first having an available store of knowledge. This knowledge, however, can be used more creatively and effectively if initially learned with a "creative" set rather than a "memory" set.

About Teaching

Because Parnes believes that creative behavior can be learned, he obviously believes that educators can and should teach creative behavior. According to Parnes, when his problem-solving process is taught to students in school or to adults in an institute, the individuals develop a set of skills that can be applied to all kinds of practical problems. These include improving relationships with others, making decisions about activities or programs, managing resources, and planning personal or career goals. He believes that by participating in the process, creative leaders can learn to use CPS successfully with groups ranging from elementary school children to adults. In short, Parnes feels that CPS is simple to learn, easy to teach, and highly transferable.

Parnes (1967) makes an important distinction between creative teaching and teaching for creativity. A teacher who is creative will be imaginative in the use of materials (films, posters, tapes) and strategies (demonstrations, unique experiences), whereas a teacher who teaches for creativity will encourage students to express themselves and stimulate them to develop their own productivity. Consequently, the latter teacher will listen more than talk and guide rather than direct. Individuals who teach for creativity do not need to be creative in their methods of imparting information. To develop an atmosphere conducive to the learning of creative behavior, a teacher must (a) establish a climate of psychological safety for the free expression of ideas, (b) encourage playfulness, (c) allow incubation, and (d) seek quantity as well as quality of ideas.

About Characteristics and Teaching of Gifted Students

Although not stated, an implicit assumption made by Parnes is that individuals who are intellectually gifted have the potential to be more creative than those who are not gifted. Gifted people also can benefit from learning how to use the creative problem-solving method in artistic, social, and scientific areas. Following from this assumption is the recommendation that in teaching the gifted, educators should use a method such as CPS much more frequently and earlier because of the greater potential of gifted learners to benefit from its use. Following this line of reasoning, gifted students also have greater amounts of information they must organize, manipulate, and evaluate. As a result, gifted individuals need to use the creative problem-solving process much more often than those who are not gifted.

ELEMENTS/PARTS

Since first encountering Alex Osborn's program in 1963, Parnes has worked toward the establishment of the most comprehensive program possible for nurturing creative behavior. Using Osborn's model as a base, he added parts of existing theories and programs, as well as approaches recently developed. The model consists of six steps—mess finding (objective finding), data finding, problem finding, idea finding, solution finding, and acceptance finding—usually followed in sequential order. Parnes feels that the resulting process is easy to follow, and once the procedures have been learned, the components of understanding the problem (Steps 1–3), generating ideas (Step 4), and planning for actions (Steps 5–6) are quite flexible and can be adapted to the particular needs of the group and the task (Parnes, 1988). These six steps, along with activities for each step, are described in Table 6.1.

The traditional conceptualization of movement through the six steps is illustrated in Figure 6.1. The illustration seems to be of a unitary, linear, sequential process; however, Parnes stresses that the model is flexible and suggests that, for specific purposes, some steps of the model may be used alone.

A different way to conceptualize the six steps is by categorizing them into three basic stages of operation: clarification, transformation, and implementation (Puccio & Gonzalez, 2004). Within clarification are two substages: exploring the vision and finding the challenges. The purpose of the exploring the vision substage is to articulate what the goal or future state of the group or individual is. The focus in the finding the challenges substage is on problems that must be addressed to reach the goal, and a list of these challenges is produced. During the transformation stage, the group generates ideas related to meeting the most critical challenges (exploring ideas) and refines these ideas into workable solutions (finding solutions). During the exploring acceptance substage, problem solvers identify factors that may enhance or prohibit implementing solutions. These factors become key as the problem solver(s) establish actions or steps to fully implement the solution (finding the plan).

One of the unique aspects of the CPS process is the repeated pattern of divergent and convergent thinking built into the process. The diamonds in Figure 6.1 represent the divergent and convergent thinking that occurs again and again while one moves through the steps (or returns to an earlier step to try a different approach). After listing a variety of ideas (divergent thinking) that identify opportunities or challenges of the "mess" in Step 1, the individual or group rates each idea, on a scale from 0 to 10, on two dimensions: importance and probability of success. Then the two ratings are multiplied together to get an overall rating. A mess statement with a probability of success of 10 and an importance rating of 1 would receive an overall score of 10; another with an importance rating of 5 and a probability of success rating of 5 would receive an overall rating of 25. Thus, a mess statement, or objective, with a high rating of importance and a high to

TABLE 6.1

Steps in the Creative Problem Solving Process

Steps	Activities
1. Mess finding (object finding)	Analyze what is known about the "mess." List broad objectives, goals, or purposes. Generate criteria for evaluation. Select the best statement(s) or objective(s) to define the chosen task.
2. Data finding	Collect data dealing with the first objective. Act as a camera; observe carefully and objectively. Explore the facts of the situation. Recognize that feelings are part of the facts. Select the data most pertinent to the objective. Repeat the process now (or at conclusion) for other objectives.
3. Problem finding	Prioritize options based on importance and probability of success. Speculate on possible problems. Look at possible problems from different perspectives. Converge on major problem(s). Restate the problem in a form that (a) states the issue for which you really want to generate ideas, (b) encourages a flow of ideas, (c) expresses the issue in concise terms, (d) identifies the ownership of the problem, (e) is free of criteria, (f) has a stem that opens up the statement to many possible answers (e.g., "In what ways might we...? How might we...?"), (g) uses an action verb to identify the specific action recommended, and (h) has an object that identifies the specific focus of the action.
4. Idea finding	Produce ideas to solve the problem. Generate many, varied, unusual ideas; freewheel. Elaborate on ideas to make them more complete or more interesting. Brainstorm alternatives for various conditions. Defer judgment. Strive for quality. Seek combinations or hitchhiking; link new ideas with others.

(continues)

TABLE 6.1 *Continued.*
Steps in the Creative Problem Solving Process

Steps	Activities
5. Solution finding	Screen, sort, and select ideas using evaluation criteria.
	Identify promising solutions.
	List criteria, using a divergent process, for use in evaluation.
	Select criteria that are appropriate to the focus of the problem and the needs of the problem owner(s).
	Analyze, develop, and support tentative solutions.
	Objectively apply the criteria to each tentative solution.
	Select the most promising solution based on objective evaluation.
6. Acceptance finding	Consider all audiences who must accept the plan.
	Brainstorm the concerns and priorities of all these audiences.
	Develop a plan of action.
	Try out the plan on a pilot basis to see if the solution is workable.
	Revise plan, if necessary, and present it to target audience(s).
	Make contingency plans in case acceptance is not achieved.

average probability of success is identified as a promising opportunity, whereas options low in importance with an average or high probability of success are identified as distractions (Isaksen, Dorval, & Treffinger, 1994). This method helps to eliminate options of average to high importance but little probability of success and those with little importance and low to average probability of success. Problem solvers then can focus on substantial options rather than waste their time with trivial or impossible tasks.

Movement through the steps of the process is aided by some proven techniques for stimulating idea output and development, such as deferred judgment, elimination of fears, extended practice, forced relationships, brainstorming, hitchhiking, checklists, attribute listing, morphological analysis, synectics, and incubation. These are all strategies to assist in getting data out of memory storage and relating them to current situations that require problem solving. Deferred judgment, for example, is a cardinal principle in allowing the expression of as many ideas as possible. When used in a group, the principle is called brainstorming. Supplemental to this process is the procedure of hitchhiking, which means building upon or elaborating on the ideas of others. These hitchhikes are accepted simply

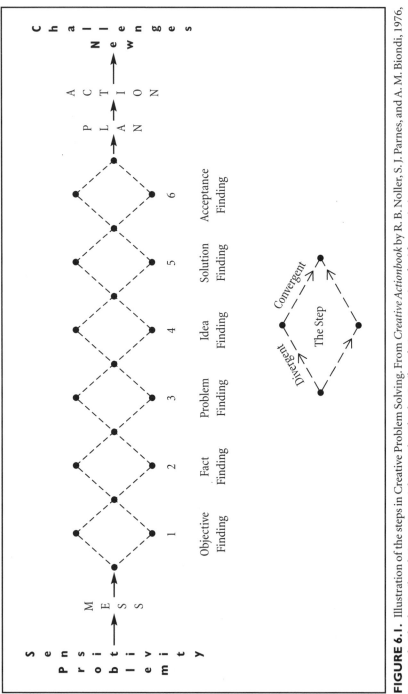

FIGURE 6.1. Illustration of the steps in Creative Problem Solving. From *Creative Actionbook* by R. B. Noller, S. J. Parnes, and A. M. Biondi, 1976, New York: Charles Scribner's Sons. Copyright 1976 by Charles Scribner's Sons. Reprinted with permission.

as additional ideas without discussion or argument as the flow of ideas continues.

Synectics is a process that involves two basic activities, making the strange familiar and making the familiar strange. The term comes from the Greek word *synectikos,* which means bringing different things into one or more unified connections. It consists of the mental activities of analysis, generalization, and model seeking or analogy. According to Wilson, Greer, and Johnson (1973), synectics is a powerful tool for use with gifted individuals, as it enables them to respond to the requirements of a rapidly changing world where traditional methods are not effective in solving new and unique problems.

Asking creative questions that can lead to unconventional solutions facilitates movement through the process. Parnes feels that this skill takes critical thinking and practice, but once acquired it enables creative problem solving to be accomplished in a minimum amount of time. John Dewey (1944) believed that "A problem well put is half solved," and throughout history noted thinkers have commented on the importance of raising new questions and possibilities. Further, rethinking and examining old questions with a new eye is important for solving problems in a creative way.

Getzels and Jackson (1962), who started the controversy over the creativity–intelligence distinction in gifted persons, describe two types of problem situations: the presented problem situation and the discovered problem situation. A presented problem situation has a known formulation, known method of solution, and known solution. A discovered problem situation is one that does not yet have a known formulation, method of solution, or solution (Type VI of the Problem Continuum discussed in Chapter 5). This latter type stimulates creative problem solving.

Getzels (1975) provides examples of the two types; the story that illustrates them briefly is of a car being driven along a deserted road when its tire has a blowout. The occupants discover they have no jack, and their question is, "Where can we get a jack?" They remember a gas station several miles back and begin walking. Another car is driving on the same road, and it too has a blowout and no jack. The occupants of the second car ask, "How can the automobile be raised?" They see a deserted barn nearby, and in the barn is an old pulley for lifting bales of hay to the loft. The car is raised, the tire changed, and the occupants are on their way again, while the other people are still walking to the service station. Getzels concludes that, in effect, the first group dealt with the dilemma as a presented problem situation: a known problem, a known method of solution, and one known solution. The second group dealt with the dilemma as a discovered problem situation. In other words, the situation could be defined in a variety of ways, and the way in which it is defined determines the solution.

In a discussion of the development of creativity in the gifted, J. J. Gallagher (1975) indicates that one of the general principles for encouraging a person to be more creative is to "remove the brakes that stop his associative mechanisms from functioning naturally" (p. 244). He continues by observing that gifted children, who often are concerned about pleasing the teacher and giving a quick answer to questions, will have difficulty inhibiting this first reaction, thinking about the problem, and allowing their associative thoughts to flow. Although this is an important observation to make, one also must consider Parnes's principle of deferred judgment. "Removal of the brakes" includes going beyond the first reaction and also requires that problem solvers free themselves from the natural tendency to judge an idea as good or bad before saying or writing it. If the idea gets a bad rating in a student's mind, he or she may decide not to say it because others might laugh or think he or she has stupid ideas. This "wild" idea may be much better than any of the conventional ones that pass the spur-of-the-moment test of value. According to Parnes, taming a wild idea is much easier than "beefing up" a conventional one. Thus, with gifted children who have been successful in school by pleasing the teacher, appearing smart, and not having "stupid" ideas, but who have the potential to create the most unique and original ideas of all, practice in using the principle of deferred judgment is essential.

Generating criteria for evaluation of problems, ideas, and solutions frequently is a difficult process for children. Using a divergent process to generate many, varied, and unusual criteria from which to choose will improve the probability of making wise choices. Criteria should be phrased as questions (e.g., "Will it be legal?" "Can 5th-grade students accomplish this task?" "Is this an underlying problem?") that can be answered with "yes," "no," or a rating. Possible convergent tools (Isaksen et al., 1994) include an evaluation matrix and a paired comparison matrix for group consensus. In an *evaluation matrix*, possible options are listed along one axis and criteria along the other (see Table 6.2). Each option is rated on an agreed-upon scale (e.g., 1 = *low* to 5 = *high* or +1, 0, −1) for each criterion. Points are totaled for each option, and options are ranked in order from high to low. In *paired comparison analysis* (PCA), each member of the decision group separately completes an evaluation matrix using an identical set of options and an identical scoring system (e.g., 1 = *low* to 5 = *high*). A group grid, prepared with options listed along one axis and group members' names along the other, then is filled in and points for each option totaled (see

Table 6.3). The purpose of the PCA is to help groups build consensus and establish priorities. The procedure also is an aid to structuring discussions and allowing members of the group to express reasons for their support (or lack of support) of options. Converging on a problem or solution might also be done in steps by using an evaluation matrix to narrow the list of alternatives and then listing advantages (strong points and positive

TABLE 6.2
Example of an Evaluation Matrix

	Criteria				
Options	I	2	3	4	Total
Wilderness	3	I	4	2	10
Riparian area	4	2	I	4	11
Homes	I	3	I	2	7
State park	3	2	2	3	10
Guest ranch	4	2	0	3	9

Note. As a group, members assign a rating to each option for each criterion. The total is the sum of the ratings given to each option.

TABLE 6.3
Example of a Paired Comparison Analysis Matrix

	Options				
Group Member	A	B	C	D	E
John	2	15	10	14	5
Sally	11	0	6	8	11
Jessica	13	7	9	12	7
David	I	10	7	15	8
Total Points	27	32	32	49	31

Note. Each group member rates each option on each criterion, totals the points for the option, and enters the total in the grid by her or his name for each option.

aspects), limitations (concerns or weak points phrased as "How to" questions), and unique qualities (novel aspects, "What does this idea have that no others have?") of the most promising options (Isaksen, 1992).

Another related idea important in the development of creative thinking in gifted children is developing and maintaining a balance between the more freewheeling, playful side of a person and the logical, judgmental, analytical side. When describing the program at SUNY (and this also applies to Parnes's creativity institutes held annually in other parts of the United States), Parnes concluded the following:

> In adapting all of the evolving programs that we have been able to synthesize with our creative problem-solving courses and institutes, we have been trying always to develop a balance in individuals—a balance between the judgment and the imagination—between the open awareness of the environment through all of the senses and the deep self-searching into layer upon layer of data stored in the memory cells between the logic and the emotion—between the deliberate creative effort and the incubation—between the individual working with the group and his working alone. The longer I [Parnes] work in this field the more the underlying problem seems to become one of developing this balance between these extremes, by strengthening the weaker aspect, not by stunting the stronger side. (Quoted in Parnes, Noller, & Biondi, 1967, p. 154)

MODIFICATIONS
OF THE BASIC CURRICULUM

Although the CPS model provides a setting for modification of content and product, the most significant (and direct) modifications suggested are those of process and learning environment. The approach itself is a process model. Therefore, by using this process or by teaching children to use it, educators modify the usual process of learning. Learners are active rather than passive, teachers are facilitators rather than information disseminators, and learners must separate their use of divergent and convergent thinking so the flow of ideas is not inhibited while evaluations are made. Each sequential step in the process initially requires divergent thinking and ends with convergent thinking.

Content Modifications

The CPS process includes content modifications of variety and methods that are appropriate for gifted students. Greater variety is possible because the problems that are identified and solved are those practical problems not usually considered in a school curriculum. The CPS method is used to identify and solve a variety of personal, social, and academic problems. Gifted students should participate in the process in group situations and learn to apply it to the solution of their own problem situations.

Process Modifications

Process modifications appropriate for gifted students are made in the following five areas: (a) higher levels of thinking, (b) open-endedness, (c) freedom of choice, (d) variety, and (e) group interaction. The development of higher levels of thinking (i.e., the use rather than the acquisition of information) is facilitated through this process: exploring the "mess," generating questions or objectives, identifying facts about the situation, defining the problem, developing ideas for solving the problem, evaluating the ideas, and developing a plan for implementing the solution. Although these steps are sequential rather than hierarchical, they progress from recalling facts (i.e., Bloom's knowledge level; see Chapter 3) to analyzing the situation, creating new ideas (i.e., Bloom's synthesis), and evaluating (i.e., solution finding), and then "back" to synthesizing (i.e., acceptance finding). Open-endedness also is an important process modification made by CPS. Both teacher and student questions at all steps of the process must be open-ended to facilitate divergent answers. The process even includes components to assist participants in devising their own open-ended questions at the problem-finding step. As shown in Figure 6.1, each step in the process contains both a divergent and a convergent aspect. Participants are taught through the process when each type of thinking is appropriate for problem solving.

The CPS process encourages freedom of choice and suggests the use of a variety of methods at different steps. With regard to freedom of choice, participants usually are encouraged to choose a problem of interest to them. Although they are expected to follow the basic approach, individual variations are possible, especially at the problem-finding and idea-finding steps. For example, at the idea-finding step, a variety of idea-stimulating questions and techniques are presented, and individuals can later choose those that work best for them in a particular situation. Because many methods are available and are suggested at each step, the principle of variety also is incorporated.

CPS is frequently used within the context of small groups working together on a project of mutual interest. This provides group interaction as students proceed through the steps to reach the resolution to their selected and self-defined problem situation.

Product Modifications

The CPS model provides for product modifications in all areas appropriate for gifted students. Addressing problems that are real to and interesting for gifted students is very much a part of this method. Although some teachers may be directive in their use of the method with students, the first three steps are designed to assist participants in identifying and stating a problem as they see it. If this product modification is not made, the problem is in the implementation, not the process itself.

A second modification, directing products toward real audiences, is made through the acceptance-finding step. At this step, the problem solver attempts to anticipate how those who must accept the solution will react to it. Based on this analysis, a plan is developed to implement the solution. Some detailed suggestions are given for assessing audiences, developing plans, and implementing solutions.

Another product modification is appropriate evaluation. In the process, both teacher and student learn how to develop criteria for product evaluation and how to apply these criteria to the selection of solutions. When developing criteria for evaluation, for example, problem solvers should consider the problem from the viewpoint of many individuals and judge the possible solutions on criteria other than their own personal preferences. Often decisions and evaluation depend very much on this subjective aspect of judgment. This and other suggested techniques help students develop skills in making appropriate evaluations. The techniques also provide methods for peers and audiences to use in evaluating products presented to them.

Variety and self-selected formats also are essential components of the CPS model, because the form of the solution must fit the problem definition and is determined solely by the problem solvers.

The final product modification, transformation rather than summary, is made easily through application of CPS. Throughout the process in solving problems, students must manipulate information, seek a variety of new data, combine information in new ways, and view situations from new perspectives. Particularly in the idea-finding step, emphasis is on development of original ideas—that is, combining old ideas to form new ones, substituting parts of one idea, and other similar techniques.

Learning Environment Modifications

To facilitate movement through the problem-solving process, the leader must establish and maintain an environment that is similar to that recommended for gifted students in most of the dimensions. Of particular importance is establishing an environment that is learner centered, independent, open, and accepting.

To implement CPS, the teacher must have a learner-centered environment. Learners should identify the problems to be solved and generate the ideas for solving them. Selecting solutions and developing plans for implementation also are the students' responsibility. Appropriate implementation of CPS requires that the leader serve as a facilitator of the process rather than as a person who instructs or "leads" the process. Thus, the teacher asks open-ended questions, plans activities to stimulate idea production, and enforces the rules of brainstorming. Because the teacher is not offering or judging ideas, he or she does not become the center of the discussions. When CPS is implemented in other than a total class setting, the teacher cannot assume control or dominate the group.

Independence is fostered by encouraging individuals and groups to apply the process on their own and to use it as a procedure for solving everyday personal and social group problems, as well as academic ones. In that the ultimate goal of those who teach the process is to see it used by individuals to solve their own problems, this modification is an important aspect of the creative problem-solving process.

Parnes provides specific guidelines for the development of an open and accepting environment. For example, the rules of brainstorming should be strictly enforced at all times when generating ideas or when the activity requires divergent production. As a way to assist in the idea-finding step, Noller, Treffinger, and Houseman (1979) provide the following suggestions for conducting and participating in brainstorming: The teacher must foster a climate of appreciation and understanding of the creative process. For example, the teacher must encourage and appreciate the need for incubation, allowing subconscious concentration on the problem. As students focus on a problem and search for ideas, they consciously defer judgment and allow free-flow to the associative mental processes. Parnes (1967) believed that these associations also may occur in the preconscious, before a student is aware that they are being formed. By detaching from direct involvement in a problem, preconscious activity occurs, where links that may otherwise be inhibited are allowed to form. Individuals often become consciously aware of these subconscious associations in an "Aha!" experience; a new idea suddenly appears when they are not consciously thinking about the problem. Teachers must not only provide for incubation but also encourage and appreciate the need for it even when it does not fit into the daily lesson plan.

Examples of Teaching Activities

The following text exemplifies a student's progress through the steps of CPS. Table 6.4 shows how the CPS process can be used to write a term paper on polychlorinated biphenyl (PCB).

☞ **Objective Finding.** Generate one or more "mess" statements. From the question, "How will I write my term paper?" the student identifies purpose(s) of this CPS process.

☞ **Fact Finding.** Collect all data surrounding the problem. The student gathers information related to the selected topic (see "Known" column in Table 6.4).

☞ **Problem Finding.** Restate the problem in a more solvable form. For most students, gathering the information is perhaps the most formidable of the tasks required to write a substantive paper. Restating the problem provides new perspectives on the situation and may help to define the problem. Questions such as the following are helpful at this point:

• In what ways might I get the information to write this paper?
• What information will I use to write this paper?
• In what ways might I write this paper?
• Who will help me write this paper?

TABLE 6.4
Example of Using CPS To Write a Term Paper on Polychlorinated Biphenyl (PCB)

Known	Like To Know	Sources
PCBs are linked to some kinds of cancer and other serious diseases. Some manufacturers in this community discarded waste containing PCBs for a number of years. PCBs are in the groundwater on the south side of this community. This community depends on groundwater as its primary source of water. "Pockets" of high incidence of cancer and other serious diseases exist in the south side of this community.	What diseases are most common in the areas of the community where PCB levels are highest? What level of PCB in drinking water is considered safe? Are fatality rates higher in the affected areas? What research has been done related to this issue? What governmental action, if any, has been taken? Does length of residence in affected area appear to have an effect on general health of a person?	Local university, Department of Hydrology Newspaper archives Internet Community-based organizations in affected areas Interviews with victims and survivors Books and journal articles on PCB

The first question is the most pressing and, therefore, the one students may attempt first. It is critical for students to find out early on whether they will be able to access sources of information and whether there is a body of knowledge to support their research.

☛ **Idea Finding.** Brainstorm and defer judgment in an attempt to develop as many ideas as possible for solving the problem. Asking the question, "In what ways might I get the information to write this paper?" and listing possibilities are helpful at this point. A list such as the following might result:

• Conduct an Internet search.
• Call the hydrology department at the university; get the name and number of one or more professors who are knowledgeable about PCBs in the water supply.

- Set up an appointment to meet with a professor.
- Prepare interview questions.
- Check newspaper archives to identify community groups that may be useful.
- Check school and local libraries for books and journals related to the topic.

At this point, a few of the idea-spurring concepts suggested by Osborn (1963)—magnify, minify, rearrange, combine, substitute, and put to new uses—can be applied to the ideas and to the questions resulting from the fact-finding process. These might result in expanding or shifting the ideas to another perspective. Ideas such as the following might result:

- Ask librarian to help with Internet search.
- Call one of the alleged polluters to see if anyone will give an interview.
- Call the university hydrology department.
- Talk to people who have researched this issue previously.
- Talk to teacher: Is this topic too broad?
- If the teacher says the topic is too broad, how might it be narrowed?
- Who might be able to help narrow the topic (a hydrology professor)?
- Would the teacher be willing to let students work together on research, if each person wrote a paper?

☛ **Solution Finding.** Produce (divergent) criteria for evaluating solutions and then select (convergent) the most useful criteria to evaluate each idea or potential solution. Choose the best solution. In a situation such as this, students need to identify some possible ways to judge their ideas. Such factors as time, cost, effectiveness, safety, ease of access, acceptability to the teacher, and uniqueness might be considerations. For a student writing a term paper, probably the most important criteria are time, effectiveness, and acceptability to the teacher. Table 6.5 contains a grid for rating possible solutions from the idea-finding step. Assigning a point value of 1 for bad ideas, 2 for medium, and 3 for good ideas provides a way to quantify the suitability of each idea. Each idea is rated on each criterion, and the points are totaled. According to this rating, the student has several good solutions, including the following: ask

TABLE 6.5
Example of Criteria Rating Grid

Possible Solutions	Time	Effectiveness	Acceptability	Total
Ask librarian for help	3	3	3	9
Call alleged polluter	1	1	3	5
Call hydrology department	2	3	3	8
Talk to people (previous researchers)	1	3	3	7
Talk to teacher (topic too broad?)	3	3	3	9
Talk to teacher (how to narrow?)	2	2	3	7
Hydrology professor help narrow?	2	3	3	8
Students work together?	3	1	1	5

the librarian for help, talk to the teacher about the possibility that the topic is too broad, call the hydrology department, and, if necessary, ask the hydrology professor for help in narrowing the topic.

☞ **Acceptance Finding.** Make the solution more appealing (acceptable) to all parties involved; make it more workable. Plan, implement, evaluate the results, and provide corrective action as needed. Because asking the librarian for help conducting an Internet search and calling the hydrology department (for information and possibly topic narrowing) seem to be promising, these steps could be taken first. The results from these first two steps determine which of the other steps should be pursued. The end result, a well-researched term paper, presumably will be acceptable to the teacher and result in the good grade for which the student was aiming.

Table 6.6 provides a summary of teacher and student activities and roles for each step in the CPS process.

(*text continues on p. 217*)

TABLE 6.6

Summary of Student and Teacher Roles and Activities in the Creative Problem Solving Model

Step, Type, or Level of Thinking	Student		Teacher	
	Role	Sample Activities	Role	Sample Activities
Mess finding (objective finding)	Active participant Idea generator	Explore the "mess." List potential objectives. Generate criteria. Select objectives.	Facilitator Resource	Develop or select exercises to lead students in exploration of the "mess" and generation of potential objectives. Develop or select exercises to lead students in generation of criteria. Develop or select exercises to lead students through an evaluation of potential objectives based on selected criteria. Lead students through exercises individually or in groups.
Data finding	Active participant Idea generator	Differentiate what is known from what needs to be known. Collect needed information. Observe carefully. Act as objectively as possible.	Facilitator Resource	Develop or select exercises to assist students in a process of finding out the known and unknown data about a situation. Lead students through exercises individually or in groups. Help students identify new sources of information and select relevant from irrelevant data.

(continues)

Problem finding	Active participant	Look at the problem from several viewpoints.	Facilitator	Help students speculate on possible problems.
	Idea generator	Generate many potential problems.	Resource	Develop or select exercise to assist students, individually or in groups, to narrow the problem, select the most important problem, state it in solvable form, and look at it from different viewpoints.
	Evaluator	Select the most important problem(s).		
		Restate the problem in more solvable form.		Provide examples of action verbs to assist students in structuring a more solvable statement of the problem.
				Encourage students to use action stems (e.g., "In what ways might I...?" "How might we...?").
Idea finding	Active participant	"Incubate" on the problem for an extended time.	Facilitator	Develop or select ideas that will assist students, individually or in groups, to generate a wide variety of useful and original ideas.
	Idea generator	Generate many, varied ideas.	Resource	
		Defer judgment until all ideas are expressed.		Provide idea-stimulating questions (i.e., "How might we magnify/minify/rearrange/combine/modify...?") to help students generate many, varied, unusual ideas and add to their ideas.
		Hitchhike on ideas of self and others.		Enforce the rules of brainstorming (i.e., quantity over quality, hitchhiking is desired, no evaluation of ideas).
		Strive for quantity.		Maintain a psychologically safe environment to encourage the free expression of ideas.

(continues)

TABLE 6.6 *Continued.*

Summary of Student and Teacher Roles and Activities in the Creative Problem Solving Model

Step, Type, or Level of Thinking	Student		Teacher	
	Role	Sample Activities	Role	Sample Activities
Solution finding	Active participant Idea generator Evaluator	Develop criteria for solution evaluation. Choose alternatives with the greatest potential for solving the problem. Objectively apply criteria to selected alternatives. Support chosen solution with evidence of reasoning.	Facilitator Resource	Develop or select exercises to enhance students' abilities to (a) generate criteria for judging a solution, (b) select relevant criteria, and (c) objectively apply criteria to selected alternative solutions. Lead students in exercises individually or in groups. Assist in the identification of possible criteria for evaluating ideas. Demonstrate the use of decision matrix or other convergent tools. Ask for support of chosen solutions.
Acceptance finding	Active participant Idea generator Evaluator	Brainstorm ways to gain acceptance of ideas or solution. Consider all audiences. Develop a plan of action. Try out plan on a pilot basis. Evaluate and revise plan as needed. Present plan to target audience(s).	Facilitator Resource	Develop or select exercises to help students identify all audiences concerned with the solution. Develop or select exercises to help students formulate an action plan. Develop or select activities to help students implement solutions. Lead students through exercises individually or in groups. Enforce the rules of brainstorming. Maintain a psychologically safe environment.

MODIFYING THE MODEL

When modifying the CPS model to make it more appropriate for gifted students, educators should make changes mainly in how the approach is used rather than in the method. The majority of suggestions are in the content area, with a few in the area of process. To make these changes, one effective method is to combine CPS with Bruner's Basic Structure of a Discipline (Chapter 4), whereas another would be to make each separate change as described below.

Content Modifications

The CPS process does not include content changes appropriate for the gifted in the following areas: abstractness, complexity, organization for learning value, and study of people. CPS can be combined with other approaches to achieve several of these changes. To implement changes in abstractness and complexity, the teacher should encourage gifted students to select complex, high-level problem situations rather than mundane or simple problems. Examples of complex problems involving abstract concepts include current ecological problems, the current economic situation, talent development in an egalitarian society, diversity within populations, rising populations and shrinking land availability, and industrialization or exploitation of underdeveloped countries by world powers. In all of these situations, information or facts need to be gathered from a variety of sources across disciplines for both definition and solution of problems. No one viewpoint or set of information provides the necessary background. In addition, the concepts involved in understanding the situations and in devising possible solutions are abstract. The materials available from the Future Problem Solving program (Hoomes, 1986; Torrance, Williams, & Torrance, 1977), particularly the practice problems, are excellent sources of complex, relevant problem situations.

Using CPS in any area of study will contribute an element of complexity. Because problem solvers must integrate a variety of information from several points of view in the identification of problems and development of solutions, complexity is automatically added. Creative solutions to problems often require that information from seemingly remote fields be brought together in an original way.

The modification of organization for learning value is not suggested by the CPS approach but can be incorporated readily. If the content is arranged around key concepts or themes, the problem situations to which CPS is applied can involve these concepts directly. For example, in Chapter 3, activities were developed around the following generalization: "Every society has rules, written or unwritten, through which social control over individual conduct is maintained." Students can, of course, identify many problem situations that are related to this idea and should be encouraged to do so; however, the teacher also can present problem situations for further examination through CPS. Some problem situations related to this generalization are prison riots, the death penalty, government intervention in crisis situations, rehabilitation of prisoners, moral and ethical development through education, the present court system, the juvenile justice system, how to develop appropriate parent–child relationships, and society's changing values.

If the content is not already organized around key concepts and generalizations, it can be organized around problem situations. CPS then can be used as the overall method for gathering information, identifying subproblems for study by small groups of students, and combining old information with new ideas to form new, creative solutions. Complex problems involving abstract concepts should be selected as organizers; most current local and national problems would be excellent. The students can identify with the problems, select subproblems of interest to them, and develop end products (e.g., solutions, research reports) that are directed toward real audiences and represent their creative thinking and original research.

The study of creative, productive people can be incorporated within CPS. Students can identify problems faced by these individuals and use CPS to develop solutions for them. They then can compare their solutions with the ones actually developed and implemented by the famous individuals. This comparison definitely should include a look at the differences and similarities between each individual studied and the gifted students themselves, along with similarities and differences in the social situation now and during the life of that individual.

Process Modifications

Process changes not suggested directly by the CPS model are discovery, evidence of reasoning, group interaction, and pacing. The issue of pacing does not seem relevant to the implementation of CPS with gifted students because new material is not being presented and participants have much opportunity to set their own pace in solving problems. When the process is used in a group setting, however, the teacher should attend to the appropriate pacing of discussions during most of the steps. During idea finding, the teacher should be careful to allow plenty of time for thought, because students are producing rather than acquiring or remembering information.

Discovery

Although CPS is not a strategy for discovery learning in the sense that we define *discovery*, it is closely related. The methods employed in the first five steps of CPS also can be used by students to structure their process of discovery or inquiry. For instance, fact finding is an important way to gather information from the situation that is relevant to the generation of hypotheses. At the problem-finding step, learners sift through the information to identify those aspects that are most relevant, and the idea-finding step is used for the generation of hypotheses. Solution finding provides a framework and methods for evaluating and selecting hypotheses.

Evidence of Reasoning

Asking students to explain their reasoning or provide evidence for their inferences is easily incorporated into the CPS process; however, questions such as these must be asked only at certain times. Otherwise, the idea-production phases of each step will be inhibited. During brainstorming, fact finding, and phases of the process involving divergent thinking, questions calling for explanations of reasoning would be completely inappropriate. During selection of problem statements, selection of criteria for evaluation, and decisions about action plans, however, such questions are highly appropriate and will facilitate understanding of the process and its use in solving problems at any of the convergent stages.

If teachers fear that the asking of "why" questions will inhibit the process, they can use the structure of Hilda Taba's Application of Generalizations Strategy (see Chapter 10). In this strategy, students brainstorm their predictions without any interruptions by the teacher except to clarify ambiguous ideas. After the ideas have been listed, the teacher goes back and asks for reasons why each prediction might be made. This strategy is not appropriate at the idea-finding step but works well during solution finding and acceptance finding.

Group Interaction

If the CPS process is used in a whole-class setting, it can provide a situation for observation and analysis of group interaction. To implement this curricular modification, the teacher should tape the process or appoint observers willing to stay out of the discussion. Through this method, however, only one type of group interaction can be observed—that is, participation in group problem solving. The process also can be used as an adjunct to the observation of group interaction by using it as a method for developing solutions to interaction situations that are problematic.

Learning Environment Modifications

Learning environment changes that are not suggested by the CPS method are complexity and high mobility. These aspects of the environment become important when students are developing sophisticated products and conducting original research. They can be crucial at the fact-finding step of the process if students need to gather information from a variety of sources for the solution of certain types of problems. The environmental dimensions of complexity and high mobility may vary in relation to the type of problem to be solved and the stage of the problem-solving process. If students are preparing a presentation for a real audience (e.g., a legislative subcommittee), mobility is of crucial importance.

Although independence already has been discussed as a learning environment modification included in CPS, a few more ideas are helpful. CPS provides an excellent process for use by students in solving their own problems and in developing solutions to classroom management problems. Students need to be taught the methods thoroughly, however. This training involves working through several sample problems with substantive content, discussing the implementation of the process, learning a variety of facilitative techniques that can be employed at each step of the process, and speculating on the application of CPS in other contexts. This conscious attention to the purpose and procedures of the problem-solving process contributes to metacognitive development and transfer of learning to other situations. Finally, students need supervised practice in the use of CPS in individual and group situations.

DEVELOPMENT

Sidney Parnes was greatly influenced by Alex Osborn's techniques, which are presented in *Applied Imagination* (Osborn, 1963). Parnes extended and elaborated on Osborn's work through research on identifying and nurturing creativity. He developed a course and later a programmed text that has been highly effective in developing the creative behavior discussed by Osborn. Since launching the interdisciplinary Center for Creative Studies, now called the Center for Studies in Creativity, and developing the Creative Problem Solving Institute, Parnes has continued to incorporate new ideas and research into CPS. In 1985, Isaksen and Parnes proposed a six-step model, which split fact finding into objective finding and data finding. In 1993, the six steps were conceptualized as three components (Isaksen et al., 1994): problem definition, idea generation, and planning for action.

RESEARCH ON EFFECTIVENESS

With Nongifted Students

The CPS model has been the subject of extensive research. This research has focused on two different but related issues, creativity and problem solving (James, 1978). As the two terms often are used interchangeably, this leads to confusion and inconsistency in research. Parnes uses CPS to produce a set for solving problems, then evaluates its effectiveness using measures of general creativity. He assumes that creativity enhances the whole problem-solving process. Others (see Mansfield, Busse, & Krepelka, 1978) have evaluated the effectiveness of the solutions and found that other problem-solving methods are just as effective as CPS. For example, some studies have shown that other methods, such as the use of Program Evaluation and Review Technique (PERT) charts and conventional (nondeferred judgment) methods of problem solving are just as effective in developing ability to solve problems as CPS (Mansfield et al., 1978). However, these other programs do not seem to cause increases in performance on measures of creativity.

In 1957, Parnes began an extensive research effort to evaluate the effectiveness of his program. For the first 10 years, the research was concentrated in the following four areas:

1. The effects of a semester course in stimulation of creativity
2. The relative effects of a programmed course used alone or with instructors and class interaction
3. The effects of extended effort in problem solving
4. The effectiveness of the principle of deferred judgment

In general, the results of several studies have indicated that the program is highly effective. Some of the major findings were as follows (Parnes, 1975):

1. The semester programs resulted in increases in quantity and quality of ideas produced. These increases (over a control group) held up even when students were tested from 1 to 4 years after taking the course.
2. The results of research on the effectiveness of the programmed course also were positive. The instructor-taught groups were superior to the other two groups, whereas the group using the programmed materials alone was superior to the control group receiving no creativity training.
3. Extended effort in idea production resulted in a greater proportion of good ideas among those produced later.
4. Individuals instructed to defer judgment during idea production produced significantly more good-quality ideas (criteria included uniqueness and usefulness) than did individuals instructed to judge concurrently with idea production. In addition, subjects trained to use the principle of deferred judgment produced significantly more good quality ideas under the deferred judgment condition than did subjects who were not trained. Groups also produced more and better ideas when using this principle than did either group or the same number of individuals working independently while using concurrent evaluation.

After these initial studies, which concentrated heavily on development of the process, Parnes and his associates began a longitudinal investigation, the Creative Studies Project. They hypothesized that students who complete a four-semester sequence of creative studies courses will perform better in the following areas than otherwise comparable students who do not take the courses: (a) measures of mental ability, problem-solving capability, and job performance; (b) tests measuring the creative application of academic subject matter; (c) achievement in other than academic areas calling for creative performance; and (d) measures of personality characteristics associated with creativity. Parnes (1975) provides the following brief summary of the results:

1. Students in the courses were significantly better able to cope with real-life situational tests, including production, evaluation, and development of useful ideas.
2. In the semantic and behavioral half of Guilford's Structure of Intellect (SOI) model of intelligence (Guilford, 1967), students in the courses performed significantly better on three out of five mental operations: cognition, divergent production, and convergent production. Students showed significant year-to-year gains over comparable controls and performed similarly to the controls on the other two mental operations—memory and evaluation—and also in the symbolic and figural half of the SOI model.
3. Most of these students believed that they had become more creative and productive and that the program had been helpful in other college courses and in their everyday lives. Those continuing for 2 years in the program felt that this improvement was shown in their more active participation in class discussions and in their ability to cope with everyday problems.
4. In nonacademic areas calling for creative performance, these students showed a growing tendency to become more productive than students not enrolled in the program.
5. Measures of personality characteristics showed that students taking the courses were changing in ways that made them more like highly creative persons.
6. Because the demographics of the students in both the experimental (Creative Studies Program) and control groups were similar to those of students at most colleges and universities, the results of this research should generalize to many other situations.
7. The Creative Studies Project participants also showed improvements in convergent processes and on ultimate criteria, as did participants in several other studies.

In a review of research on the effectiveness of creativity training programs, Mansfield et al. (1978) reported that of all the creativity programs reviewed, the CPS program is the most effective. They were not as positive as Parnes about the results, as they believed that several of the CPS studies showing gains suffered from serious methodological flaws, such as confounding of instructor effects with program effects, massive sample attrition, and volunteer subjects for the instructed but not for the control groups. Parnes and his colleagues, however, disagreed with this assessment except in the case of volunteer subjects in experimental but not control groups in their first study. These concerns were dealt with in other studies. One extensive, well-designed study showed very positive results: High school students in an instructor-taught course performed significantly better on all 10 verbal tests of divergent thinking (4 of fluency, 2 of flexibility, 2 of originality, and 1 each of elaboration and sensitivity) than did students in the control group. In the same study, students using the programmed text without an instructor were inferior to the instructor-taught groups but superior to the controls who had no instruction.

Torrance (1972) also reviewed studies testing the effectiveness of programs designed to develop creativity in children. Approaches were separated into nine categories, including (a) CPS and other disciplined approaches, (b) training in general semantics, (c) complex programs involving packages of materials, (d) the creative arts as vehicles, (e) media and reading programs, (f) curricular and administrative arrangements, (g) teacher–classroom variables, (h) motivation, and (i) testing conditions. Of these approaches, the CPS process and other disciplined approaches showed by far the highest percentages of success—91% and 92%, respectively. The next highest percentages were 81% for the creative arts as vehicles and 78% for the media and reading programs.

In a meta-analysis of long-term creativity training programs, Rose and Lin (1984) concluded that such training enhances creativity. Innate abilities can be stimulated and skills can be developed through creative problem solving. CPS training significantly improves the interaction among members of small groups (Firestien, 1990). Members of the trained groups also produce a significantly greater quantity and higher quality of ideas generated for real problems.

Puccio and Avarello (1995) identified creative thinking as one of the main qualities that produces resiliency in at-risk youths. Additionally, training in creative thinking strategies has been shown to improve the chance that school dropouts will find a successful life path (McCluskey, Baker, O'Hagan, & Treffinger, 1995).

In summary, creativity training and specifically CPS are effective in improving performance on tests of divergent thinking, which are an important aspect of creativity. Certain specific principles, such as deferred judgment and extended effort, also are effective in producing more and better ideas.

With Gifted Students

Although gifted students are included in the groups studied by Parnes and his associates, little research has concentrated on the effectiveness of CPS with only the gifted. Schack (1993) investigated the effects of a creative problem-solving curriculum on gifted, honors, and average students. The curriculum produced substantial gains in problem-solving ability in all three groups.

Harkow (1996) used a combination of strategies that included CPS encounters to improve thinking skills in 2nd- and 3rd-grade gifted students. The students met the projected increase of 80% or above in overall figural and verbal creativity, verbal originality, and verbal flexibility.

CPS is a popular model that enjoys widespread use. Rash and Miller (2000) surveyed 62 Idaho teachers and discovered that more teachers used CPS to organize curricular experiences than any other single model.

A significant body of research related to the topic is concerned with relationships between creativity and intelligence. Because a review of this literature could fill volumes, however, only a few of the more significant results are presented. In a classic study of the creativity–intelligence relationship, Getzels and Jackson (1962) found a low correlation between IQ scores and performance on tests of creativity in gifted students (average IQ 132). They also found that those who scored highest on tests of creativity but not highest on IQ tests (average IQ 132) scored just as well on achievement tests as did those who were highest on IQ tests (average IQ 150) but not highest on tests of creativity. Wallach and Kogan (1965) also measured the performance of those who were highest on measures of both creativity and intelligence. They found, as did Getzels and Jackson, that the "high creatives" did just as well on achievement tests as the "highly intelligent." They also found, however, that the highest achievers and most versatile individuals were those who were both highly creative and highly intelligent. Another important finding of this study is that those who scored high on IQ tests but not on tests of creativity have a "disinclination" rather than an "inability" to perform well on tasks calling for divergent thinking. The subjects appeared to be reluctant or fearful of being original rather than unable to be original.

Meador (1994) compared creativity scores of gifted and nongifted kindergarten students who had special training in synectics and those who did not receive the training. She found significant improvement in creativity for the experimental group compared with the control group, but not more for gifted than nongifted students.

The results of these studies have important implications for the use of CPS or other such techniques with gifted children. If intellectually gifted but not necessarily creative children have the potential to be more original than they are, and if these children can be more effective achievers when they use both their intelligence and their creativity, then teachers must provide experiences that will increase these children's use of all their potential abilities.

Several researchers have studied the effects of the Future Problem Solving (FPS) program, which was designed to develop students' problem-solving skills. Torrance (1977) found that those who participated in FPS showed increased concern for the future and an awareness of the interdependence of people and of knowledge as a source of power. Tallent (1985) found that the gifted FPS program participants performed better on futuristic ill-structured problems than did those who had not participated. Finally, Tallent-Runnels and Yarbrough (1992) found that gifted 4th-, 5th-, and 6th-grade students who participated in FPS differed from those who did not participate in the following ways: perceptions of their control over the future, concerns about the future, and types of concerns cited most frequently. FPS participants were interested in more global issues and were more positive about their control over the future. In general, these are important, positive effects and suggest that gifted students of many ages can benefit from the program.

JUDGMENTS

Advantages

The major advantages of the CPS model in programs for the gifted are its versatility and validity. The CPS process can be used in any content area, as a method both for learning about the content area and for arriving at creative solutions to significant problems proposed by scholars in that field. The process also can be used to solve the practical problems encountered in classrooms, business, industry, and daily life. The skills transfer easily from one situation to another and can be taught to children of all ages. For the teacher, the advantages also include a wide variety of materials and teacher training that are readily available, and the experience is personally and professionally rewarding. The goals of CPS are explained easily and are defensible to parents and school personnel, and gifted children enjoy participating in the process.

With regard to its validity, although only a few comparative studies have assessed the effectiveness of the method with gifted students, the CPS model is consistent with the characteristics of gifted learners. It builds on their capability for developing unique products and provides for the development of the "inclination" to use their creative potential. Parnes defines creativity in specific behavioral terms and provides a structure and process for increasing these behaviors. Thus, the goals, procedures, and evaluative measures are clear. Research indicates that when this process is followed, the results are positive. Continuing research and evaluation of the process by Parnes and his associates ensure that new developments will be incorporated into the process to enhance its effectiveness.

A final, important advantage is the multitude of excellent materials available for use in a variety of situations. Manuals for leaders, sample problems, and how-to books for problem solvers are readily available.

Disadvantages

The major disadvantage of the model is that it was not designed specifically for use with gifted individuals, and in fact may be equally effective with those who are not gifted. For this reason, a gifted program based only on the CPS model may be difficult to justify as "qualitatively different" from the basic school curriculum that includes CPS. One cannot create a rationale for concentrating on particular aspects of the process with gifted students, as with certain other models (e.g., Bloom's and Krathwohl's Taxonomies; see Chapter 3). The use of the taxonomies in programs for gifted students can be justified by the rationale that the educator is concentrating on the higher rather than lower levels of thinking. In this way, the program is qualitatively different for gifted students, whereas each CPS step is equally important for all learners. Thus, when used by itself, CPS does not provide a comprehensive, qualitatively different program for gifted students unless it is used as a model for attacking complex, societal problems. Although the program is supported by extensive positive research, methodological problems are present in several important studies. The major problem is in measuring creativity. Most studies equate divergent thinking with creativity, even though this type of thought process may be only a small part of creative behavior. A related problem is that most studies use standardized measures of creativity as the criterion, rather than long-term assessment of transfer effects. For example, a critical question involving the transfer effect of risk taking might be "Will students who engage in creative problem solving exhibit fluency, flexibility, and originality in situations in which their ideas may be subject to criticism?" (Bodnar, 1974, p. 4).

For many years, advocates of the CPS model tended to overemphasize the inspiration and imagination required in the idea-generation phases of the process and neglected the actual implementation phase, with its requirements of high degrees of motivation, self-discipline, self-criticism, and hard work. If the model is used alone as the basis of a program for gifted students, this emphasis on the divergent phases of the process can be a disadvantage. A few authors (e.g., Isaksen et al., 1994; Lewis, 1991), however, have focused on planning for action and implementing proposed solutions in the real world. With that approach, the emphasis on inspiration and imagination in the CPS process adds a positive and enjoyable dimension to a comprehensive program for gifted students.

CONCLUSION

As a total approach to curriculum development for the gifted, the CPS model is difficult to justify as qualitatively different or comprehensive. The model, however, can be combined easily with other approaches in a way that can minimize or eliminate its disadvantages. Teachers also can emphasize different uses of the process, complex societal problem solving, and application of the process in interdisciplinary studies to make CPS more appropriate as a strategy in program development for gifted students.

RESOURCES

Background Information

Berger, S. (2000). Surfing the net: Children + problem solving = giftedness. *Understanding Our Gifted, 13*(4), 24–26.

Isaksen, S. G., Dorval, K. B., & Treffinger, D. J. (1994). *Creative approaches to problem solving.* Dubuque, IA: Kendall/Hunt.

Parnes, S. J. (Ed.). (1992). *Source book in Creative Problem Solving: A fifty year digest of proven innovation processes.* Buffalo, NY: Creative Education Foundation Press.

Treffinger, D. J. (1994). *The real problem-solving handbook.* New York: Center for Creative Learning.

Instructional Materials and Ideas

Jackson, J. B., Crandell, L., & Menhennett, L. (1997). *Future problem solving: Connecting the present to the future.* Washington, DC: Zero Population Growth.

Kobert, D., & Bagnall, J. (1991). *Universal traveler: A guide to creativity, problem-solving, and the process of reaching goals* (7th ed.). Menlo Park, CA: Crisp Publications.

Lewis, B. A. (1991). *The kid's guide to social action: How to solve the social problems you choose—and turn creative thinking into positive action.* Minneapolis: Free Spirit.

Noller, R. B., Treffinger, D. J., & Houseman, E. D. (1979). *It's a gas to be gifted or CPS for the gifted and talented.* Buffalo, NY: DOK.

Two international programs that provide students with experience with the creative problem-solving process are Future Problem Solving and Odyssey of the Mind. Training for coaching for both programs is available in most of the United States and many other countries.

Future Problem Solving Program
315 West Huron, Suite 140-B
Ann Arbor, MI 48103-4203
http://www.coe.uga/torrance/problem_solving.html

Odyssey of the Mind
P.O. Box 27
Glassboro, NJ 08028
http://www.odysseyofthemind.com

CHAPTER 7

Problem Based Learning

Problem Based Learning (PBL) was first used in medical schools in the 1970s after medical educators at McMaster University in Canada noticed that what students learned in classrooms was consistently and markedly different from the skills and knowledge used by practicing physicians. This led to the development of an innovative model that educates medical students in an environment similar to the physician's examining room, where ambiguous situations are encountered and where asking good questions may be a matter of life or death. The question-asking orientation creates a dynamic interaction, with the physicians being ready to change their minds and form new conceptions of the possible diagnosis. The opposite frame of mind occurs when medical students memorize facts and make them fit as best they can to the question or the illness. Expert physicians were able to filter out unnecessary information and keep only the pertinent; previously, medical students did not know which information was applicable in a given situation (S. A. Gallagher, 1997).[1]

PBL incorporates four elements: (a) an ill-structured problem, (b) substantive content, (c) student apprenticeship, and (d) self-directed learning. It is a good model for discipline-based problem solving in any field; students experience content, thinking skills, habits of mind, and concepts relevant to the discipline. An important point in developing curriculum is that problems must be structured carefully so students encounter worthy bodies of knowledge, the problems are central to their field of study, and the

---

[1]Unless otherwise noted, the primary source for this chapter is Gallagher (1997). Throughout this chapter, text cites mentioning Gallagher refer to S. A. Gallagher; however, initials are not repeated through the chapter.

curriculum is designed around specific educational goals. Since its inception, PBL has been used in various fields, including education at all levels, and research results support its effectiveness.

PBL curricula should be structured to provide students with guided experience in solving ill-structured, complex, real-world problems. The original goals of PBL follow: (a) to construct an extensive and flexible base of knowledge; (b) to develop effective problem-solving skills; (c) to develop self-directed, lifelong learning skills; (d) to teach collaboration skills; and (e) to inspire students to become intrinsically motivated to learn (Barrows & Kelson, 1995, cited in Hmelo & Ferrari, 1997).

The PBL structure is closely aligned with its curriculum goals, which were developed from its original goals. The curriculum goals and critical components of the model follow:

Curriculum Goals
- Acquisition, retention, and use of knowledge
- Intrinsic interest
- Multidisciplinary perspective
- Conceptual learning
- Adaptation to change
- Reasoning/problem-solving process
- Self-directed learning
- Collaborative learning

Critical Components
- Problem is designed to lead to investigation that will incorporate core content.
- Problem is representative of a real problem that occurs within a discipline or that has intrinsic interest to students.
- Viable solution to problem requires consideration of many viewpoints or information from many fields.
- Problems bring students into contact with the basic structures of the disciplines under study.
- New information requires that the problem be redefined or reformulated, perhaps several times.
- Teacher–facilitator helps students to identify and understand the procedures used in various disciplines to solve problems.
- Teacher–facilitator encourages and allows students to become academically self-directed.
- Group process is an important part of the PBL process.

Based on her own work and that of several others in the field of gifted education, Gallagher (1997) presented a further refinement of PBL goals, which follows:

1. fostering problem-solving skills
2. enhancing acquisition, retention, and use of knowledge
3. improving students' self-directed learning skills
4. developing students' intrinsic interest in subject matter and, subsequently, their motivation to learn
5. developing students' capacity to see problems from multidisciplinary viewpoints, integrating information from many different sources
6. facilitating the development of effective collaborative learning practices
7. emphasizing for students the importance of learning for understanding rather than for recall
8. improving flexible thought and the capacity to adapt to change

These goals are appropriate for gifted learners and are found in the goals of many programs for gifted students. Reaching these goals requires a major transformation of the current curriculum and instruction practices of most schools and many programs for gifted students. Reaching the goals is well worth the pain and effort of this transformation; the will to do so must come from educators, parents, and students.

ASSUMPTIONS UNDERLYING THE MODEL

About Learning

Although the development of PBL predates much of the body of knowledge about teaching and learning and virtually all of the brain research related to learning, the research of the last 30 years has supported the following assumptions of PBL:

- Learning is more effective when it is hands-on and in a meaningful context that builds on prior knowledge.
- Problems will motivate students to explore many topics related to the core curriculum in greater depth.

- Real-world problems are ill-structured, and thus support the thinking and skill development that students will encounter in their careers. Well-structured problems do not teach and may indeed prevent development of the skills needed to solve real-world (ill-structured) problems.
- Learning and motivation increase when curriculum contains thoughtful questions and significant, real problems.
- Acquiring a positive attitude toward learning may be one of the most important attributes of learning to think critically.
- Curriculum content that is designed around significant concepts provides the best foundation for understanding and retention of knowledge.

About Teaching

In PBL, the teacher becomes a facilitator and coach to students, stepping completely away from the role of the giver of knowledge. As facilitator of students in PBL, the teacher moves the group through the stages of PBL; monitors individual and group progress and participation; and encourages students to externalize and analyze their own thinking, and to interact with each other's findings and ideas.

Metacognitive Coaching

Metacognition is an important element of PBL, and the teacher–facilitator needs to develop the mind-set and skills to help students become aware of their thinking processes. Students must learn to review these processes, describe them, and modify them when they are not effective. Reflection and evaluation of one's thinking processes ultimately result in better reasoning. Barrows (1988, cited in Gallagher, 1997) sees metacognition in PBL as the "executive function" in thinking—that is, reflecting on the problem, or reviewing what is known and remembered, creating hypotheses, deciding what decisions need to be made, considering other sources of information, and reviewing and reflecting on the meaning of what has been learned and what needs to be done next.

The most critical role of the tutor in PBL is to give voice to metacognitive questions—that is, to incorporate them into classroom dialogue so that students become familiar and comfortable with them, attend to and appreciate them, and then adopt their use as the students become increasingly independent, self-directed learners. Questions such as the following should be consistently put forth by the tutor: "What other perspectives might you consider?" "What assumptions are you making?" "What step should you take next?" and "Have you been thorough in your thinking?" Modeling and requiring metacognitive thinking processes are important aspects for the tutor–facilitator.

The tutor also should model expert inquiry through use of questions that (a) demonstrate good critical thinking, (b) probe student understanding of ideas or issues, and (c) assess students' learning needs. These questions help the tutor understand how to modulate the level of challenge for current and future problems (Barrows, 1988, cited in Gallagher, 1997).

Procedural Coaching

Procedural coaching includes the skills and finesse of all great teaching:

- ensuring that the learning environment supports student learning and success
- matching the challenge of the problem with the abilities of the learner(s)
- pacing that allows students to reach a reasonable resolution in a sensible period of time
- making sure that all students are involved in the process
- monitoring group behavior
- bringing group problems to the table as necessary
- assisting in procuring authentic assessment (Barrows, 1994, cited in Gallagher, 1997)
- debriefing students and providing information as to how experts might approach and resolve the problem (Norman & Schmidt, 1992, cited in Gallagher, 1997)

About Characteristics and Teaching of Gifted Students

One might suggest that given the origins of PBL (schools of medicine), the approach obviously would be appropriate for gifted learners because a high percentage of students in medical school probably are gifted. Gallagher (1997) draws on numerous sources to specify established characteristics of gifted students that make PBL especially appropriate for them. According to her, gifted students

- acquire and use knowledge in broader and deeper ways than nongifted peers,
- use more sophisticated strategies than others their age,
- are better at regulating and evaluating their own thinking,
- transfer previously learned strategies more easily than others,
- deal with novelty comfortably, and
- have more functional and adaptive motivation toward school tasks and perceive greater control over their success and failures than others.

The open-ended structure of PBL, which makes it less efficient for many students, commends it for teaching the gifted. These students are more motivated, reflective, and strategic than other learners. PBL offers a rich context within which to construct knowledge. The novel real-world problems and social contexts within which they are embedded are highly suited to gifted students (Sternberg, Ferrari, Clinkenbeard, & Grigorenko, 1996).

ELEMENTS/PARTS

PBL is composed of four elements: (a) an ill-structured problem, (b) substantive content, (c) student apprenticeship, and (d) self-directed learning.

The Ill-Structured Problem

The ill-structured problem encompasses the doubt, uncertainty, and difficulty that a person encounters in any human endeavor or subject of inquiry (Barell, 1995). Characteristics of ill-structured problems include the following: (a) more information is needed than is initially available, in order to understand the situation and decide on possible resolutions; (b) no single formula exists to solve the problem; (c) the problem changes as new information becomes available; and (d) students can never be absolutely certain that they have made the "right" decision (Barrows, 1985, cited in Gallagher, 1996). Other characteristics of ill-structured problems include that they are generative—that is, they immediately engage students and cause the problem solver to ask questions; they lead to inquiry in most disciplines; they must be rationally investigated before they can be defined and criteria for a successful solution established; criteria can emerge that conflict with each other; different solutions may be arrived at by various students, all using rational thought and thorough investigation (Boyce, VanTassel-Baska, Burruss, Sher, & Johnson, 1997; Gallagher, 1997; Simon, 1978, cited in Stepien & Pyke, 1997).

Substantive Content

One of the most stinging criticisms of curricula in programs for gifted students regards substantive content. As noted many times in numerous places, gifted students frequently have been provided thinking exercises and strategies separated from core curriculum objectives and other classroom learning. The use of substantive content is critical in any program for gifted students, and the structure of PBL may assist educators in integrating substantive content and mandated curricula.

Ill-structured problems abound in life; they surround and engage individuals with their unknowns and possible consequences. Trained teachers are able to select ill-structured problems that students will find engaging. The teachers' task then becomes to guide students in those directions that not only help them formulate a solution, but that also require them to use (learn, if necessary) core curriculum concepts, skills, and objectives. Needless to say, the investigation and solution of ill-structured problems span various disciplines.

Transforming ill-structured problems into appropriate curricula requires skill and planning. Gallagher (1997) suggests that a more accurate name for the PBL problem might be a "well-constructed, ill-structured problem." This means that the problem must (a) be designed to ensure coverage of specific, predefined knowledge, preferably from various disciplines; (b) help students learn important concepts, ideas, and skills; and (c) hold intrinsic interest or importance (B. Ross, 1991, cited in Gallagher, 1997).

Student Apprenticeship

The teacher's role of facilitator or coach is key to students taking charge of their own learning. Motivation and the development of metacognitive skills are critical to the self-directed learner; therefore, the development of these skills is one of the primary responsibilities of the teacher–facilitator in PBL.

By definition, ill-structured problems used as a basis for curricula have an intrinsic interest that motivates students, and Carr and Borkowski

(1986) and Sternberg and Davidson (1985), both cited in Gallagher (1997), believe that the central skill to becoming self-directed is to become "hyper-conscious" of thought, and metacognition—thinking about thinking—is the basis for this consciousness.

Self-Directed Learning

As defined by Gallagher and Stepien (1996), the stakeholder in a PBL situation has some level of responsibility, authority, and accountability for re-solving some aspect of the problem. Being in a specific role places students in the shoes of professionals and helps achieve the goals of PBL. They learn

- the way people in different disciplines approach problem solving;
- the biases, perspectives, and paradigms of interpretation that different professionals bring to the problem-solving process;
- the subjective element that is always present in real-world problem solving;
- the necessity of appreciating many approaches to interpreting a problem situation; and
- the complex process of weighing the priorities of different constituents in the problem who have equally compelling, but conflicting, goals. (Gallagher & Stepien, 1996, p. 262)

Table 7.1 provides a summary of teacher and student roles and activities in PBL.

MODIFICATIONS
OF THE BASIC CURRICULUM

PBL requires significant modifications of the educational approach. These modifications include alteration of (a) the curriculum content and processes, (b) expectations for student products, and (c) the entire learning environment. They extend beyond merely implementing a constructivist curriculum to a true *transformation* of curriculum and instruction that requires different roles for students and personnel and an entirely fresh approach to learning.

TABLE 7.1
Summary of Student and Teacher Roles and Activities in Problem Based Learning

Steps in Starting a New Problem	Student		Teacher	
	Role	**Sample Activities**	**Role**	**Sample Activities**
Problem selection	Active participant	Take part in discussion of potential school or community problems and give input as appropriate.	Resource Facilitator	Develop list of potential problems that are relevant and intriguing to the students. Facilitate discussion of problems.
Role decisions within groups	Active participant in assigning roles	Discuss individual strengths as prequel to deciding on appropriate roles.	Resource Facilitator	Facilitate students' discussion of individual strengths and the assignment of roles.
Learning objectives set	Active participant in choosing or defining learning	Brainstorm list of concepts and skills students want to learn from working on this problem.	Resource Facilitator	Facilitate brainstorming sessions. Plan structure for students to reach learning objectives.
Problem presentation	Active participant	Scribe lists: facts, ideas, learning issues, and action plan.	Resource Facilitator	Guide students as they seek factual information. Ask proof-of-reasoning and probing questions during discussions. Assist students in finding and accessing community resources.
Problem processing	Active participant	Independently gather, analyze, and synthesize information related to	Resource Facilitator	Guide students as they seek factual information. Ask proof-of-reasoning and probing questions

(continues)

TABLE 7.1 *Continued.*

Summary of Student and Teacher Roles and Activities in Problem Based Learning

Steps in Starting a New Problem	Student		Teacher	
	Role	Sample Activities	Role	Sample Activities
Problem processing (*continued*)		selected problem; participate in group discussions; and share information gathered.		during discussions. Assist students in finding and accessing community resources.
Problem follow-up	Active participant	Participate in group discussions; apply new knowledge and synthesize, revise hypotheses; and identify new action plan if necessary.	Resource Facilitator	Lead discussions and ask proof-of-reasoning questions. Help students locate resources if necessary.
Solution presentation	Active participant in developing a presentation within a small group	Work independently and within group. Develop presentation that demonstrates synthesis and transformation.	Resource Guide Facilitator	Assist students by helping to locate materials and people who are willing and able to assist in evaluation of the presentations.
Post-problem reflection	Active participant	Reflect and determine how to demonstrate what has been learned.	Facilitator Guide	Provide a structure for reflection and self-evaluation. Assist in self-critique of process and product through questioning.

Content Modifications

The extent to which curriculum content is transformed becomes apparent when one considers that students encounter curriculum content in a meaningful context; must define and search for information they need; have a stake in the resolution of a problem; and need to actively interact with information, other students, and experts in various fields. Ill-structured problems have numerous abstract aspects, are incredibly complex, and include a wide variety of concepts, disciplines, interactions with others, and content areas. The well-constructed, ill-structured problem serves as a way to organize content for learning value, and the study of methods of the disciplines becomes necessary to progress toward a solution. The study of people is not intrinsic to PBL, but could be incorporated easily, especially as experts in their fields are needed to give information or shed a different light on proposed solutions.

Process Modifications

Gallagher's (1997) recommendations for modifying curriculum and instruction for gifted students, which overlap significantly with those of Maker (1982b) and Maker and Nielson (1995), follow:

1. advanced content
2. complex concepts
3. interdisciplinary connections
4. good reasoning, habits of mind, and self-directed action
5. conflicting ethical appeals

Adaptations are built into the problem and drawn out during instruction. As students define, research, redefine, discuss, modify, and work toward a workable solution to a complex problem, they engage repeatedly in higher level thinking, interact with a group, and encounter a wide variety of ideas and strategies. The role of the facilitator–teacher includes the tasks of modulating the challenge level and coaching at an appropriate level. For gifted students, the levels should include more complex kinds of reasoning.

By definition, PBL is open-ended, includes discovery learning, and requires evidence of reasoning as students challenge and are challenged about information gathered, conclusions drawn, and ideas inferred. Students also have opportunities to make a number of choices—about tasks, responsibilities, direction of inquiry, and strategies. As they continuously interact with other students, as well as experts in their field, they choose their focus, which information to use, and how to present what they have learned to the group.

Pacing of the PBL process ultimately becomes the responsibility of the teacher–facilitator. Motivation, challenge level, skills, and expectations all affect the pace of learning, and a skilled and experienced instructor is able to find the fine line between challenging and overwhelming that will assure appropriate pacing for gifted students.

Product Modifications

Students tackle real, relevant, and substantive problems in PBL, which easily leads to directing solutions to real (and appropriate) audiences. Product (solution) evaluation is a process, but the end product needs to be self-evaluated by individual students, by the group, and by the instructor, based on predetermined criteria. Evaluation by experts can be determined by (a) the adoption of part or all of the proposed solution; (b) feedback in response to specific, predetermined questions; or (c) a questionnaire based on predetermined criteria.

Learning Environment Modifications

To support PBL, the learning environment must be structured to include all of the characteristics detailed by Maker (1982b) and Maker and Nielson (1995). The teacher's role as facilitator requires that the classroom, the interactions, the direction of investigations, and the topics be student centered. Students are encouraged to be or become independent as they acquire the necessary skills and knowledge to apply to developing a solution. The atmosphere and inquiries are open; no correct solution to the problem exists, and the problem very well may be frequently redefined, as more information becomes available. Acceptance of information and ideas without immediate judgment is more likely to occur when everyone is collaborating on a solution. All new ideas initially should be given a level playing field.

As noted previously, complexity is an inherent part of PBL. The environment must include a variety of tools and materials suitable for use when pursuing complex ideas. The extension of the learning environment beyond the classroom, school, and perhaps community is an obvious component of PBL; thus, the requirement of high mobility for gifted students is met.

Students working through the PBL process work alone at times, within a small group, and within a larger group or whole class. These flexible groupings allow students exposure to the ideas, strategies, and personalities of others and may assist them in accepting and valuing ideas and personal traits that are different from their own.

IMPLEMENTATION

The implementation of PBL requires that three simultaneous changes be integrated into content-rich curriculum: (a) a well-constructed, ill-structured problem; (b) students being encouraged to take control of their own learning; and (c) students being placed in a stakeholder position (Gallagher & Stepien, 1996). Within PBL, the tutorial groups provide the context for much of the student learning, so understanding the tutorial process is critical to implementing the approach (Hmelo & Ferrari, 1997). Students working through the PBL process work alone at times, within a small group, and within a whole-class or large group. These flexible groupings allow students exposure to the ideas, strategies, and personalities of others and may assist them in accepting and valuing ideas and personal traits different from their own.

Starting a New Group

As with any group, members must get to know each other, establish ground rules, and develop a collaborative climate for learning. At an initial meeting, each student and the facilitator need to introduce themselves by giving a brief self-description. This exercise will reveal possible areas of expertise and personal characteristics that may be useful as the process continues. Another important function of the pre–problem-solving phase is to establish a nonjudgmental climate in which the students and facilitator can recognize and articulate what they do and do not know (Barrows, 1988, cited in Hmelo & Ferrari, 1997). Additionally, PBL roles, including that of facilitator, must be presented and explained (Hmelo & Ferrari, 1997).

Starting a New Problem

To start a new PBL problem, the facilitator presents minimal information about a complex problem to a group of students. This presentation should approximate how the problem would appear in the real world, and the problem must be interesting to the students. The problem must be authentic and relevant to engage the students and motivate them toward its solution. Newspapers and news magazines are good sources of complex, interesting problems. For example, the report in a local newspaper that the childhood leukemia rate in a nearby community is twice the national rate might pique students' interest and make them want to investigate the discrepancy (Uyeda, Madden, Brigham, Luft, & Washburne, 2002). Other possible topics include the spread of a virulent virus or immigration-related issues, such as (a) the high mortality rate of Mexican citizens illegally crossing the Arizona–Sonoran border or (b) the impact on the economy of those immigrants who successfully reach the interior of the country. Language issues, such as the English-only movement, provide complex problems, as do many civil rights issues and movements.

After selecting a problem, the group needs to agree on who will perform the role of scribe. The scribe records the groups' problem-solving ideas and information on whiteboards or butcher paper. Four columns— the *Facts* of the problem, the students' *Ideas* or hypotheses, the *Learning Issues,* and the planned *Actions*—are formed, and ideas must be listed and updated as appropriate. The scribe needs to keep the information current if the group is to proceed toward resolution in an efficient and orderly way.

At this point, students and the facilitator jointly agree on their objectives for the problem. The facilitator might ask, "What do you want to learn from this problem?" to help the group set learning goals and work toward common objectives. These objectives can be used by the facilitator to monitor and focus or refocus student direction (Barrows, 1988, cited in Hmelo & Ferrari, 1997), as well as for student and facilitator evaluation after the process is completed. The objectives also might indicate the need to modify or reformulate goals.

As students work through a problem, they discover concepts they do not understand fully and therefore need to learn more about. The facilitator's questions help them to clarify the learning issues and to decide whether new issues need to be added to the growing list. When the group understands the problem to the point that further progress is impeded by lack of knowledge, group members divide up and individual students begin researching the learning issues they have identified (Barrows & Kelson, 1995, cited in Hmelo & Ferrari, 1997). The Facts column lists information students have gathered from research and experimentation, a growing synthesis relevant to their hypothesis that is shared when they come together. In the Ideas column, the scribe records student conjectures that may include causation, effects, and possible resolutions. This helps students keep track of their evolving hypotheses. The Learning Issues column lists questions for further study—that is, what students believe they need to know or understand to resolve the problem. The Action Plan column includes tasks that need to be completed to solve the problem.

The consistent use of white boards or chart paper supports the PBL process, leading to scaffolding of ideas and information. The scribe records the group's problem solving, including group deliberations. The four columns, Facts, Ideas, Learning Issues, and Action Plan, help students keep a record of where they began and where they are going in the PBL process (Hmelo & Guzdial, 1996, cited in Hmelo & Ferrari, 1997). This running record aids in the iterative process of problem definition, information gathering, and solution synthesis (Gallagher, Sher, Stepien, & Workman, 1995; Hmelo, Narayanan, Hubscher, Newstetter, & Kolodner, 1996, cited in Hmelo & Ferrari, 1997).

Problem Follow-Up

In the problem follow-up phase of PBL, students come together to share knowledge, reconsider hypotheses, and generate new hypotheses based on new information. They discuss and critique resources used and reassess the problem, applying what they have learned; resynthesize information; and possibly revise the hypothesis list. For example, if the investigation were centered on the spread of the West Nile virus, knowledge of mosquitoes, the pattern of the spread of the disease, communities especially hard hit and those spared, medical information, and prevention and control measures taken might be investigated and shared. The ensuing discussion might result in modification of the original hypotheses, or the need for an entirely new hypothesis might become apparent.

This process and the interaction help students apply new knowledge to the problem and to co-construct their solution. An important part of this process is self-evaluation and evaluation of information presented by other students. They examine and critique sources of information, which assists them in becoming self-directed learners (Hmelo & Coté, 1996).

Performance Presentation

The PBL emphasis is not only on students developing a solution to the problem, but also on their developing an understanding of the cause of the problem. The problem statement includes student roles and the product or performance expected as the result of their work. This statement helps students identify a finite goal and standards they must meet to know they have reached completion of their task. The end product must have a clear and real relationship to the problem. Students must synthesize the information gathered and use a variety of formats in their problem presentation. Typically, formats include mathematical analyses, graphs and charts, oral presentations, and dramatic performances.

Post-Problem Reflection

Post-problem reflection is a deliberate reflection designed to identify and articulate what was learned. Students need to consider connections between the problem under consideration and previous problems, and how this problem is similar to and different from others they have encountered or worked on (Barrows & Kelson, 1995, cited in Hmelo & Ferrari, 1997). During this reflection time, students are able to generalize information and find applications for their learning (Salomon & Perkins, 1989, cited in Hmelo & Ferrari, 1997).

The Role of the Problem

Needless to say, the problem is a critical component of PBL, and research and experience have resulted in identifying characteristics of a good problem, as detailed by Hmelo and Ferrari (1997). For students to learn the desired thinking skills, problems must

- be complex, ill-structured, and open-ended;
- be realistic and resonate with students' experiences;

- be complex enough to have many interrelated parts, each important for a good solution;
- motivate students and encourage them to learn;
- afford feedback that allows students to evaluate their knowledge, reasoning, and learning strategies; and
- promote conjecture and argumentation.

Additionally, problems in a PBL curriculum should be chosen so that concepts are revisited across the curriculum, enabling students to construct flexible knowledge (Koschmann, Myers, Feltovich, & Barrows, 1994).

The Role of the Facilitator

Individuals who are trained to help students learn through PBL act as teacher, facilitator, and coach as they move the group through the stages of PBL. The facilitator monitors the group process, assuring that all students are involved and encouraging students to voice their own thinking and to comment on that of others (Koschmann et al., 1994). Metacognitive coaching requires appropriate questions to individual students, encouraging the justification of thinking and the externalizing of self-reflection. By asking metacognitive questions, the coach assists students in learning what questions they need to ask during different steps of problem solving. "In general, cognitive questions address domain-specific knowledge and procedures needed to solve the problem; metacognitive questions are domain general and refer to planning, monitoring, controlling, and evaluating the problem-solving process" (Hmelo & Ferrari, 1997, p. 412). For example, cognitive questions are those such as "What are the causes of the West Nile virus disease?" "Where in the world is it most prevalent?" and "How is it spread?" Metacognitive questions are those such as "What questions do you need to ask at this point?" "How did you arrive at that conclusion?" and "What from your research leads you to believe that?"

Collaborative Learning in PBL

As discussed in regard to other teaching models, collaborative learning is an important part of the educational experiences of gifted students, and small-group problem solving is a key feature of PBL. This structure takes advantage of the strengths and knowledge of various individuals and makes it possible to apply the group expertise to tasks that might be too difficult for individual students. As some individuals become "experts" on specific aspects of the problem, others in the group might become especially skilled at metacognitive questioning. During group discussions, the expertise of each student contributes to the learning of the entire group and to the solution of the problem. The variety of perspectives within a small PBL group requires group members to examine their information, their thinking, and the clarity of their expression as they discuss, argue, and coordinate their findings. The whole of their expertise becomes greater than a sum of its parts.

Reflection in PBL

Reflection is critical to meaningful learning and certainly to becoming proficient in the use of the higher level thinking processes. It helps students to (a) link new information with prior knowledge, (b) mindfully extract concepts, (c) see possible applications of specific strategies to different tasks, and (d) come to understand the thinking and learning processes they have used.

Challenges for Teachers

Changing teaching styles and strategies requires great effort and significant amounts of time. Implementing PBL can seem overwhelming to the instructor who is trying to "cover the curriculum," find or develop appropriate problems, learn the necessary facilitator and coach skills, and keep students interested and on track. Gertzman and Kolodner (1996, cited in Hmelo & Ferrari, 1997) identified strategies that teachers new to PBL used:

1. *Jump starting* involves questioning students about how they are going to get started or prompting them to consider the nature of the problem on which they are working.
2. *Check-ups* are used to get students to think about how what they are doing relates to their goals.
3. *Spotlighting* occurs when the teacher focuses on a different aspect of new information, such as the source of a document.
4. *Stepping back* structures students' problem solving as they begin,

and during the process, the teacher asks them about their problem-solving goals and subgoals.

5. *Dropping hints* involves the teacher's attempts to help students move forward when the lack of correct information threatens to halt the process.

The first four of these strategies are focused on process and give a structure for metacognitive scaffolding. The fifth strategy relates to content, and is used frequently by beginning facilitators worried about not covering the curriculum content sufficiently (Gertzman & Kolodner, 1996, and Hmelo, Holton, & Gertzman, 1997, both cited in Hmelo & Ferrari, 1997).

Given that PBL was begun in medical schools, adapting the process to lower levels of education offers significant hurdles and challenges. Teachers who aspire to be facilitators and coaches must have sufficient information and help when planning, as well as access to skilled practitioners to coach them as they experience the various wonders and pitfalls of the process. They need to be trained in the process and to receive feedback and support from mentors and colleagues as they begin the implementation. Workshops, mentoring, and collegial discussions can provide the necessary supportive environment for teachers to successfully meet the challenges and embrace the opportunities that PBL offers (Hmelo & Ferrari, 1997).

MODIFYING THE MODEL

Content Modifications

A well-constructed, ill-defined problem includes many abstract and complex issues, and serves as a structure for organizing learning experiences for efficiency (learning value). Student investigations ensure a variety of topics and disciplines, and the study of methods is inherent to the pursuit of the problem. The study of people needs to be incorporated, and is an easy and logical addition. As students gather information, they will encounter people, or the names of people, who have contributed to the field of study. With teacher encouragement and guidance, students can find learning more about the person and his or her life and contributions a fascinating part of their study.

Process Modifications

A significant part of the PBL model requires higher levels of thinking and discovery. Real problems are open-ended, complex, and contain a variety of aspects and issues that demand multiple cognitive strategies. During the small-group meetings, students are interacting and must support their findings or conclusions with evidence of reasoning. Students choose a topic or subtopic, and their investigations are self-paced to a certain degree. If the teacher or facilitator monitors individuals and groups, as is desirable, PBL meets the process needs of gifted students.

Product Modifications

By definition, PBL addresses real problems, and the products are presented to real audiences using a self-selected variety of formats. Such products and presentations require a transformation of information and have an evaluation component as well.

Learning Environment Modifications

The successful implementation of PBL requires all of the environment modifications recommended by Maker (1982a) and Maker and Nielson (1995). The learning environment is learner centered and open, and high student mobility is necessary. Student independence is encouraged, and students work within small groups and large groups of varied composition. Teachers and students all need to be accepting of each other's unusual ideas and personal strengths and weaknesses. Setting up a classroom or space to facilitate PBL requires that the learning environment is complex, containing a wide variety of objects, research tools, experimentation opportunities, and people.

DEVELOPMENT

As mentioned previously, PBL is generally credited to a core of medical educators working at Canada's McMaster University in the 1970s (Barrows,

1994, and Norman & Schmidt, 1992, both cited in Gallagher, 1997). The impetus for this new approach was the observation of consistent differences between the medical school classrooms and physicians' examining rooms. Doctors spent much of their time with patients, dealing with ambiguous situations and asking questions. Furthermore, the observers noted that the asking of good questions was pivotal to a physician's success. In stark contrast, medical students spent their time with books, learning "known facts," and success was equated with giving the right answers. The practicing physicians, always asking questions, were open to changing their minds and forming new conceptions of what the patient's problem was, whereas the medical students were not taught to be flexible thinkers and were expected only to attempt to apply the "right answer" to the situation. When physicians received answers to their questions, they disregarded non-useful information and focused on the useful. Medical students did not know which information in their store of facts should be applied in a given situation. Expert physicians accessed new information as needed, whereas recent graduates seemed to believe they were finished with their learning, but they did not understand the relevance of that learning (Barrows, 1988, cited in Gallagher, 1997). The patient–physician interaction seemed to be at the center of the difference between the medical school classroom and the practicing physician's examining room, and the McMaster team identified a single feature of that interaction that unified all the other differences: Patients consistently needed doctors who were good problem-solvers.

Once articulated, the conception of doctor as expert problem-solver helped define the goals for a new form of medical education: Medical students needed to (a) be taught information in a way that they would remember it and apply it appropriately, (b) learn to appreciate a good question as much as a good fact, and (c) practice asking questions as a means of learning facts. Students also needed feedback on their question asking and on their skill in discriminating between relevant and irrelevant information. Most important, they needed to develop an internal gauge of the quality of their own reasoning. Recognizing that the relevance of medical students' learning should be just as apparent as an artist's apprenticeship, the context for this self-reflection was also considered important: Medical students needed to learn the skills of expert reasoning and problem solving through the process of diagnosing and treating patients (Gallagher 1997, p. 334). If one were to substitute "gifted people" for "medical students" in the previous passage, each statement would be equally appropriate. These are the skills that gifted students need to acquire as they are educated.

RESEARCH ON EFFECTIVENESS

With Nongifted Students

Content Retention

Separating the research on nongifted and gifted students is complicated by the fact that studies of medical students may indeed be considered as research on gifted students. Thus, the separation may not be strictly accurate, and is definitely arbitrary because the studies done in medical schools appear under "Nongifted," whereas those of practicing physicians are found under "Gifted."

SHORT-TERM RETENTION. The importance of retaining what has been learned is obvious, and the difference in research results between short-term and long-term retention is interesting. Norman and Schmidt (1992) found no difference in short-term retention between students in PBL situations and those given traditional instruction; they also reported an initial deficit among the students who learned through PBL. Dods (1997) reported increased retention, and in an investigation of factors that might relate to content retention, Schmidt, De Grave, De Volder, Moust, and Patel (1989) found that providing information related to a problem stem increased recall to a significant degree.

LONG-TERM RETENTION. Studies of long-term retention consistently favor PBL over traditional instruction. Martensen, Eriksson, and Ingleman-Sundberg (1985, cited in Gallagher, 1997) found no difference in short-term recall between the two approaches, but PBL students scored 60% higher on a test given 2 to 4 years after completion of the course. Stepien and Gallagher (1993) reported success in various K–12 environments, including low-income, inner-city schools. A study reported by Norman and Schmidt (1992, cited in Gallagher, 1997) found that PBL students had slightly lower short-term retention, but the difference disappeared after 2 years, because PBL students forgot less information than their traditionally instructed peers. Norman and Schmidt also reported a study by Tans and colleagues in which PBL and traditionally instructed students were given a "free recall" test 6 months after they completed their studies. PBL students recalled up to five times more concepts than their peers.

With Gifted Students

In a study of students attending a 3-year, state-supported residential school for students talented in math and science, Gallagher and Stepien (1996) found no significant differences between students instructed using PBL in their American studies class and those instructed in traditional settings. Gallagher, Stepien, and Rosenthal (1994) and Stepien, Gallagher, and Workman (1993) reported success with PBL for instructing gifted elementary, middle school, and high school students. Gallagher (1996, cited in Gallagher, 1997) found that PBL students studying a war in the Pacific tended to examine more perspectives than traditionally instructed students. Brinkerhoff and Glazewski (2000) found that PBL may be an effective strategy for gifted and talented 6th-grade students. Student scaffolding did not appear to affect achievement or student attitudes; however, teacher scaffolding appeared to increase teacher effectiveness, confidence, and attitudes.

To look at whether PBL is effective in helping students integrate knowledge from basic and applied fields, Patel, Groen, and Norman (1991) gave the same problem to practicing physicians who had been educated in traditional methods and to those who experienced PBL. The physicians who were trained in PBL were more effective at integrating basic and clinical knowledge. Boshuizen and Schmidt (cited in Norman & Schmidt, 1992) found that PBL-trained doctors took a more analytical approach to examining problems and were more successful in reaching a good diagnosis than other doctors, who tried to solve the problem by applying previously learned knowledge. Blumberg and Michael (1991, cited in Gallagher, 1997) looked for an increase in self-directed learning by examining library use. Students trained in PBL used library resources more frequently while in the classroom, and this continued into their clinical experiences.

JUDGMENTS

Advantages

The advantages of PBL are numerous and obvious. PBL curriculum engages students in qualitatively different educational experiences; the structure of the problems engages the students and demands their responsibility in working toward a solution; good, substantive content and meaningful concepts are part of the problems; and problems are large enough to require collaboration, which mimics the real-world requirement for shared expertise. The facets and structure of PBL match many characteristics of gifted students and provide defensible evidence not only of differentiated curriculum, but also of superior education that prepares students for the future.

Disadvantages

As with many excellent models, the disadvantages of PBL include the cost associated with implementation and the resistance to change by many educators and community members, including politicians. To implement PBL effectively, most teachers need to learn new skills and some need to embrace an entirely different philosophy of teaching, learning, classroom management, and student expectations. Additionally, specific training and continued coaching and support are needed as teachers work their way through the whole new educational world they have entered.

Many administrators prefer to have a building in which teaching strategies are consistent throughout and lend themselves to easy use of the teacher evaluation tools and methods currently in place. Such tools, however, typically do not lend themselves to the evaluation of nontraditional strategies, and when they are used in nontraditional classrooms, the teacher may be evaluated as not being an effective instructor.

CONCLUSION

PBL is a viable teaching model for gifted students. The fact that it has spread from its beginnings in a medical school to other medical schools and into the public school sector is encouraging and speaks to its worth. If national educational leaders continue to cry for the restructuring of schools and for constructivist learning, more teachers and school administrators may look at PBL as a possibility, especially for their advanced classes and programs for gifted students.

RESOURCES

Background Readings

Berger, S. (2001). Surfing the net: Creativity on the World Wide Web. *Understanding Our Gifted, 13*(4), 24–26.

Boyce, L. N., VanTassel-Baska, J., Burruss, J. D., Sher, B. T., & Johnson, D. T. (1997). A problem-based curriculum: Parallel learning opportunities for students and teachers. *Journal for the Education of the Gifted, 20*, 363–379.

Giftedness: How can ill-structured problems take advantage of a child's natural curiosity? *Understanding Our Gifted, 13*, 23–26. (ERIC Document Reproduction Service No. EJ621397)

Hmelo, C. E., & Ferrari, M. (1997). The problem-based learning tutorial: Cultivating higher order thinking skills. *Journal for the Education of the Gifted, 20*, 401–422.

Ngeow, K., & Kong, Y. (2001). Learning to learn: Preparing teachers and students for problem-based learning. *ERIC Digest.* (ERIC Document Reproduction Service No. ED 457524)

Stepien, W. J., & Pyke, S. L. (1997). Designing problem-based units. *Journal for the Education of the Gifted, 20*, 380–400.

Torp, L. T., & Sage, S. (1997). What does it take to become a teacher of problem-based learning? *The Journal of Staff Development, 18*(4), 32–36.

Torp, L. T. & Sage, S. (2002). *Problems as possibilities: Problem-based learning for K–16 education* (2nd ed.). Alexandria, VA: Association for Supervision and Curriculum Development.

Curricular Materials

The Center for Gifted Education (CGE) at the College of William and Mary (P.O. Box 8795, Williamsburg, VA 23187-8795; http://cfge.wm.edu) offers a problem-based science curriculum for Grades K–8, all published in 1993. The unit titles include *Small Ecosystems: Planet X; What a Find: Archaeology and Historical Systems; Acid, Acid Everywhere; Electricity City; Agriculture, Pollution, and Politics: How They Interact Within the Chesapeake Bay Ecosystem; No Quick Fix: The Body, Disease, and the Immune System;* and *Hot Rods: Nuclear Energy and Nuclear Waste.*

Center for Problem-Based Learning, Illinois Math and Science Academy Web site: http://www.imsa.edu/team/cpbl/problem.html

College of William and Mary. (1997). *Guide to teaching a problem-based curriculum.* Dubuque, IA: Kendall/Hunt.

Gallagher, S., Stepien, W. J., Sher, B. T., & Workman, D. (1995). Implementing problem-based learning in science classrooms. *School Science and Mathematics, 95,* 136–146.

Greenwald, N. L. (2000). Learning from problems. *The Science Teacher, 67,* 28–32.

Mortality and Morbidity Weekly Report on the Web site (www.cdc.gov.mmwr/) for the Centers for Disease Control.

Stepien, W. J. (2002). *Problem-based learning with the Internet: Grades 3–6.* Tucson, AZ: Zephyr Press.

Stepien, W. J., Senn, P. R., & Stepien, W. C. (2000). *The Internet and Problem-Based Learning: Grades 6–12.* Tucson, AZ: Zephyr Press.

Treffinger, D. J., Isaksen, S. G., & Dorval, K. B. (1994). Creative problem-solving: An overview. In M. A. Runco (Ed.), *Problem finding, problem solving, and creativity* (pp. 223–236). Norwood, NJ: Ablex.

Uyeda, S., Madden, J., Brigham, L. A., Luft, J. A., & Washburne, J. (2002). Solving authentic science problems. *The Science Teacher, 1,* 24–29.

CHAPTER 8

Joseph S. Renzulli: The Enrichment Triad Model Joseph S. Renzulli and Sally M. Reis: The Schoolwide Enrichment Model

Educators of the gifted and critics of special provisions for the gifted have long been concerned about providing "qualitatively different" learning experiences for these students. Renzulli (1977) devised a research-based enrichment model that can be used as a guide in developing defensible programs for the gifted. Additionally, Renzulli and Reis (2002) developed an enrichment model that provides for gifted students while including all students in a school.

For over two decades the Enrichment Triad Model (ETM) has been used in schools across the country and around the world. Over the years, educators and parents have found unusually large numbers of examples of creative productivity by young people in these programs. Through field testing and further research, the Schoolwide Enrichment Model (SEM) has evolved and been disseminated widely (Renzulli & Reis, 2002). Although the SEM is based on the ETM, they are similar but separate models and will be treated separately in this work unless statements apply to both.

ENRICHMENT TRIAD MODEL

Unlike most teaching–learning models considered in this volume, the Enrichment Triad Model (Renzulli, 1977) was developed specifically to provide differentiated education for gifted students. Although the first two components of the triad—general exploratory activities and process thinking—are deemed appropriate for almost all children, the third component

—individual or small-group investigation of real problems—is considered most appropriate for gifted learners.

Renzulli (1978) proposes a three-ring conception of giftedness as the interaction of above-average intellectual ability, creativity, and task commitment, and believes that creativity and task commitment are developmental objectives to be fostered in intellectually able students. He proposes that *gifted* be used as an adjective and asserts that gifted behaviors also are contextual; creative or gifted performances are dependent on the interaction of people, circumstances, time, and place. As a result, the ETM, designed to move gifted students through awareness (Type I activities), learning of processes (Type II activities), and development of real-world projects (Type III activities), is complemented by the Revolving Door Identification Model (Renzulli, Reis, & Smith, 1981). Using this combined approach, 15% to 20% of the students in a school are identified as a talent pool (i.e., those who have well above average ability either in a general sense or in a specific performance area). Students in the talent pool participate in Type I and Type II activities, as do most students in SEM programs, and may revolve out for a period of time to do qualitatively different Type III projects of interest to them.

"Qualitatively different," according to Renzulli, means more than freedom of choice, lack of pressure, absence of grading, and individualization of rate or pace, although all of these are important in programs for gifted students. Additionally, modifications are needed in curriculum content, learning style must be taken into account, and teaching strategies must be matched to learning needs.

The simplest form of enrichment, sometimes referred to as vertical enrichment or acceleration, consists of introducing gifted students to advanced courses early. This practice takes care of the gifted student's need to be challenged and to interact with equally advanced peers and a more specialized instructor. Thus, through accelerated placement, the advanced ability of the learner is considered. According to Renzulli, however, two other dimensions of learning in enrichment activities must be respected: the student's content interest and preferred style of learning. These are important components of the ETM.

Two main program objectives are recommended for guiding the education of gifted and talented students and are incorporated into the ETM:

1. For the majority of time spent in gifted programs, students have an opportunity to pursue their own interests to whatever depth and ex-

tent they want, and they are allowed to pursue these interests in ways that are consistent with their own preferred styles of learning.
2. The primary role of the teacher in these programs is to provide each student with assistance in (a) identifying and structuring realistic, solvable problems consistent with the student's interests; (b) acquiring the necessary methodological resources and investigative skills for solving these particular problems; and (c) finding appropriate outlets for student products (Renzulli, 1977).

Historically, superior intelligence, or an extremely high ability score on a test, has been the major criterion for admitting students into programs for the gifted. Renzulli offers a rationale for using more than one criterion. He believes that three clusters of characteristics are important in students who can benefit from his model: (a) above-average intelligence, (b) above-average creativity in the area of interest, and (c) task commitment (motivation or persistence). The interaction of these three clusters results in superior performance.

SCHOOLWIDE ENRICHMENT MODEL

Because most gifted students spend the majority of their time in regular classrooms, Renzulli and Reis (1985) adapted and expanded the ETM to create the Schoolwide Enrichment Model, a plan to promote educational excellence and school reform. The major difference between the two models is that the SEM involves a much greater number of teachers and children in Types I and II enrichment activities and requires that all personnel at a participating school buy into the philosophy of the model. An added benefit is that the involvement of almost all students in Types I and II activities seems to lessen the charges of elitism often directed toward gifted students who are involved in special projects.

The SEM addresses three major goals that accommodate the needs of gifted students, as well as providing challenging learning experiences for all students. These goals are as follows:

- To maintain and expand a continuum of special services that will challenge students with demonstrated superior performance or the potential for superior performance, in any and all aspects of the school and extracurricular program.

• To infuse into the general education program a broad range of activities for high-end learning that will: (a) challenge all students to perform at advanced levels and (b) allow teachers to determine which students should be given extended opportunities, resources, and encouragement in particular areas where superior interest and performance are demonstrated.

• To preserve and protect the positions of gifted education specialists and any other specialized personnel necessary for carrying out the first two goals. (Renzulli & Reis, 2002, p. 9)

Renzulli and Reis (2002) suggest consideration of two types of giftedness: "schoolhouse giftedness" and "creative–productive giftedness." They emphasize that (a) both types are important, (b) usually the two types interact, and (c) special programs should encourage both types and provide for the many times the two interact.

ASSUMPTIONS UNDERLYING THE MODELS

About Teaching and Learning

Enrichment Triad Model

When developing the ETM, Renzulli (1977) made major assumptions about the regular curriculum and about enrichment activities. Inherent in his approach and following from his stated premises are implicit and important assumptions that must be recognized and accepted before the approach can be implemented appropriately. The following assumptions are clear from discussions of the model's development:

1. Certain basic competencies should be mastered by all students so they can adapt effectively to the culture in which they live. This mastery process should be as exciting, relevant, and streamlined as possible.

2. Talent pool students are capable of mastering one or more subjects in the regular curriculum at a faster pace than average or slower students. "Curriculum compacting" (Renzulli & Reis, 1985, 2002)

should be used to enable students to progress through the basic curriculum as rapidly as possible.

3. A student's content interests and style of learning must be respected in any enrichment situation. Student interests should be the point of entry for all enrichment activities. Educators must take the time and develop the skills to assist students in the discovery of areas of true interest.

4. Enrichment experiences and activities may be integrated with regular curriculum themes but must be above and beyond the scope of the standard curriculum. Exploratory activities (Type I enrichment) allow students to interact with a particular person, concept, or bit of knowledge; stimulate interest; and open up opportunities for exploration. Varied thinking processes and information-management strategies (Type II enrichment) must be learned so that students can conduct self-directed investigations and develop products and ideas.

5. Enrichment experiences can take place in almost any setting and involve one child or many children. Any student with potential for superior performance and a sincere interest should have the opportunity to pursue the topic(s) in depth.

Most of these assumptions are related to the educator's concept of providing "enriching experiences" for gifted students. All children participate in the regular curriculum, but gifted students need experiences that are above and beyond those provided for all children. Renzulli assumes that gifted students should participate in the regular curriculum for some part of their school experience, or at least demonstrate the minimum competencies that are required as a part of this regular curriculum. An implication of this assumption, very important for those planning to implement Renzulli's ideas, is that the ETM may need some major modifications if it is to be used as a basis for curriculum planning in a self-contained program for the gifted.

The last assumption about the physical setting carries with it some important considerations that go beyond the usual concerns in a classroom setting. To implement the model and its requirement that a student who has a superior potential for performance in a particular area of interest be allowed to pursue topics therein to "unlimited levels of inquiry" (Renzulli, 1977) means that administrative flexibility is absolutely essential. Enrichment activities may take place in the regular classroom, in a special resource room, in an independent study carrel in the library, or in the community. They may involve one child or several children and must not be limited to any one place. For example, students should be able to study with a college professor if that is the best way for them to pursue their topics to unlimited levels of inquiry.

Schoolwide Enrichment Model

Because the SEM is based on the ETM, they share the same basic assumptions. The SEM, however, operates on the premise that *all* students can benefit from experiences with Type I and Type II activities, and that "a rising tide lifts all ships" (Renzulli & Reis, 2002). The current atmosphere in education and the reform initiatives afoot have created a more receptive atmosphere to more flexible approaches that challenge all students, which is what the SEM is designed to do.

Extensive use of Enrichment Clusters is essential to the SEM. Enrichment clusters consist of experiences, knowledge, and guided investigation in an area of interest. A small group of students might choose a topic such as American Sign Language, or the bacteria passed from hands to surfaces and other hands, or a perceived problem related to the school or community. A teacher (or other person) who has a strong interest and some level of expertise provides instruction, hands-on learning, guest speakers, and perhaps field trips that allow students the opportunity to explore this topic. Further, they identify some issue or problem to investigate and develop a presentation or other product that addresses the issue or suggests a solution to the problem. Through these experiences the students are enriched by their findings, interactions, and investigations.

Schoolwide use of Enrichment Clusters is based on the major assumption that "every child is special if we create conditions in which that child can be a specialist within a specialty group" (Renzulli, 1994, p. 70). Further assumptions include that (a) each learner is unique, (b) learning is more effective when enjoyable, (c) learning is more meaningful and enjoyable when it occurs within the context of a real problem, and (d) knowledge and thinking are enhanced through the application of students' own knowledge and thinking as they construct their own meaning (Renzulli & Reis, 2002).

About Characteristics and Teaching of Gifted Individuals

Enrichment Triad Model

The major assumption Renzulli (1978) makes about the characteristics of the gifted follows from his reviews of research on characteristics of successful or eminent individuals. He reviewed the research of Roe (1952), Wallach (1976), Terman and Oden (1959), Hoyt (1965), and MacKinnon (1965). From these and other studies, he concluded that gifted individuals possess three interlocking clusters of traits, as discussed previously in this chapter. The clusters—above-average ability, task commitment, and creativity—may not be equally important in all instances. Someone with great task commitment may be able to compensate for average ability, and someone with superior creativity may produce a superior product without superior task commitment. Interaction among the clusters, not one single cluster, is necessary for creative or productive accomplishment.

Schoolwide Enrichment Model

Renzulli and Reis (2002) point out that in the field of gifted education, a spectrum of ideologies exists, from conservative to liberal. These terms refer to the degree of restrictiveness used in determining which students are included in special programs. The SEM is liberal and casts a wide net; the talent pool in effect is the entire student body.

Above-Average Ability

ENRICHMENT TRIAD MODEL. Above-average cognitive abilities include those characteristics often measured by intelligence, aptitude, or achievement tests. Renzulli, however, is highly critical of a unitary conception of giftedness (IQ) and argues that gifted behaviors also include other abilities not measured on traditional tests (e.g., superior performance in a specific ability area). In the selection of students for a talent pool, Renzulli recommends selection of all students who score at or above the 92nd percentile (using *local* norms) on one or more subtests of standardized instruments. Teachers then are asked to nominate additional students whose academic or creative performance may not be assessed accurately by psychometric instruments. Additional students are identified through a case study approach to ensure that highly able students from divergent populations are not excluded.

SCHOOLWIDE ENRICHMENT MODEL. As mentioned previously, Renzulli and Reis (2002) believe that giftedness must be considered within the context of cultural and situational factors. Using a variety of measures, a talent pool of 15% to 20% of the school population is identified. The measures may include achievement tests, teacher nominations, and assessment of potential creativity and task commitment, as well as alternative paths to entrance, such as self- or parent nomination.

Furthermore, students in the talent pool may opt to participate or not to participate in Type III activities.

Task Commitment

ENRICHMENT TRIAD MODEL. Of the three clusters, task commitment seems to be the most misunderstood by individuals attempting to implement the ETM. Educators seem to equate the concept of task commitment with either a global concept of motivation or a more specific concept of a child who is "motivated" to do a teacher-chosen task. What Renzulli has in mind is different. The kind of motivation he discusses is a refined or focused commitment and ability to take energy and concentrate it on something very specific (e.g., a problem situation, a creative project, a research project). Some of the characteristics included in this cluster follow: persistence in the accomplishment of goals, integration toward goals, drive to achieve (Terman, 1959), enthusiasm, determination, and industry (MacKinnon, 1965). An important point to emphasize is that these characteristics were observed when the individuals were involved in work of their own choosing—their life work—and not in a teacher-designed task.

SCHOOLWIDE ENRICHMENT MODEL. In the SEM, motivation is most likely to surface in the enrichment clusters. These clusters consist of mixed-grade groups of students with a common interest or interests. They meet during specifically designated time blocks during the school day and are led by an adult who shares an interest and has some advanced knowledge and expertise in the area.

Creativity

ENRICHMENT TRIAD MODEL. Creativity is the ability to look at problems in new and unusual ways; to generate a large number of ideas; to challenge the existing ways of doing things (in school or in a field of study); and to be speculative, playful with ideas, and willing to take risks. Included in this cluster of characteristics are such traits as "originality of thinking and freshness of approaches," ingenuity, and "ability to set aside established conventions and procedures when appropriate" (Renzulli, 1978, p. 184). As with motivational traits, however, caution must be exercised in assessing creativity in students. Creative performance on a test of divergent thinking may have little or no relation to creativity in a person's life work. Educators may be able to observe some characteristics in children that would lead them to believe these children have the potential to become creative adults, but the persistence required to return to an idea repeatedly and the creativity necessary to generate relevant solutions to a pressing problem daily may be something entirely different.

SCHOOLWIDE ENRICHMENT MODEL. As in the ETM, in the SEM *creativity* refers to creativity within an area of interest or the production or presentation of a product. This creativity becomes apparent in the enrichment clusters, when students tackle real-world problems and struggle to find workable solutions. New ideas and approaches are frequently necessary in solving such problems.

ELEMENTS/PARTS

Enrichment Triad Model

As mentioned previously, the ETM has three types of enrichment. In Type I enrichment, the teacher (or school team) plans general exploratory experiences on new and exciting topics, fields of knowledge, or ideas not included in the regular curriculum to "invite" students to greater involvement with areas of study. Students have opportunities to explore a variety of content and perhaps discover an area of fascination that may lead to a Type III activity. Type I enrichment also helps teachers decide what types of activities should be selected for Type II. Although much exploratory freedom is needed, students should be aware from the beginning that they are expected to have a purpose when exploring and that eventually they will be conducting further study in one of the areas of interest to them. An important point to remember in relation to Type I enrichment is that general exploratory activity is a cyclical and ongoing process, and even if students are involved in a specific project, they should be given continuous opportunities to keep generating new interests.

Type II enrichment activities are strategic and consist of activities, methods, materials, and instruction designed to develop higher level thinking processes, affective behavior and processes related to personal or social development, and specific research methodology and reference skills. These processes often are scheduled on a regular basis but also may be taught when a specific need is identified during Type III investigations. Thinking and feeling processes have been the focus of many programs for the gifted in the past, because research shows that certain thinking and feeling processes provide students with skills and abilities that are applicable or transferable to new learning situations and other content areas.

Attention should be given to ensure that thinking and feeling processes are used only as necessary tools to facilitate investigations. If not used as tools, they will become ends, rather than means. Process should go hand in hand with the content, as both are critical to meaningful learning. Even if thinking and feeling processes cannot be defended as being exclusively appropriate for the gifted, they can be defended as an essential part of a total enrichment model for the following reasons: (a) they provide an opportunity for gifted students to reach the levels of thinking and feeling that their natural abilities allow; (b) they have the potential for introducing students to more advanced kinds of study and inquiry; and (c) they provide the gifted student, who is characterized by a wide range of interests, with the skills and abilities to solve problems in a variety of areas and new situations.

Type III enrichment, individual or small group investigations, should account for about half the time students spend in enrichment experiences. The main characteristics of Type III activities include the following:

- The student takes an active part in formulating both the problem and the methods by which the problem will be attacked.
- No routine method of solution or recognized answer exists, although appropriate investigative techniques upon which to draw and criteria by which a product can be judged often are available.
- The area of investigation is of sincere interest to an individual or small group, rather than being a teacher-determined topic or activity.
- Students use raw data rather than the conclusions reached by others as their information in reaching conclusions and making generalizations.
- The student engages with a producer's rather than a consumer's attitude and, in so doing, takes the necessary steps to communicate results in a professionally appropriate manner.
- A tangible product often is presented to a real (rather than a contrived) audience but products are not necessarily the major goal of programs using the ETM (Renzulli, 1988).

Schoolwide Enrichment Model

The SEM includes the same three types of enrichment activities as the ETM, with the main difference being that in the SEM all students are provided Type I and Type II activities and have opportunities to engage in

Type III activities in the enrichment clusters. The difference is in the scope of the program; the same elements are included in both models.

MODIFICATIONS
OF THE BASIC CURRICULUM

Content Modifications

Enrichment Triad Model

Content is modified in the ETM in that students learn not only facts about an area but also the methods of inquiry within that discipline. The student also is exposed to a wide variety of topics within a discipline before selecting what to investigate. Content is modified based on the student's interests. Students are encouraged and allowed to select topics of interest to them. Teachers assess student interests continually and attempt to provide experiences that build on these interests.

The ETM provides for some modifications in all aspects of the curriculum—content, process, environment, and product—to make it more appropriate for the gifted. An important note, however, is that the model provides a framework for integrating a variety of content and process changes to meet the learning needs of gifted students. Teachers can ensure that students are dealing with substantive content by providing guidance in the enrichment activities and especially in the choice of problems and the avenues followed in pursuit of a solution.

Schoolwide Enrichment Model

The SEM influences regular curriculum in three ways:

1. The challenge level of required material is differentiated through processes such as curriculum compacting and textbook content modification procedures.
2. Systematic content intensification procedures should be used to replace eliminated content with selected, in-depth learning experiences.
3. Types of enrichment recommended in the Enrichment Triad Model (Renzulli, 1977) are integrated selectively into regular curriculum activities. (Renzulli & Reis, 2002, p. 10)

Although the enrichment clusters and other SEM modifications help meet individual needs, they do not meet all the learning needs of gifted students. For total talent development, supplementary services such as individual or small-group counseling, direct assistance in advanced-level work, mentorships, and other types of connections between students, their families, and out-of-school persons, resources, and agencies are necessary (Renzulli & Reis, 2002).

Curriculum modification techniques in the SEM are designed to (a) adjust the levels of required learning so that all students are challenged, (b) increase the number of in-depth learning experiences, and (c) introduce enrichment into the regular curriculum. Procedures include a planned approach to introducing curricular material of greater depth (Renzulli & Reis, 2002).

Process Modifications

Enrichment Triad Model

As mentioned before, in the ETM, process is a means and not an end. The teacher chooses different processes according to the students' interests and needs, to equip them with the tools and skills to do an independent investigation.

The major process modification directly suggested by the ETM is freedom of choice. In all the areas—content, process, product, and learning environment—students choose activities that are of interest to them. Either individually or in small groups, students should select the topic or area of study, decide on the methods and tools needed to carry out the investigation, and develop a product directed toward an appropriate audience of their choice. Students also should be able to conduct the study in any appropriate environment inside or outside the school. Freedom of choice is encouraged in the three types of enrichment activities, to different degrees. In Type I exploratory activities, the students often choose among options created by the teacher. (The students, of course, played a part in determining the original options when the teacher assessed their interests.) In Type II activities, the students perhaps have less choice, although the kind of investigations in which they are engaged will influence the Type II activities provided. With Type III investigations, students have complete freedom to choose topics, methods, products, and environments.

Higher level thinking is a process modification implied by the structure of the ETM. A need exists for the development of problem-solving skills and of operations that help students deal more effectively with content. These operations or processes include critical thinking, reflective thinking, inquiry, divergent thinking, and productive thinking. Renzulli specifically mentions the Taxonomies of Educational Objectives (see Chapter 3) as a model that can be used in implementing the ETM.

A second process modification indirectly suggested by the ETM is open-endedness. Renzulli emphasizes that Type II experiences should have the power to elicit advanced levels of thinking from gifted students.

Discovery learning is another process modification suggested by the ETM. Although this approach does not provide for the use of guided discovery, discovery learning is certainly an aspect of Type III investigations. Because students are expected to use the techniques of real inquirers in making their own investigations, they are practicing discovery learning in a real-world context. The ETM, however, does not provide teachers with strategies for developing activities that will facilitate discovery learning or the use of inductive reasoning, important components of this curricular modification.

A final process modification included in the ETM is variety. Teachers are encouraged to use a wide range of methods, including field trips, observation of real professionals at work, simulations, learning centers, lectures, and other methods or opportunities that may arise. Another aspect of variety is that a wide range of thinking and feeling processes are developed through Type II activities. This necessitates the use of many different methods.

Schoolwide Enrichment Model
The process modifications of the ETM are included when the SEM is implemented. The primary difference, as previously mentioned, is that the SEM is applied to an entire school. Therefore, all students have learning opportunities that require higher level thinking and other process modifications.

Product Modifications

Enrichment Triad Model
Product modifications are inherent in the ETM. Renzulli, with his emphasis on creative productivity, has made more impact in the area of product modifications than any other theorist or practitioner in the field of education of the gifted. In the early development of the model, he suggested that no investigation was a true Type III activity unless a tangible product was

presented to a real audience. Products are not the goal of ETM; rather products afford a means to bring together the complex cognitive, affective, and conative skills students learn to apply to planning, organization, resource use, and time management. Products are viewed as "the assembly plants of the mind" that require developing, applying, and making meaningful a wide variety of advanced-level processes. These processes were purposefully designed to be the antithesis of prescribed, presented learning. Products are designed to solve real problems of interest to the students, employ methods appropriate to the field of study, and use raw data to generate unique conclusions. An important aspect of the process is that students are acting as producers rather than consumers of information. The students are not merely emulating professionals; they are engaging in tasks as professionals.

Renzulli and Reis (1985) provide implementation guidelines for Type III activities. These guidelines make appropriate modifications for gifted students and include strategies for identifying and focusing student interests, such as interest development and identification, the Interest-A-Lyzer, and interest refinement and focusing. Finding appropriate outlets for student products, providing students with methodological assistance, and developing a "laboratory environment" are necessary, as well. Renzulli and Reis provide suggestions for reference books and materials, along with methods and strategies.

Schoolwide Enrichment Model
The enrichment cluster dimension of the SEM is based on an inductive approach to solving real problems through the development of authentic products and services. Enrichment learning and teaching use the ETM to create a learning situation that requires students to use methodology, higher order thinking skills, and the application of these skills in a creative and productive way (Renzulli & Reis, 2002).

Learning Environment Modifications

Enrichment Triad Model
Renzulli makes numerous suggestions for developing environments appropriate for gifted students. He advocates a student-centered atmosphere in which independence is encouraged, few restrictions are present, complexity is essential, and high mobility is a must. In the learning environ-

ment appropriate for implementing the ETM, the teacher's major goal is to identify, focus, and facilitate student interests and ideas. In fact, student interests guide the selection of both content and process activities developed by the teacher.

In this atmosphere, the teacher cannot possibly be an information giver, except when asked by the students. Although the teacher may direct certain activities, at least half will be determined by the students because half their time should be spent in Type III investigations. Students must learn to be independent in other than academic settings, since many of them will be involved in small-group activities during their investigations. They should solve their own disputes when they arise, and assist the teacher in planning and implementing Types I and II activities that interest them.

Environmental openness requires that few, if any, restrictions affect the students' participation. Students should be encouraged to develop new ideas, produce different products, and use different investigative techniques. The physical environment must permit new people, exploratory discussions, and freedom to change directions when necessary. Renzulli encourages complexity in the learning environment through his suggestion that specialized equipment, a wide variety of reference materials, and sophisticated materials be available (Renzulli, 1977). To enable the teacher to develop a true laboratory environment, a variety of types of workspaces also must be provided, including tables, study carrels, soft areas for discussions, easels for painting, computer hardware and software, and Internet access.

High mobility is necessary to the implementation of the ETM. Students must be permitted to conduct their investigations in any environment that facilitates the process. Renzulli suggests that teachers develop a laboratory environment in which students are engaged actively in gathering some form of relevant information that is to be used in the development of a particular product. Examples given by Renzulli are (a) a street corner where children recorded the number of automobiles that failed to stop, then analyzed the data for a presentation to the commissioner of public safety, and (b) the school cafeteria where students collected leftover food and unused napkins in an antiwaste campaign (Renzulli, 1977). In these cases, the students could not have conducted investigations of their problem situations if they had been confined to a classroom. Thus, an environment that permits free movement is essential in implementing Type III investigations.

Schoolwide Enrichment Model

The SEM provides a structure for a learning environment similar to that necessary for the implementation of the ETM. For students with higher level abilities engaged in Type III activities, the learning environment must be open to the community and to the world at large.

IMPLEMENTATION

Type I Enrichment Activities

Three procedures the teacher can use to allow students to explore a diversity of areas are interest centers, visitations or field trips, and resource persons or guest speakers. Interest centers should include a wide range of topics or areas of study, material that is stimulating, and information regarding methods of investigation in the field. Previously completed student investigations and products may serve as provoking or stimulating materials.

Visitations should include places where dynamic people are actively engaged in problem solving and the pursuit of knowledge. During these visits, gifted learners should have "escalated experiences"—that is, opportunities to look into and become involved with what is on display, being presented, or being produced. For example, students should be able to interact with artists, curators, engineers, and other professionals by seeing them at work and taking part in some of their activities. Guest speakers should be actively engaged in the advancement of art or knowledge in their respective fields; examples are local historians, poets, dancers, architects, photographers, and scientists.

The major role of the teacher in Type I enrichment is to develop interests and identify areas for further study; the teacher also must assist students to analyze their own interests. Students can examine their present and potential interests by using the Interest-A-Lyzer (Renzulli, 1977, pp. 75–82). This instrument consists of a series of hypothetical situations in which the student is asked to respond to open-ended questions. By looking at the responses, the teacher can analyze consistencies and detect general patterns of interest.

Furthermore, the teacher needs to expose students constantly to new areas for creative expression. For example, when recruiting community resource persons as guest speakers, teachers should choose those who are in professions and activities that are different from those with which the students are familiar. A community survey may identify people who might follow up an exposure activity and become involved with groups of students. Additionally, a survey might identify individuals who would be willing to become mentors. A sample form for surveying community resources is the Community Talent Miner (Renzulli, 1977, pp. 82–86).

Interest development centers, field trips, and resource persons are organized approaches to Type I enrichment. Students also should be given informal opportunities to examine topics for possible study. For example, they should be encouraged to browse in libraries or bookstores, encouraged to read how-to books, and provided opportunities for structured and unstructured group discussions.

Type II Enrichment Activities

Any model or strategy that provides systems for organizing thinking and feeling processes and factors that are essential for human learning can be used effectively as a Type II activity. Some examples include the Cognitive Taxonomy (Chapter 3), the Affective Taxonomy (Chapter 3), Creative Problem Solving (Chapter 6), and the Hilda Taba Teaching Strategies (Chapter 10). An important aspect of Type II activities is that they be selected according to student interests and that they integrate the thinking processes with substantive content and issues.

The ultimate goal of Type II activities is for students to develop the thinking and feeling processes necessary for Type III investigations. Students must acquire the process skills and abilities that will enable them to solve problems in a variety of areas. The following are examples of process skills (Renzulli, 1977, p. 25):

Brainstorming	Comparison	Elaboration
Observation	Categorization	Hypothesizing
Classification	Synthesis	Awareness
Interpretation	Fluency	Commitment
Analysis	Flexibility	Value clarification
Evaluation	Originality	

Other Type II activities for talent pool students include (a) advanced reference and research skills; (b) inquiry processes such as research design and collection and interpretation of data; (c) planning, hypothesizing, and decision making; (d) specialized process training (e.g., digital photography); (e) minicourses in methods of the specific discipline (e.g., oral history techniques); and (f) advanced computer programming or graphics production and specific technical skills needed for projects.

Type III Enrichment Activities

In Type III enrichment, the teacher's role is to be a manager in the learning process and to know when and how to enter into this process. The teacher thus has the following major responsibilities when managing Type III activities:

- identifying and focusing student interests
- finding appropriate outlets for student products
- providing students with methodological assistance
- developing a laboratory environment

Successful Type III enrichment activities depend on the interaction of these four basic responsibilities.

General interests must be refined and focused to enable students to identify a real and solvable problem. During this process, the teacher must make certain that students apply the proper investigative strategies so they do not report instead of investigate. Teachers also must be careful not to rush students through the process or impose a problem on them.

Students must be allowed to make their own decisions, and teachers need to help them find appropriate outlets for their products. One of the major characteristics of a real problem (as opposed to a training exercise or simulation) is that the producer is attempting to inform, entertain, or influence a relatively specific but real audience. This need to have an impact is one of the reasons why creative and productive persons are highly product oriented; they always have an audience in mind. Because real-world audiences frequently are grouped together by topical interests, teachers can look for interested groups as potential audiences for the creative work of their students. Examples of audiences include historical societies, science clubs, dramatic groups, and persons interested in preserving a certain species of wildlife or promoting a particular social action. Another potential outlet consists of children's magazines that include the work of young people. The third responsibility of the teacher in Type III enrichment is guiding student application of the tools of inquiry—that is, the methodological techniques that are necessary to solve a problem. The teacher should help students locate books or mentors that offer step-by-step guidance in methodological activities. Students also must learn about the existence, nature, and function of different types of reference materials. These include bibliographies, online databases, dictionaries, glossaries, indexes, atlases, reviews, abstracts, periodicals, surveys, almanacs, anthologies, nonbook reference materials (e.g., art prints, videotapes, filmstrips, charts, maps, slides), and software. The use of reference materials requires a systematic plan so that students are continuously learning where and how information is stored. Analyzing the level of methodological references compared to the reading and conceptual levels of the student is a critical teacher task, as well as serving as a translator when a particular concept is beyond the student's level of comprehension.

The development of a laboratory environment, where the students inquire or investigate, is also important in the implementation of Type III enrichment. A laboratory is not necessarily a physical place. It is the psychological environment, the mood and atmosphere, that encourage investigative activities. What determines the presence of a laboratory environment is whether students are able to gather, manipulate, and use raw data or existing information to produce something that is new and unique.

An additional issue that must be addressed is the quality of products. Teachers should make their students aware that the creative–productive process goes beyond generating ideas and that the students must work hard to refine each product before it is considered final. Students should avoid circulating or presenting products that have not been revised, edited, and polished (i.e., that do not meet professional standards). Some specific examples of possible outlets and products in Type III follow:

- writing a journal article
- making a conference presentation
- issuing a statement to legislators
- producing a television program
- publishing a book
- writing a play
- developing a new theory
- developing a lattice

- writing a brochure
- writing a computer program

A good strategy for teachers to use to get students started with investigative activities is a Management Plan (Renzulli, 1977, p. 71; Renzulli & Reis, 1985, p. 439). This document, a somewhat simplified version of a proposal, provides a format for planning a project. It requires students to think ahead about the purpose of the investigation, the questions to be answered, the format of the product, where and to whom the product will be presented, the methodological resources to be used, and the criteria to be used in evaluating the product.

Reis and Schack (1993) provide a very helpful step-by-step process for teachers to assist students in developing qualitatively differentiated products:

1. Assess, find, or create student interests.
2. Conduct an interview to determine the strength of the interest.
3. Help students find a question or questions to research.
4. Develop a written plan.
5. Help students locate multiple resources and continue working on the topic.
6. Provide methodological assistance.
7. Help students decide which questions to answer.
8. Provide managerial assistance.
9. Identify final products and audiences.
10. Offer encouragement, praise, and critical assistance.
11. Escalate the process.
12. Evaluate.

Using the Triad and the Schoolwide Enrichment Models

In the following examples, the activities are organized around this generalization: Every society has rules, written or unwritten, through which social control over individual conduct is maintained.

Type I Student Activities
- Observe a city council meeting and conduct interviews afterward with selected officers and members.

- Observe a legislative session.
- Actively listen to a lecture by a state or local legislator.
- Visit and interact in learning centers with copies of constitutions of various countries, books about constitutional issues, newspaper articles about constitutional and legal issues, and books about sociological analysis (i.e., how to study societies and their means of social control).
- Actively listen to a lecture by a sociologist describing his or her work in investigating methods of social control.
- Read biographies of famous historians, sociologists, anthropologists, and statespersons.
- View a film about Margaret Mead and her work.
- Actively listen to a lecture by a historian about the historical development of codes and how he or she has studied their development.
- Actively listen to a lecture by a cultural anthropologist about what kinds of things he or she does (e.g., types of projects and methods used).

Type II Student Activities

- Participate in a guided discussion of a moral dilemma, based on Kohlberg's model (Chapter 12), that involves an issue in which someone must break a law to save a life.
- Participate in discussions structured on the Hilda Taba Interpretation of Data Strategy (Chapter 10) to examine stories about various societies and their laws.
- Engage in the Creative Problem Solving process (Chapter 6) using a problem situation related to the study of a society or how to settle a problem regarding the breaking of a rule.
- Participate in simulations in which students create a society.
- Lobby the state legislature, city council, or board of education.
- Analyze the methods used by the different historians, anthropologists, and sociologists, including the eminent individuals studied and those who have been guest lecturers or who have been observed.
- Study methods used by cultural anthropologists (e.g., learn how to use observation forms to decide who is in a position of authority based on how others react to this person).
- Compare the characteristics of current state legislators and famous statespersons.
- Study the use of sociograms (i.e., what information may be gleaned and how to develop one).

- Predict the reactions of different societies to the imposition of certain laws or codes of conduct in the past. Afterward, check the accuracy of predictions through the use of historical sources. Participate in an Application of Generalizations (Chapter 10) guided discussion of societal reactions to varied restrictions.
- Using Williams's visualization strategy (Chapter 12), examine certain laws and social codes from the perspectives of (a) law enforcement officers, (b) lawmakers, (c) prisoners, and (d) the general public.
- Participate in a discussion, based on Krathwohl's Taxonomy (Chapter 3), of the differing values of varied investigators and how these values influence the choice of investigative strategies.

Type III Student Activities

- Compare the Mexican and U.S. processes of developing and implementing rules to govern society. Identify similarities and differences, and relate these to cultural, economic, societal, and political variables.
- Conduct a survey of all classrooms asking for opinions on (a) the school rules most needed and (b) the rules most often broken. Prepare and present a proposed disciplinary code to parent and school district governing boards.
- Research the amount of eye contact between people in a shopping center as a way to investigate some of the unwritten rules governing behavior. Report findings in a paper to submit to an anthropology journal.

These are only suggestions for activities. The students' interests and needs determine the learning experiences provided by the teacher or developed by the students. Teaching activities and strategies for the two models covered in this chapter are so similar that they will be treated as one. For a summary of teacher and student roles and activities in these models, see Table 8.1.

MODIFYING THE MODELS

The ETM and the SEM are in many ways frameworks for providing curricular modifications in all areas for gifted students. All of the content and process modifications suggested by Maker (1982b) and Maker and Nielson (1995) can be incorporated easily into a program that uses the ETM or the

(*text continues on p. 282*)

TABLE 8.1

Summary of Student and Teacher Roles and Activities in the Enrichment Triad and Schoolwide Enrichment Model

Step, Type, or Level of Thinking	Student		Teacher	
	Role	Sample Activities	Role	Sample Activities
Type I: General exploratory activities	Active participant Observer	Work in learning centers. Go on field trips. Explore new ideas. Interact with practicing professionals. Take an active part in activities of professionals. Read about famous person or people in area of interest.	Planner Organizer Interest stimulator	Develop a supportive learning environment. Plan experiences to expose students to new fields of inquiry and the methods used in those fields. Plan continuous experiences to put learners in contact with topics or areas of study in which they may develop a sincere interest. Encourage students to visit the library. Develop interest centers. Arrange for visitations, field trips, and guest speakers. Choose *active* professionals as speakers. Provide (or encourage) informal opportunities for exploration.

(continues)

TABLE 8.1 *Continued.*

Summary of Student and Teacher Roles and Activities in the Enrichment Triad and Schoolwide Enrichment Model

Step, Type, or Level of Thinking	Student		Teacher	
	Role	Sample Activities	Role	Sample Activities
Type I (*continued*)				Provide (or encourage) informal opportunities for exploration.
				Collect biographies and autobiographies for a reading or "Study of People" center.
Type II: Group training exercises	Active participant	Participate in simulations.	Trainer	Plan group and individual activities that will develop thinking and feeling processes.
	Thinker	Answer thought-provoking questions.	Facilitator	
		Do thinking skill activities.	Discussion leader	Select thinking and feeling processes that can be used in a variety of investigations.
		Identify interests.		
		Identify thinking process needs.		Plan process experiences to meet both individual and group needs.
		Discuss ideas and methods.		
		Analyze and compare methods of inquiry used historically and currently in discipline of interest.		Plan activities to develop higher-level thinking skills.
				Plan activities to develop divergent as well as convergent thinking skills.
				Plan activities designed to develop affective and organizational skills.

(*continues*)

| Type III: Individual and small-group investigation of real problems | Problem finder
Data gatherer
Problem solver
Producer
Inquirer | Identify a problem of real concern (interest).
Develop a management plan.
Conduct an investigation of a real problem.
Work individually or with a small group.
Develop a product that is new and unique.
Identify a real audience for the product. | Manager
Resource | Maintain a supportive learning environment.
Assist students to identify and focus personal interests.
Help students develop a management plan.
Identify mentors.
Identify appropriate outlets or audiences for student products.
Provide students with methodological assistance.
Wait for students to make their own decisions.
Assist in locating information.
Encourage students to go beyond the school environment to locate and collect data.
Assist students in revising and "polishing" their work. |

SEM as a framework. The models themselves imply modifications in all product areas and in almost all environmental dimensions. The changes suggested are designed to illustrate how the ETM or SEM approach can be implemented more effectively to achieve the purposes of a comprehensive program for gifted students.

Content Modifcations

Suggestions for content changes to these models fall mainly into the areas of variety and methods of inquiry. Abstractness, complexity, organization for learning value, and the study of people are not included in these models. As shown in the sample activities, however, modifications can be made easily. Previously in this chapter, we described how activities can be organized around an abstract, complex generalization, and students can be encouraged to explore a variety of related topics or issues. We described many different types of experiences from various disciplines, chosen carefully to illustrate key concepts and to expose students to a variety of methods. Additionally, the sample activities illustrate the integration of the study of eminent or famous people. Type I activities include exposure to biographies and autobiographies of famous individuals who made significant contributions. Type II activities include an analysis of the methods used by present investigators, comparing them with those employed by the eminent people studied and comparing the characteristics of present lawmakers with statespersons of the past.

Process Modifcations

The design for Type II enrichment activities encourages teachers to incorporate many process models into their teaching, and suggests that the selection of such activities be based on the students' interests and needs. Renzulli (1977) and Renzulli and Reis (1985) suggest process modifications that should be made in the areas of higher levels of thinking, openendedness, and discovery. They offer numerous guidelines for providing freedom of choice and for the use of a variety of methods.

Higher Levels of Thinking
Skills in the use rather than acquisition of information are developed through the following Type II activities within the theme of societal laws:

(a) Discussions of Moral Dilemmas related to the law (Chapter 12), (b) discussions of societies and their laws (Chapter 10), (c) the problem-solving approach applied to the breaking of laws (Chapter 6), and (d) a discussion of values and their influence on methods used by those engaged in research (Chapter 3).

Open-Endedness

Many of the activities included as both Types I and II are designed to be open-ended and to stimulate the interests of students in investigating related problem situations. By using sound questioning practices (Schiever, 1991), the Hilda Taba Teaching Strategies (Chapter 10), and Discussions of Moral Dilemmas (Chapter 12), teachers can ensure that open-endedness is a significant element of all Type II experiences.

Discovery

Discovery learning is an important aspect of all Type III activities, as students are acting as inquirers and producing rather than consuming information. Guided discovery, supervised or practiced, in the inquiry process can be incorporated through the use of Hilda Taba's Interpretation of Data or Application of Generalization strategies (Chapter 10), which lead students through a process of examining data, inferring causes or effects, developing supportable conclusions, generalizing to new situations, predicting, inferring necessary conditions for predictions, and inferring consequences. In a discussion of values based on the structure of the Affective Taxonomy, as recommended in Chapter 3 for use with gifted students, guided discovery also is included.

Evidence of Reasoning

The process modification of requiring evidence of reasoning can be incorporated easily into discussions and activities by asking the "why" question. Some models, such as the Hilda Taba Teaching Strategies (Schiever, 1991; Chapter 10 of this book) and discussions based on Kohlberg's Discussions of Moral Dilemmas model (Chapter 12), include the asking of questions to elicit explanations of reasoning. Chapters on the various models describe how this process change can be accomplished.

Group Interaction

Structured group interaction is accomplished through simulations. Group participation can be observed by a small group of students, or the entire activity can be taped for later viewing by everyone. Analysis of group participation can include assessment of the roles assumed by individuals and their effectiveness in carrying out these roles. Analysis also can include an attempt to identify individual values and the level of development of those values by using the Affective Taxonomy (Chapter 3) as a guide for observation. The group may want to spend some time brainstorming procedures for more effective participation, or students may wish to discuss values and their effect on various interactions between people.

Pacing

As a process modification, pacing is particularly important during Types I and II activities, when new material or ideas are presented to the students. Guest speakers should be reminded that these are gifted students and they can absorb material quickly. Guests should be prepared to answer in-depth questions from students about their work and use terminology appropriate to their field of inquiry.

Learning Environment Modifications

One learning environment dimension not modified directly by the ETM and SEM is acceptance versus judgment. This dimension is important as a support for developing student products that truly belong to the students rather than the teacher. The teacher must encourage (and assist) students to develop criteria for evaluation, implement the project, and make their own mistakes and analyze the effects of these mistakes. Then they need to redesign, revise, or improve products as needed. An effective way to develop an environment appropriate for gifted students who are engaged in Type III activities is to follow the suggestions made by Parnes (Chapter 6): to encourage elaboration and clarification prior to evaluation and encourage students to use self-evaluation techniques.

Although neither ETM nor SEM addresses the group participation aspect of Type III activities, a few more suggestions about the independence dimension need to be made. To implement the learning environment modification of independence in both academic and nonacademic areas, students should be encouraged to develop their own group-management procedures. They also should develop their own solutions to problems using Creative Problem Solving (Chapter 6) or the Hilda Taba Resolution of Conflict Strategy (Chapter 10).

Summary

The ETM and SEM lend themselves to developing a program that is comprehensive in providing curricular modifications that are appropriate for the gifted. By integrating several process models and by organizing Types I and II activities around abstract, complex ideas, the content and process modifications not suggested by the ETM and SEM can be included.

DEVELOPMENT

Enrichment Triad Model

For many years, Joseph Renzulli has worked with programs for the gifted, both as a consultant in program development and as an evaluator. Based on these experiences and a growing concern for comprehensiveness and defensibility of programs, he developed the ETM. His reviews of research on characteristics of individuals who are eminent and successful in their adult lives revealed the three well-defined clusters of characteristics: above-average intelligence, creativity, and task commitment. Because these three clusters of traits must interact to manifest themselves, an individual must have some type of real problem to investigate. Renzulli considered the following in the development of the ETM: (a) Roe's (1952) classic study of 64 eminent scientists, in which she concluded that the most important factor in their decisions to become scientists was the sheer joy of discovery; (b) Ward's (1961) fundamental principles underlying differential education for the gifted, one of which is that superior students should become acquainted with the basic methods of inquiry within the various fields of knowledge; and (c) Phenix's (1964) conclusion that learning different methods of inquiry is valuable because they are modes of active investigation. Renzulli also was influenced by Bruner's (1960) belief that young children are able to engage in critical inquiry.

Schoolwide Enrichment Model

The SEM is based on the ETM, which was developed and refined through extensive research. Although grounded in that research, it is expanded to include entire school populations. The model is based on successful practices that originated in special programs for gifted students and were validated through research. Continuing research has resulted in a detailed blueprint for school improvement that allows individual schools to develop unique programs based on local resources, demographics, school dynamics, and staff strengths and abilities (Renzulli & Reis, 2002).

RESEARCH ON EFFECTIVENESS

Enrichment Triad Model

Much research was incorporated into the formulation of the ETM, and numerous studies of its effectiveness have been published. For example, Reis and Renzulli (1982) compared the effectiveness of the model with 1,162 elementary students from 11 school districts. Students who scored at or above the 95th percentile on a standard achievement test were placed in Group A; Group B included those students who scored 10 to 15 percentile points lower. Double-blind rating of the students' products on eight specific and several general characteristics of quality revealed no significant differences between the two groups. Schack (1986) and Starko (1988) found that children who participated in the program showed greater creative productivity and improved self-efficacy. Roberts, Ingram, and Harris (1992) compared performance on the *Ross Test of Higher Cognitive Processes* (J. D. Ross & Ross, 1976) by gifted and average students at a treatment school who participated in Types I and II activities with comparable students at a nontreatment school. In the pretest, no significant differences were found between students at the two schools. On the posttest, gifted students at the treatment school scored significantly higher ($p < .02$) than gifted students at the nontreatment school and higher ($p < .01$) than average students at the treatment school. Although gifted students at the nontreatment school scored higher than average students at the treatment school, when pretest scores were subtracted from posttest scores, the average gain significantly ($p < .05$) favored average-ability students.

Studies have shown that isolated aspects of the ETM are effective. For example, a good Type II activity would be teaching students to use the Creative Problem Solving process (see Chapter 6). Another well-documented part of the ETM is the independent study aspect, which is present to a great

degree in Type III activities. Studies show these procedures to be highly effective when used in programs for the gifted (Renzulli & Gable, 1976).

Schoolwide Enrichment Model

Renzulli and Reis (1985) addressed key questions of organization and
implementation in the design of the SEM. Olenchak (1988, cited in
Renzulli & Reis, 2002) and Olenchak and Renzulli (1989) found that use of
the SEM resulted in more positive attitudes of teachers and students,
numerous high-quality creative projects, and increases in student-centered
enrichment activities. Olenchak (1990) found that students enrolled in
SEM schools had significantly more positive attitudes toward learning than
comparable students in schools that did not employ SEM. Factors contributing to more positive attitudes included curriculum compacting,
opportunities to study in areas of interest, greater understanding of the purpose of the program, and fewer people who felt the program was restricted
to a select few.

In a review of the research on the SEM, Renzulli and Reis (1994) concluded that use of the model (a) influences teachers' instructional practices
in a favorable way; (b) improves teachers' attitudes toward gifted students
and elementary students' attitudes toward learning; (c) is associated with
positive changes in many aspects, including instructional activities and
student projects; (d) encourages creativity and task commitment; (e) encourages diverse and sophisticated student products; (f) provides appropriate intervention for special populations of gifted students, including
underachieving students; (g) assists many students to plan appropriate career choices; and (h) can provide an appropriate curricular framework for
all students. They also reported that model implementation may improve
classroom climate, instructional processes, students' self-concept, and attitudes toward learning, as well as administrative support and staff morale.

Reis, Westberg, Kulikowich, and Purcell (1998) looked at the effect of
curriculum compacting on 336 high-ability students in Grades 2 through
6. On the *Iowa Test of Basic Skills* (ITBS), the scores of those students who
had compacted curriculum did not differ significantly from those students
who were taught the regular curriculum. Students' scores did not decline
even when the replacement (compacted) curriculum was not in the same
content area.

Hebert (1993, cited in Renzulli & Reis, 1994) conducted a longitudinal
study of nine senior high students who had been in an SEM program. The

major findings include that (a) Type III interests of students affect their postsecondary plans and (b) Type III processes serve as important training for later products.

In a comprehensive synthesis of the research on the SEM, Reis and Renzulli (2003, pp. 34–35) concluded that the use of the SEM

1. favorably influences teachers' practices
2. improves teachers' attitudes toward the education of gifted students and of elementary students' attitudes toward learning and self-concept
3. is associated with positive changes in many aspects of schooling including instructional activities and student projects
4. encourages creativity and task commitment in targeted students
5. encourages more diverse and sophisticated products
6. provides appropriate intervention for special populations of gifted students, including [those with learning disabilities] and those who are identified as underachieving
7. assists many students in traditional programs for the gifted as well as high-ability students in vocational/technical schools to plan appropriate career choices
8. can provide an appropriate curricular framework for all students, especially when the implementation of SEM includes the use of learning styles, interests, and curriculum compacting
9. can increase attitudes toward reading, as well as reading fluency and comprehension

JUDGMENTS

Advantages

Enrichment Triad Model
The most important advantage of the ETM is that it was designed specifically for use in programs for gifted students and, as such, is based on research about characteristics of gifted people who achieve. A related advantage is that it takes into account that programs for the gifted must be related to the regular curriculum, and they must build on or expand on the basic competencies taught to all children. With the ETM, the relationship

between the gifted and regular programs must be considered. Because it was designed specifically for use with the gifted, the ETM directly addresses the issue of and need for a qualitatively differentiated educational program for the gifted. Other models may modify one or two aspects of the curriculum, but most do not provide as comprehensive an approach or framework as does the ETM.

Another advantage of the ETM is that it provides an overall program framework, including guidelines for program philosophy, definition of giftedness, identification of the gifted, teaching activities, and strategies for program evaluation. A number of program alternatives and curricular approaches shown to be effective with gifted students can be integrated easily into the ETM, making it a defensible and effective approach. Also, the model is straightforward enough for parents, administrators, and students to understand easily.

Schoolwide Enrichment Model

In addition to the advantages of the ETM, the SEM influences the regular curriculum in numerous positive ways (Renzulli & Reis, 2002). Additionally, it is effective in schools with widely differing socioeconomic levels and school organizational patterns (Olenchak 1988; Olenchak & Renzulli, 1989), and its modifications provide many services to meet individual needs (Renzulli & Reis, 2002).

Disadvantages

Enrichment Triad Model

The most obvious disadvantage of the ETM is that educators have sometimes adopted the model without seriously considering the philosophical approach necessary for its implementation. Too often, the framework has been adopted and existing curricula have been incorporated into the framework, but few educators have made the philosophical and programmatic commitments that make the model effective.

Another disadvantage is that the ETM emphasizes the selection of children who show the most potential to succeed (according to society's definition of success) rather than, for example, children who (a) show an educational need for services based on their intellectual deviation from the average or (b) need a differentiated program because of their unique learning styles. A further disadvantage is that most of the research on which the three-ring conception of giftedness is based was done with adults. One cannot determine whether these characteristics were the causes or results of success. This disadvantage has serious consequences, particularly in the selection of children from certain subgroups of the population. Some of the more practical disadvantages of the ETM include difficulty in assessing task commitment and creativity, the fact that teachers are not trained to implement a model such as this (i.e., they are not scholars or methodologists in scholarly fields; they are trained to teach content rather than guide investigations), and the fact that the model appears to be deceptively simple.

Schoolwide Enrichment Model

Most of the disadvantages of the ETM have been eliminated in the SEM. The philosophical approach of enriched learning experiences and higher level thinking for all students is in line with current calls for and attempts at school reform. Research that addresses the concern of only looking at successful adults has been conducted in schools where the ETM or the SEM is in place.

In the SEM, assessment of students casts a wide net, allows for parent or student self-nomination, and provides the opportunity for "hidden" gifted students to surface through their participation in Type II activities or desire to engage in Type III activities. The main disadvantage remaining is personnel. Many teachers and administrators have yet to become comfortable with empowering students to direct their own learning and to study fewer topics in depth rather than covering the textbook. Additionally, legislators have become focused on accountability and measuring student achievement, and many districts and states mandate curricula that are aligned with standardized assessments. These assessments typically measure the memorization of factual information and force teachers to spend instructional time in traditional memorize-and-regurgitate lessons.

CONCLUSION

Enrichment Triad Model

The ETM has its drawbacks, but with careful consideration of its philosophical base, along with its specific strategies and how these fit with diverse student populations, teachers can implement it appropriately. Such a program also can have benefits for the overall program at the school, increasing student-centered opportunities and developing more favorable attitudes toward talent development in all students.

Schoolwide Enrichment Model

The SEM possibly could become the wave of the educational future. Its strengths—(a) building on the research and implementation of the ETM, (b) including the entire school in Types I and II activities, (c) offering specific structures and strategies for all teachers, and (d) including a response to many trends and issues of the school reform movement—may allow it to be more and more widely implemented. If this happens, the philosophy of the "rising tide lifting all ships" may be the hope of education and the promise of the future.

RESOURCES

Background Information

Reis, S. M., & Renzulli, J. S. (1985). *The secondary triad model: A practical plan for implementing gifted programs at the junior and senior high levels.* Mansfield Center, CT: Creative Learning Press.

Renzulli, J. S. (1994). *Schools for talent development: A practical plan for total school improvement.* Mansfield Center, CT: Creative Learning Press.

Renzulli, J. S., & Reis, S. M. (1985). *The schoolwide enrichment model: A comprehensive plan for educational excellence.* Mansfield Center, CT: Creative Learning Press.

Renzulli, J. S., & Reis, S. M. (1997). *The schoolwide enrichment model: A how-to guide for educational excellence.* Mansfield Center, CT: Creative Learning Press.

Renzulli, J. S., & Reis, S. M. (2002). *The schoolwide enrichment model: Executive summary.* Retrieved March 18, 2002, from http://www.sp.uconn.edu/~nrgt/sem/semexec.html

Instructional Materials and Ideas

Alvarado, A. E., & Herr, P. R. (2003). *Inquiry-based learning using everyday objects.* Thousand Oaks, CA: Corwin Press.

Green, T. D. & Brown, A. (2002). *Multimedia projects in the classroom.* Thousand Oaks, CA: Corwin Press.

Kettle, K. E., Renzulli, J. S., & Rizza, M. G. (1998). Products of mind: Exploring student preferences for product development using My way … An expression style instrument. *Gifted Child Quarterly, 1,* pp. 48–61.

Useful Web sites:

http://www. corwinpress.com

http://www. zephyrpress.com

CHAPTER 9

Shlomo and Yael Sharan: Group Investigations Model

Cooperative learning is a controversial issue among educators of gifted students. Although the benefits of collaboration and the importance of group interaction are widely recognized, many educators, parents, and students themselves feel that gifted students are exploited in most models of cooperative learning (Feldhusen & Moon, 1992; Mills & Durden, 1993; Robinson, 1991). The asymmetrical relationships built into peer tutoring approaches have negative consequences for both tutors and tutees (Foot, Morgan, & Shute, 1990). Furthermore, interactions among students in mixed-ability groups reveal three persistent challenges: inclusiveness, enacting the ideal, and monitoring growth (J. A. Ross & Smyth, 1995).

One significant exception is a model developed in Israel. Group Investigations, a student-centered approach to cooperative learning, is based on John Dewey's (1938, 1902/1943) philosophy that active experience, inquiry in a social setting, and reflective thinking are the tools of intellectual development. The Group Investigations model also derives theoretical support from research in cognitive development, social-learning theory, and group processes. In this view, learning is conceptualized as a dynamic, reciprocal process embedded in social, cultural, physical, and psychological environments. The ways people communicate and construct meaning, the kinds of knowledge valued, and individual access to knowledge all depend on social interaction and cultural context (Heath, 1983; Newman, Griffin, & Cole, 1989; Rogoff, 1990; Vygotsky, 1978).

The Group Investigations model is designed to incorporate students' interests, abilities, and past experiences in the planning of small-group activities. In this model, peer collaboration and student choice of projects is emphasized. Students form groups on the basis of friendship or interest in a topic or project, or to meet agreed-upon classroom goals (e.g., learning to value cultural diversity). Each student may belong to several different groups during a school term and has the freedom to leave one group to join another in the early stages of an investigation. Students are active in planning and evaluating their learning experiences as well as in the performance of learning tasks, experiences that promote self-efficacy and individual responsibility. Learning and cooperation are viewed as inherently satisfying. Mutually beneficial activities are emphasized, self-efficacy is promoted, and students' unique abilities and learning goals are respected (Sharan & Sharan, 1976).

Major goals of the Group Investigations model are to nurture democratic participation, develop students' skills in differential social roles, differentiate work assignments so that students need not duplicate each other's work, help students develop social skills that enable group members to work cohesively and deal effectively with differences or conflict. The model has a strong process orientation and aims to help students develop both cognitive and cooperative interaction abilities. Group Investigations is an ambitious and complex approach to cooperative learning that may not be appropriate for all subjects or all students (Sharan et al., 1984); however, the emphasis on complex content, student choice and planning, and its process-oriented structure makes Group Investigations an excellent collaborative-learning model for gifted students.

ASSUMPTIONS UNDERLYING THE MODEL

The Group Investigations model is based on the belief that cooperation and communication among students are keys to achieving the more important goals of learning and teaching. Students learn concepts and strategies best and enjoy learning more when they are engaged directly in activities in a social context. The goal of Group Investigations is to create a "group of groups" and transform the class into an active, inquiring community of learners.

Several assumptions about social relationships are intrinsic to this model. Friendship and mutual respect grow out of constructive cooperation in which goals and tasks are interdependent. Learning is best facilitated in small groups where members hold a personal attraction for each other and the tasks of the group are compatible with an individual's own values, goals, and interests. Finally, working together on mutually satisfying tasks can help students learn to value classmates from diverse racial or ethnic groups and break down cultural stereotypes.

About Learning

Learning is a natural process of social inquiry. Satisfying curiosity about the world, gaining a measure of control over one's several environments, and growing in the ability to make sense of perceptual data are as natural to a child as breathing. In classrooms, learning is most likely to occur when

- children have a role in planning and implementing learning tasks,
- competition and performance anxiety are reduced,
- communication and cooperation are encouraged,
- learning tasks are relevant to the individuals involved, and
- self-evaluation and reflective thinking are part of every project.

Learning and cooperation, interdependent primary goals of Group Investigations, are intrinsically rewarding. As a result, competition for extrinsic rewards is unnecessary.

About Teaching

The Group Investigations model fundamentally changes the relationship between teachers and students. The teacher is neither the main dispenser of knowledge nor the sole judge of products. Instead, the teacher's role is to act as a guide and adviser to help students investigate issues and solve problems. A teacher's role might be compared to Vygotsky's (1978) conception of a more skilled partner in thinking and problem solving. Initially, the teacher provides considerable structure and support in selection and design of learning activities. As students become more skilled in the use of inquiry processes and develop effective social interaction skills, the teacher gradually withdraws from the leading role and transfers many planning, decision-making, and group-maintenance responsibilities to students. This nondirective approach to teaching and learning is crucial to the development of self-directed, collaborative learners.

In the Deweyian tradition, a teacher must be an active inquirer and a reflective thinker. Examining experiences, beliefs, new information, and changing purposes is a critical factor in personal growth and thoughtful collaboration with others.

About Characteristics and Teaching of Gifted Students

The Group Investigations model, like many excellent teaching–learning models, was not developed for gifted students. Instead, the intent of the developers was to reform educational practice for all students through a variety of small-group learning methods. Group Investigations is an elaborate model that also was designed to improve relationships between racial and ethnic groups in integrated schools. Sharan and Sharan (1976) emphasize the importance of interest in a topic or friendship, rather than ability, in creating groups. Several researchers, however, have emphasized the importance of collaboration with peers (Damon, 1984; Doise & Mugny, 1984). The highest achieving students in mixed-ability cooperative learning groups gain limited benefit from helping others understand the material. Gifted students tend to ask questions regarding complex problem-solving processes and are more motivated to learn when able to advance at their own pace, as when they are grouped with similar-ability students (Garduno, 2001). Children of similar abilities, working together, make greater gains in achievement in conceptual development than do children in whole-class instruction or in peer tutoring situations (Phelps & Damon, 1989). In cooperative learning settings, students are constantly exposed to others' ideas, allowing them to listen to and reflect on the thinking and the solutions of fellow students (Garduno, 2001). Peer cooperation is essentially a dialogue between equals and incorporates many features of critical thinking—verification of ideas, clarity of communication, strategic planning, and contemplation of new patterns of thought (Damon, 1984). Students learn from each other because they are matched closely in knowledge and ability, no authority relationship exists between or among them, and they pool their efforts to work out a solution to a problem or understand a concept.

ELEMENTS/PARTS

Four broad dimensions are essential in the Group Investigations model. First, topics for investigation must be broad and general so that a number of related subtopics can be identified. Second, subtopics must be sufficiently challenging that a meaningful subdivision of labor and interdependence among group members is possible and necessary. Third, frequent communication within and between groups is essential as students plan, coordinate, collect information, analyze data, and integrate their work with that of other students and groups. Finally, the teacher must create a learning environment that stimulates interaction, search, and communication while maintaining an indirect, facilitative style of leadership.

Organization of the Classroom into a "Group of Groups"

Students organize into ad hoc groups with three to six members and investigate different aspects of a general topic, theme, or issue. The length of time scheduled for an investigation depends on the complexity of the topic, the maturation level of the students, and the format(s) selected for sharing results. As students work on different aspects of the topic, a steering committee composed of representatives from each group may be necessary to coordinate between-group planning and decision making. At other times, informal discussions are sufficient to maintain contact and exchange information with other groups.

Facilitating effective social relationships among group members, a complex and constantly evolving process, is essential to the achievement of group goals. In collaborative groups, learners provide academic and psychological support, encouragement, and constructive feedback to each other. Together, they monitor progress toward group goals. If students have little experience working in groups, teachers should not begin collaborative inquiry with Group Investigations. Sharan and Sharan (1976) suggest a range of small-group activities (e.g., discussions, communication activities, creative problem solving) to help students acquire the experience necessary to regulate their own learning and work cooperatively with peers. Teachers also can conduct a series of small-group seminars in which students observe and practice effective behaviors for discussion, goal setting, planning, decision making, and conflict resolution.

Multifaceted Tasks

Topics for Group Investigations must be sufficiently complex that a single student cannot complete the investigation alone. Learning tasks that do not require coordination of viewpoints, mutual exchange of views, or interdependence among group members are not appropriate. Topics are best organized as problems or questions that can be explored from several perspectives and have a variety of possible solutions (e.g., "Acts of civil disobedience are a result of institutional abuse of power"). The use of abstract generalizations can ensure that problems or questions are appropriate.

Multilateral Communication and Active Learning Processes

In Group Investigations, students must engage in a variety of communicative processes. Reading, summarizing, efficiently using reference materials, and collecting data are even more important than in traditional instruction because each student does a different part of the investigation. In the social context of the group, students plan together and decide what they will study, who is responsible for each part of the work, and how they will integrate their data. Students collect data from a variety of sources; therefore, strategies for interviewing, research design, analysis and organization of data, and procedures for evaluation must be negotiated among group members or demonstrated by a mentor. Integration of the varied data collected by individual group members into a coherent whole for presentation also requires listening, reflecting on and elaborating another's ideas, clarifying statements, and choosing the final format.

Teacher Behavior: Guiding and Communicating with Groups

For students to develop the autonomy necessary to carry out group investigations, teacher leadership must be indirect. Important teacher behaviors include the following:

- facilitating research
- consulting with a group or an individual about a specific aspect of a topic or process
- asking questions or suggesting ideas to help a group clarify a problem
- demonstrating a skill (e.g., polling methods) when a group requests assistance
- helping groups coordinate their activities

In addition, the teacher and students organize the classroom environment to facilitate communication, mobility, and access to information sources. One major purpose of Group Investigations is to build a community of learners in which academic work is coordinated, shared, and purposeful.

When a classroom is structured to promote choice, active planning, and decision making by students in a relaxed social atmosphere, the teacher's role changes from active direction of student learning to facilitation and guidance of multivariate group activities. Relinquishing control does not mean that the teacher abandons students to their own devices once groups are organized. In this model, the teacher assumes the responsibility for overall planning and selection of materials, structuring the learning environment, and teaching processes that help students organize a learning team. Students need guidance, but the adoption of a nondirective role by the teacher is prerequisite for changing learning from passive acceptance of information to an active decision-making and responsibility-sharing role. For many teachers, the most difficult task may be to recognize the necessity of freeing students to investigate problems or work out solutions in their own way and at their pace.

MODIFICATIONS
OF THE BASIC CURRICULUM

In the Group Investigations model, social inquiry in small groups, multilateral communication and cooperation, and active exploration of ideas and objects are emphasized. This approach dramatically changes curriculum and instructional practice. The traditional notion that information can be transmitted from a teacher (or other expert source), received by students, and evaluated through objective tests is totally rejected. Cooperative learning can be implemented only to the extent that traditional whole-class teaching is supplanted, not merely altered (Sharan, 1990).

Content Modifications

General topics, broad concepts, themes, or persistent issues are the content of Group Investigations. This approach to learning through collaboration requires that content be complex, multifaceted, and abstract. Methods of inquiry, particularly the scientific method, are integral, and variety is assured through the investigation of different subtopics by each small group. The study of methods comes about when the teacher instructs students on the use of techniques they need for their study, and the study of people can be incorporated easily as one facet of the selected topic.

Process Modifications

As a model of social inquiry, the structure of this model emphasizes higher level thought, open-ended questions, experimentation and discovery, group interaction, and reflective thinking. Students select their own topics and cooperatively plan investigations. Appropriate pacing and evidence of reasoning are an integral part of the group inquiry process. Because each student investigates a different aspect of a topic, variety is included as well.

Product Modifications

All students in a group collaborate on a single product but work individually on one or more facets of the product. A wide variety of products are possible, and data are transformed into a form suitable for presentations to an audience of peers and, on occasion, invited guests. Student products are designed to share information with classmates and are an integral part of the learning experience of an entire class. Student products are self-evaluated and evaluated by a jury of peers and the members of the group. If tests are given, questions are open-ended with a range of possible answers.

Learning Environment Modifications

The learning environment is modified by the teacher and students to support autonomy, mobility, group communication, and a wide variety of learning activities. During investigations, students must be free to leave the classroom to conduct research in other settings. As students work in groups, the environment is learner centered and interactive. Students work independently on varied complex tasks and participate in both self-evaluation and evaluation of group activities. With the wide variety of activities and complex, challenging tasks for gifted students, the modification of the psychological environment is assured. One recommendation is that teachers be sure that the physical environment is designed to support active inquiry and includes a rich assortment of varied equipment and materials. If these are not possible within the classroom, students must have access to them.

IMPLEMENTATION

The Group Investigations approach to collaborative inquiry learning can be adapted by teachers so that projects are appropriate for the students' abilities and backgrounds, the subjects studied, and the constraints of time and space in the classroom or school. Guidelines for implementation are organized into six stages: (a) identifying a topic and organizing research groups, (b) planning the learning tasks, (c) carrying out the investigation, (d) preparing a final product, (e) presenting the final product, and (f) evaluation individually and in small groups.

Identifying a Topic and Organizing Research Groups

The teacher designates a general subject or a broad theme based on curricular goals or persistent issues (e.g., social implications of technological development, problems of poverty and overpopulation, interdependence of all living things) important to students' educational growth. Teachers may arrange a joint experience, set aside a period of time for exploration, or both. For example, reading, viewing a film, listening to records or tapes, watching a videotape, going on a field trip, or listening to a guest speaker exposes students to a topic in advance. Alternatively, teachers may trust that students have a wealth of concepts and experience to help them make initial decisions about preference of topics to investigate. One typical way to organize a topic for investigation is to brainstorm possible subtopics, then categorize related ideas into research topics. The Taba Concept Development strategy (Chapter 10) is an excellent process to use for this purpose. Another excellent organizational tool is a web (Short & Pierce, 1990) of subtopics, as shown in Figure 9.1. The teacher and students all make suggestions during this idea-finding stage. Next, students choose a subtopic for investigation and join two or three other students with the same interest to explore and classify possible components of the subtopic and develop categories with potential for investigation. This step should not be rushed; students need time to explore and categorize ideas, assess the possibilities for investigation of a subtopic, and work out group arrangements. At this stage, three types of goals are considered: instructional, organizational, and social.

Instructional Goals

Students will

- form an overall view of the topic and its research possibilities,
- propose topics that pique their interest,
- classify suggestions into categories and subcategories, and
- focus on subtopics crucial to understanding rather than on peripheral features.

Organizational Goals

Students will

- join a group no smaller than three and no larger than six to study the topic of their choice,
- decide on ways for the groups to maintain contact and exchange ideas or coordinate activities during the course of the investigation, and
- organize the furniture and other resources in the classroom to meet their needs.

Social Goals

Groups will

- be composed of students of both genders and include students with different abilities and ethnic backgrounds whenever possible,

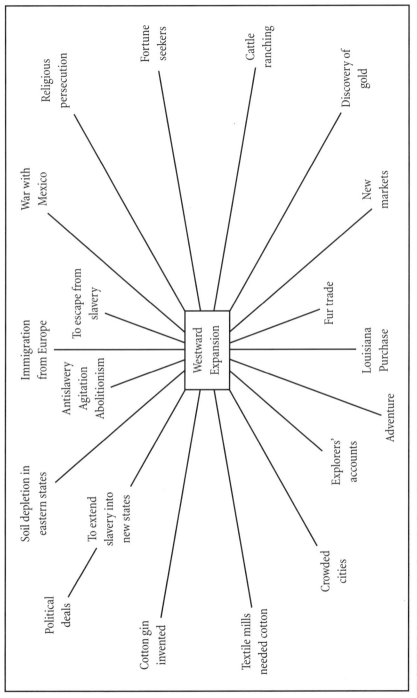

FIGURE 9.1. Example of a web of possible causes of westard expansion.

- discuss ideas to set (group) goals and identify subtopics that suit each member best,
- divide investigative tasks and establish work patterns that encourage mutual support and cooperation among members, and
- exist for the life of an investigation, not for an extended period of time. Students should work with different partners when new groups are formed to avoid cliques and to encourage social interaction.

During this organizational stage, teachers help students work through problems or difficulties encountered in stating problems and planning and organizing the project. The CPS process is a useful tool to assist students in designing an investigation project. Time spent preparing and trouble-shooting at this stage will pay off in smoother operations and more effective learning during later stages.

Planning the Learning Tasks

Each group must formulate a researchable problem about the topic chosen for investigation. Once the problem is defined, students set goals, identify sources of information, set up procedures to follow, and create a plan of action. In addition, each group must decide what parts of the investigation are best done by individual members and what parts require collaborative action. Three questions guide the planning stage of Group Investigations:

1. What shall we study? (Teachers may need to remind students that tasks for investigation are problems that can be considered in a variety of ways. Information can be obtained through a variety of sources, and a range of ideas, opinions, analyses, or solutions to the topic being studied need to be identified and explored.)
2. How do we study it? (Identify subtopics for each group member, possible resources, procedures, members' responsibilities, group participation, etc.)
3. For what purpose or goal do we study it? (How will we make sense of the information we collect? How will it be shared or presented? How will we apply the knowledge we acquire?)

Advocates of learning through a social inquiry process, such as Group Investigations, assume that a serious effort to answer these three questions will stimulate personal involvement by students. When students use inquiry processes, they actively generate ideas and construct knowledge—a process comparable to the work of practitioners in a discipline or craft.

As part of the planning process, specific areas in the classroom may be designated for special purposes. A seminar center where students can consult the teacher for special help, support, or feedback on an idea, or meet with others to communicate about work in progress, is essential. A center to house the master work schedule, resources, and materials needed for group work provides easy access to information sources and facilitates autonomy and mobility. Learning stations can be set up for viewing and listening to media, holding group discussions, conducting interviews, making graphics, and facilitating other activities needed by students during an investigation cycle. Other learning stations can be set up to provide specific kinds of information or experiences that all students need. In addition, each group should have a portable container to keep materials together.

Carrying Out the Investigation

During this stage, students implement their plans. They collect, analyze, and evaluate their data, draw conclusions, and coordinate their information with each other. This is typically the longest part of the study. It often takes longer than the teacher and students originally planned but should not be cut short as long as students are working productively.

When students are inexperienced, the teacher may have to intervene relatively frequently to steer them in more productive directions and help them overcome their insecurity and obtain needed resources, such as videotape equipment or permission to travel away from school to do an interview. Teachers also may need to demonstrate specific skills to one or more students. At times, the teacher may stop group work to help all students learn better discussion behaviors or processes to resolve conflict among group members. Cooperative and cognitive skills taught in the context of small-group collaboration are more likely to be learned and used in subsequent activities.

Collaborative learning involves multiple skills and information-management processes. Students collect data from a variety of sources; communicate with each other; discuss the implications of their data in terms of group goals; clarify ideas; and negotiate meaning. Thinking is more complex and students are involved more directly when they work to understand a concept or accomplish a mutually agreed-upon goal within a small group.

Preparing a Final Product

Once data have been gathered and analyzed, members of a group must determine how to present the information to others. This is primarily an organizational task, but it also includes processes of abstracting the essential meaning of the data, putting component parts into perspective so that others can gain an overall view of the topic, and planning a presentation that will communicate effectively and appeal to their audience.

At this stage, between-group planning must take place. What will each group present and how will it be presented? A steering committee may receive reports on each group's work, process requests for materials, create a time schedule for presentations, and make sure each group's presentation is realistic and interesting. Coordinating activities on a classwide basis requires cooperation to select and organize the overall format for presentation fairly and may require compromise on differences of opinion. Presentation formats may be jointly agreed upon, such as a mid–19th century fair or exposition (as described in Example 2 later in this chapter). At other times small groups may prefer to present, for example, a seminar, a television documentary, a simulation, or a debate.

The teacher should highlight some key ideas, such as the following, for students to consider during the design and preparation of their presentations:

- Emphasize main ideas, supporting evidence, and conclusions of the investigation.
- Identify the sources of data and other information.
- Include all members of the group in the presentation.
- Involve classmates as much as possible in the presentation. This may include giving them roles to perform or activities to do.
- Allow time for questions.
- Set and observe time limits.
- Make sure to request in advance all materials or equipment needed.

As students prepare to present the essence of what they have learned about their topic to an audience, they act as investigators, planners, decision makers, designers, and teachers. Rather than simply receiving and responding to transmitted information, students are creating and generating new knowledge for a socially valuable purpose.

Presenting the Final Product

Presentations are made to the entire class, and often to invited guests. If the presentation format were an exhibition, for example, each group might set up its display in a different part of the room or at various sites in the school or community. Groups take turns as viewers and presenters; all students in the class must participate as an audience for other groups so they can integrate all subtopics into the general concept or theme.

Presentation roles may be unfamiliar to them, but each group must communicate its ideas clearly. The teacher or a mentor may spend time with groups to demonstrate specific skills or help with technical details prior to a presentation. Some general suggestions for varied types of presentations follow:

- Speak clearly and expressively when addressing an audience but avoid lecturing.
- Practice the content of a speech and use notes only for reminders.
- Use a chalk- or whiteboard, chart, overhead projector, PowerPoint or other means to illustrate important concepts when giving an oral presentation.
- Use learning stations where classmates and visitors can do tasks or conduct experiments that have been set up to help them learn concepts or interact with the data.
- Dramatize an event or relationship that illustrates an important concept or issue from the investigation.
- Illustrate written reports or books with pictures, drawings, graphs, tables, or other visual devices that help to explain the data or illustrate the information.
- Conduct formal debates or panel discussions for an audience.
- Design a quiz program or a role-playing simulation to involve the audience (in this case, the necessary information needs to be given to the audience in advance).
- Make a videotape, slide show, or other audiovisual presentation and set up a viewing or listening station.
- Publish a newspaper or magazine to share the information with a wider audience.
- Create a simulation of a historic event or a possible future scenario.
- Conduct a trial to represent the laws and customs of a given civilization.

- Build a model in as much detail as possible and to scale, if appropriate. Label the essential features of the model and explain its function.
- Participate in an industrial fair. Showcase the group's model and compete for investors.

Making a presentation to share the results of group investigations is a powerful intellectual and emotional experience. Students demonstrate not only the knowledge they acquired during the investigation, but also their ability to plan, organize, coordinate, and produce a presentation that allows others to share that knowledge.

Evaluation

The Group Investigations model exposes students to constant evaluation by their peers and teachers throughout the study. Ideas, time spent on task, grasp of the subject, and dependability are highly visible. Interaction with peers in discussions, planning, decision making, and analysis and organization of data can be observed to assess communicative behaviors, social skills, and higher level thinking. During a group investigation, teachers may interview individual students formally or have frequent conversations with them to assess their academic growth. Teachers also may write brief observations of a student's cognitive, affective, or social behaviors on self-stick notes or labels, date them, and place the notes in student portfolios at the end of the day.

If formal tests are necessary, Sharan and Sharan suggest that each group prepare open-ended questions about the most important points of their presentation. The steering committee and the teacher work together to review questions and select two from each group for the test. If there were six groups, for example, each student would respond to 12 questions covering all aspects of the study. Students would get all the questions and have some time (1 or 2 weeks) to think about them before writing responses. This gives students time to review the topics and think about the ideas from the presentations. They can question members of other groups to clarify some data or conclusions from their investigation.

Group members become a committee of experts on their topic. Each group receives the written answers to their two questions and evaluates the classmates' answers. They can see how well their classmates understood the information presented about the topic and learn what other students thought about the ideas. Once questions have been evaluated, they are returned to the writers. Students can again discuss answers or evaluations with members of each research group. This multilateral communication and interaction is a powerful spur to intellectual development. Although this form of evaluation may be too complex for novice investigators, it is recommended for students with more experience in collaborative learning.

One form of evaluation with definite value for every student is self-analysis. At the beginning of an investigation, each student selects one or more cognitive and social goals. At regular intervals, the teacher schedules time for students to review their goals, reflect on their progress, and write a brief report for personal use. Groups map out the different steps they followed in their work, analyze factors that contributed to progress or complemented the work of other students, and make recommendations for future investigations. Using personal progress and group reports, students can reflect on their experiences, contributions to the group, and how other students contributed to their learning. This reconstructive evaluation helps students develop a broad and critical view of their own study procedures, achievement, and interactions with others. Reflection on practice is an excellent way to help students improve their ability to plan future investigations. A summary of teacher and student roles in each component of Group Investigations is given in Table 9.1.

Examples of Activities

Example 1: An Elementary Interdisciplinary Study
In an elementary classroom, students completed a study of seasons. The teacher wanted to extend the concept of "cycles" or phenomena that occur in patterned ways.

First, all students did a productive thinking activity to list many, varied, and unusual phenomena that occur or operate in cycles. Items on the list were discussed and arranged into the following categories: life, weather, economy, sports competition, holidays, reproduction, elections, mechanical devices, fashions in clothing, migration, and water.

Next, after exploring possible resources and thinking about the topic, May, Sally, Roland, and Bryan chose the topic of cycles in the economy and formed an interest group. They elected May to be their group leader and Bryan to serve on the coordinating committee. They also set up procedures to follow during the investigation and elected Sally to prepare and post a

(*text continues on p. 314*)

TABLE 9.1

Summary of Student and Teacher Roles and Activities in the Group Investigations Model

Step, Type, or Level of Thinking	Student		Teacher	
	Role	Sample Activities	Role	Sample Activities
Building discussion skills	Active participant	Speak concisely for 15 seconds.	Resource	Plan and implement experiences to assist students in the development of discussion skills.
		Listen reflectively; wait 3 seconds before responding.	Facilitator	Plan and implement training experiences for student observers.
		Reflect/summarize previous speaker's ideas before adding one's own.		Model active listening and concise speaking behaviors.
		Wait until all group members have spoken before speaking for second time.		
		Take a turn serving as an observer to note how well group members do on a specific skill.		
		Report results of observations in a constructive manner.		
Reflect on group process	Active participant	Use a Taba Interpretation of Data strategy to evaluate/reflect on group interaction: (a) identify specific behaviors that occurred during interaction, (b) analyze causes/effects of the behaviors, and (c) generalize how skills used in this session can be used in another context.	Resource	Plan and implement a small-group interaction activity, such as reaching consensus using *The Untitled Story* strategy (Graves & Graves, 1990).
	Reflective thinker		Facilitator	Review the steps and guidelines for an Interpretation of Data strategy.
	Evaluator		Planner	Have students meet their small groups to reflect on their group interactions and construct generalizations about behaviors.

(*continues*)

Students determine subtopics, organize research groups	Active participant Classifier Evaluator Decision maker	Use a decision-making strategy to (a) generate a list of many, varied subtopics; (b) generate criteria for evaluating alternatives; (c) reach consensus on several subtopics for investigation; and (d) generate support for the selection. Select a subtopic on the basis of interest. Form a group with two to five others who are interested in the same subtopic.	Planner Facilitator Resource	Plan and implement activities to assist studentsin the understanding of the main topic and stimulate interest in further investigations. Provide many, varied resources pertinent to the topic. Facilitate a discussion of possible subtopics. Assist students in generation of criteria for decision making. Allow students time to consider possible topics for investigation.
Groups plan investigation	Active participant Decision maker Planner	Identify what group members know about the subtopic and what they want to learn, and identify possible resources. Set goals for the investigation, identify resources needed, and list steps and responsibilities for the investigation.	Facilitator Resource	Circulate among groups to observe interaction, identify needs. Facilitate group thinking and organizational strategy discussions. Review specific skills as needed. Respond to student questions. Ask key questions to stimulate or redirect students' thinking.
Group members conduct research	Active participant Researcher Inquirer	Identify useful resources both in and out of classroom. Read. Observe.	Facilitator Resource	Provide resources and a possible format to assist students in data collection. Arrange for students to use resources outside the classroom for the collection of data.

(continues)

TABLE 9.1 *Continued.*
Summary of Student and Teacher Roles and Activities in the Group Investigations Model

Step, Type, or Level of Thinking	Student		Teacher	
	Role	Sample Activities	Role	Sample Activities
Group members conduct research *(continued)*	Active participant Idea finder Planner	Take notes. Organize and interpret information. Identify sources of data. Discuss data, coordinate activities with group members; integrate findings.		Respond to requests for information or help with thinking or search strategies.
Groups plan presentation		Appoint a member to the class steering committee. Identify the main idea in the group's integrated findings. (What is the main outcome of the research?) Identify a presentation format that will present ideas clearly, stimulate interest, and involve all group members. Use the Creative Problem solving strategy to plan and organize the presentation. Obtain equipment and materials required for the presentation.	Facilitator Planner Resource	Coordinate group presentation plans. Convene steering committee meetings periodically for joint planning, scheduling, and coordinating requests for special materials. Assist the committee or groups as needed to arrange for facilities and materials; clarify ideas. Ensure that all group members are involved in planning and presenting.

(continues)

Group presentation	Active participant Presenter Listener Evaluator	Present results of investigation in an interesting, well-organized manner. Respond to questions. Facilitate interactive experiences for other class members. Constructively evaluate others' work; reflect on appeal, clarity, and relevance of the presentation. Observe and select good ideas or techniques for future presentations.	Coordinator Resource Audience	Post presentation schedule. Review guidelines for audience participation and etiquette. Provide a brief evaluation form or set of questions for consideration. Sit back and enjoy the presentations. Facilitate evaluation discussions after each presentation.
Students and teacher evaluate their projects	Active participant Reflective thinker	As a group, prepare two open-ended questions about the main ideas of your findings. Answer questions from class members. As a small group, evaluate classmates' responses to your test questions. As a group, evaluate your own interactions and presentation. Individually evaluate own participation and growth. Contribute thoughtfully to "wrap up" discussion and evaluation of the project. Record ideas for new investigations.	Facilitator Resource Evaluator	Review and compile test questions. Present list of questions to all students for study. Provide criteria and facilitate evaluation of test questions by small groups. Guide discussion to integrate and "wrap up" the group investigations.

weekly schedule. Roland then led the group in a decision-making process to decide which specific aspects of the economy would be studied. The group made a list of many, varied alternatives, then asked the following questions about each alternative:

1. Will there be enough information available on this aspect of the economy?
2. Will studying this aspect of the economy help us learn more about cycles?
3. What other aspects of the economy could be integrated with this one?
4. Will this aspect contribute interest to our presentation?

After some reflection, May chose to investigate seasonal retail sales, Roland chose the causes and effects of consumer confidence, Sally chose the causes and effects of depressions, and Bryan chose the causes and effects of discovery and exploitation of a scarce resource (e.g., oil).

The students then used the Creative Problem Solving process (Chapter 6) to engage in fact finding, selecting their problem statement and proposed presentation project, and identifying the roles and responsibilities of each member of the group. They also set time schedules for group meetings to coordinate their joint investigation. For the next 3 weeks, students read, observed, and interviewed members of their community to learn more about their topics. In group meetings, they explored the application of the law of supply and demand to their specific subject and chose to design a boom-and-bust simulation for their presentation. During the fourth week, they wrote a scenario, created various roles for participants, and designed materials to be used in the simulation. At the same time, they prepared comparison charts to summarize their new knowledge at the end of the simulation.

While this group was exploring economic cycles, other groups investigated other subtopics from the list generated by the class. The coordinating committee met with the teacher periodically to plan schedules and review plans so that presentations would go smoothly. Because the economy group planned an interactive simulation, the coordinating committee scheduled the presentation near the end of the day so the classroom could be rearranged to provide space for the activity.

After the group completed the boom-and-bust simulation, Roland led a discussion of feelings that participants had experienced during the activity. After the discussion, he summarized the feelings that had been expressed and linked them to the main ideas discovered in the investigation and summarized in the comparison charts.

In the final step of the group investigation, the four group members jointly evaluated the strengths and limitations of their project, assessed their own contributions to its success (or limitations), and summarized what they had learned and what they still wanted to know. All other groups followed a similar procedure.

Example 2: A Secondary Interdisciplinary Unit

☛ **Broad Theme:** Westward expansion

☛ **Generalization:** Many apparently unrelated social, economic, political, and personal factors led to westward expansion in the United States and, in turn, were affected by the westward movement.

☛ **Goal:** Students will make connections between historical, scientific, economic, literary, cultural, and religious movements of the first half of the 19th century and infer their influence(s) on the exploration and settlement of western North America.

☛ **Presentation Format:** A mid–19th century fair or exposition

Figure 9.1, shown previously in this chapter, illustrates a web of causes or factors leading to westward expansion in the United States. High school students generated this web after an introduction to the theme and an opportunity to examine several sources of information (e.g., texts, novels, biographies, newspapers, videotapes, realia). (An alternative generative process is the Taba Interpretation of Data strategy; see Chapter 10.)

Following the web discussion, students reflected on the subjects and signed up for a group based on their interest(s). Group size was capped at six; if all the student slots for a subtopic had been taken, a student could choose to work on another area of interest or, in rare instances, propose an independent project in the area of interest. In small groups, students used a fact-finding strategy (see Chapter 6 on Creative Problem Solving) to assess prior knowledge of group members, forecast additional information they wanted to discover, and made a plan to guide the investigation. The Taylor Multiple Talent Model (Maker, 1982b; Maker & Nielson, 1995) includes four steps for planning: (a) a clear statement of purpose and questions to guide the investigation, (b) a list of resources and materials needed, (c) a sequence of steps needed to reach the goal, and (d) a list of possible problems and at least one alternative way to solve or bypass each problem. The next step is to discuss the plan with the teacher (or a mentor), show how the small-group goal is related to the theme goals, and reach consensus on the plan.

A group investigating the abolitionist movement, for example, might plan to have each of four students select a leading abolitionist and study his or her life using biographies, fiction, the abolitionist's own writing, and contemporary views. Students then prepare to participate in a symposium as the abolitionist they had studied. One person would focus on abolitionism as a social reform movement, using history and fiction to gain a broader view of the topic, then moderate the symposium.

Each student pursues an individual study with an interdependent goal. In group meetings, students discuss progress toward the goal, share information they discover, make decisions, and plan the presentation. In private, each student reads, reflects, and writes a position paper for the symposium that incorporates the language and ideas of the abolitionist he or she had chosen. The time plan for this group includes more time for reading and writing than would the work of a group that chose, for example, to build a model of a textile mill to demonstrate the economic connections between cotton growers in the South and milling towns in New England. Members of the mill group also would do research to learn about textile mills in New England but probably would spend more time designing and constructing the model. In each case, tasks and goals are interdependent.

MODIFYING THE MODEL

The Group Investigations model incorporates most of the content, process, product, and learning environment modifications recommended for gifted students. Care should be taken to select abstract or complex topics, themes, or persistent issues that challenge the thinking of gifted students and pique their interest. The authors of the model have recommended process changes comparable to those recommended by Maker (1982b), Maker and Nielson (1995), and Renzulli and Reis (1985). Teachers, however, must look at other models to find guidelines for developing complex thinking processes. The levels of analysis, synthesis, and evaluation in the Cognitive Taxonomy (Chapter 3) are essential for this approach. In addition, the Creative Problem Solving process (Chapter 6) and the Hilda Taba Teaching Strategies (Chapter 10) are excellent models to help students organize their investigations, make sense of their data, resolve conflicts, and communicate more effectively.

Product and learning environment changes recommended for Group Investigations are essentially the same as those recommended for gifted students. In programs for the gifted, greater emphasis is placed on submitting products to appropriate audiences, such as magazines, newspapers, community groups, government representatives, or other decision makers, in addition to making presentations to other students.

DEVELOPMENT

Sharan and Sharan (1976) based their small-group learning models on the theories of John Dewey, with his emphasis on the importance of experience and the interdependence of members of a community, and those of Jean Piaget, who theorized that a child actively constructs meaning through interaction with objects and others in the environment. Dewey (1943) advocated changes in instructional practice and classroom organization to respond to children's natural learning abilities and recommended changes that allow students to communicate with others, actively observe, research, experiment, discover information, and reflect on real experiences. He strongly believed that democratic principles must be taught and experienced in classrooms designed to support active communication (Dewey, 1944) if students were to be prepared to function effectively in democratic societies. He also pointed out that the words *communication* and *community* have common linguistic roots and that learning to communicate effectively requires participation in a variety of social interaction experiences.

Piaget (1963) hypothesized that development is an ongoing process of assimilation of sensory data, accommodation (modifying existing cognitive structures when data no longer fit), the experience of disequilibrium when new ideas and old structures are in conflict, and integration (revising or transforming cognitive structures that are no longer useful in explaining natural or social phenomena). Like Dewey, Piaget believed that peer interaction facilitates development. He argued that cognitive conflict among peers helps learners see a concept from different perspectives and, thus, construct more adequate representations.

Social learning and group contact theories also are important to the Group Investigations model. Following school integration, many educators, concerned about wide disparities in achievement between students from dominant social groups and those from lower socioeconomic or ethnic minority groups, designed a number of approaches to reform educational practice.

Several cooperative learning programs have been developed and tested in classrooms in the United States and other countries over the past 30-plus years. Model developers claim many and varied benefits for cooperative learning (e.g., improved achievement for all students, improved social skills, improved peer relations). Cooperative learning models, however, differ radically in structure and philosophy (Kagan, 1985). Phelps and Damon (1989) identify three approaches:

1. Peer tutoring, in which an "expert" student teaches a "novice" to master objectives determined by teacher or text
2. Cooperative learning teams, in which children work jointly on the same problem or separately on individual components of the same problem
3. Peer collaboration, in which relative novices work together to complete tasks or solve problems that none of them could do alone

In collaborative learning, peer relationships are more symmetrical; cognitive development and knowledge or skill needed to solve problems is more equivalent than in the highly structured forms of peer tutoring or cooperative learning. The peer tutoring approach to cooperative learning is an integral part of several methods developed by Robert Slavin (1983). His Student Teams Academic Divisions model is used in this chapter as an exemplar of peer tutoring. An example of cooperative learning teams is the original Jigsaw model developed by Aronson, Blaney, Stephan, Sikes, and Snapp (1978). Group Investigations (Sharan & Sharan, 1992) is an outstanding example of the third approach, peer collaboration. Theories from sociology and group dynamics also have been incorporated by the Sharans to create a model that still maintains the philosophical and theoretical approach of their small-group teaching methods.

RESEARCH ON EFFECTIVENESS

With Nongifted Students

Numerous studies on cooperative learning in small groups with students in almost all grades have been conducted (see Johnson, Johnson, & Maruyama, 1983, for a meta-analysis of these studies). In an early study of small-group teaching methods with children in Grades 2 through 6, Sharan, Hertz-Lazarowitz, and Ackerman (1980) compared the achievement of children working cooperatively in small groups with that of peers in traditional whole-class instruction. Students working in small groups scored significantly higher on questions that required higher level thinking or creativity. Scores on lower level questions did not differ significantly. Behavior patterns established through cooperative learning experiences were found to transfer and operate in contexts and situations other than those found in classrooms (Hertz-Lazarowitz, Sharan, & Steinberg, 1980).

In a large-scale investigation, Sharan et al. (1984) studied the effects of participation in either of two different models of cooperative learning—Group Investigations (GI) and Student-Teams Academic Divisions (STAD) (Slavin, 1980)—or traditional whole-class instruction (WC) on academic achievement and interethnic relations of junior high school students. In general, the achievement of students in either of the cooperative learning classes was superior to that of students in whole-class instruction. Students in STAD and WC had slightly higher scores on low-level test questions; students in GI had significantly higher scores on questions that required more complex thinking. These findings were consistent across all ability levels and in all ethnic groups. However, a finding that the most advanced students, previously ability-grouped in English classes, made smaller achievement gains than had been expected is disturbing to advocates for gifted children. The authors suggested that this result may have been due to the abolition of ability grouping during the study, but they have no data to confirm or deny that inference. The authors reported some methodological problems with the research in literature classes but concluded that trends suggest that the GI method is better for developing higher level thinking than it is for helping students to acquire specific information.

In general, students who participated in GI were most cooperative, those in STAD were somewhat less so, and those in WC were most competitive.

The GI method clearly was superior in promoting cross-ethnic cooperation. The distinction between the two methods of cooperative learning appears to hinge on the ways in which peer relationships are structured by the method. In STAD, academically successful pupils help less successful pupils, usually of a lower socioeconomic or minority ethnic group, to master subject matter assigned by the teacher. The status of students in a STAD group basically is the same as that in the classroom or the society as a whole.

The key to the superiority of the Group Investigations model in improving social relationships is in the design of the group task and the structure of peer interactions. Each group member performs a different task, mutual assistance is required to meet group goals, and all members of the group are equally important to the success of the project. Peers are potential sources of ideas and information. Subjects for investigations and plans of operation for each group differ, so less social comparison and competitive behavior is present than when all members of the class have the same task to do.

Sharan and Shachar (1988) compared language and achievement of (a) 8th-grade students using the Group Investigations method and (b) students in whole-class instruction in ethnically mixed geography and history classes. They used pretest and posttest measures of achievement and videotaped discussions of 27 groups of students (3 groups of 6 students selected randomly from each of 9 classrooms). Data about students' interethnic cooperation and verbal and intellectual behaviors were extracted from the videotapes and analyzed by two judges. Students from the GI classes showed a very superior level of academic achievement on questions requiring both low-level and high-level answers, greater interethnic cooperation, and greater equality in the frequency of speech acts by members of the two ethnic groups. The data obtained from group discussions correlated highly with the results of achievement tests, indicating that small-group study leads to significantly higher performance on tests of academic achievement. Other significant findings were that ethnic minority students in the GI classes showed greater language proficiency and used more complex thinking strategies than did ethnic minority students in traditional whole-class instruction.

With Gifted Students

Research using the Group Investigations model with gifted students would be valuable, but at this time few studies have been reported. A notable exception is Coleman and Gallagher's (1995) study comparing gifted middle school students in cooperative learning programs with those in schools successfully blending the school reform initiative with gifted education. They identified the following strategies to differentiate cooperative learning for gifted students (p. 377):

- different tasks that vary in complexity;
- open-ended tasks where students set their own outcomes;
- assigning multiphase tasks where some of the work is completed independently;
- assigning self-paced tasks like the Team Assisted Instruction in math;
- Team Games Tournaments asking advanced bonus questions;
- expert groups that allow gifted students to work together;
- interest-centered groups where students cluster around topics they choose;
- homogeneous groups within the heterogeneous classroom;
- Jigsaw content materials with more difficult materials for gifted students;
- assigning the gifted students a specific role (i.e., teacher–facilitator);
- cross-grade grouping so that younger gifted students can work with older students;
- Team Games Tournaments competition among same-ability performance levels; and
- self-selected groups where students choose their own groups.

Many of these strategies were "created" by teachers in the studies in response to perceived student learning need. Some strategies require differentiation of the task assigned to the cooperative learning groups, as noted here:

- varying the complexity level for the group
- providing open-ended activities that allow students to set their own limits
- allowing students to pace themselves at their own learning rate through the content (Team Assisted Instruction in math)
- encouraging the creation of products that require several types or levels of skills
- giving assignments requiring multiple phases and including some independent components

- asking more complex or difficult "bonus questions" (Team Games Tournament)
- expecting some students to become "experts" to share particular knowledge within the cooperative learning groups

Coleman and Gallagher (1995) concluded that cooperative learning is an appropriate strategy to meet the needs of gifted students when it is carried out in a supportive learning environment and it includes the elements and strategies discussed above.

JUDGMENTS

Group Investigations is an excellent model for collaborative learning in classrooms for the gifted. When gifted students lack the opportunity to attend homogeneously grouped classes, this model also can be used to structure small-group learning activities that offer greater opportunities for gifted students.

Advantages

Most of the curriculum modifications recommended for gifted students are integrated into the Group Investigations model. Students have freedom of choice and opportunities to engage in complex and functional thinking, investigate real problems and issues, interact with peers, and create a variety of products for real audiences. Students have many opportunities to learn social interaction skills, deepen their conceptual understanding, and express their creativity. Students participate in inquiry in the same ways that professionals in a field would do. Thus, their activities and products are authentic and functional. Student participants in Group Investigations report satisfaction with this approach and consistently show greater achievement on tests of higher level thinking or creativity. In addition, students report a wider circle of friends and greater appreciation of the talents of others.

The Group Investigations model differs from other models of cooperative learning in several essential ways. Students select topics of interest and plan investigations rather than performing a teacher-prescribed task in a group setting. Complex and functional thinking skills are integrated with interesting and challenging content. Finally, students are evaluated by their own individual products and on group projects. The emphasis is on self-evaluation of real products and contributions to group success rather than scores on basic skills tests. Based on an extensive analysis of the research on cooperative learning, Robinson (1991) made five recommendations for the use of cooperative learning with gifted students (pp. 7–8):

1. Cooperative learning in the heterogeneous classroom should not be substituted for specialized programs and services for academically talented students.
2. If a school is committed to cooperative learning, models which encourage access to materials beyond grade level are preferable for academically talented students.
3. If a school is committed to cooperative learning, models which permit flexible pacing are preferable for academically talented students.
4. If a school is committed to cooperative learning, student achievement disparities within the group should not be too severe.
5. Academically talented students should be provided with opportunities for autonomy and individual pursuits during the school day.

With the exception of the first recommendation, the Group Investigations model meets these standards and can be used effectively in programs for gifted students.

Disadvantages

The lack of recent or ongoing research on this model is a disadvantage. The model is research based, but apparently little research has been done in recent years.

Because of its complexity, the Group Investigations model may not be appropriate for young gifted students. Some experiences in group processes, conflict resolution, planning, decision making, and organizational skills are prerequisite to participation in this approach to collaborative inquiry. Unless students have mutual respect and a disposition to work together to meet group goals, interdependence can be a problem when one or more students fail to fulfill their responsibilities. Problems can be solved by careful planning and formulation of research questions, but teachers and students must be prepared to deal with uncooperative individuals.

Availability of resources and mentors may be a problem in many schools. This approach to learning requires a variety of information sources and the ability to move freely from the classroom to other sites. School rules or transportation problems may interfere with freedom of access to needed information. In some cases parents may be able to assist, but this again requires careful coordination and scheduling.

One factor that may concern some teachers and parents is that the Group Investigations model discourages competition for grades and does not focus on acquisition of specific information. All students do not study the same content, and some students may not do as well on achievement tests; research results are mixed on this point. To avoid criticism for lack of rigor, teachers must be prepared to document student progress with portfolios, examples of sophisticated products, examples of professional behavior, and results of assessment using measures other than traditional standardized tests.

CONCLUSION

Collaborating with peers in social inquiry is recognized by many cognitive psychologists and educators as the most effective means of intellectual and social development. Group Investigations is an excellent model for this purpose, but it does require careful organization, planning, and multilateral coordination in the classroom, school, and community. Although gifted students can learn to make many of the arrangements necessary for access to information, cooperation from parents, school officials, and community mentors still is necessary for the success of a complex inquiry project. A relatively simple investigation can be completed in as little as 2 weeks. Investigations of more complex concepts, themes, or issues may involve students for several weeks or longer.

A key to the success of collaborative learning is the competence and preparation of teachers. With this model, teachers can create conditions that are more conducive to learning, that motivate students to learn and achieve at higher levels, and that foster more positive social relationships.

These are primary goals of differentiated education for gifted students as well. The Group Investigations model, although embedded in the paradigm of cooperative learning, includes most of the recommendations for differentiated curriculum for the gifted. Students develop research skills, focus on open-ended tasks, create new ideas or construct products that challenge existing ideas, and participate in functional, socially viable projects. The multitude of possibilities for content, process, and product modifications and the opportunities for mutually reinforcing experiences make this model of collaborative learning an important addition to teaching–learning methods for gifted students.

RESOURCES

Background Information

Robinson, A. (1991). *Cooperative learning and the academically talented student: Executive summary*. Storrs, CT: National Research Center on the Gifted and Talented.

Sharan, S. (Ed.). (1990). *Cooperative learning: Theory and research*. New York: Praeger.

Sharan, S., Hare, P., Webb, C. D., & Hertz-Lazarowitz, R. (Eds.). (1980). *Cooperation in education*. Provo, UT: Brigham Young University Press.

Sharan, Y., & Sharan, S. (1992). *Expanding cooperative learning through Group Investigations*. New York: Teachers College Press.

Instructional Materials and Ideas

Booth, D., & Thornley-Hall, C. (1992). *Classroom talk: Speaking and listening activities from classroom-based teacher research*. Portsmouth, NH: Heinemann.

Dalton, J. (1992). *Adventures in thinking: Creative thinking and cooperative learning talk in small groups*. Portsmouth, NH: Heinemann.

Fleisher, P. (1993). *Changing our world: A handbook for young activists*. Tucson, AZ: Zephyr Press.

Kagan, S. (1989). *Cooperative learning: Resources for teachers*. San Juan Capistrano, CA: Resources for Teachers.

Sharan, S., & Sharan, Y. (1976). *Small group teaching.* Englewood Cliffs, NJ: Educational Technology Publications.

Short, K., & Burke, C. (1991). *Creating curriculum: Teachers and students as a community of learners.* Portsmouth, NH: Heinemann.

Short, K., & Pierce, K. (Eds.). (1990). *Talking about books: Creating literate communities.* Portsmouth, NH: Heinemann.

Useful Web sites:

http://www.CriticalThinking.com

http://www.zephyrpress.com

CHAPTER 10

Hilda Taba
Teaching Strategies

The Hilda Taba Teaching Strategies are structured, generic methods in which the teacher leads students through a series of sequential intellectual tasks by asking open-ended but focused questions. The four strategies are (a) Concept Development, (b) Interpretation of Data, (c) Application of Generalizations, and (d) Resolution of Conflict (also called Interpretation of Feelings, Attitudes, and Values). Although the strategies were developed as structures for discussions, they can be used to develop curriculum. Parts of strategies may be used as learning activities, and entire strategies, singly or in combination, can be used as the foundation on which instructional units may be built.

The four strategies, although not designed to be hierarchical or sequential, can be used sequentially because they build on each other. Within each strategy, however, the questions have a definite sequence, with a theoretical and practical justification for the order. A close associate of John Dewey, Taba incorporated many of his ideas along with the research and writings of Jean Piaget, Jerome Bruner, and Lev S. Vygotsky in developing her approaches to teaching and curriculum development. Although her strategies are of a generic nature and are appropriate for use in any content area, because of her social studies curriculum (Ellis & Durkin, 1972), Taba's methods are viewed by some as social studies techniques. As can be seen by examining the theoretical and empirical bases for the strategies, however, they are techniques for developing thinking skills, or in Piaget's terms, methods for arranging the environment so that maximum cognitive growth can occur.

On a personal note, C. June Maker's involvement with the Hilda Taba Teaching Strategies has been interesting and rewarding. After the first series of training in their use, Maker's reaction was similar to an "Aha!" experience.

Another immediate reaction was that these strategies, particularly the second, Interpretation of Data, were close to what Maker had always attempted to do in her teaching, although her methods always were lacking in some way. Taba had perfected these methods and even had data to show that they were effective. Furthermore, the methods that Taba developed for training teachers were the best Maker had encountered: demonstrations and modeling; analysis of the demonstrations; step-by-step planning; team planning and team tryouts; and classroom tryouts, taping, and self-analysis. Both the teaching strategies and the teacher-training process have had a profound, positive effect on Maker's teaching and her writing.

ASSUMPTIONS UNDERLYING THE MODEL

In developing the teaching strategies, Taba rejected the following assumptions commonly made about children's thinking because they tend to retard progress in developing thinking skills:

- An individual must accumulate a great deal of factual knowledge before thinking about this knowledge base.
- Thinking skills are developed only through "intellectually demanding" subjects (e.g., physical sciences, math, and foreign languages).
- Abstract thinking is an ability that can be developed only in bright or gifted children.
- Manipulation of the environment will not improve or cause growth in thinking skills because cognitive growth is locked into a predetermined developmental time sequence.

These ideas were rejected and more positive alternatives proposed due to the results of Taba's three research projects (Taba, 1964, 1966; Wallen, Durkin, Fraenkel, McNaughton, & Sawin, 1969).

About Learning

Probably the most basic idea underlying the Taba strategies is acceptance of Piaget's (1963) beliefs about cognitive development. He believed that an invariant sequence of cognition occurs at particular ages and that specific types of thinking are exhibited at each developmental stage. Although discussing all of Piaget's ideas in this chapter is impossible, we briefly present a few of the general principles necessary to understanding the teaching strategies.

Sequence

Cognitive development is sequential and does not vary from this sequence. Children begin at the sensorimotor stage and progress sequentially, without skipping any stages, through preoperational to concrete operations. Finally, they achieve formal operations at about age 11. Change, or cognitive growth, occurs through children's interactions with the environment and their attempts to construct their own reality or organize their world. As children interact with the environment and attempt to interpret it using increasingly sophisticated ways of thinking, the phenomenon of disequilibrium occurs; they experience discomfort because they begin to recognize previously unnoticed inconsistencies. When this happens, they attempt to consolidate and integrate various schemes for interpreting what is seen to achieve equilibrium (and be "comfortable") again.

Assimilation and Accommodation

The concepts of assimilation and accommodation are related closely to equilibrium and disequilibrium and are crucial to understanding pacing in the Taba model. A somewhat simplistic, but effective, way of explaining the two ideas begins with the conception of a person's mind as a filing system with file folders representing categories (e.g., dogs, furniture, books). When new information comes in, it needs to be filed somewhere in the system. The individual doing the filing essentially has the following three choices: (a) fit the information as it is into one of the existing categories; (b) change the information in some way so that it fits into the existing system; or (c) change the system in some way so that it can handle the new information. This change can be a small one, such as adding a new category, or it can be more extensive through redefining a whole series of categories or even reorganizing the whole system.

In this example, filing the information as it is represents a form of assimilation. Changing the information is another form of assimilation, which occurs when the item does not fit but there is no desire to change the system. Accommodation is represented by some change in the system, from limited (making a new category) to extensive (revising the entire structure). The changed system that results from an extensive revision is a more sophisticated one. Thus it is with cognitive growth. Individuals experience disequilibrium when they recognize inadequacies in their existing organization of reality, so they make changes that improve that organization. They now experience equilibrium again. Intellectual growth, then, can be seen as a progression of assimilation, attempted assimilations that will not work, necessary accommodations, and then new assimilations at a higher order.

Developmental Trends

As children progress through the stages of cognitive development, they become increasingly able to use more formal systems of logic and to rely on symbols of meaning. A second trend is away from egocentrism or an egoistic view of the world toward the ability to differentiate the self from the rest of the world. A third related trend in development is toward internalization and "interiorization." Actions become less overt and more internal. In this movement, individuals go through distinct stages. The thought processes of previous stages are incorporated into the thinking at higher levels, but at each higher level, the processes are qualitatively different from those at lower stages. As children mature, they develop cognitively at their own rate, with movement through the stages determined by the interaction of both internal and external factors.

Facilitating Cognitive Growth

The one aspect of Piaget's theory not accepted by Taba is environmental influences on cognitive growth. Although Piaget recognized the importance of a child's interaction with the environment as the growth processes occur, he believed that deliberate manipulation of the environment to enhance development or to quicken its rate is a futile exercise. In other words, educators can do nothing to hasten or improve the quality of a child's cognitive development. They must wait for these natural changes to occur. Experiences that provide for horizontal elaboration (e.g., enrichment within stages) can be helpful, according to Piaget, but vertical elaboration (e.g., enrichment at different levels) is neither helpful nor desirable.

In contrast, Taba's basic assumption is that the environment is extremely important; it can and should be manipulated so that maximum horizontal and vertical elaboration occurs. In other words, she agrees with the sequence identified by Piaget but disagrees with his deterministic assumptions about how growth occurs.

One of the most important ideas underlying the Taba strategies is that thinking involves an active transaction between an individual and the information with which he or she is working. This idea has numerous implications for the learning process. It means, for one thing, that children do not develop their thinking skills by memorizing the products of adults' thinking. Children develop these skills by manipulating ideas, examining them critically, and trying to combine them in new ways. Data become meaningful only when individuals perform certain mental operations on those data. Even if children reach exactly the same conclusions as an adult after reviewing certain materials, the process of manipulating the information is necessary and valuable. This is not to say that children should not read the conclusions of others. They certainly should, but they also should be encouraged to reach their own conclusions and to examine the data of others critically to see if they would draw the same conclusions.

A second assumption relates content and process. Although Taba believes that thinking skills can be developed through any subject matter (i.e., not just through the so-called intellectually demanding subjects), process cannot be separated from content. The "richness" and "significance" of the content with which children work will affect the quality of their thinking, as will the processes used and the initial assistance given in developing these processes. Because of this belief, every lesson has a content and a process purpose that are interrelated and can be accomplished by the particular strategy. Selection of content that is rich and significant enough to be appropriate for developing thinking skills then becomes an important aspect of learning the teaching strategies, as does the organization of that content.

Another relationship between content and process centers around Taba's ideas about "thought systems" in each content area. Although the precise nature of the relationships between content areas and the processes used by scholars in those areas is unclear, Taba hypothesizes both generic processes of inquiry cutting across all types of content and specific processes of conceptualization in each area. For example, all areas deal with such processes as inferring cause–effect relationships. In the social sciences, however, multiple causation and probabilistic reasoning are much more important than in the physical sciences, where phenomena are more easily predicted. In short, the nature of the content and the thought systems in each content area determines in part the most important thinking skills to be practiced by the students.

About Teaching

Unfortunately, not all teaching results in learning. Because teaching is a complex process requiring an infinite number of decisions that must meet many criteria, different analyses and teaching strategies may be required to meet varied objectives. Generic strategies, however, can be applied across disciplines to meet multiple learning objectives.

The Importance of Specific Strategies
Productive teaching involves "developing strategies that are focused sharply on a specific target while at the same time integrating these specific strategies into an overall strategy that accommodates the generic requirements of multiple objectives" (Taba, 1966, p. 42). In other words, many thinking skills can be taught, and particular methods can be used for developing different thinking skills. Before teachers can be successful in developing thinking skills, they must have a clear idea of how these thinking skills are manifested and what methods can be used to develop them. One specific effect of this idea on Taba's methods is that each teaching strategy and each step in each strategy has specific "overt" and "covert" objectives. In other words, she pinpoints the behavioral (overt) manifestations of the underlying (covert) thinking processes.

Related to the development of thinking skills and following from her agreement with Piaget's sequence of cognitive development is Taba's (1964) assumption about the sequencing of learning experiences. If educators assume a sequential order in the development of thought processes, learning experiences also should be sequenced so that each step develops skills that are prerequisites for the next step. This sequence applies to day-to-day learning experiences provided for children, as well as to experiences spanning a single school year or a number of years.

Teacher Questions
A crucial factor in developing thinking skills and the sequencing of learning experiences is appropriate questioning by the teacher. Important aspects of teacher questions include open-endedness, pacing, and sequencing and patterning. Open-ended questions allow for and encourage responses at different levels of abstraction, sophistication, and depth, and from different perspectives. Pacing refers to the match between students' capacity for mastering the skills at each step and the time allowed for them to do so. Sequencing and patterning are accomplished through use of the strategies and are particularly important in that the "impact of teaching does not lie

only in the frequency of single acts" (Taba, 1966, p. 43) but also in the ways these single acts (questions) are combined into sequences and patterns.

Based on Taba's work, literature, research, personal experience, and taped classroom discussions, Schiever (1991) developed 10 principles of effective questioning that can be applied to all content areas, classroom and playground problems or situations, and informal interactions between teachers and students:

1. Questions are focused.
2. Questions are open-ended.
3. Questions require the use of information.
4. Proof-of-reasoning questions are asked.
5. Wait-time is allowed.
6. Discussion is appropriately paced.
7. Individual student responses are accepted without teacher comment.
8. Student responses are not repeated by the teacher.
9. A variety of ideas and student interactions are sought.
10. Clarification and extension questions are asked as needed.

The first four principles apply to both written and oral questions; the last six apply to oral questions, especially in the context of a guided discussion.

Rotating Learning Experiences

Taba's belief in the value of "rotating" learning experiences that require assimilation and accommodation also is based on an assumption about how development occurs (Taba, 1966). Putting this idea into practice requires alternating experiences in which children absorb information with those experiences that challenge their current mental schemes for organizing the information. Primitive or inadequate schemes can be challenged by having children consider information that is "dissonant with their current schema" (p. 23) so they are required to revise their present conceptualization. The teacher's task is not to correct the student or to point out these inconsistencies but to present or otherwise arrange the situation so that students encounter the dissonant information in activities with potential for causing change. Students must manipulate data themselves. To be successful, however, this process of rotating experiences must "offer a challenge that is sufficiently beyond the student's present schema to induce accommodation, and yet not so far removed that the student cannot make the leap" (p. 23). This underlying idea of rotation and challenge is related closely to Taba's concept of pacing, which is discussed later.

Organization of Content

Because content is an important aspect of the learning process and sets limits on the kind of learning and on the teaching strategies that can be used, it must be organized to develop thinking skills. Suggested organizational schemes are those advocated by Jerome Bruner (1960, also see Chapter 4), Ward (1961), and Taba (1962). Basic concepts and ideas provide the underlying system of organization rather than chronology or type of information.

About Characteristics and Teaching of Gifted Students

Taba's assumption that "All school children are capable of thinking at abstract levels, although the quality of individual thinking differs markedly" (Institute for Staff Development, 1971a, p. 148), resulted from her research. When growth was measured, results showed that students with low IQs gained as much from the teaching strategies as did those with high IQs. In the teaching strategies, pacing is important. With learners who may not learn as quickly as some, new material is not presented rapidly, and sufficient opportunities are provided for concrete operations before transitions are made to abstract operations with symbolic content. With faster learners, pacing is different. In short, the same basic intellectual tasks can be used with gifted and nongifted children and can be effective in developing their abstract-thinking capabilities; however, the pacing of assimilation and accommodation activities and the frequency of the rotation between them must be different.

Taba does not make statements about the most effective grouping of students to achieve appropriate pacing for all students. She assumes that, at least during some parts of the day, children need to be grouped according to learning rate. In many of the classrooms in which the teaching strategies were tested, however, many discussions involved the whole class rather than small groups within it. Perhaps the reason few differences were found between gifted and other learners in Taba's research is that gifted children were always in groups with all ranges of ability. Thus, the pacing of the discussion may not have met their learning needs.

Those who use Taba's strategies in programs for the gifted emphasize that although the strategies can be used with all children (and should be used part of the time with groups consisting of varied ability levels), having gifted children grouped with other gifted children part of the time is essential for maximum cognitive growth to occur. A theoretical justification for this idea comes from Piaget's (Piaget & Inhelder, 1969) statements about the importance of peer interaction in fostering cognitive growth. Because Taba accepts Piaget's assumptions about how cognitive development occurs, and because the teaching strategies are designed to foster development along the lines suggested by Piaget, his ideas form an implicit assumption, even though Taba does not make that fact explicit.

In discussing the importance of peer interaction, Piaget emphasizes that children learn from each other. They learn content (specific facts or pieces of information) and reasoning processes (logic or ways of handling information). An important way in which cognitive growth occurs is through exposure to higher levels of reasoning; however, these higher levels must be only slightly higher than the child's present level of reasoning for the child to incorporate this reasoning into his or her repertoire. In addition, this learning from others is beneficial only when the child is ready, which usually means when the child is in some transitional stage of development. Extending this idea to the use of the Taba strategies with gifted children, then, suggests that they need to be grouped with their gifted peers at least part of the time. One or two gifted children in a heterogeneous 4th-grade classroom will not learn as much from each other as will 9 or 10 gifted children drawn from all the 4th-grade classrooms in a school. A further extension of the idea suggests the value of multiage grouping of gifted students.

Because Piaget's theory of cognitive development forms a theoretical basis for the Taba strategies, his possible conception of giftedness needs to be considered. Although Piaget makes no direct references to giftedness, educators and psychologists often have interpreted his ideas without a full understanding of them. Most psychometric (measurement) conceptions of giftedness emphasize the importance of rate of development: A child who talks earlier, reads earlier, thinks abstractly at an early age, and does tasks normally accomplished only by older peers is considered more intelligent. Often, this same idea is carried over into interpretations of giftedness in Piaget's developmental scheme: Those who progress through the stages more quickly will be (and are) more intelligent.

This perception of intellectual development, however, ignores a concept important in Piaget's theory: horizontal elaboration. According to this idea, an individual who passes through all the periods of development more rapidly may not be as capable intellectually as a person who has passed through the periods more slowly. The individual who has moved more slowly and has interacted with a variety of resources will have more time to develop cognitive structures at each stage, and thus the individual will have a better base for the next higher stage because of the interaction with a greater variety of content. Although Taba does not address this Piagetian concept directly, it seems to be an underlying idea that has influenced her perception of giftedness.

Summary of Assumptions

The major ideas underlying the Taba strategies can be summarized as relying heavily on Piaget's developmental theory, including the sequence of development, the major stages, and the importance of interaction with the environment. Her major disagreement with his theory, however, forms the basic rationale for the Hilda Taba Teaching Strategies program: Thinking skills can be taught. If educators are familiar with the various thinking skills and their behavioral manifestations, and if they use precise teaching strategies designed to enhance these skills in students, they can arrange the environment so that maximum cognitive growth occurs.

ELEMENTS/PARTS

Four separate but related teaching strategies make up the Hilda Taba Teaching Strategies: Concept Development, Interpretation of Data, Application of Generalizations, and Resolution of Conflict. Each has specific cognitive tasks, a rationale for the use of the strategy, and a rationale for the steps in the strategy. An incidental benefit of discussions using the strategies is that students become better listeners. They may discover classmates who have insightful and interesting contributions to make, and may find that working with such students is intellectually stimulating and makes learning more exciting.

Concept Development

The Concept Development strategy deals with the organization and reorganization of information, and with the labeling of categories (Institute for

Staff Development, 1971a). The name "concept development" indicates the planned end result—that is, the derivation of fundamental ideas or major concepts from broad categories of data that are related in some way. Students classify data and support their classifications. Concepts are formed, clarified, and extended as students respond to questions that require them to enumerate items, notice similarities and differences that form a basis for grouping items, label groups in a variety of ways, regroup items in different ways, and give reasons for all groupings. In all cases, students must perform these operations for themselves; teachers must be able to ask focusing questions at the appropriate time and recognize when to employ other tactics to extend, clarify, refocus, or support a discussion that will foster the students' conceptual development.

Rationale for the Concept Development Task
Concept development is considered the basic form of cognition on which all other processes depend. Closely related to assimilation and accommodation, the process allows each student to clarify ideas (through expressing personal thoughts) and extend concepts (through building on ideas and thoughts expressed by others). Concept development enables students to participate at their own levels but also provides a model to which they can aspire. For example, one student may group items on the basis of descriptive attributes (e.g., color, shape), whereas another may make abstract groupings (e.g., fruit, animals). Still another may be at an even higher level, adding or multiplying classes (e.g., putting things together that are either wood or blue, or putting things together that are both wood and blue).

From a content standpoint, the strategy assists students and teachers in organizing data or information to be studied into units that are meaningful to the students and that can facilitate further investigation. When used in this way, the task also helps teachers assess the breadth and depth of the students' concepts so they can plan individual and group experiences that will expand students' concepts. In general, the strategy helps students to develop (a) greater openness and flexibility in thinking and (b) better processes for developing and organizing data.

Rationale for the Steps
Each step in the Concept Development strategy has a rationale for inclusion and a rationale for its placement in the sequence. The first step, listing, involves the process of differentiating relevant from irrelevant information, an important skill upon which all other skills will be built. Each student can make a useful contribution, and each can learn from the contributions

of others. Students gain ownership by having their contributions included. The discussion leader's role at Step 1 is to be sure that specific, factual data make up the list. If a student response is unclear or too broad, the leader needs to ask for an example or for clarification of the response. If broad, inclusive ideas are listed at Step 1, Steps 3 and 4 become difficult to impossible to execute.

At the second step, grouping, students become involved in the cognitive task of noticing common attributes and putting items together on the basis of these commonalities. They not only make their own groupings but also see the different groups made by other students. This promotes identification of multiple attributes and stimulates openness and flexibility in thinking (e.g., seeing many sides of an issue). Making certain that the reasons for groupings are clear to all students is important to (a) help students clarify their reasoning to themselves and others and (b) enable students to build on others' ideas by adding to a group made by someone else.

Labeling, the third step, is an abstracting or synthesizing process in that a student must find a word or a phrase to express the relationship or commonality among diverse items. The more accurate and inclusive a person's labels are, the more efficient that person is in handling a variety of information. When a teacher consistently asks for variety in labels, students improve in vocabulary development and creativity. Should a student suggest a label that seems inappropriate to the teacher, the label is accepted and listed; the support question should provide the child's reasoning, establishing the link the child perceives.

The fourth step, subsuming, provides another opportunity to see different relationships and new attributes of the items. Perhaps more important, however, is that this step helps students see hierarchies in the relationships. When deciding what labels can fit under other labels, students begin to analyze the inclusiveness of each label.

At the fifth step, all the previous steps are recycled. This not only accomplishes the same purposes already mentioned, but also promotes openness and flexibility in thinking because it emphasizes that one can always find fresh ways to look at the same data.

Many teachers and discussion groups have expressed a desire for closure after Step 5 of a Concept Development discussion. The authors have dealt with this expressed need with a suggested Step 6. Although not in the original strategy, Step 6 offers an opportunity for participants to further process the information and reach personal mental closure. This opportunity allows participants to reflect on how their thinking about the target concept has changed; to organize the information as they now see it through making an outline of the concept or topic based on their new insights; or to write a paragraph, essay, or part of a major paper. The focus question for Step 6 is, "Reflecting on our discussion, how has your thinking about _____ changed, or what new insights did you have?" Asking students to share these reflections and their proof of reasoning further enriches the learning of the students.

Interpretation of Data

As the name implies, the Interpretation of Data strategy deals with gathering information and making inferences about it (Institute for Staff Development, 1971b). Based on class discussions, students derive conclusions and form generalizations about similar situations or events. Through processing of information, students make inferences about cause–effect relationships and defend the statements they make. A critical element of the Interpretation of Data strategy is that students have meanings for their interpretations and recognize the significance of these data in relation to other events in the past, present, or future.

Rationale for the Interpretation of Data Strategy
The Interpretation of Data strategy is a "discovery" or "inquiry" technique that provides a sequential method for helping children use the observable data in their own experience as a starting point for developing their own conclusions and generalizations. In this strategy, students process the data in their own way and also have the opportunity to observe how others process the same information.

Rationale for the Steps
At the first step, listing, the same purposes are served as in the Concept Development Step 1. Students have the benefit of their collective observations, and they must decide what is relevant and what is not. As in Concept Development, the data listed must be "small ideas" and relatively concrete.

At the second step, inferring causes and effects, students apply their own reasoning, experience, and knowledge to the data to arrive at and give support for their inferences. By listening to different interpretations that often are equally justifiable, students learn to attend to and seek out the basis for differing ideas. Providing support for inferences helps students clarify their reasons and develop the habit of justifying their ideas.

The process of making inferences is carried further in the third step, inferring prior causes or subsequent effects. At this step, the fact that cause–effect relationships are usually complex and interrelated rather than simple and linear is emphasized. The fact that many influences are far removed from the immediate data or situation also is stressed.

In the fourth step, students are required to reach conclusions. Even though they may not have all the information they would like, they must make the soundest conclusion possible and support it. Step 4 requires that they sift through what they know and what has been said, evaluate the ideas, and decide what they think is the most important cause or effect of the situation or topic of the discussion. Furthermore, they are asked to tell *why* that cause or effect is the most important. Step 4 acts as a bridge from the previous steps to Step 5; it brings students cognitively to the point from which they may be able to generalize.

Generalizing, the fifth step, is an efficiency-building technique similar to labeling. This task provides practice in transferring knowledge gained in one situation to other situations where it might apply. Students rarely have opportunities to practice this essential skill, and to become more accurate and more tentative in their generalizing. At this step, students reach their own generalizations, justify them, have the opportunity to review critically the general statements developed by others, and also have their own generalizations examined critically.

Application of Generalizations

In the Application of Generalizations strategy, the major objective is to help students apply previously learned generalizations and facts to other situations (Institute for Staff Development, 1971c). Students use these generalizations to explain unfamiliar events and to make predictions about what will happen in hypothetical or proposed situations. For example, if students are asked, "What will happen if our country continues to pollute our streams and lakes?" they must apply previous knowledge about the causes of pollution and the conditions present now in the water supply and knowledge of the previous effects of pollution on lives and environments. In this strategy students develop the ability to make predictions about things that will happen in the future and are enabled to apply what they have learned.

Rationale for the Application of Generalizations Strategy

In the Application of Generalizations strategy, students apply previously learned facts, principles, or processes in new situations to explain new phenomena or to predict consequences from known conditions. This process is an important vehicle for transfer of knowledge, enabling students to get more "mileage" out of their direct experiences. The Application of Generalizations strategy allows for and encourages divergent thinking in making predictions; however, students also are required to establish the parameters of data and logical relationships by which to judge the validity of predictions. These established parameters also are judged on their completeness; students must generate the chain of causal links that will connect the conditions and the predictions.

Rationale for the Steps

At Step 1, predictions, students are encouraged to use their creativity in predicting the possible results of some hypothetical situation. It requires the logical proposition of "If _____, then _____." They then are asked to explain the possible reason(s) for making a particular prediction. Explaining the relationship they see between the situation and a stated prediction gives students practice in clarifying their own thinking and expressing their thoughts distinctly; listening to the predictions and thinking of others helps them to extend and deepen their own understanding.

The second step, inferring conditions, brings the discussion to a reality base by requiring that students build a logical, justifiable chain of relationships. This process strengthens and expands the students' understanding of multiple causality as they understand that no consequence directly follows from a given situation and that many other factors also must be present.

The next step, inferring consequences and conditions, is essentially a recycling of the first two steps and, as such, serves the same purposes. Additional purposes also are served, however, in that each time the processes are recycled, the predictions and conditions are extended further from the original situation and are therefore more complex and probabilistic in nature.

At the fourth step, conclusions, the same purposes are served as in Step 4 in the Interpretation of Data strategy. Students are required to consider all the predictions, conditions, and reasons that were discussed and make a judgment on their own about which conditions they think are likely to prevail and lead to a particular prediction coming true.

Step 5, examining a generalization, strengthens students' abilities to form their own general statements and to look critically at others' statements. Generalizations may be too general, inaccurate, or unqualified. After students have some experience developing general statements, teachers need to offer some instruction on how to develop valid generalizations.

Resolution of Conflict

The Resolution of Conflict strategy, originally called Interpretation of Feelings, Attitudes, and Values, leads students through a process that is helpful in resolving conflict situations (Institute for Staff Development, 1971d). The Resolution of Conflict strategy is an extension of all the other strategies, using human behavior as the data to be interpreted. The primary purpose is to help students deal more rationally and effectively with situations encountered in life by giving them practice in exploring the feelings, attitudes, and values behind people's behavior. Students are encouraged to take the viewpoints of all individuals involved in a conflict situation and discuss their possible motives, feelings, and reasons for feelings before talking about what each individual can do to resolve the conflict situation. They are asked to generate alternatives for action by each person and then to analyze these alternatives in relation to their general consequences and effects on all the other people involved in the situation. Based on the discussion, students evaluate the alternatives and make individual judgments about the most appropriate action that should be taken. After explaining their judgment and considering its possible long-range consequences, students are asked to consider a similar situation experienced by a member of their own group. The same process is followed with this situation, from exploration of reasons for behavior through evaluation of alternatives. Finally, on the basis of this discussion and prior experiences, students are asked to form a generalization about how people usually handle conflict situations of the type discussed.

Rationale for the Resolution of Conflict Strategy
The Resolution of Conflict strategy, as an extension or combination of two previous strategies, serves the same purposes as those tasks; however, the subject matter being interpreted and the principles being applied are particularly subjective because human behavior and emotions are the target areas. This strategy provides practice in assuming the viewpoints of others,

an ability that, according to Kohlberg (1971) and Selman (1971), is a necessary prerequisite for advanced moral reasoning to occur.

Rationale for the Steps

At the first step, listing, the same purposes are served as in the other strategies. Students learn to differentiate relevant from irrelevant data. The step also builds the idea that a person must understand the facts and know what actually happened in a situation before taking any action.

In Step 2, inferring reasons and feelings, the same purposes are served as in the inference steps of other strategies. Additionally, this is the major aspect of perspective taking.

Generating alternatives and examining their consequences is Step 3. Through the Resolution of Conflict strategy, students learn to realize that effective decision making and conflict resolution require careful consideration of all contributing factors and the likely consequences of each alternative course of action.

At Step 4, evaluation, students are asked to decide the most appropriate action. This involves much the same processes as the conclusion step in the other strategies because students must think carefully about the discussion and interpret it in their own ways.

In the next phase of the discussion, Steps 5 through 8, students are asked to apply the same processes of listing facts, inferring reasons and feelings, generating alternatives and consequences, and evaluating alternatives in a situation in their own lives or in the life of one of their peers. This heightens the transfer effect and provides additional emphasis on the validity of these processes in handling the day-to-day situations these students may encounter.

At the last step, generalizing, students are asked to form an abstract statement about how people usually handle such situations. The same purposes are served through the generalization process as in the previous strategies.

Supporting Behaviors

Although the particular steps in each strategy are different, certain teacher behaviors are necessary at all steps of discussions. For example, teachers must always ask questions that are both open-ended and focused. Except for the listing step, they must always ask students to provide evidence or reasoning to support inferences, unless the student provided support when answering.

General Behaviors

At all steps of Taba discussions, the teacher needs to encourage participation by all students and ask open-ended questions that will permit and encourage a variety of answers. Teachers must follow the appropriate sequence of steps and must avoid negative acts such as (a) giving opinions or value judgments about student ideas; (b) rejecting, ignoring, or cutting off a student response; (c) doing the task students are supposed to do; and (d) editing or changing a student's idea. Other general supporting behaviors are accomplished through the following four types of questioning techniques.

QUESTIONS CALLING FOR VARIETY. Teachers should ask questions that encourage students to think of completely different responses from those already given.

- What else might happen?
- What are some *completely different* ways these items can be put together?
- What are some *completely different* things he or she could do?

QUESTIONS CALLING FOR CLARIFICATION OR EXTENSION. Other questions encourage students to explain the meaning of statements or words, provide specific examples, or elaborate on an idea to extend its meaning.

- What do you mean by freedom?
- How is your idea different from Sally's?
- What do you mean when you say _____?

QUESTIONS CALLING FOR REASONS OR SUPPORT FOR IDEAS. Questions that call for reasons or support for ideas are used at all steps of discussions except listing. They encourage students to explain or cite reasons for their inferences, conclusions, or generalizations. Because asking for reasons or support is initially threatening to students, teachers need to advise students in advance that they will be asking "why" questions so that everyone can share their thinking. Additionally, questions should be clearly expressed and used carefully.

- What are your reasons for grouping these items together?
- In what way are these items alike?
- Why do you think these items go together?
- What are you thinking that makes you say that?
- What leads you to believe that?
- How do you know that _____ causes _____?
- What makes you believe that _____ would be an effect of _____?
- What from our discussion led you to that conclusion?

FOCUSING QUESTIONS. The initial questions that focus students on the task at a particular step are called focusing questions. They should be worded carefully to be both open-ended and clear in their focus. If students stray from the topic or focus, the initial question needs to be restated to bring them back on task. Following are some examples of different focusing questions for specific purposes.

Grouping Questions
- Which items could you put together because they are alike in some way?
- Which items would you put together in a group because they are similar?

Causes and Prior Causes
- What are some factors contributing to _____?
- What do you think prevented _____?
- How did _____ happen?

Effects and Subsequent Effects
- What do you think has happened because _____?
- What do you think were the results of _____?
- What do you think might have been some of the consequences of _____?

Supporting Behaviors for Specific Steps or Types of Tasks
As shown in Table 10.1, similarities exist among the types of tasks, teacher and student roles, and activities in the four Taba Teaching Strategies.

When getting the data, the teacher's main task—other than general support behaviors (e.g., encouraging variety or seeking clarification)—

TABLE 10.1

General Supporting Behaviors in Taba's Teaching Strategies

Task	Teacher Role	Strategy	Student Role
Gathering information	Ask focusing questions. Request clarification. Seek variety. Make sure only data are given.	All	List relevant items. Clarify as necessary. Identify facts.
Organizing data	Ask focusing questions. Request reasons and support. Request clarification. Refocus students as needed.	All	Organize data (e.g., grouping, labeling, subsuming). Identify relationships. Give reasons and support.
Making inferences	Ask focusing questions. Ask for reasons and/or support. Ask for clarification. Refocus. Broaden patterns of thinking; seek variety.	All	Explain relationships. Justify inferences. Infer causes—effects, Identify conditions. Infer consequences. Listen actively. Subsume labels.
Generating alternatives	Ask focusing questions. Ask for reasons and/or support. Ask for clarification. Refocus.	All	Generate alternatives. Provide reasons and support. Consider consequences of varied actions. Listen actively.
Making conclusions	Ask focusing questions. Seek variety. Ask for clarification.	All	Conclude about causes—effects. Conclude about predictions. Conclude about alternatives. Support conclusions.
Making generalizations	Ask focusing question. Ask for clarification. Broaden patterns of thinking. Seek variety.	All but concept development	Form generalizations based on data, inferences, predictions. Support generalizations or evaluate provided generalizations.

is to make certain that students stick to the data rather than make inferences. In the Concept Development task, students must give specific examples rather than categories. Otherwise, no items are available for grouping at the later steps.

Organizing data is a task that requires teachers to pay careful attention to the data and the ways students are organizing them if the discussion is to meet its learning goals and objectives. With younger children, writing the items on mountable tagboard strips is critical for classification and grouping, as items actually can be moved. At the middle school and high school levels, students can work within small groups, with each group having cards or strips with the items written on them. The groups can share with the whole class as deemed appropriate by the teacher.

Encouraging the whole group to participate is another important aspect of class discussions aimed at organizing data. For example, the teacher should encourage adding to the groups that have been formed, based on the reasons the groups were initially made. Also, the whole group should be involved in recalling the reasons why groups were formed.

To subsume is to classify into a larger category or under a more general principle. The subsuming task often is difficult for children to understand. They may need examples and, if so, the teacher should provide only one or two, subsuming items, ideas, or labels unrelated to the current discussion.

The task of making conclusions often is difficult for students, and they may tend to summarize the discussion. Conclusions must show evidence of synthesis and personal reflection rather than summarize or simply recount what was said. The statement should carry a personal conviction. To this end, the teacher should accept students' summaries but push them for a conclusion (e.g., "Yes, that's what we said. Now, what do you think is the most important idea from our discussion?").

Generalizing also is a difficult task for children. It requires careful thought, so they should be given time to think about and write their ideas before sharing them orally. Often, telling students to write a complete sentence will help. More important, however, the teacher's focusing question must be narrow enough that students' responses are relevant to the discussion. For example, after an Interpretation of Data discussion about the effects of differences between types of solvents, the following question would be appropriate: "Based on our discussion, what general statement can you make about solvents? Write your statement as a complete sentence, and think of three supporting statements." The focus of the generalization question is provided by reference to the preceding discussion.

Table 10.2 is an example of an Interpretation of Data lesson plan. Note the behavioral objectives and the focus questions related to each objective. Data are listed, and causes and prior causes of specific data are inferred and supported, providing the base for conclusions and generalizations. Step 3, prior causes, is based on Step 2, causes that are directly related to the data. Each step leads to more abstract thinking than the prior step(s). The further removed the focus question is from the data, the higher the level of thinking.

Summary of Steps and Activities

Learning to use the Hilda Taba Teaching Strategies is not easy. The strategies are complex, and differences between an appropriate and inappropriate focus question or behavior are subtle, but can be deleterious to learning. The description of the strategies in this chapter is not sufficient to allow a person to use them effectively. Demonstration discussions, practice followed by critiques from experienced leaders, classroom tryouts, and self-analysis are necessary components of the learning process. Many teachers feel that years of practice have been necessary for them to perfect their techniques; however, they also attest to the effectiveness of the strategies when implemented appropriately. Table 10.3 presents a summary of student and teacher roles and activities in each type of task in the Hilda Taba Teaching Strategies.

MODIFICATIONS OF THE BASIC CURRICULUM

Use of the Taba model provides content, process, product, and learning environment modifications that are appropriate for gifted students. Although primarily a process approach, Taba's (1962, 1964) comprehensive approach to curriculum development and implementation provides for many changes that are important in programs for gifted students. Content modifications suggested by the model are in abstractness, complexity, organization for learning value, and methods of inquiry. Process changes include an emphasis on higher levels of thinking; open-endedness; use of

(*text continues on p. 356*)

TABLE 10.2

Sample Discussion Plan for Interpretation of Data Lesson

Discussion Purposes

Content: To draw warranted conclusions about the following relationships:

People and their
physical environment   +   The ways people
meet their needs

Process: To make and support cause–effect inferences, to draw warranted conclusions, and to generalize from specific instances to other such instances.

Topic: The Bedouin of the Negev

Level: Intermediate

Prediscussion Procedures:

Arrange students in a semicircle. Have chalkboard and chalk or butcher paper and markers available.

Materials:

Library resources on the Bedouin people.

Behavioral Objectives	Focusing Questions	Support Procedures
Step 1. Data Students will enumerate what they know or have read about the ways the Bedouin people meet their basic needs for survival.	What are some things you know about the Bedouin people? What are some things you have learned about the ways Bedouin people meet their basic needs for food and shelter?	Encourage students to list data about the lifestyle, food, shelter, and habits of the Bedouin people. Seek a variety of observations. Focus on and record facts (rather than inferences).
Step 2. Causes a. Students will state inferences about the causes for the ways Bedouin people meet their basic needs.	a1. What are some possible causes for (e.g., the Bedouin people moving from place to place)? b1. Why would that (e.g., dry climate) cause them	Choose data to follow up that provides the most promise of eliciting causes relating to the environment and people.

(continues)

TABLE 10.2 *Continued.*

Sample Discussion Plan for Interpretation of Data Lesson

Behavioral Objectives	Focusing Questions	Support Procedures
Step 2. *Causes (continued)*		
b. Students will cite evidence or reasoning to support their inferences.	to move around? a2. What causes (e.g., children learning mainly from their parents)? b2. Why would moving from place to place cause (e.g., children learning mainly from their parents)?	Seek a variety of causes for each item of data. Ask for support for inferences immediately after inferences are given. The basic question when seeking support is "Why does (cause) cause (data)?"
Step 3. *Prior Causes*		
a. Students will state inferences about the prior causes of selected causes given at Step 2.	a1. Why do you think (e.g., the pastures are picked over by summer)? b1. Why do you think (e.g., winter rains would cause pastures to be picked over by spring)?	Step 3 can be repeated many times. Depth of thought is developed through asking for prior causes of the prior causes.
b. Students will cite evidence or reasoning to support their inferences.	a2. What are some of the causes of (e.g., each man having several wives)? b2. Why would (e.g., needing a large family cause men to have several wives)?	Choose causes and prior causes that elicit answers relating the environment to the people. Ask for a variety of prior causes for each selected cause. Seek support for all inferences. The basic question is "Why does (prior cause) cause (cause)?" Step 3 answer Step 2 answer
Step 4. *Conclusions*		
a. Students will state conclusions about the causes for the Bedouin lifestyle.	a. Thinking back over our discussion, what would you say are the most important causes for	Encourage each child to reach his or her own conclusions.

(continues)

Step 4. Conclusions (continued)

b. Students will cite evidence or reasons for their conclusions.

the Bedouin people meeting their basic needs in the ways that they do?

b. Why do you think (e.g., the climate) is an important cause for the Bedouin lifestyle?

Encourage a variety of conclusions.
Ask for clarification of ideas when needed.
Encourage synthesis of inferences about cases rather than summaries.
Conclude about *causes*.

Step 5. Generalizations

a. Students will generalize about the causes for the ways most people meet their basic needs.

b. Students will cite support for their statements.

a. What would you say generally about what causes all people everywhere to live the way they do?

b. Why do you think (e.g., the characteristics of people and their environment) determine the ways people meet their basic needs?

Allow time for students to jot down some ideas before asking for responses.
Ask students to write a complete sentence or statement.
Encourage each student to write a statement.
Ask for clarification when needed.
Encourage students to consider information about other peoples they have studied.

Cognitive Map

Planning Generalization: Interaction between people and their physical environment influences the ways they meet their basic needs.

Possible Prior Causes	Possible Causes	Possible Data
Winters are cold.	They must continually move to find grass.	The Bedouins live in tents.
There are no rains in spring.	There is little rain.	Barley crops are planted in the fall.
Most have large herds.	The desert is dry and doesn't support much grass.	The Bedouins move from place to place except in winter.
Rains come in winter.	Pastures are depleted by summer.	

(continues)

TABLE 10.2 *Continued.*

Sample Discussion Plan for Interpretation of Data Lesson

Possible Prior Causes	Possible Causes	Possible Data
Cognitive Map (continued)		
They store their heavy tents in the summer.	Winters are cold and rainy.	The whole family helps with the harvest.
They stay in one place in the winter.	They live in heavy tents in the winter.	Winter is a social time.
A large family is needed to care for animals.	Most of the year, they are moving.	Baby animals are born in the winter.
Some social life is needed.	They seldom see each other except in winter.	They seldom go to the marketplace to buy goods.
Each man has several wives.	Often, the religious month comes in winter time.	Children learn mainly from their parents.
The land supports very few people.	Families live together.	Money is made from selling animals.
They must constantly look for food and water.	Children are needed to help with crops and animals.	
The country is not technologically advanced.	Families move around.	
	There are few towns and cities.	
	Meeting basic needs takes most of their time.	

Possible Conclusions

The climate of the desert causes the people to live the way they do.

The Bedouin have to live in tents and move around because they must follow the grass with their herds.

The Bedouins live together in tents because they are in a lonely desert and must have some time and opportunities to socialize.

The major causes of the Bedouin's nomadic lifestyle are the climate, the terrain, and the traditions of the people.

Possible Generalizations

People everywhere develop ways to meet their needs for survival that depend on the environment in which they live.

The inherited traits, traditions, and religion of a people and the characteristics of the environment in which they live determine the ways in which food, shelter, and clothing are obtained and the type of food, shelter, and clothing that are needed.

TABLE 10.3

Summary of Student and Teacher Roles and Activities in the Hilda Taba Teaching Strategies

Step, Type, or Level of Thinking	Student		Teacher	
	Role	Sample Activities	Role	Sample Activities
Getting the data	Observer	Notice what happened.	Presenter	Present a situation, provide information to read, or initiate some other "intake" experience.
	Active participant	Recall events or knowledge from past experience.	Questioner	Ask focusing questions to get students to recall specific facts or data from past experience or the intake experience.
	Listener	Generate ideas.	Facilitator	Ask for clarification when needed.
			Active listener	Ask refocusing questions when needed.
				Strive for a variety of specific facts or data.
Organizing data	Active participant	Group like items together.	Questioner	Ask questions that invite students to group, label, subsume, and recycle.
	Listener	Provide labels for groups.	Active listener	Ask for clarification when needed.
		Subsume items under labels.	Facilitator	Seek variety.
		Subsume labels under labels.		Ask refocusing questions as needed.
		Explain reasons for grouping, labeling, and subsuming.		Ask for support or reasoning for all answers given.
		Listen to the ideas and reasons of others.		Encourage student-to-student interaction.
		Think of different ideas.		

(continues)

TABLE 10.3 *Continued.*
Summary of Student and Teacher Roles and Activities in the Hilda Taba Teaching Strategies

Step, Type, or Level of Thinking	Student		Teacher	
	Role	Sample Activities	Role	Sample Activities
Making inferences	Active participant Listener	Make inferences about causes and prior causes of data. Make inferences about effects and subsequent effects of data. Explain reasoning on which inferences were made. Make predictions about a hypothetical situation. Infer conditions necessary to make a prediction come true. Infer consequences of predictions. Listen to the ideas and reasoning of others. Think of different ideas.	Questioner Active listener Facilitator	Ask questions that stimulate students to make inferences and focus on the task. Ask for clarification when necessary. Ask for support or reasoning for all answers given. Ask refocusing questions when necessary. Seek variety.
Generating alternatives	Active participant Listener	Develop alternative courses of action for each individual involved in a conflict situation. Think of new ideas. Listen to ideas of others.	Questioner Active listener Facilitator	Ask questions to focus students on the task. Divide class into pairs or small groups. Ask for clarification when needed. Seek variety.

(continues)

	Student roles	Student behaviors	Teacher roles	Teacher actions
Drawing conclusions	Synthesizer Listener Active participant	Evaluate alternatives for action. Think about the discussion and reach a conclusion about the most likely outcome. Explain reasons for conclusions. Reach a conclusion about important causes or effects. Listen actively to the ideas of others; react thoughtfully to them.	Questioner Active listener Facilitator	Ask questions to focus students on the task. Ask for clarification when needed. Ask refocusing questions when needed. Accept summaries, but ask for interpretations and conclusions. Encourage student-to-student interaction.
Making generalizations	Synthesizer Generalizer Active participant	Make general, abstract statements about causes, effects, or human behaviors. Examine the general statements made by others; thoughtfully react to them. Explain reasons for general statements or evaluations of statements of others. Write generalizations in complete sentences.	Questioner Active listener Facilitator	Ask questions that focus or refocus students on the task. Ask for clarification, extension, and elaboration when necessary. Encourage student-to-student interaction. Wait for students to think. Present a generalization for students to examine or ask students to make and support generalizations based on the discussion.

discovery, requiring students to verbalize their reasoning or evidence; group interaction; and pacing. One product modification, transformation, is suggested. Four learning environment changes are suggested: learner centeredness, independence, openness, and acceptance.

Content Modifications

A good example of the content changes suggested by Taba is the social studies curriculum (Ellis & Durkin, 1972) developed and field-tested during the same time period as the teaching strategies. Because Taba assumed an interactive relationship between content organization and quality and the processes taught, these components are integral to this curriculum.

In the social studies curriculum (Ellis & Durkin, 1972), three levels of knowledge serve different organizational functions: key concepts; main, organizing, and contributing ideas; and content samples. These are explained in the following passages.

Key Concepts

The most abstract knowledge level is key concepts. These represent highly generalized abstractions selected because they embody the synthesis and organization of large numbers of specific facts and ideas. Key concepts are developed in a more abstract and complex way at each higher grade level and form threads running throughout the curriculum. Some examples of key concepts are causality, conflict, cultural change, differences, institutions, interdependence, and modification.

Main, Organizing, and Contributing Ideas

The second level of knowledge consists first of main ideas—that is, ideas the students will need to remember after they forget specific facts. Each year's work centers around several main ideas, which may be treated as a hierarchy reappearing at several grade levels. The main idea expresses a relationship that applies both to the content being studied and to parallel examples of human behavior in other settings. Interdependence is an example of a main idea.

Content Samples

The lowest level of knowledge, specific facts or content samples, provides the means for illustrating, explaining, and developing main ideas. Content samples (e.g., an in-depth study of human behavior) are selected because they demonstrate the main idea. They are sufficient in depth, richness, and breadth to provide the opportunity for students to develop their own generalizations, which approximate the main and organizing ideas.

Abstract key concepts and generalizations are used as the organizing framework for the content presented to students. These concepts and generalizations also need to be complex in that they must include several traditional content areas and integrate methods of study or "thought systems" into the study of a particular discipline.

Process and Product Modifications

Process modifications appropriate for gifted students are integral parts of the Hilda Taba Teaching Strategies. Higher levels of thinking are developed through the sequential tasks (in response to teacher questions) in each of the strategies and by each strategy as a whole. Open-endedness is necessary because during discussions teacher questions are open-ended and because the focusing and extending questions also are provocative. Having students verbalize their reasoning and support for inferences is also an integral, required aspect of the strategies. Taba provides many suggestions for appropriate pacing in discussions, and she supplies specific techniques for facilitating interaction among students in a group.

In the Taba model, direct product modifications are made only in the area of transformation. Emphasis is placed on student participation in analysis of content, and students are encouraged to organize, interpret, and evaluate the information they receive, and then develop their own conclusions and generalizations. Because of this active involvement, if the teacher is using the strategies appropriately, the products developed will be transformations. During this process, students also learn skills in appropriate evaluation of their own products and the products of others. They are encouraged to critique and react to others' logic and products.

Learning Environment Modifications

Correct and frequent implementation of the Hilda Taba Teaching Strategies ensures that the learning environment will be learner centered. Because the strategies were designed as discussion techniques, the teacher who uses them consistently will present few lectures. Also, with the major focus placed on student ideas, the teacher is not the central figure in discussions. Most of the general support behaviors discussed earlier ensure a learner-centered classroom. Asking open-ended questions and questions calling for variety, avoiding opinions or value judgments, encouraging student-to-student reactions and interaction, and waiting for students to think before responding demonstrate that students and their thinking are the primary emphasis.

Independence is fostered by the emphasis placed on student ideas. Students are encouraged to explain and justify their ideas, and teachers are trained not to express their opinions and not to edit or change student ideas when recording them. Specific skills involved in interpersonal independence also are taught through the strategy Resolution of Conflict.

An open environment is developed through appropriate implementation of the strategies. Teachers encourage and push for divergent ideas through their methods of questioning, and place no restrictions on the kind of generalization(s) that can be developed and stated as a result of a discussion.

Acceptance rather than judgment is another integral aspect of the Taba strategies. Teachers are cautioned against providing an opinion or value judgment of a student's idea. They are to accept all ideas and encourage the students to look at their own statements by asking questions of clarification, extension, and support. Student ideas are not edited or changed when they are recorded. Teacher questions are designed to develop understanding of, clarification of, and support for student ideas rather than criticism of them.

MODIFYING THE MODEL

Content Modifications

Although the Taba model makes many of the content, process, and learning environment changes recommended for gifted students, the model is more appropriate for use with these students if certain additions are made. For example, the two content changes not made by the model are (a) the study of people and (b) variety. The study of people can be integrated easily by using the strategies as methods to study the lives of productive, eminent people. The Interpretation of Data strategy can be used to make inferences about the causes for the characteristics of eminent people or to make inferences about the effects these characteristics had on their products or their careers. The Application of Generalizations strategy can be used to predict what would have happened to a famous or eminent individual if that person lived today or in a different period of time. Resolution of Conflict can be used to examine conflicts in the lives of individuals— either inner, personal conflicts or conflicts between individuals. The students can then discuss similar situations in their own lives.

A second content change, variety, can be accomplished in a way that is similar to the modification of Bruner's approach described in Chapter 4. Using a worksheet similar to Bruner's for building content plans (see Table 4.6), the teacher can write the key concept at the top (see Table 10.4, which provides an example using the ideas presented earlier in this section). The main idea becomes the generalization. Instead of listing the concepts involved in the generalization, the teacher can list the contributing ideas. Organizing ideas and content samples that pertain to the main idea are then listed as data, either data taught in the regular curriculum or data that need to be taught in the special program.

Process Modifications

Only two process modifications need to be incorporated into the Taba model: freedom of choice and variety. To ensure freedom of choice of topics, one teacher of the gifted (Maker, 1982b; Maker & Nielson, 1995) allows the students to choose general topic areas for discussion several weeks in advance. She then selects the planning generalizations and reading materials and plans a Taba discussion on the topics chosen. Other ways of integrating freedom of choice are the following: (a) in the Concept Development strategy, they might choose either the concepts to be discussed or the data to be used at the listing step; (b) students could collect data on a topic of their choice and use the Interpretation of Data strategy to process and organize it; (c) in the Application of Generalizations strategy, students may choose one or more of the predictions given at the first step and develop reasons, conditions, and consequences for it; and (d) in the Resolution of Conflict strategy, students might choose conflict situations to discuss, select alternatives to develop, and write about similar situations of their own choice.

Another way to incorporate freedom of choice is to allow students to choose areas of study, investigate them independently, and then organize discussions so that all students "pool" their knowledge and findings. These are processes used in the Autonomous Learner Model (see Chapter 2), Problem Based Learning (Chapter 7), Group Investigations (Chapter 9),

TABLE 10.4

Sample Worksheet for Overall Curriculum Design—Building Content Lessons
Based on the Regular Curriculum

Key Concept:

Interdependence

Main Idea 1:

Interaction between people and their physical environment influences the ways in which they meet their needs.

Contributing Ideas (CI):

1. People living in a desert area may be able to meet their needs by modifying their behavior.
2. People living in a desert area may be able to make a living through modification of their environment.
3. The seasons influence the way in which nomadic people living in a desert meet their needs.
4. The products of an agricultural group allow its producers to meet many of their needs.
5. A specialized society requires a medium of exchange.
6. A specialized society fosters interdependence among its people.

Organizing Ideas and Content Samples

Regular Program	Special Program
Farmers in the western United States modify their environment and their behavior to meet their needs (CI 2).	The Bedouin people modify their behavior and their environment to meet basic needs for survival (CI 2).
Farmers	The Bedouin
irrigate their crops.	move regularly to get food and water.
build very few fences.	use animals for transportation.
use large ranches rather than small farms.	herd animals adapted to the desert
organize cooperative groups to supply water to all.	environment.
	plant some crops to feed animals.
Farmers of the United States sell their crops to provide money for needed goods and services (CI 6).	store grain and food for winter.
	The Yoruba craftsmen exchange services (CI 6).
Farmers buy	The blacksmith makes hoes for farmers.
specialized equipment for harvesting.	The leatherworker makes drum pieces for the drummer.
materials for building homes.	
veterinary services.	
repair services for equipment.	
fuel for equipment.	

and Thinking Actively in a Social Context (Chapter 11). In the social studies unit, for example, each student or group of students could select the people of interest to them. Using the basic plans for the lessons presented as examples, each student or group would list data at Step 1 that pertained to the group of people they were studying. After the first step, all students should be encouraged to make inferences about all data, not only the information they reported. In this way, not only do students have freedom to study topics of interest to them, but they also learn a variety of information from other students.

Variety in methods is integrated through alternating different methods with the basic discussion strategy. The first step, getting the information, is a part of each strategy. Students can get the information they need to participate in a discussion in many different ways, such as by participating in a simulation, reading an article, listening to a tape, participating in a role-playing incident, listening to a lecture, watching a film, watching a television program, or making observations. C. June Maker once conducted a lesson on prejudice in which the students' task was to observe and record evidence of prejudice through taking pictures, taping conversations, or making notes on things they had heard or seen. These observations were then used as a basis for Concept Development, Interpretation of Data, and Resolution of Conflict discussions.

The same intellectual tasks can be accomplished when students work in small-group or individual settings. Another way to vary any of the strategies is to alternate small- and large-group activities and to integrate individual activities. With the Application of Generalizations strategy, for instance, students can work in small groups to develop their predictions. The groups then share these predictions and discuss reasons. The Resolution of Conflict strategy lends itself to small-group or individual work when the task is to generate alternatives. Students also might develop a "similar situation" in this strategy through a writing assignment.

The easiest way to vary the Taba strategies is to alternate between small and large groups or to vary the groupings. Because interaction with at least a small group is important, any individual work should be shared in a discussion setting at some point.

Product Modifications

Because the model provides for direct changes in only one area (transformation), the Taba strategies should be used differently to provide product modifications. One of the most important ways is to teach students the steps involved in each strategy. This can be done by having "debriefing" sessions after the discussions to indicate to students the steps (intellectual tasks) and the questions asked by the teacher at each step. After participating in several discussions, the students learn the processes and will be able to use them in their individual investigations and product development.

The teacher should show students how the different strategies can be helpful to them in their product development. The Concept Development strategy is useful at the beginning of a project to organize questions about a topic. C. June Maker often has used this strategy with graduate students as a way to help them develop thesis or dissertation topics. The graduate students first list or brainstorm all the questions they have about a topic, then they group, label, subsume, and regroup these questions. Often this exercise helps them to clarify what they want to investigate and to select the major and minor questions to be addressed.

Concept Development also is useful as a process for organizing a final product. For articles, chapters, and even longer pieces, the process can be used in the following way: (a) list all the important information that needs to be included, as specifically as possible; (b) group the similar items together; (c) develop titles for the groups; (d) subsume items; (e) examine each category to see whether all the essential information has been included; and (f) try another regrouping of all the information in an attempt to find a better organization. The titles for the groups become subheadings, and the items within each category are then combined and explained or discussed to form the text.

The Concept Development strategy also can be used in research to analyze the content of responses to open-ended questions. All of the responses to a particular question can be listed, preferably one response to a note card. These cards can then be sorted by one person into piles containing similar items. After the card groupings have been completed, titles are given, and then the subsuming task is undertaken. A second person can then take the titles of the groups along with a description of the groups and attempt to classify the items into the groupings established by the first individual. The degree to which they classify items into the same groups is the index of agreement. If the index of agreement is high, the groupings remain the same, perhaps with minor changes, but if their agreement is low, completely new groupings may need to be formed.

The Concept Development strategy was important to the development of the DISCOVER Assessment (see Chapter 5). Hundreds and hundreds of observed behaviors were grouped based on similarities, labeled, and subsumed. The strategy provided a structure to deal with volumes of data and to organize them so they could be put into a usable and practical format.

The Interpretation of Data strategy is useful as a technique for developing discussions and conclusions after an experiment or demonstration has taken place. The data collected comprise the information used at Step 1. The investigator, observer, or writer then develops inferences about either causes or effects of the data or both causes and effects. Prior causes and subsequent effects also are listed, as are conclusions and generalizations. These inferences, conclusions, and generalizations are used as the basis of discussion of and conclusions about the research. Use of this strategy before actually beginning the task of writing can make the writing easier and can ensure that many different aspects of the experiment will be considered rather than just the most obvious.

The Application of Generalizations strategy is useful for developing products that involve making predictions or forecasting future events. As such, it is an extremely useful tool in developing hypotheses to guide experimental research. In addition to the development of hypotheses, the strategy can be used to predict how audiences might react to a certain product. Each individual can use the process when developing a product, or the teacher can lead group discussions to assist each student in the development of products acceptable to different audiences.

When students are involved in group investigations or development of products, conflicts are bound to arise. The Resolution of Conflict strategy is an excellent process for solving these problems. It also can be used to develop fictional stories involving some kind of conflict between people.

In summary, the Hilda Taba Teaching Strategies can provide useful processes for students and teachers in the development of products that address real problems, that are directed toward real audiences, and that are evaluated realistically.

Learning Environment Modifications

The only two learning environment modifications not implied by the Taba strategies are complexity and high mobility. Students need a variety of complex references and equipment for their use, or ready access to such items. Movement in and out of the classroom is necessary for access to supplies and environments not housed within the classroom. Flexible grouping arrangements also are necessary so that interaction with gifted peers can occur during discussions.

Summary

Although the Hilda Taba Teaching Strategies make many of the content, process, and learning environment changes recommended for gifted students, certain modifications and additions still need to be made if the model is to be used as a comprehensive curriculum structure for gifted students. The model can be combined easily to yield a comprehensive curriculum with the Autonomous Learner Model (Chapter 2), the Basic Structure of a Discipline (Chapter 4), DISCOVER (Chapter 5), Problem-Based Learning (Chapter 7), the Enrichment Triad Model or Schoolwide Enrichment Model (Chapter 8), Group Investigations (Chapter 9), or Thinking Actively in a Social Context (Chapter 11).

DEVELOPMENT

Two aspects of Taba's approach discussed in this chapter—the specific teaching strategies and the social studies curriculum—were developed along separate but related lines. The Hilda Taba Teaching Strategies model (Institute for Staff Development, 1971a, 1971b, 1971c, 1971d) resulted from the refinement of the teaching strategies and teacher training program used in three studies of the effectiveness of teaching strategies in the development of children's thinking (Taba, 1964, 1966; Wallen et al., 1969). The Taba Program in Social Science (Ellis & Durkin, 1972) was developed concurrently with the strategies but was more complete than were the strategies before the studies of children's thinking were completed. In the research projects, as in Taba's theoretical orientation, content and process were somewhat separate entities but played complementary roles. For instance, in the research projects, Taba's (1964) overall objective was "to examine the development of thought under the optimum training conditions" (p. 27). These optimum conditions included the following: (a) a curriculum designed to develop thinking skills, (b) teaching strategies focused specifically on the mastery of certain thinking skills, and (c) an adequate time span for a developmental sequence in training.

Development of the social studies curriculum that was published by Addison-Wesley (Ellis & Durkin, 1972) was begun much earlier, with Taba's involvement in the development of a social studies curriculum for Contra Costa County, California. Development of the teaching strategies program began with the first research project in 1964. Hilda Taba's untimely death in 1967 left much of her work incomplete. Several of her associates, however, completed the different projects: Norman Wallen and his associates at San Francisco State College completed the research project in 1969; Lyle and Sydelle Ehrenberg, with the help of other associates of Taba, completed the teacher-training and teaching strategies program and founded the Institute for Staff Development to provide this training nationwide; and Kim Ellis and Mary Durkin were primarily responsible for the completion of the curriculum in social science.

In the research projects, which provided the setting for development of the strategies and refinement of the curriculum, emphasis was on how thought could be developed best in elementary school children. The first study (Taba, 1964) was exploratory, serving as a setting for the development of the methodological tools (e.g., methods of categorizing thought processes, methods of coding classroom interaction, and criterion measures [tests] necessary for studying the development of thought). During the course of this study, teaching strategies became the most important variable being studied. Thus, throughout the first study and subsequent ones, the following three dimensions of classroom interaction were studied: (a) behavior of the teachers, (b) behavior of the students, and (c) the content or product of the interaction. Although the first study was concentrated only on the effects of strategies of trained teachers (in 20 classrooms from Grades 2 through 6), the second study (Taba, 1966) compared the classrooms of trained teachers with classrooms of untrained teachers. The final study involved the training of leaders around the country who in turn provided training for teachers. Thus, the strategies were revised and refined through a long process of trial and error, assessment of effectiveness, and input from numerous classroom teachers with different teaching styles and skills.

RESEARCH ON EFFECTIVENESS

To assess the effectiveness of the teaching strategies (Taba, 1964), two kinds of instruments were devised and used in conjunction with the *Sequential*

Tests of Educational Progress (STEP) (Educational Testing Service, 1972) social studies achievement test. The first was an objective test, the *Social Studies Inference Test* (Taba, 1964), in which students were presented with a series of stories followed by a list of statements (inferences) about the story. Students read the story and the statements and decided whether each statement was probably true or probably false, or whether a person cannot tell from the story that the statements were true or false. Scores were provided on the dimensions of inference: (a) correctness (i.e., students select correct inferences), (b) caution (i.e., students are overly cautious and select the "cannot tell" alternative frequently), (c) overgeneralization (i.e., students make inferences that are not warranted by selecting an inference when they should choose the "cannot tell" alternative), and (d) discrimination (i.e., students can discriminate between the items given in the test problem).

The second measure developed for assessing the effectiveness of the teaching strategies was a system for coding and analyzing classroom interaction using audiotapes of discussions held during the year. The system of coding included scoring each "thought unit" (i.e., a remark or series of remarks expressing a complete idea) by three different sets of codings. The first coding was a designation of the sources—that is, whether it came from the teacher or student, and whether the person was seeking or giving information. The second coding was function and included two large groups, managerial or content-free (e.g., agreement, approval, disagreement, disapproval, management, reiteration) and content-related (e.g., focusing, refocusing, change of focus, deviation from focus, controlling thought, extending thought on the same level, and lifting thought to a higher level). The third type of coding identified the level of thought. The same system was used for both teacher and student behavior, and a different system was developed for each cognitive strategy: grouping and labeling, interpreting and making inferences, and predicting consequences. Within each strategy, the specific tasks were ordered from low to high levels whenever possible. A procedure also was developed for relating the levels of thought across cognitive tasks.

To analyze interaction patterns, several measures were obtained for each child, each classroom, and each grade level, and across all classrooms and grade levels. The following patterns were included: amount of participation, interaction between teaching strategies and thought levels, frequency of success of extending and lifting functions, amount and effect of other teacher functions, and amount of thinking at three levels across the three types of strategies. Children also were classified as high or low participators. Finally, these aspects of children's participation in the discussions were compared with their performance on the *Social Studies Inference Test* and with the other variables assessed (i.e., IQ scores, mental age, social studies achievement, reading achievement, and socioeconomic status of the family).

With All Children

Taba's research was conducted in classrooms of heterogeneously grouped children of wide ranges of ability. The following are some of the general conclusions of the studies that have implications for the teaching of all children:

- Formal operational thinking appears much earlier than Piaget assumed but follows the sequence he identified. Steady growth occurs in formal thinking from Grades 2 through 6, with this type of thinking occurring in about one sixth of all thought units in Grade 6 (Taba, 1964).
- The most marked influence on cognitive performance of the children was the teaching strategies. Of these strategies, two variables were of particular importance: teacher questions and the sequencing or patterning of teacher acts. Teachers got what they requested most of the time. If they asked for thinking at a low level, the children generally responded on a low level. When teachers asked for thinking at a high level, the children generally responded at that level. Students' level of thinking, however, was affected not only by the single teacher question preceding it but also by the whole pattern of teacher behavior prior to the student's response (Taba, 1964).
- The teacher function of reiteration (e.g., the habit of restating or repeating what children have said) is used abundantly by teachers and constitutes almost half of all teacher functions (46%) but has little impact on the course of discussion (Taba, 1964).
- Students in experimental groups performed better on tests and in discussions than did students in the control groups (Taba, 1966).
- Trained teachers had a greater success rate in getting students to respond at the higher levels than did the untrained teachers (Taba, 1966).
- Teacher training is more effective when directed toward specific strategies rather than overall improvement in teaching (Taba, 1964).

Other researchers also have studied use of the Taba strategies. Betres, Zajano, and Gumieniak (1984) examined the effects of two different preinstructional activities on cognitive achievement by elementary school students in social studies. The authors concluded that the effects of both approaches were significant, but that the students who were taught using the Taba strategies scored higher than students taught with the other approach and higher than those taught with inquiry and expository methods. Hanninen (1989) studied 192 students in Grades 6 through 11, and reported that the use of the four Hilda Taba Teaching Strategies had a significant impact on the creative and critical thinking behaviors of students. Pryor (1994, cited in Lori, 1999) reported on the use of two strategies, Concept Development and Interpretation of Data, in addition to questions based on Bloom's Taxonomy (see Chapter 3). Her conclusion was that all children benefited from the use of higher level questioning strategies, and that 5 of the 6 gifted students in the classrooms studied showed great increases in their cognitive abilities. Al-Shwailan (1997, cited in Lori, 1999) found that use of the Concept Development strategy positively influenced the cognitive growth of students in her study. Scores of students who were taught using the strategy scored better on the posttest.

With Gifted Students

One of the most surprising findings of the first study (Taba, 1964) was the generally low relationship between the level of thinking and traditional variables that influence thought (i.e., IQ, achievement, reading comprehension, and economic status). When growth was measured, the relationships were almost nonexistent. To explain this phenomenon and justify the use of the strategies with homogeneous groups of gifted children at least part of the time, further explanation of the results of the research is necessary. The patterns of teacher functions—particularly extending and lifting—and the pacing of these functions in the total discussion were critical to students' cognitive growth. An important aspect of the use of the Taba strategies is to pace the discussion and rotate assimilation and accommodation activities so that all children can participate. For this reason, the discussion must remain at the lowest level until an adequate basis is found for moving as a group to the next level. The timing of the extending and lifting is critical to the cognitive development of the students. A discussion begins at the lowest level with a process such as listing. Teachers must keep the discussion at this level by extending (i.e., asking for additional ideas, examples, new ideas, or explanations of ideas given) until they feel the group has an adequate basis for the discussion. Then, they ask a question that "lifts" the level of thought required (e.g., moving from listing to grouping in the Concept Development strategy, or moving from listing to inferences about causes or effects in the Interpretation of Data strategy). If teachers remain too long at a low level, the discussion may never reach the higher levels. On the other hand, if they attempt to move students too quickly from lower to higher levels, often the children are unable to make the leap requested, so they return to the lower level.

Taba (1964) described four class discussion patterns. In Pattern A, the teacher attempts to raise the level of thinking early in the discussion and continues to attempt to lift it without providing an adequate basis at the lower levels. The children are unable to maintain these levels and keep returning to the lowest level. Pattern B represents an effective discussion in which the teacher remains at the lower levels long enough to accumulate an appropriate amount of information before moving the children to higher levels. The teacher is generally effective in keeping the discussion moving upward. In Pattern C, the teacher constantly attempts to move the discussion too high and too quickly without much basis at the lower levels or any steps in between. The result is that the children repeatedly return to the information level. Pattern D represents still another ineffective strategy. The teacher is constantly changing the focus of the discussion, which results in the children being unable to accumulate enough information about any focus to be able to move to higher levels and remain there. These patterns indicate that when gifted children are grouped with other gifted children, discussions can be paced much more rapidly. Not as much time must be concentrated on the lower levels before moving upward.

C. June Maker's, Shirley Schiever's and other teachers' experiences verify the validity of this idea. Perhaps the most significant reason for the fact that the growth in cognitive skills of children with low IQs was as great as that of children with high IQs was that most discussions had to be paced so that all children could move upward together. This pacing increases the boredom and decreases the challenge of the tasks for gifted children.

Research on the Taba strategies indicates that they are effective with gifted students. High and Udall (1989) found that gifted students' perception that the teacher was using strategies to teach higher level thinking skills and the use of the strategies resulted in meaningful learning.

Schiever (1986) and Brooks (1988) reported positive results of the Taba strategies with gifted students. Schiever (1986) compared the cognitive growth effects on students in six groups using a model × treatment design: two service delivery systems (gifted students in either self-contained or once-weekly programs) and three teaching models. She found a significant model $\times$ treatment interaction ($p < .0001$), with significant differences between daily treatment and control groups and between the Taba self-contained and once-weekly service delivery models. Brooks also measured to assess growth in conceptual complexity and cognitive maturation among 97 seventh-grade gifted students in self-contained classes in an existing school program. Two of four social studies classes for the gifted were designated as experimental groups; the remaining two served as control groups. The same teacher taught all classes. The results provide support for the effectiveness of the Taba strategies with gifted students; additional comparative studies still are needed.

Lori (1999), in a study of academically gifted Bahraini students that extended over two semesters, found a mean score gain between pretest and posttest of 11.29. Furthermore, he found significant differences between the mean scores of five groups, based on the level and frequency of teacher implementation. The students whose teachers used the strategies (cor-rectly) the most times scored significantly higher than the other groups. The level of implementation was highly related to student posttest scores.

JUDGMENTS

Advantages

The Hilda Taba Teaching Strategies program has many advantages for gifted students. Perhaps the most obvious is its strong research base, which supports the effectiveness of the strategies in developing higher levels of thinking in children. This research not only provides general information about its effectiveness, but also has resulted in the development of specific strategies and clear methods for applying them to achieve the desired ob-jectives. An excellent teacher-training program and specific procedures for teacher self-evaluation, for analysis of classroom interaction, and for stu-dent evaluation also have been developed during the course of the research. Additionally, a curriculum organized to facilitate the development of think-ing and designed for use with the strategies has been developed.

Another advantage of the teaching strategies is the ease with which they can be generalized or transferred. Once learned, many aspects of the strategies can be incorporated into a total approach that goes beyond the use of specific strategies. For example, asking open-ended but focused questions is an extremely important skill for use with gifted children, as are appropriate pacing of discussions and asking questions that require children to verbalize their reasons. After learning the Taba strategies, many teachers say they internalize the skills and consistently apply them. Also, this approach can be combined easily with others used in programs for the gifted. Because Taba's ideas about the organization of content are almost identical to Bruner's (Chapter 4), the combination of Bruner-based curricula with the Taba strategies is an easy one. This combination can enhance the effectiveness of both approaches, because few curricula have been developed built around Taba's approach, but numerous ones are based on Bruner's ideas. Also, the Taba strategies fill a definite "process" need not addressed in depth by Bruner. Furthermore, they provide a nice addition to the Autonomous Learner Model (Chapter 2), DISCOVER (Chapter 5), Problem-Based Learning (Chapter 7), the Enrichment Triad and Schoolwide Enrichment Models (Chapter 8), Group Investigations (Chapter 9), and Thinking Actively in a Social Context (Chapter 11). The strategies also can be combined with moral developmental (Kohlberg, 1966) and emotional developmental models (Dabrowski & Piechowski, 1977), as the interdisciplinary concepts recommended in the Taba Social Studies Curriculum are both affective and cognitive.

Another advantage is the comprehensiveness of the Taba approach when both the curriculum and teaching strategies are used. This program provides almost all of the content, process, and psychological learning environment modifications advocated for gifted children. It provides one of the product changes and sets the stage for others to be made. The relationships of content and process are made explicitly clear when combined in the Hilda Taba Teaching Strategies.

An additional advantage can be secured when teachers and others who develop curricula learn the strategies and use them, in part and in whole, as a structure for curricula. The resulting curricula easily meet state and national standards and make learning more fun and interesting for students.

A final advantage is that researchers continue to demonstrate its effectiveness with all students, in a variety of settings. The body of research also supports the appropriateness and effectiveness of its use with gifted students.

Disadvantages

Because the Taba strategies are complicated and require the learning of overt as well as subtle teacher behaviors, they are difficult for many teachers to learn. For some, a complete change in style is required and may take a long time to internalize. In C. June Maker's and Shirley Schiever's teacher-training program, for example, at least one 3-hour semester course is necessary to learn to teach the strategies. The semester is intense, but gratifying for most as they practice the strategies by taping class discussions, analyzing their own performance, and receiving evaluations of their performance.

One problem with the training and later use of the Taba strategies is that the training manuals (one for each of the four strategies), which in the past could be purchased by trained leaders for use in teaching teachers, are now out of print and few trained seminar leaders are available to conduct staff development sessions. Furthermore, Schiever's (1991) text, *A Comprehensive Approach to Teaching Thinking*, which includes an overview of the Taba strategies, clear explanations of each strategy, extensive examples, and complete lesson plans adapted from the Institute for Staff Development training manuals, is also out of print. Likewise, developmental information regarding the strategies and their use is extremely difficult to find. The research reports are out of print, which make the research difficult to replicate and the information difficult to disseminate.

CONCLUSION

The advantages of Taba's approach far outweigh its disadvantages. In the years since publication of this book in its original form, use of the Taba strategies has spread widely, nationally and internationally. We anticipate that this trend will continue, as the leadership of underdeveloped countries continues to realize the importance of critical and creative thinking in their educational programs.

RESOURCES

Background Information

The following materials are out of print and difficult to locate. They are included, however, to provide information for those who may wish to search in academic libraries or curriculum archives for more information than is found in books currently in print.

Schiever, S. W. (1991). *A comprehensive approach to teaching thinking*. Boston: Allyn & Bacon.

Institute for Staff Development. (1971). *Hilda Taba teaching strategies program: Unit I, Unit II, Unit III, and Unit IV*. Miami: Author.

Ellis, K., & Durkin, M. C. (1972). *Teacher's guide for people in communities (The Taba program in social studies)*. Menlo Park, CA: Addison-Wesley.

Instructional Material

Instructional materials are available from various retail sources. Some of their Web sites are listed, along with a sampling of the materials they offer.

A. W. Peller (http://www.awpeller.com)
Architecture Activities for Ancient Egypt, Greece & Rome
As It Was Series: An Interdisciplinary Approach to History

Prufrock Press (http://www.prufrock.com)
Creating History Documentaries: A Step-by-Step Guide to Video Projects in the Classroom
Simulation Series

Zephyr Press (http://www.zephyrpress.com)
Begin with the Brain: Orchestrating the Learner-Centered Classroom
The Parallel Curriculum: A Design To Develop High Potential & Challenge High-ability Learners
Synergetics: Differentiating with Science
Synergetics: Thinking & Math
Synergetics: Independent Study
Synergetics: Literacy
The Parallel Curriculum

CHAPTER 11

Belle Wallace
and Harvey B. Adams:
Thinking Actively
in a Social Context

ASC, the acronym for Thinking Actively in a Social Context (Adams & Wallace, 1991; B. Wallace & Adams, 1987, 1993[1]), was developed in response to concerns regarding underachievement, dropout rates, and the standard instructional practice of rote memorization in KwaZulu/Natal schools in South Africa. The model provides a structure for curriculum development that includes instruction and practice in necessary skills, and the use of these skills to solve relevant problems.

TASC is a multiphase problem-solving model that incorporates basic thinking skills and tools for effective thinking. It offers a flexible structure within which teachers and students can develop curriculum to meet the needs of diverse populations (Adams & Wallace, 1991). The teaching principles of TASC are based on worldwide research about how children learn and best teaching practices. Although rigorous, these principles can be modified to meet learning needs and student interests (Wallace, 2002b). These principles include the following:

1. Adopt a model of the problem-solving process and explicitly teach this.
2. Identify a set of specific *Basic Skills* and *Thinking Tools* and give training in these.
3. Develop a vocabulary to suit the learner.
4. Give ample practice in both *Basic Skills* and the *Thinking Tools.*
5. Give attention to the motivational aspects of problem-solving.

---

[1]Throughout this chapter, text cites mentioning Wallace refer to B. Wallace; however, the initial is not repeated through the chapter.

6. The progression of teaching is from modeling by the teacher to guided activity by the learner, and eventually autonomous action by the learner.
7. Every effort must be made to enable the learner to transfer *Basic Skills* and *Thinking Tools.*
8. The emphasis is on cooperative learning in small groups.
9. Teachers should encourage pupils' self-monitoring and self-evaluation.
10. Students should be encouraged to develop their metacognitive knowledge (Wallace & Adams, 1993, p. 63).

As a beginning project, the following were aims of TASC (Adams & Wallace, 1991):

1. improve attitudes toward and motivation for learning
2. improve student self-concepts
3. help students learn to take on and solve problems in all facets of their lives that had a bearing on their performance in school
4. improve student learning and achievement
5. provide students opportunities to learn and practice decision making and leadership roles
6. prepare students to be successful citizens in a society bound to experience rapid and profound changes in the foreseeable future
7. help disadvantaged students to assume societal roles never envisioned by those in their families and neighborhoods

Based on pilot projects and further use of the model, these initial aims have been revised and extended to become general aims that focus on student development, teacher training, and curriculum development. The general aim for the students is to maximize their ability to make sense of their experiences and to learn from them. The general aim for teachers is to improve their efficacy as facilitators of their students' learning. Both short- and long-term general aims exist for the curriculum. The short-term general aim is to modify existing syllabi to maximize achievement of the general aims for teachers and students. The long-term general aim is to reconstruct the curriculum to achieve short- and long-term general aims for teachers and students (Adams & Wallace, 1991).

TASC originally was developed for students in their mid-teens (those who are in high school in the United States). Its effectiveness for all ages has resulted in its spreading to virtually all age levels and to numerous countries. The strength of the structure has made this possible and indeed inevitable. A critical aspect of TASC is that it is intended to be only a starting point, one of many, for teachers to lead students to identify and formulate problems that are relevant to them, and then to help them learn the skills needed to work effectively toward solutions.

ASSUMPTIONS UNDERLYING THE MODEL

About Learning

The essential belief of Adams and Wallace (Adams, 1985, 1986; Adams & Wallace, 1988) is that classroom teachers and students should have a major voice in the development of curriculum. Therefore, the model is intended to be used as a *framework* for courses in problem solving, based on student experiences, needs, and interests (Adams & Wallace, 1991).

Assumptions underlying the model include that (a) teachers and students can learn to design and implement relevant and effective curriculum; (b) learners mature mainly through interactions with others and personal reflection; (c) development is dynamic and ongoing; (d) intelligent behavior is related to real-life situations and problem-solving abilities, which can be continuously developed; (e) learners gain control through metacognition; (f) modeling is an important aspect of learning; (g) a positive self-concept is necessary to becoming self-directed; and (h) transfer of learning occurs with constant practice within the learning context (Wallace & Adams, 1993). Additional assumptions about learning include the following (Adams & Wallace, 1991):

1. Language is the major tool for communication and learning, and home language needs to be accommodated and extended to language for formal learning.
2. Senior learners need to scaffold experiences for young learners until they are able to proceed independently.
3. The best environment for learning includes trust, acceptance, and encouragement.
4. All people can learn to plan their learning effectively and monitor it efficiently (Wallace, 2002b).

5. Thinking skills can be systematically developed, making it possible for all learners to become more efficient.
6. An information processing approach incorporating basic skills is efficient.
7. A structure within which students and teachers can incorporate problems that are important to them will enhance learning and motivation.
8. Explicit training is necessary to learn higher order thinking processes.
9. Student motivation is related to self-confidence, as well as to becoming an efficient learner and problem solver.

About Teaching

A critical assumption of the TASC model is that teachers' actions have an important influence on student behaviors, including thinking and problem solving. Therefore, if teachers model and provide instruction in positive social and academic behaviors, including metacognition, these behaviors can facilitate the development of advanced skills in students, who can then become independent learners. Further assumptions include that (a) the incorporation of issues and problems that are relevant to the learners is motivational and leads to transfer of skills to real-life problems; (b) motivation is instrumental toward developing a sense of self-worth, internal locus of control, and belief in the self as an effective learner (Adams & Wallace, 1991); and (c) teachers can acquire the skills to design curriculum that is motivational and relevant to their students.

About Characteristics and Teaching of Gifted Students

Gifted students are noted for their extraordinary grasp of concepts and principles and their store of knowledge. Additionally, they thrive on being involved in choices about their learning. Generally, they are able to process information quickly and to see ideas and possibilities others do not see. Examining the extended aims of the TASC program reveals a good fit with characteristics of gifted students. The extended program aims to develop the following: (a) attitudes that include an active approach to thinking and problem solving, avoidance of impulsivity, perseverance, internal locus of control, and a positive self-image; (b) thinking skills such as the ability to make comparisons and categorize, and stable spatial and temporal relationships; (c) tools for effective thinking and problem-solving strategies; and (d) metacognitive strategies and the skill to know when to use these strategies (Adams & Wallace, 1991).

ELEMENTS/PARTS

The elements of TASC are defined as follows (see Figure 11.1):

☞ **Thinking:** Effective thinking is necessary to achieve learning.

☞ **Actively:** Thinking must be practiced, and knowledge about thinking must be applied.

☞ **Social:** Thoughts and ideas are operational when they are communicated to, or shared with, another person(s).

☞ **Context:** Thinking always occurs in a context, and the purpose, meaning, or situation underlying an action or idea should be understood (van der Horst, 2000).

Dimensions

As presented in Figure 11.2, four basic thinking categories are included in TASC. These are knowledge, attitudes and motivation, metacognition, and skills and processes.

Effective Thinking Tools

The TASC framework has three levels: a range of *Basic Thinking Skills* that all learners need, such as making comparisons, sequencing, developing a thinking language, and so on; *Effective Thinking Tools*, which are more complex thinking strategies; and the *Problem Solving Framework*, in which

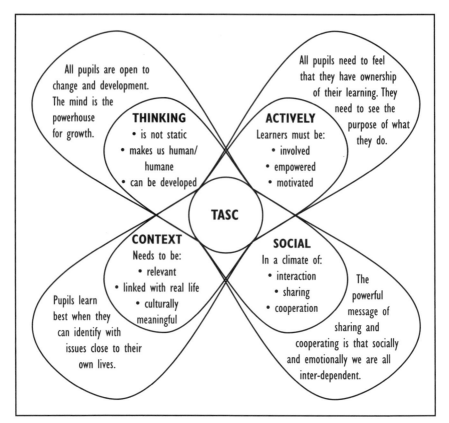

FIGURE 11.1. Elements of TASC. From *Teaching Thinking Skills Across the Middle Years: A Practical Approach for Children Aged 9–14*, by B. Wallace and R. Bentley (Eds.), 2002, London: David Fulton. Copyright 2002 by David Fulton Publishers. Reprinted with permission.

the first two levels are embedded (B. Wallace, personal communication, March 11, 2004). Figure 11.3 provides an example of the application of both Basic Thinking Skills and Effective Thinking Tools during a problem-solving process. The process begins with exploration of a potential problem situation, and continues through the stages necessary for developing, evaluating, and transferring the skills and knowledge to students.

Table 11.1 provides a summary of teacher and student roles and activities in the TASC model. Comparing teacher and student roles across models helps readers evaluate the models contained in this volume and to choose the most appropriate for implementation in their situation.

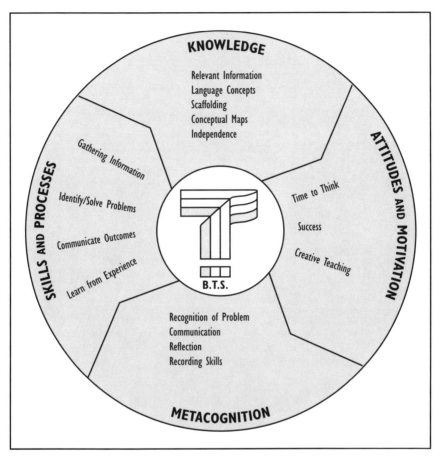

FIGURE 11.2. Basic thinking skills. From *TASC: Thinking Actively in a Social Context,* by B. Wallace and H. B. Adams, 1993, London: AB Academic Publishers. Copyright 1993 by AB Academic Publishers. Reprinted with permission.

MODIFICATIONS
OF THE BASIC CURRICULUM

Content Modifications

The TASC structure includes the choice of real problems and provides variety; complexity and abstractness also may be incorporated, depending on problem selection. If the model is used as proposed, with thematic

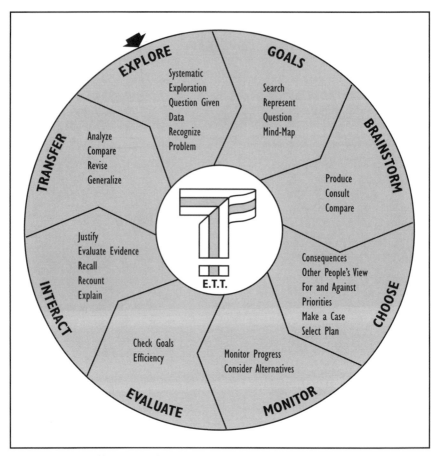

FIGURE 11.3. Effective Thinking Tools. From *TASC: Thinking Actively in a Social Context,* by B. Wallace and H. B. Adams, 1993, London: AB Academic Publishers. Copyright 1993 by AB Academic Publishers. Reprinted with permission.

planning, material will be organized for learning value. The study of people is not included but can be added easily. For example, solving a problem might require consulting experts in one or more disciplines. Students who show a particular interest in a discipline might want to learn about one or more prominent persons in the field. This situation also offers the opportunity for students to study the methods of the disciplines. As students struggle with defining a problem, which might require researching the history of the problem, they might discover individuals whose lives would be of interest and value to them.

(*text continues on p. 386*)

TABLE 11.1
Summary of Student and Teacher Roles and Activities in the TASC Model

Elements	Student		Teacher	
	Role	Sample Activities	Role	Sample Activities
Gather/Organize	Active participant in establishing what is known about problem situation	Brainstorm information or ideas. Participate in mind-mapping with entire group. In small groups, work on organizing available information.	Guide / Resource / Facilitator	Establish ground rules for brainstorming. Lead students in mind-mapping brainstormed list. As student interest becomes apparent, begin gathering materials and resources. Monitor small groups by circulating and asking questions or pointing out ideas.
Identify	Active participant	In small groups, identify and refine the aspect of the problem of most interest.	Facilitator / Resource	Monitor small groups. Ask proof-of-reasoning questions as appropriate. Observe dynamics of small groups and entire class discussions.
Generate	Active participant	In small groups, brainstorm possible solutions to selected aspect of problem situation. Share ideas with whole group.	Resource / Facilitator	Record small groups' ideas (no repetition). Ask clarification questions or for examples as necessary.
Decide	Active participant in selecting criteria and	In small group, establish criteria for selection. Using these criteria, select and rank-order the three best ideas from the shared class list or	Resource / Guide / Facilitator	Assist students in setting criteria for choosing three best ideas. Facilitate sharing of small groups' best ideas with entire group. Ask proof-of-reasoning

(continues)

TABLE 11.1 *Continued.*
Summary of Student and Teacher Roles and Activities in the TASC Model

Elements	Student		Teacher	
	Role	Sample Activities	Role	Sample Activities
Decide *(continued)*	prioritizing three best ideas, with support for selection and prioritization	from within the group. Establish support for selection and order.		questions about best ideas and priorities.
Implement	Active participant	Plan the solution to selected problem situation. Develop criteria for judging the solution and the interactions of individuals within the group. Within small group, assign tasks in a fair way and using student strengths. Work independently and share with small group the results and information gathered. Refine, re-define, and modify the problem and solution as necessary.	Organizer Facilitator	Plan realistic amounts of time for individual work, small group meetings, and class sharing. Assist in the development of criteria, unless students are experienced with this process. Monitor individuals and small groups, helping or guiding as necessary. Lead class discussions for maximum learning. Ask proof-of-reasoning questions as appropriate.
Evaluate	Active participant	As individuals, self-evaluate process, interactions, and contributions based on the criteria. As a small group, apply criteria to group interactions, process, and product.	Instructor Facilitator	Assist individuals and groups with evaluation based on criteria. Monitor students' need for information, help, or guidance.

(continues)

| Communicate | Active participant in selecting information to be presented and methods of presentation
Active participant in preparing for presentation | Assist in preparing small-group presentation that uses a variety of media, that reflects what was learned, and in which everyone in the group has a part. | Resource Facilitator Manager | Gather materials students need for presentations. Allow time for groups to practice presentations, and assist them in meeting time allotment. Instruct entire class in providing constructive feedback to each other, based on the criteria. |
| Learn from experience | Active participant in self-reflection on what was learned and areas for improvement, and within small group as to how they might improve next time. | Reflect on the process and the product, interactions with others, and the most important thing learned from the project. Record reflections in a journal. | Resource Facilitator | Establish calm and positive environment, especially as related to the recent project. Provide some prompts (e.g., "As I thought about this project, I...."; "Next time, I think I will...."; "My small group...."; "The most important thing about this project for me was/is...."). |

Process Modifications

Most of the recommended process modifications for gifted students are included in the TASC model. Higher levels of thinking are taught and practiced in context; the problems are open-ended; learning occurs within small, interactive groups; and students must provide evidence of their reasoning to their small group and possibly to the entire class when a solution is developed. Students make choices within the context of the problem; and in finding the solution, a variety of processes are used, and students are discovering information as they seek solutions. The pacing appropriate for gifted students is not necessarily part of the TASC processes, but the sensitive, knowledgeable teacher can easily ensure that the composition of the small groups is such that gifted learners are not being held back by others.

Product Modifications

The comprehensive and specific TASC manuals currently do not contain much information related to student products. Delightful samples of student products adorn the covers of some journals and the pages of the teaching manuals, but this dimension of TASC has not been developed as fully as other dimensions. When students select a problem that is relevant to their lives, one would assume that when a solution has been formulated, it would be presented to the appropriate "real audience." This is an easy and natural component to add, and evaluation can be included as well. Developing criteria and identifying appropriate evaluators early in the process and revisiting these regularly enables students to stay on track *or* to modify criteria and audience as necessary. Variety, self-selected format, and transformation of information need to be included in the criteria for evaluation. All of these can be incorporated easily into the existing TASC structure.

Learning Environment Modifications

When teachers have been trained in TASC philosophy, principles, and strategies, their classrooms will be learner centered, flexible, open, and accepting, and will allow high mobility. Students are taught basic thinking skills and metacognitive strategies to motivate and enable them to become independent learners. As small groups of students work through the problem-solving process, their needs, materials, resources, and activities will contribute to the complexity of the environment. Because students are not in small groups for all of their instructional time, varied student groupings occur. Teachers need to vary the composition of the small groups to facilitate personal, social, and intellectual or academic growth.

Examples of Teaching Activities/Strategies

The following are teacher guidelines for instruction and learning experiences based on TASC:

1. Adopt a model of the problem-solving process, and explicitly teach this.
2. Identify a set of specific skills and strategies, and give training in these.
3. Develop a vocabulary—including verbal labels and visual mnemonics suited to the age and social background of the students.
4. Give ample practice in both the skills and the strategies, using situations which are significant and relevant to the learners.
5. Give attention to the motivational aspects of the problem-solving. (Adams & Wallace, 1991, p. 107)

Throughout the TASC process, teachers need to monitor and be aware of their roles and function. These include (a) moving from teacher-modeled behavior to guided activity and then autonomous action by the learner, (b) placing an emphasis on cooperative learning within the small groups, and (c) encouraging self-monitoring and self-evaluation by the students. Students need to be (a) transferring the skills and strategies they are learning to other situations, (b) making observable progress toward becoming autonomous learners, (c) engaged in self-monitoring and self-evaluation, and (d) developing metacognitive skills and knowledge (Wallace & Adams, 1991).

Although during the introductory days or weeks of using TASC, teachers introduce open-ended problems to the students (B. Wallace, personal communication, March 11, 2004), other critical elements— problem choice and definition—are not included. These elements are critical to motivation, relevance, and the transfer of skills. To add this element, students can brainstorm problems related to the classroom, school, community, neighborhoods, city, state, or nation. After recording the list of problems, the group should develop criteria for the problem on which they will focus. Criteria need to include high interest to all or most of the group members, importance of the underlying issue, feasibility of using the problem-solving process on the problem, and feasibility of the undertaking. The teacher needs to ensure that the groups select a *well-constructed, ill-structured* problem (See Chapter 7) that can be used to achieve curricular objectives and include interdisciplinary explorations.

Problem definition is an important step and may be an evolving entity as the group learns more about the problem. Small groups work on defining their problems and bring their definitions to the entire group for discussion and critique. The teacher needs to give input, and may need to share with students learning objectives and curriculum goals so they are aware as they select, define, and solve the problem.

The TASC Flexi-Think Program is an example of how to help students develop basic thinking skills as they acquire knowledge and participate in activities. According to van der Horst (2000, p. 106), students need to learn to use key words and phrases and to use tools for effective thinking.

Using Key Words and Phrases
- knowing directions, shape, size, volume
- looking for similarities and differences
- separating into parts
- putting parts into a whole

Tools for Effective Thinking
- brainstorming
- making mind maps
- being in someone else'e shoes
- thinking about consequences
- deciding order or importance

IMPLEMENTATION

Thinking skills need to be embedded in all contexts of the learners' lives, permeating all experiences until learners are empowered and sufficiently confident to select, apply, and assess their thinking, recognizing that efficiency constantly increases with practice followed by reflection upon practice (Wallace & Adams, 1993, p. 75). Wallace and Adams (1993) suggest a twofold approach to the implementation of TASC. They advise that an initial course in thinking skills and problem solving be conducted in a series of sessions that equal up to 25 hours of instruction and practice. The next step is to incorporate the Basic Thinking Skills, the Tools for Effective Thinking, and the Problem-Solving Model into the curriculum in a holistic and integrated way.

Bentley and Johnstone (2002) provide an example of how they implemented the TASC model. After deciding what they wanted to accomplish, they developed the following list:

- Introduce students to the TASC model and enable them to apply an understanding of the problem-solving process within a range of problem contexts.
- Be fast, flexible, and fun.
- Include teacher training component, as well as teaching the process to students.
- Form a basic "introductory package" that teachers and schools could build on.
- Embed a range of curricular experiences within the problem-solving strategies.

For the purposes of this text, discussion of Bentley and Johnstone's implementation focuses only on how the model is introduced to the students.

The "fast, flexible, and fun" approach is helpful in generating enthusiasm for a new approach that may require risk-taking and stepping out of the established routine. "Fast" is important so students (and their teachers) do not feel overwhelmed by the perception of a lengthy project. "Flexible" is necessary to accommodate the range of interests and strengths in the group. And the reason for "fun" is that students are more motivated, learn more, retain information longer, and resist the work less when they are enjoying activities.

Bentley and Johnstone (2002) organized a 2-day introduction to TASC for students and their teachers. The following example focuses on the TASC processes, offers a brief overview of the types of activities included in TASC, and demonstrates some of the many ways this model can be used across the curriculum. It includes a description of the objectives and activities for each day of this introductory experience.

Day I

Prepare a TASC Problem-Solving Wheel suitable for presenting to a class. This can be a poster, transparency, or any other representation. Explain the wheel and its supportive nature and tell the students that they are going to learn the skills of the wheel by participating in fun learning activities. A basic TASC Problem-Solving Wheel appears in Figure 11.4.

Activity I. Memory Search: The Brain

☛ **TASC Focus:** Gather/Organize

☛ **Modeling Focus:** Organize, Classify, Group Responses

☛ **Student Objectives:** Students will see that
  • an efficient starting point for any problem is noting what is known about the situation;
  • the knowledge of the group is greater than that of individuals; the group is a useful source of information and ideas;
  • performance can be improved through practice; and the brain can be trained.

Divide the class into groups of four students and ask them to think about what they know about the brain. Allow 4 or 5 minutes for each group to create an oral list. Take feedback from the entire group, listing responses on chart paper or a whiteboard. Using a different colored marker, ask students which of the ideas and responses link together, and draw lines that reflect the linkages.

This activity demonstrates the potential for revising and reorganizing information after "first thoughts" are shared and the potential for "hitch-hiking" on someone else's idea.

Activity 2. Using Your Bottle

☛ **TASC Focus:** Gather/Organize, Generate, Decide

☛ **Modeling Focus:** Discuss, Listen, Prioritize, Justify Prioritization, Think Creatively

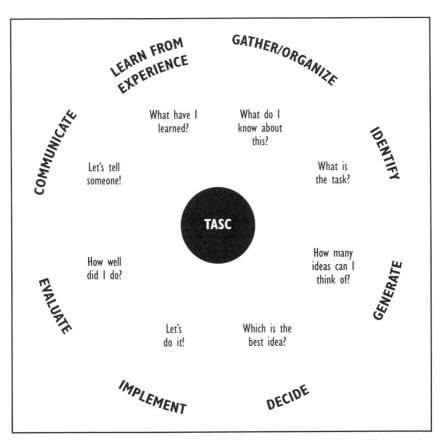

FIGURE 11.4. TASC Problem-Solving Wheel. From *Teaching Thinking Skills Across the Early Years: A Practical Approach for Children Aged 4–7,* by B. Wallace and R. B. Bentley (Eds.), 2002, London: David Fulton. Copyright 2002 by David Fulton Publishers. Reprinted with permission.

☞ **Student Objective:** Students will become more comfortable about offering and building on suggestions.

In groups of four, with one student acting as recorder, students are to brainstorm and list all the uses they can think of for a 2-quart (or 2-liter) plastic bottle. When the groups have had sufficient time to develop a list, give them a few minutes to choose their three best ideas. As a class, have each group give its best, second-best, and third-best ideas. List these on a flip chart, butcher paper, or whiteboard. Emphasize that no repetitions will be recorded on the class list.

This activity is designed to provide students further practice with the skills from Activity 1, help them become more confident in offering unusual ideas, and encourage creative thinking. This helps establish a classroom environment in which students are comfortable taking risks. Some of the ideas may include using the bottle as another container (serving the same purpose), changing the shape by cutting or melting, or adding to the shape (e.g., rocket fins). Each idea entails a different type of thinking, and the sharing of ideas with the entire group provides for broader thinking horizons for individual students. Additionally, teachers may note new strengths in students, providing opportunities for future development.

Activity 3. Preparing for a Day's Hike Through Hills, Jungle, Desert, or Rainforest

☛ **TASC Focus:** Gather/Organize, Identify, Generate, Decide

☛ **Modeling Focus:** Decide, Justify, Generate

☛ **Student Objectives:** Students will
- repeat and practice skills included in Activities 1 and 2;
- clarify the task and examine many possibilities; and
- experience being in different situations, which prepares them for role playing and being empathetic.

In groups of four, have students brainstorm what they know about hiking through a specific bionomic region (hills, jungle, desert, rainforest, etc.). Ensure that the task is clarified—they need to consider all factors, based on what they know about the region. Ask questions as necessary to ensure the development of a comprehensive list (see Figure 11.5). In their small groups, instruct them to brainstorm a list of everything they need to take with them for their hike. After they have a brainstormed list, have each group decide which are the five most important items on their list, in order of importance. They also must justify their prioritization. Note that Activities 1, 2, and 3 have taken students through four segments of the TASC Problem-Solving Wheel. Additionally, they have prepared students for Activities 4 and 5, and the completion of the wheel.

FIGURE 11.5. Questions to develop thinking in the TASC problem-solving model. From *Teaching Thinking Skills Across the Early Years: A Practical Approach for Children Aged 4–7,* by B. Wallace and R. B. Bentley (Eds.), 2002, London: David Fulton. Copyright 2002 by David Fulton Publishers. Reprinted with permission.

Activity 4. Saving the Erar

☛ **TASC Focus:** Completion of TASC Problem-Solving Wheel

☛ **Modeling Focus:** Using empowering language, such as "You decide…," "No right answer…," "What do you think?" "That's up to your group to decide…," "Why did you decide to…?" (Bentley & Johnstone, 2002, p. 36)

☛ **Student Objectives:** Students will
  • bring together previously practiced skills within a different group;
  • experience the entire TASC wheel;
  • develop skills of implementation, evaluation, communication, and drawing on experience;
  • tackle a real problem (that is fictional) to put problem-solving skills into a real context;
  • meet, through evaluation, the concept of criteria and measurement issues (agree on measures and measuring strategies); and
  • interpret deliberately limited instructions and data and make detailed decisions.

The students are to work in groups of four or five (a different group composition from previous activities) to build a freestanding structure, as tall as possible, to transport an Erar egg to the ground as slowly as possible. They have the following information to provide the context for the problem:

> The Erar is a very unusual and rare bird, which builds its nest on the ground. That sounds OK, but on this occasion it hasn't laid its single egg in the nest but has chosen, instead, to lay it on the branches of a tree. To save this bird from extinction the students need to build something to transport an Erar egg carefully from the branch to the ground. (Bentley & Johnstone, 2002, p. 35)

Materials available to the students are limited to the following:

2 sheets of 9" × 12" tagboard	ping-pong ball or plastic egg
8 large paper clips	4 strong rubber bands
8 plastic drinking straws	48" masking tape
4-8½" × 11" scrap paper (for recording plans)	2 pairs of scissors

Additionally, each group should have access to a stopwatch to time the descent using their constructions.

Some students or groups tend to rush into action without planning, and others want specific guidance (teacher instructions) for completing the task. These behaviors indicate areas in need of growth, and the students may need reminders at this time and mini-lessons or activities in the future.

Day 2

Linking Activity To Begin Day 2

Using the version of the TASC Problem-Solving Wheel in Figure 11.5, lead the students around the wheel by asking the questions in each segment. The approach is designed to answer the question, "What did we learn from yesterday, about ourselves as thinkers and about problem solving?" (Bentley & Johnstone, 2002, p. 36). Focus on the vocabulary of each segment, and point out how different questions are helpful to assess their progress separately. Prior to beginning Activity 5, tell students that the new task will test their expertise, but that the wheel is designed to help them navigate the task successfully.

Activity 5. The Persuaders: Selling Your Idea

☛ **TASC Focus:** Whole TASC Problem-Solving Wheel

☛ **Modeling Focus:** Vocabulary associated with whole wheel

☛ **Student Objectives:** Students will see that
- the first idea may not be the best idea, and sometimes ideas have to be abandoned;
- to complete the task they need to work within a genuine collaboration and to use each other's ideas;
- communicating ideas succinctly is important and they need to be able to justify their group's decisions;
- role-playing and seeing things from another person's perspective provides an advantage, as does presenting in role to a "real" audience;
- evaluation is important, and various ways to make judgments exist; and
- revisiting and improving a product after evaluation is an important step.

The task for today is creating a family game that has the power to communicate a message and to sell. To do this, students will consider a variety of games and assess their qualities.

STAGE 1: LOOK AT AND PLAY A SELECTION OF BOARD GAMES. The following issues need to be considered, but the criteria need to be elicited from the students. In other words, rather than asking the questions listed, base questions on the students' experience playing the games, and start with questions such as these: What did you like about the game you were playing? What did you *not* like? Who might like this game? Why might they like it? The information sought is related to the following questions:

- Does it have a specific setting?
- What type of game is it?
- Who is it designed to be played by?
- What skills are required of the players? (Are these appropriate for the age range specified?)
- To what extent does it depend on chance?
- Does it look attractive?
- Would you buy it? What in particular attracts you or puts you off?
- Who might purchase it? (Parents, children, relatives, schools?)
  (Bentley & Johnstone, 2002, p. 37)

STAGE 2: DEVISE A GAME OF YOUR OWN. In groups of three or four, students design a board or other family game that is a potential best seller. The students should aim to be in a position, by afternoon, to present and justify their design to a panel representing a company that manufactures games. The game must

- convey a social message (an example is a message relating to an aspect of conservation);
- be appropriate for a range of family members and age groups;
- be usable in a family context (not a computer game); and
- be potentially marketable world-wide. (Bentley & Johnstone, 2002, p. 37)

Of particular importance, the emphasis must be on *ideas*, not on making the game. The actual games that students played earlier need to be in a teacher-controlled area to avoid "modification" of existing games and wasting time. The activity is one of thinking and planning; not enough time will be available to make the games.

STAGE 3: SELECT ONE DESIGN TO BE PUT FORWARD TO THE MANUFACTURING COMPANY'S PANEL IN THE AFTERNOON, AND PREPARE THE PRESENTATION. Each small group of students will join with one or two other groups for this stage. Each small group will have to explain its original game to the combined group. Students in the combined group are to come up with a *composite* game that incorporates aspects of the games of the smaller groups. Each person in the combined group must have a role in the preparation of the presentation or the actual presentation. For example, a group recorder is chosen to record the features selected for the final product and the reasons the group chose those features.

The teacher's role is to circulate to listen and perhaps remind groups that their task is to select the best details or features of each game, which will result in a composite of all the games. Also, the teacher may need to remind students to designate roles by asking questions such as, "What will (e.g., Melinda's) role be?" or perhaps remind a group of strengths they might want to consider as they decide on roles. The critical factor is that the teacher does not direct, but rather guides students to accomplish their assigned task.

STAGE 4: PREPARE A 10-MINUTE PRESENTATION OF THE GAME (USING PROVIDED MATERIALS) FOR A MEETING WITH THE GAME MANUFACTURER'S PANEL. Students have 1 hour to prepare their presentation. The whole group will be at the meeting, and each person will introduce him- or herself and state briefly what he or she contributed to the game. Every member of the group needs to be prepared to answer questions about the game. The presentations are to be no more than 10 minutes long, so students need to keep to the most critical points. The games may be presented in any way students choose, but suggestions for their consideration include the following:

- design of the box, or package, and rules of the game
- use of a poster or storyboard of a television advertisement (decisions must be made regarding what appears in the visual component and what information must be included in the sound byte)
- design of a poster or billboard advertisement

STAGE 5: PRESENT THE GAME TO THE PANEL. Each group presents to the panel in turn. The panel consists of students taking various roles. Panel roles can be, for example, design/marketing director, finance director, and parent/family consultant. In addition to a family consultant, some firms use children in a similar role, so all those students not involved in the presentation may be child advisers and score games (as presented) against the previously agreed-upon criteria.

After the presentation, the panel asks some presentation-specific questions to clarify the product. The student designers justify and expand on points as requested. The panel provides feedback and discusses how each game was evaluated based on the predetermined criteria.

MODIFYING THE MODEL

Although TASC was developed to meet the learning needs of diverse groups of students, it lends itself easily to the necessary modifications for gifted learners. It is primarily a process model, but content and product modifications are not difficult to incorporate within the structure and processes of TASC. Wallace (personal communication, March 11, 2004) believes that thinking processes are the same for all people, but the more able need to embed the processes in complex content with greater depth and breadth. They easily learn the process, and it soon becomes automatic. The less able can use the same processes but in simpler content; the TASC framework, which exemplifies the processes of an expert thinker, is used as a "crutch" to guide their thinking.

Content Modifications

None of the content changes indicated for gifted students are inherent to the TASC model. By using a thematic approach to curriculum development, however, a teacher can include all of the changes. For example, using the theme of systems, social, political, environmental, or global systems can be explored using the TASC model. The students' level determines how abstract a system is appropriate for study. Very young children can focus on family, school, and community systems or systems in nature. Older students might explore political systems as related to cultures or history.

Table 11.2 provides an example of civics curriculum for middle school students using the TASC structure. The topic, political (governmental) systems, brings abstractness and complexity to the learners; the thematic approach organizes content for learning value; and allowing small groups to explore different types of governmental systems provides variety. The study of people is easily incorporated because political systems are about people—the governed and those who govern. Those who govern are generally gifted in one way or another, and thus of interest to gifted students. Qualities of leaders and types of leadership are ways in which students might study people within the thematic framework. The study of methods is less obvious, but inviting sociologists and politicians to be guest speakers will provide a look at methods used within and from the outside to assess political systems and elements of these systems.

Process Modifications

The TASC model includes open-endedness, discovery, freedom of choice, variety, and group interaction. Higher levels of thinking and proof of reasoning can be added through questioning practices of the teacher and, later, the students. Pacing is determined by the teacher, and variables related to pacing include (a) the composition of the small groups, (b) the timeline established for activities and projects, and (c) the organization of the classroom and curriculum.

Product Modifications

Students are expected to discover, define, and work to solve real problems within the TASC model. Evaluation is part of the model, as are variety and self-selected format. Transformation is not specified as part of the model, but teacher guidance when students develop criteria for their projects and their presentations will ensure that it is included. Presenting solutions to real audiences is at least implied by the model, and teachers of the gifted can ensure the inclusion of this component without difficulty.

TABLE I I.2
Example of Using TASC as a Structure
for Exploring Political Systems at the Middle School Level

National Standard: Limited and unlimited governments. Students should be able to describe the essential characteristics of limited and unlimited governments (Center for Civic Education, 1994, p. 47).

TASC Segment	Learning Activity	Teaching Strategies
Gather/Organize	Within small group, select country or type of government of most interest. Begin gathering data related to U.S., British, Cuban, Saudi Arabian, or other government systems of interest. Use Concept Development Strategy to organize data as a means of determining paths for further pursuit.	Assess student research skills, and determine what needs to be taught. Provide interesting bits of information about a variety of selected governments to pique students' interest. Facilitate small groups' selection of country on which to focus. Ensure availability of a variety of resources. Teach students Taba's Concept Development Strategy (Chapter 10).
Identify	Identify unique aspects of chosen governmental system. Investigate possible sources in areas of most interest (most unique or intriguing aspects).	Assist with locating resources. Stay alert for individual and group skill needs; teach as appropriate. Bring entire group together occasionally for sharing.
Generate	Develop questions to be answered in investigation. Brainstorm ways information might be shared.	Instruct students in principles of constructing good questions (Chapter 10).
Decide	Select most promising questions for further investigation. Develop criteria for evaluation of information gathered and final product. Decide on individual responsibilities for project.	Assist students as needed to develop viable criteria. Observe individual and group effort and interactions. Meet with each small group to ensure readiness for further research.

(continues)

TABLE 11.2 *Continued.*
Example of Using TASC as a Structure
for Exploring Political Systems at the Middle School Level

TASC Segment	Learning Activity	Teaching Strategies
Implement	Research selected questions. Meet with (small) group regularly to share information; refine or redefine research questions and criteria as necessary.	Provide support—sources, technology, people, online assistance, access to tools of researchers.
Evaluate	In small group, evaluate information and select critical or key ideas based on criteria from previous steps.	Meet with each small group to review their critical or key ideas.
Communicate	Plan presentation to entire class, referring to criteria to select information and presentation format. Gather materials, practice, and polish presentation. Make presentation and ask for feedback from classmates and teacher.	Provide necessary support—materials and equipment. Circulate and observe planning process, providing feedback or suggestions as necessary. Schedule presentations; assist students in achieving a realistic time frame for presentations. Prepare entire group for roles of self, small group, and observer.
Learn from experience	Reflect on experience from perspective of self, small group members, classmates, and teacher. Identify strengths and weaknesses of individual and group performance. Note areas for future growth.	Provide time for guided and spontaneous evaluation. Lead Interpretation of Data and Application of Generalizations class discussions (Chapter 10) to assist students in assimilating information learned in this project.

Learning Environment Modifications

All of the learning environment modifications recommended for gifted students, except acceptance and complexity, are necessary for the implementation of TASC. Acceptance of diverse people, ideas, and cultures is necessary, however, to establish a comfortable environment for risk-taking, which is part of the TASC model. The complexity comes about through the availability of a variety of resources, tools of the disciplines, and the encouragement of complex ideas and undertakings.

Summary

Although many of the modifications recommended for gifted students are not explicit to the TASC model, all of them can be included easily. The Hilda Taba Teaching Strategies (Chapter 10), Problem Based Learning (Chapter 7), and the Enrichment Triad and Schoolwide Enrichment Models (Chapter 8) can be used to complement the model when developing curriculum for gifted students.

DEVELOPMENT

The TASC model was developed to meet the perceived needs of Black students and teachers in KwaZulu/Natal schools (Adams & Wallace, 1988, 1991; Wallace & Adams, 1988). The model, however, has potential for use in other situations as well (Maltby, 1993). According to Wallace and Bentley (2002), the theories that were most influential in the development of this model are (a) Vygotsky's (1978) belief that the development of higher levels of thinking is based on social transaction, (b) Feuerstein's (1980) theory of cognitive modifiability and the concept of mediated learning experiences, (c) Sternberg's (1988) triarchic theory of intelligence, (d) Borkowski's (1985) general model of intelligence, and (e) Bandura's (1971, 1977) Social Learning Theory.

In the mid-1980s, Belle Wallace and Harvey B. Adams surveyed the available thinking skills packages and visited major thinking-skills projects around the world. They decided to take an eclectic approach and adopt the most successful elements of the programs to be used to conduct action research with groups of disadvantaged learners and their teachers over the next 10 years. The researchers, participating teachers, educational psychologists, and students evaluated and reflected on the strategies and methods being tried. The quality of the reflections, the rethinking, and the revisiting of thinking skills and problem-solving strategies contributed to the development of this model. The process culminated in the publication of *TASC: Thinking Actively in a Social Context* (Wallace & Adams, 1993).

The strong grounding in valid learning theories and the action research have resulted in a model that can be modified to benefit diverse student populations and learning environments and retain its integrity. TASC provides a flexible framework for designing problem-solving courses according to the needs and experiences of the participants. The general purpose for students is to "make sense of and learn from experience" (Maltby, 1993, p. 45).

RESEARCH ON EFFECTIVENESS

With Nongifted Students

Carter and Rickarby (2002) reported that learning and using the TASC Problem-Solving Wheel gave young students a framework to structure and express their thinking and writing. They reported that the students were able to gather pertinent information, identify the nature of a task, generate a range of ideas, decide what to write about, and implement the task. After the students wrote a draft, they knew that the writing would be shared with others and evaluation of some type was probably going to occur. Reflection gave them the opportunity to review what they had written and to decide whether the task had been achieved successfully. At the end of the term in which the Problem-Solving Wheel was introduced, teachers reported that the quality and quantity of children's writing had improved. Figure 11.6 shows the modification of the TASC Problem-Solving Wheel that these teachers used for their young students.

Maltby and Cowan (1995) conducted a small study with two similar groups of ten 7- and 8-year-old students. Their task was to fold three circular and two rectangular pieces of paper into sixths. Group 1, the experimental group, received training in thinking skills between paper-folding activities. Additionally, they were encouraged to engage in the following cognitive strategies: (a) avoid impulsive actions, (b) avoid hurrying, (c) think of all possible folds first and carefully select the best ones, (d) check possible folds and (e) try another way if you need to next time. The TASC elements were arranged as a "stepladder," with the initial step at the bottom and each step a spoke of the TASC Problem-Solving Wheel. The stepladder was explained to

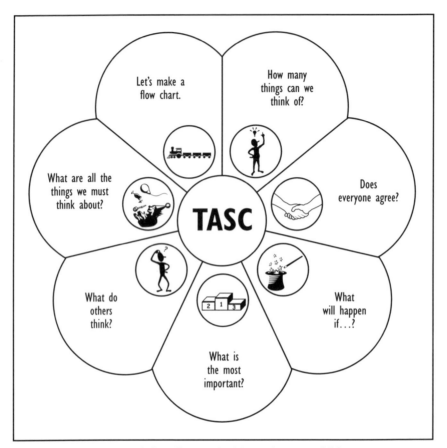

FIGURE 11.6. TASC Tools for Effective Thinking with Young Children. From *Teaching Thinking Skills Across the Early Years: A Practical Approach for Children Aged 4–7*, by B. Wallace and R. B. Bentley (Eds.), 2002, London: David Fulton. Copyright 2002 by David Fulton Publishers. Reprinted with permission.

students, and they were encouraged to use it to remind them of the process. Group 2 had no strategy training, and between tasks played a relaxing game while Group 1 had some training and reinforcement of the stepladder steps.

After 4 days, students were assigned two tasks: (a) to cut or fold two circular pieces of paper into thirds and (b) to cut or fold three rectangular pieces of paper into ninths. Students worked individually on these tasks. The two groups were separated as they were previously, with Group 1 receiving strategy training and Group 2 playing the same game as before. The researchers reported that compared with students in Group 2, students in

Group 1 (a) made fewer repeats of ineffective folds, (b) showed more decreases in folds, (c) had fewer increases in folds, and (d) experienced more than twice as many successes. The data indicated that training in thinking and problem-solving strategies improves students' success in problem-solving tasks.

Case study support for TASC can be found in Wallace (2002a, 2002b, 2002c) and in Wallace and Bentley (2002). Evaluation of the data has been qualitative: Teachers assess the framework, use it in their classrooms, review and evaluate, and reflect (the classical spiral of qualitative action research). The students also evaluate their experiences within TASC (B. Wallace, personal communication, March 11, 2004), and sample mind-maps and comments are found throughout the four previously mentioned texts. As evidenced in these publications, the model is teacher friendly, provides a structure for children's learning across the disciplines, and can result in sophisticated student products.

With Gifted Students

Maltby (1993) developed a 3-day course in mathematics for high-ability children in Grades 5, 6, and 7. Although no formal measurement was attempted, parents, observers, and teachers were enthusiastic about the course and the excitement it generated about math. Students were reluctant to leave their work at break times, and they displayed high levels of concentration and thought. Examination of the videotapes of the 3 days supported the belief that higher order thinking levels were necessary for children to solve the problems. Despite the difficulty of the tasks, the motivation and achievement of the children were high.

In another instance, Maltby (1995) reported on a study that demonstrated the effectiveness of TASC on two groups of 10 students, ages 7 and 8. The students demonstrated improved problem-solving strategies and higher level thinking skills. Maltby and Beattie (1996) developed an extension program through Telematics, which is the delivery of instruction to remote sites using electronic media. This program incorporated TASC, Telematics, and preparation for participation in the Tournament of Minds for Year 6 and 7 students. A case study of this program revealed that students enjoyed the challenges and were able to develop metacognitive strategies, a particularly worthwhile accomplishment. They found it difficult at first, but soon were eager to contribute. Through verbalizing their thinking processes and strategies, they learned new strategies from each other, gained an appreciation of individual differences, developed self-appreciation and respect for others, and developed more effective communication skills.

JUDGMENTS

Advantages

The TASC model has many advantages. Originally designed to raise the learning, thinking, and achievement levels of all students, it has been shown to be effective with both nongifted and gifted. As a multiphase problem-solving model that incorporates basic thinking skills and tools for effective thinking, it offers a flexible structure within which teachers and students can develop curricula to meet the needs of diverse populations (Adams & Wallace, 1991). The teaching principles of TASC are based on global research about how children learn and best teaching practices. Although these principles are rigorous and require excellence in classroom practices, the model can be modified to meet diverse learning needs, level of skills, and student interests (Wallace, 2002b).

Disadvantages

The disadvantages of TASC are similar to those of other problem-solving models. These include entrenched teachers, parents, administrators, school governing bodies, and regional or state legislatures. Any good instructional strategy requires well-trained teachers, which requires willing teachers, qualified trainers, and the expenditure of money. An unnamed fear on the part of the public in general is that any nontraditional approach to learning will not increase achievement as reflected on standardized tests. This fear is supported to a certain extent: Standardized tests assess the level of facts students have memorized, not how well they can think and solve problems. However, when students become motivated about school and learning, and become comfortable with problem solving, their scores on standardized tests also rise (Baum, Owen, & Oreck, 1996; Maker, 2001; Maker, Rogers, Nielson, & Bauerle, 1996) TASC is in good company when one notes which teaching models share its disadvantages—that is, DISCOVER, Enrichment Triad Model, and Problem Based Learning. The task of educators is to educate the public at large about what meaningful learning is and how it occurs.

Qualitative action research supports the effectiveness of TASC through teacher reflection on the changes in pupil motivation, behavior, and enjoyment of and dedication to tasks (B. Wallace, personal communication, March 11, 2004). What is needed is longitudinal research that (a) covers a significant time span, (b) demonstrates that basic skills can be mastered within the TASC structure, and (c) reveals the depth and mental longevity of information learned.

CONCLUSION

With a few additions, TASC can be used as the major model for curriculum for gifted students. Some content and process modifications need to be added, and products need to be real and presented to real audiences. Most learning environment modifications are implied if not stated, but overall TASC is an exciting addition to teaching models for use in programs for gifted students. With education under fire, as it virtually always seems to be, such a model is indeed refreshing and promising. This is a model grounded in respected theory, developed by use in classrooms with appropriate reflection and modification, and embodying the best of constructivist principles. TASC is an exciting and potentially influential model.

RESOURCES

Background Readings

Adams, H. B., & Wallace, B. (1991). TASC: A model for curriculum development. *Gifted Education International, 7*(3), 104–113.

Maltby, F., & Beattie, J. (1996). A TASC for Telematics. *Gifted Educational International, 11*(3), 149–155.

van der Horst, H. v. R. (2000). A problem solving strategy for gifted learners in South Africa. *Gifted Education International, 14*(3), 104–110.

Wallace, B., & Adams, H. B., with Maltby, F., & Mathfield, J. (1993). *TASC: Thinking actively in a social context.* Bicester, Oxfordshire, Great Britain: A B Academic Publishers.

Curricular Materials

Adams, H. B., & Wallace, B. (1991). A model for curriculum development. *Gifted Education International, 7*(3), 104–113.

Maltby, F. (1993). Teaching mathematics through "Thinking Actively in a Social Context." *Gifted Educational International, 9,* 45–47.

Maltby, F., & Cowan, E. (1995). The use of TASC to develop a selection of tools for effective thinking. *Gifted Education International, 11,* 18–23.

Wallace, B. (Ed.). (2002). *Teaching thinking skills across the early years.* London: David Fulton.

Wallace, B. (Ed.). (2002). *Teaching thinking skills across the primary curriculum.* London: David Fulton.

Wallace, B. (Ed.). (2002). *Using history to develop thinking skills.* London: David Fulton.

Wallace, B., & Adams, H. B., with Maltby, F., & Mathfield, J. (1993). *TASC: Thinking actively in a social context.* Bicester, Oxfordshire, Great Britain: A B Academic Publishers.

Wallace, B., & Bentley, R. (Eds.). (2002). *Teaching thinking skills across the middle years: A practical approach for children aged 9–14.* London: David Fulton.

CHAPTER 12

Other Models

LAWRENCE KOHLBERG:
DISCUSSIONS OF MORAL DILEMMAS

The development of values, moral reasoning, ethical behavior, and virtuous action has always been a concern of educators. Some educators have been interested primarily in the development of values and assisting students to clarify their values through the processes advocated by individuals such as Raths (1963) and Raths, Harmin, and Simon (1966). Educators and parents often are concerned about developing ethical behavior in children and, in the past, have attempted to do so through religious education, Boy Scouts, Girl Scouts, and other approaches that emphasize to children that the virtuous person is honest, loyal, reverent, just, and altruistic. Children are told that if they acquire these virtues, they will be happy, well respected, and fortunate.

Kohlberg's (1966) theory of the development of moral reasoning and his approach to moral education is a response to the failure of indoctrination programs and disagreement with the idea of ethical relativity as a basis for values education (Kohlberg, 1971). Kohlberg rejected the most fundamental idea of ethical relativity, on a philosophical base. His key idea (Kohlberg, 1971), which in part is based on the writings of Kant (1929/1965) and the contemporary moral philosopher John Rawls (1971), is that, although different values relating to personal choice (e.g., what clothing to wear, the most appropriate way to spend time) are equally appropriate, different values relating to basic moral questions (e.g., the sanctity of life, the equality of all people) are not equally appropriate. In other words, certain universal ethical principles do exist. For example, even though an individual arrives at the decision that all Blacks should be slaves because they are an inferior race using the seven-step process of values clarification, this conclusion is not as appropriate as the conclusion that slavery is wrong for everyone. A conclusion such as the latter is based on universal ethical principles such as the worth of every person and the equality of every person relative to certain rights and freedoms. Such ethical principles as respect for the worth of all individuals, justice and liberty for all, and inalienable rights are embedded firmly in and necessary to a democratic way of life. As educators and individuals participating in a democracy, teachers can and should assist children in developing moral reasoning that will consider these higher philosophical principles in decisions involving basic moral questions.

In contrast to the attempts to develop ethical behavior is values clarification, wherein the school's and teacher's responsibility is not to indoctrinate children as to what values they should hold but to assist them in thinking seriously about what values they hold and what values they should hold. Perhaps the values clarification approaches were formulated as a reaction to the ineffectiveness of indoctrination or as a 1960s reaction to adults' attempts to manipulate children through developing certain moral values advocated by the educational establishment. The teacher's role in the process is nonjudgmental and involves posing questions and planning activities that will lead children through the processes of choosing (e.g., choosing freely, choosing from alternatives, choosing after thoughtful consideration of the consequences of each alternative), prizing (prizing and cherishing oneself, affirming publicly), and acting (acting on choices, repeating the action in a pattern over time) (Raths et al., 1966). A fundamental idea behind this approach is that of "ethical relativity": No universal ethical principles can be identified because values and ethics are relative. As long as a person has followed the processes of choosing, prizing, and acting, all values developed are equally valid.

ASSUMPTIONS UNDERLYING THE MODEL

About Learning

Kohlberg assumes that moral reasoning can be learned. The thought or wish that follows is that moral behavior will result from learning and using higher levels of moral reasoning. A further assumption is that through the use of structured discussions about moral dilemmas, students can be exposed to and eventually internalize higher levels of moral reasoning.

About Teaching

That which can be learned can be taught. Therefore, moral reasoning can be taught if appropriate strategies and engaging topics are offered to students. Teachers can be educated regarding levels of moral reasoning and provided with demonstrations and examples of classroom discussions that center on moral issues.

About Characteristics of Gifted Students

Although Kohlberg and his colleagues have not written specifically about gifted students, educators of the gifted have long been concerned about the moral and ethical development of bright students. If these children are to become future leaders, they should serve as models of the highest ethical behavior in addition to being models of intellectual and productive behavior. Ward (1961) believes that intellectually superior individuals have a greater capacity than average individuals to develop consistency between their ethical ideals and their actual behavior. Many of the characteristics of the gifted (e.g., their ability to foresee consequences of their own behavior, their ability to choose long-term benefits over short-range consequences, and their greater capacity to generalize learning from one situation to another) suggest that a concentration on moral reasoning and the development of an understanding of universal ethical principles is an effective approach to the development of ethical behavior.

According to Ward (1961), gifted students should be instructed in "the theoretical bases of ideal moral behavior and of personal and social adjustments" (p. 202). He suggests that gifted individuals should examine critically the historical development of societal philosophies and values, and that they should study the effects of these ideas on the development of societies. This examination also should include the analysis and classification of values, with an emphasis on the individuals' development of their own "reasoned synthesis" of values. This approach differs from values clarification in that individuals have examined high ideals and considered their appropriateness rather than simply looking within themselves for these ideals. The approach is somewhat similar to values clarification in that individuals must go through a process of self-examination and develop personal conclusions.

Some relatively recent approaches to education of the gifted, such as Problem Based Learning (Chapter 7), are designed to give students practice in examining all aspects of a problem, including ethical and moral issues. Kohlberg's ideas can be incorporated easily into this strategy. The model fits well with Problem Based Learning because the emphasis is on reasoning, with the objective of ultimately reaching a level at which certain universal ethical principles or ideas guide behavior. An analysis of the philosophical and theoretical bases of the ethical principles related to the issue being investigated adds an important dimension to the process.

ELEMENTS/PARTS

The most important aspect of Kohlberg's approach to the development of moral reasoning is the Discussion of Moral Dilemmas. Dilemmas are chosen or created on the basis of several criteria: (a) A central character must decide between alternative possibilities for action, (b) at least one moral issue is involved, and (c) society lends some support for any of several actions that could be taken by the protagonist. Dilemmas are presented to students, and a discussion follows. Moral discussions can be based on current events, literature, or ethics in various disciplines. A suggested six-step process for moral discussion follows.

☛ **Step 1. Present the dilemma.**

Moral dilemmas abound in life, and a pertinent and provocative situation may be found in any number of sources. Discussion of moral issues may evolve out of school, community, and world events; media articles; and student conflicts. Students can be asked to role-play conflict situations prior to such discussions.

☛ **Step 2. Have students clarify the facts of the situation and identify the issues involved.**

The teacher asks for information about what happened relevant to the focus situation. Students summarize the events, identify the principal characters, and describe the alternatives open to the protagonist. This part of the discussion takes a short period of time.

☞ Step 3. Have students identify a tentative position on the action the central character should take and state one or two reasons for that position.

The teacher asks students to choose from the identified alternatives what the character should do and the major reason for this choice. This can be done in writing to ensure that students will think for themselves and develop a position. While students are writing, the teacher can walk around the room to get an idea of how the class is thinking. After each student has developed a written opinion, the teacher then asks for a show of hands on the various alternatives to get an idea of differences or similarities. This information also is used to guide the organization of the next step.

☞ Step 4. Divide the class into small groups.

In small groups, students share their reasons for the positions they have taken. Shy students and those who may feel threatened by the teacher's presence find a small group setting more comfortable for sharing their ideas. Small-group discussions with four to six members should take approximately 10 to 15 minutes. To organize these small groups for maximum effectiveness and interaction among students, the teacher should consider how the class is split on the issue. If the class splits unevenly on the issue, students can be divided into groups that have taken the same position. They can discuss their reasons and decide on the two best reasons for the position. If the class splits evenly on the issue, students can be divided into groups with an approximately equal number that agree with each position. In groups, students discuss both positions and choose the best reasons for each. If the class agrees about one position, the students can be divided into groups based on the similarity of their reasons for supporting a position. Each group can then decide why the reason they prefer is the best one. In this situation, students also can be divided according to differences in reasons. The small groups then discuss their reasons and decide on the best two or three to support their decision.

During these small-group discussions, the teacher should move around the class to make certain that students understand the task and that they focus on reasons rather than argue about the facts or some aspect of the situation. While observing the groups, the teacher gathers ideas for opening the discussion in the large group.

☞ Step 5. Reconvene the class for a full class discussion of the dilemma.

This part of the process should take the majority of class time. The class should be seated in a circle, with the teacher included, to encourage a maximum amount of student-to-student interaction. Although student interaction is the most important aspect of this discussion time, the teacher's role is crucial in encouraging interaction among students with different points of view, establishing an atmosphere in which students feel free to express different ideas, and keeping the discussion focused on the reasons and positions rather than side issues or facts of the situation.

A full class discussion can be initiated in several ways: (a) having each group write its position and supporting reasons on the board or chart paper, and then asking opposing groups to respond to each other; (b) asking for oral reports from each group, beginning with those who seemed to function well in the small-group setting, and then asking for comments from those with opposing viewpoints after each report; or (c) opening the discussion to all, asking the question, "What do you think the central character should do?" And "Why should he or she do that?" The teacher should pace and guide the discussion for maximum student interaction and learning.

During this part of the discussion, teacher questions are crucial for keeping the conversation focused on reasons, encouraging shy students to participate, encouraging interaction among students who are reasoning at different stages, and encouraging students to think about reasons at stages higher than their own. Teachers can ask the following types of questions at this step:

- *Clarification*—When you say _____, what do you mean? Please give us an example of that. Who can put what Suzanne just said in their own words?
- *Student interaction*—How is what you are saying different from what Carlos told us? How do you think your view compares to that of Sergio?

- *Focus*—When, if ever, do you think a person is justified in breaking a law? When, if ever, do you think breaking the moral code (we are discussing) is okay?
- *Perspective-taking*—How do you think _____ felt about that? Who else might be really upset by (this event or situation)?
- *Proof of reasoning*—Why do you think that? What from our discussion led you to believe that? How did you come to that conclusion?

While listening to the discussion, the teacher should identify reasoning at a particular stage and then encourage a student who has expressed reasoning at a higher stage to respond. The teacher also should prepare questions that stimulate students to consider reasoning that is at a higher level than anyone in the class has expressed. If the teacher knows from past discussions the levels of reasoning usually employed, such provocative or lifting questions can be prepared in advance.

☞ **Step 6. Ask students to reevaluate their original positions individually.**

After the large-group discussion, the teacher should ask students to review the discussion and answer the following two questions privately: (a) "Now what do you think the main character should do?" and (b) "What is the most important reason for this action?" The teacher should not attempt to get the group to reach consensus about the dilemma or to suggest that one reason or position may be better than another, but the reevaluation is important. The teacher can collect these responses along with the original written position to see if any significant changes occurred. Individual responses should be evaluated according to their stage so that growth over a period of time can be assessed.

To keep the process interesting and stimulating, teachers can and should vary their methods of presenting and discussing moral dilemmas. In the *Values in a Democracy* and *Values in American History* series (Guidance Associates, 1976a, 1976b), the following different ways of presenting dilemmas are used: (a) a list of statements about an issue, each followed by *agree, disagree,* or *can't decide,* with instructions for students to indicate their position and then write the most important reason for it; (b) one or two paragraphs about an issue with four reasons supporting an action and four opposing it, with instructions for students to choose their preferred reasons; (c) a short description of a dilemma with a list of five arguments at each of five stages supporting an action, which students rank according to their preference; and (d) three arguments supporting a different position on an issue from which the students choose a preferred argument and expand on it.

With these varied presentations of a dilemma, teachers need to modify the six-step process. In all of them, however, opportunities should be provided for students to discuss their reasons. The teacher should set up the situation so that students are interacting and being exposed to reasoning at higher stages than their own. In the first presentation, in which students respond to statements indicating their agreement or disagreement, only Steps 5 and 6 are appropriate, and the procedures at Step 5 should be modified. A way to facilitate discussion in this situation is to consider each of the five statements in turn, asking students who have taken each position (*agree, disagree, can't decide*) to state their reasons for the position. As the discussion proceeds, the teacher can ask questions in the same manner outlined previously for this step. Step 6 is much the same except that students should be asked to choose the statement they prefer and write the major reason for this preference. Other modifications of the process can be made to enhance interest. The major part of each, however, is whole-class discussion of the issues and reasons (Step 5), with small-group discussions at different times to encourage more interaction among students.

MODIFICATIONS
OF THE BASIC CURRICULUM

Discussions of Moral Dilemmas include mainly content and process modifications that are appropriate for the gifted. For teachers to implement these changes effectively, however, the psychological learning environment must be centered on student ideas, permit independence, be open to new ideas and new viewpoints, and be accepting rather than judgmental.

Content Modifications

Discussions of Moral Dilemmas include content modifications appropriate for the gifted due to their focus on moral and ethical issues rather than the usual subject matter content. Because the content is different, the principle of variety is met. However, more important modifications are suggested in the areas of abstractness and complexity. Because the ultimate goal of these discussions is to encourage students to consider ideas at higher stages, which by definition are more abstract, more complex, and more universal, and because gifted children are capable of reaching these stages more quickly than others, discussions should concentrate on these abstract ideas. Guidelines also are given for selecting dilemmas that have no simple solution and those whose solutions must take into consideration several complex issues with no clear-cut societal solution.

Process Modifications

Process modifications suggested by the model include emphasis on higher levels (stages) of thinking, concentration on reasoning, group interaction, and variety in methods. Open-endedness also is emphasized. Kohlberg suggests a step-by-step procedure for accomplishing these purposes during a discussion. Because the emphasis is on presenting reasoning at levels higher than the students' predominant ones and specific descriptions of the type of thinking at each stage are given, the goal of developing higher levels of thinking should be achieved.

Although Kohlberg's discussion procedures do not emphasize the asking of open-ended questions, the element of provocativeness is included in the entire method. The whole approach is designed to promote cognitive conflict and further thought about a moral issue, resulting in positive change or movement through the stages. At Step 5, a great deal of emphasis is placed on provocative questions, especially issue-related, role-switch, and universal-consequences questions. Teachers should use these questions to stimulate further and higher level thought from students.

Almost by definition, the procedure makes the process modifications of proof of reasoning and group interaction. The model is focused on encouraging students to express moral reasoning at higher levels than they had previously, and a basic assumption is that this reasoning reaches higher levels because students have interacted with each other. Students at a lower stage have listened to the reasons presented at higher levels, and because they tend to prefer higher level reasons, they will adopt the higher level. The teacher's major task at Steps 4 (small-group discussion) and 5 (full-class discussion) is to keep the group's attention focused on a discussion of reasons for actions. Several types of questions recommended at Step 5 are designed to force students to listen and react to the ideas presented by other members of the group (e.g., perception-checking questions and inter-student participation questions).

Variety of methods is accomplished through the varied means of presenting and discussing dilemmas. In each method, the six-step process needs to be modified.

Product Modifications

The Moral Dilemma discussion strategy does not include product modifications appropriate for gifted students. Products of these moral discussions, however, can be letters to the editor; projects to alleviate, improve, or do away with situations; or the lobbying of governmental bodies.

Learning Environment Modifications

Kohlberg's Discussions of Moral Dilemmas make provisions for developing a learner-centered environment. Because the class is divided into small groups for a portion of he time (Step 4), student talk must be emphasized without the teacher as the center. No opportunity is provided for the teacher to talk during a discussion of this type. Teachers must exercise care, however, to avoid becoming the center of the discussion during Step 5. The central position can be avoided by (a) liberal use of perception-checking and interstudent participation questions to encourage student reaction to student ideas and (b) avoiding a response to every student idea. Changes in the learning environment also can be made by using Kohlberg's concept of the development of "communities" that govern themselves (Muson, 1979). In these communities, the emphasis is on having group members develop their own rules of government, solve their own problems, and enforce their own rules. According to Kohlberg, the principles of democracy cannot be taught in an autocratic school or institution. These principles must be practiced on a daily basis and developed in a setting in which individuals can observe the effects of their decision making. Unfortunately, in most schools, rather than learning democratic principles, students learn obedience to authority and to arbitrary rules made and enforced by adults.

Communities have been developed in several high schools and prisons as an experiment in rehabilitation. Members discuss solutions to their problems based on "fairness and morality." In other words, instead of discussing hypothetical dilemmas, such as the ones used to study moral development, communities discuss their own real problems. Although the communities have not escaped criticism, Kohlberg views them as a success, especially those operating in high schools. Students have been able to develop a sense of community and govern themselves responsibly. They have their problems, however, when the wishes of the group conflict with state or federal laws or with school policy.

Regardless of the criticism, the basic idea of the community applies directly to the development of learning environment changes appropriate for gifted students, especially in the dimension of independence and in openness and acceptance. With regard to independence, students are encouraged to develop their own management and government rather than relying on the teacher to develop and implement solutions to their problems. The element of openness is present because the students are free to develop and implement their own procedures and to express themselves freely. Teachers present their ideas, but as equal members of groups. The teacher, according to the theory, should present moral reasoning at a higher level than the students so they can be exposed to the highest levels. Acceptance is an important part of the process in that the teacher must be a member of the group and model the kind of behavior expected from students. This behavior includes attempting to understand another person's perspective and ideas, accepting the ideas, clarifying the ideas (an important aspect of moral dilemma discussions), and challenging the ideas. The challenging is valuable in Kohlberg's strategy, because growth is believed to occur through cognitive conflict. As the communities operate for a long period of time and develop mutual trust, the challenging of ideas can be integrated easily.

DEVELOPMENT

Kohlberg's (1966) theory of the development of moral reasoning and his approach to moral education is a response to the failure of indoctrination programs and disagreement with the idea of ethical relativity as a basis for values education (Kohlberg, 1971). In the late 1920s, a classic study of children's cheating and stealing by Hartshorne and May (1930) shocked the educational community by showing that indoctrination approaches were ineffective. Children who attend Sunday school, who participate in Boy Scouts and Girl Scouts, and whose parents emphasize ethical behavior do not behave more ethically than children whose parents do none of these things. Other results of this study, also confirmed by later research, are that (a) the world cannot be divided into honest and dishonest people because almost everyone cheats at some time; (b) if a person cheats in one situation, whether the person will cheat in other situations cannot be predicted (in other words, cheating seems to be determined by the situation); and (c) the moral values expressed by people do not necessarily govern their actions; people who express extreme moral disapproval of cheating will, given the "right" situation, cheat as much as those who do not verbally express disapproval of cheating.

RESEARCH ON EFFECTIVENESS

With Nongifted Students

Kohlberg (1966) studied the development of moral reasoning by interviewing 50 boys over a period of time. He posed moral dilemmas to them and asked them to tell (a) what would be morally right for the individual to do and (b) why this action would be right. He found that children's reasoning about moral issues proceeds through certain stages in a sequential order and becomes more sophisticated at each stage. Subsequent to the research on these developmental stages, numerous individuals, including Kohlberg, his colleagues, and his students, have studied how this development can be facilitated. They have concluded that educators can encourage the development of higher levels of moral reasoning through methods emphasizing class discussion of moral dilemmas.

Other researchers have examined emotion and moral reasoning (Helmuth, 2001); compared students' and ethicists' moral reasoning (Keefer & Ashley, 2001); established a framework for turning students into ethical professionals (Gorman, 2001/2002); examined moral reasoning as affected by sex role orientation, gender, and academic factors (Elm, Kennedy, & Lawton, 2001); and conducted moral reasoning comparative studies (Windsor & Cappel, 1999). As science and technology continue to expand the boundaries of what is possible, more research is likely to be conducted. With continued research, the hope is that educators may have more definitive information as to how to develop ethical and moral behavior in all students.

With Gifted Students

Although an online search reveals numerous studies of the moral reasoning of individuals in various professions and situations as mentioned previously, no research on gifted individuals per se was located.

JUDGMENTS

Advantages

Advantages of the Kohlberg model are the content changes brought about by the discussion of abstract, complex moral issues. The concentration on ideas and issues of the type suggested by Kohlberg's model should be not only interesting and stimulating, but also valuable in producing the kind of cognitive conflict or disequilibrium that causes growth to occur. Encouraging students to consider these big ideas as early as possible should contribute to higher quality thought about them in the future.

Another advantage is in the possibilities for combining discussions of moral dilemmas with other areas of the curriculum to achieve effective organization for learning value. In social studies classes, for example, when students are studying some of the abstract ideas that form the basis of governmental systems, discussions of historical and current moral dilemmas involving these ideas can bring an added dimension to the students' understanding of governance.

The Kohlberg approach to moral education presents a better alternative for use with gifted students than those of indoctrination and values clarification. The indoctrination approach, often seen in the form of behavior modification, has little effect on ethical behavior and no effect on moral reasoning. Values clarification, on the other hand, with its emphasis on a process of examining values, is an important technique to use with gifted students and can help them develop valuable critical thinking skills; however, it does not go far enough in the areas of examination of moral and ethical issues. In the area of personal choice, the approach or the underlying philosophy of values clarification is appropriate, but in the area of moral and ethical issues, the underlying philosophy of ethical relativism is difficult to accept. Kohlberg's model goes one step further in recognizing that certain universal ethical principles are important for students to develop.

Disadvantages

The major disadvantages of Kohlberg's model lie in the process and the ways moral dilemma discussions are implemented. The use of Discussions of Moral Dilemmas may facilitate growth in moral reasoning; however, the results of research are mixed and rather unspectacular. A related weakness is that no structure or sequence is provided for discussions. Through extensive research on the development of children's abstract thinking, Taba (1966) found that the type and sequence of teacher questions are important in achieving growth in cognitive abilities. Not only the question immediately preceding a child's answer but also the whole sequence of teacher questions and acts leading up to the question determine the quality of thinking exhibited by the answer. This research suggests that a particular sequence of teacher questions might be most valuable for questioning in a moral dilemma discussion. Kohlberg discussions, however, have not been developed with the same attention to sequence as have the Hilda Taba Teaching Strategies (Chapter 10).

A related disadvantage is in the lack of guidelines for selection of dilemmas. If Kohlberg is right about the developmental sequence of moral reasoning, certain dilemmas are more appropriate for discussions at particular stages. An optimum sequence of issues (e.g., discussing stealing before discussing killing) also is important.

Finally, a major disadvantage of the model is its basis in research involving only boys. Gilligan (1982) presented convincing evidence that women reason differently from men and raised serious questions about the use of a model derived entirely from research on men and boys. One can hold discussions about dilemmas, but making judgments about the level of reasoning of female students is suspect from this perspective.

CONCLUSION

Because the major advantages of the Kohlberg model are in the area of content modifications and its major disadvantages are in the process area, it is a valuable approach to use in programs for gifted students when combined with one of the process models, such as the Hilda Taba Teaching Strategies (Chapter 10). It also could be combined effectively with Prism (Chapter 12), Creative Problem Solving (Chapter 6), Problem Based Learning (Chapter 7), or TASC (Chapter 11) if moral or ethical problems relate to the definition and solution of the problem. Although research is inconclusive about the validity of Kohlberg's developmental stages, the model does provide a valuable goal for programs for the gifted: the development of sophisticated moral reasoning.

FRANK E. WILLIAMS: TEACHING STRATEGIES FOR THINKING AND FEELING

The Williams model (Williams, 1972) was not developed specifically for use with gifted students. In fact, its major purpose is to provide a model for enhancing the cognitive and affective processes involved in creativity and productivity in all children. The thinking processes of fluency, flexibility, originality, and elaboration, along with the feeling processes of curiosity, risk-taking, complexity, and imagination, are developed through traditional subject matter content. The teacher uses a series of 18 strategies or modes of teaching. For optimum learning to occur, a proper mix of interaction must occur among three basic elements: (a) the curriculum (subject matter content), (b) what teachers can do with both the curriculum and the students (teacher behaviors), and (c) what children can become (pupil behaviors). In any teaching situation, all three elements interact (see Figure 12.1). Because of this interaction, learning experiences should include all three elements.

ELEMENTS/PARTS

Based on his philosophy, Williams (1970, 1972) developed a morphological model with three dimensions: (a) curriculum, (b) teaching strategies, and (c) student behaviors. As with other morphological frameworks, this model depicts the components as interrelated parts of a whole. No hierarchy of strategies or behaviors is either implied or intended. The framework can be used as a structure for curriculum planning, instruction, and teacher training. In short, it provides a vehicle for intersecting a given subject area with any teaching strategy to produce student behavior that is creative.

Dimensions

Curriculum
The curriculum dimension includes the traditional content areas—that is, art, music, science, social studies, arithmetic, and language. Other content areas used in a particular setting can be substituted. In a program for gifted students, Williams (1972) notes, the teacher can substitute topics such as ecology, marine life, population growth, or career options.

Strategies
The strategies dimension includes the situations, techniques, or methods (Williams, 1972) that teachers use in their classrooms in all subject matter areas. Williams lists 18 methods or processes; however, only the following seven strategies named as being most effective to use with more able students are discussed in this chapter: (a) exploring discrepant events, (b) asking and seeking answers to provocative questions, (c) exploring examples of change and habit, (d) developing skills of search, (e) learning to tolerate ambiguity, (f) teaching for development rather than adjustment, and (g) learning to evaluate situations. Definitions and examples of these strategies are provided.

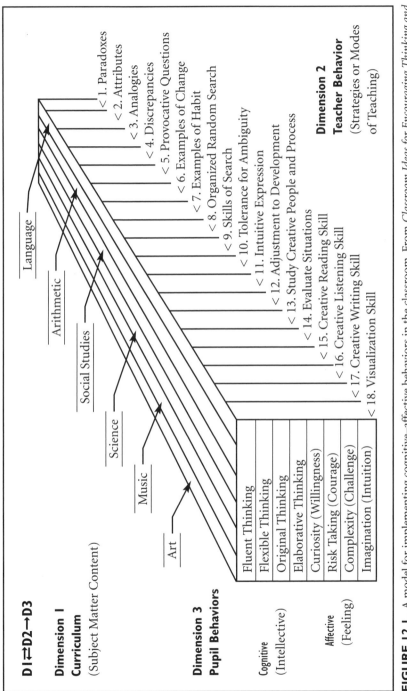

FIGURE 12.1. A model for implementing cognitive–affective behaviors in the classroom. From *Classroom Ideas for Encouraging Thinking and Feeling* (2nd ed.), by F. E. Williams, 1970, Buffalo, NY: DOK. Copyright 1970 by DOK. Reprinted with permission.

- *Explore discrepant events and information.* Discrepancies include gaps in knowledge, unknown information, contradictory events, or "missing links." *Examples:* Ask students to think of all the things they do not know about people from another country and list all the ways this information could be found. Have students think about life in a glass house and list ways their lives might be different if they lived in a glass house rather than a regular house.

- *Ask and seek answers to provocative questions.* These are questions intended to get students excited about inquiry and get them to explore and to discover new knowledge. *Example:* During a unit on living things, ask students to list all the things that can be learned about a tree by looking at its leaves. Then ask, "What do you think the world would be like if all the trees were destroyed?" (Williams, 1970).

- *Explore examples of change and habit.* Demonstrate to students how dynamic the world is or can be. Provide situations for making substitutions or modifications. *Examples of change:* Discuss ways people preserve things (e.g., freezing fish or bronzing baby shoes). Ask students to think of a list of things that are preserved, kept, or sustained. Then have them think about how and why these things are preserved. Pursue the ideas of change in content areas (earth formations, life cycles, language evolution, mathematical concepts, etc.). *Examples or habit:* Discuss the habitual use of a base-10 numbering system. After using other bases, have students think of situations in which other bases would be more appropriate. During a unit on transportation, explore the effects of tradition and habit-bound thinking on innovations. Pose questions such as why engines are usually placed at the front of a car, propellers are usually placed on the front of engines, and drive wheels are placed on the rear of a car. Then discuss some results of breaking out of these patterns of thinking.

- *Develop skills of search.* This strategy includes teaching several ways of searching for information, including (a) a historical search, or looking for ways something has been done before; (b) a trial-and-error search, and describing how it was done; and (c) an experimental search, or controlling experimental conditions and reporting the results. *Example:* After talking about seeds and variables related to growth, have students experiment with different kinds of seeds and manipulate variables to determine critical elements for growth.

- *Build a tolerance for ambiguity.* Provide situations that are challenging and intriguing. Present open-ended situations that do not encourage or force closure. *Examples:* Read a story and stop at an interesting part. Have students tell or write what they think the ending might be. Emphasize that stories can have many endings, and no "right" way can be found to end a story. Ask students to think about what might happen if certain natural cycles changed (e.g., seasons following each other in a different order or ocean tides changing every week).

• *Teach for development rather than adjustment.* Model and provide a structure for looking at how failures or accidents have been positive, how to learn from mistakes, and how to develop or change rather than simply adjusting. *Example:* After studying how the government functions and making field trips to government offices, have students design an ideal government. Ask them to decide what qualities ideal governments should have and how the necessary changes might be achieved.

• *Encourage students to evaluate situations.* Choose solutions by careful consideration of consequences and implications, and predict from the results of ideas and actions. *Examples:* Beginning with a random collection of items, have students predict which ones will sink or float. Have them tell why the prediction was made and then try out items to see whether their predictions were accurate. In social studies, after a unit on exploration showing that movement is always from east to west, have students consider the possible causes and effects of westward movement.

Pupil Behaviors

Student behaviors are divided into cognitive (intellect) and affective (feeling). Based on research on the behaviors involved in creativity, Williams (1972) identifies eight clusters of behaviors, four cognitive and four affective. The cognitive behaviors include fluency, flexibility, originality, and elaboration. The affective behaviors are being observant and inquisitive, having a strong imagination, being challenged by complexity, and being a courageous risk-taker. Following are Williams's descriptions and examples of these behaviors (adapted from Williams, 1972, pp. 35–39 and pp. 70–73).

COGNITIVE (INTELLECTUAL) BEHAVIORS

1. *Fluency in thinking* is indicated by students who usually come up with the most ideas, responses, solutions, or questions. They can produce a quantity of ways or suggestions for doing things, and they virtually always think of more than one answer. *Examples:* Students who

- have a flow of answers when a question is asked,
- draw several pictures when asked to draw one,
- usually have several ideas about something while others struggle for one idea, and
- ask many questions.

2. *Flexible thinking* is demonstrated when a student is able to produce a variety of ideas, responses, questions, or solutions. Such students seek many different directions or alternatives and have the ability to shift approaches or change

direction in thinking about things. Flexible thinkers need not necessarily be fluent, but each idea will be of a different variety. *Examples:* Students who

- can apply a principle or concept in subjects other than the one in which it was introduced;
- shift and take another point of view or consider situations differently from others in the class;
- when discussing a situation, always take a different position from the rest of the class; and
- when given a problem, usually think of a number of different possibilities for solving it.

3. *Original thinking* is evidenced by students who are usually able to think of novel, unique expressions. They have clever ideas, rather than common or obvious ones. Their thinking is unusual and they choose to figure things out and express them in new ways. An original thinker has the capacity to combine pieces of the usual into a new and unusual whole. *Examples:* Students who

- are nonconformists who cannot help being different and always have a new twist in thinking or behavior;
- enjoy the unusual and will rebel against doing things the way everyone else does them;
- deviate from others to do things their own way;
- after reading or listening to a problem solution, will go to work on inventing their own new solution; and
- not only question the old way but always try to figure out a new way.

4. *Elaborative thinking* is exhibited by students who usually want to add to or elaborate on ideas or productions. These students love to stretch or expand upon things, and they seek to embellish materials or solutions by making them more elegant and interesting. Elaborators may not be originators, but once they get a new idea, they modify or expand upon it. *Examples:* Students who

- sense a deeper meaning to an answer or solution and therefore produce more detailed steps,
- will accept an idea or someone else's work but will always want to "jazz it up," and
- are uninterested in things that are barren or plain and always attempt to add detail to make them more beautiful.

AFFECTIVE (FEELING) BEHAVIORS

1. *Curiosity* is demonstrated in students who are keenly observant and inquisitive by nature. They are always curious about people, objects, and situations,

and they like to wonder, explore, ask questions, and puzzle over things. *Examples:* Students who

- question everything and everyone,
- love to explore mechanical things,
- constantly search for "why,"
- question why things are not done differently than the usually accepted way,
- use all of their senses to understand things,
- are sensitive to problems, and
- are alert to details that produce meaning.

2. *Imagination* is evident in students who can visualize and dream about things that have never happened to them. They can deal with fantasy, and know the difference between that and reality. *Examples:* Students who

- can feel intuitively something that has not yet happened,
- like to build images of things they have never seen, and
- can see things in a picture or drawing that no one else has seen.

3. *Complexity* is indicated in students who thrive on complicated situations. They like to tackle difficult problems, and they have a preference for "digging in" to intricate solutions and things. *Examples:* Students who

- appreciate complex ideas or problems;
- become intrigued with messy situations;
- choose a more difficult way out;
- want to figure things out for themselves, without help;
- thrive on trying again and again to gain success; and
- seek more difficult answers rather than accepting an easy one.

4. *Risk-taking* is demonstrated in students who are willing to make guesses. These students usually are not afraid of failure or criticism. They play on hunches just to see where these will take them. Such children are not bothered by uncertainty, the unconventional, or lack of structure. *Examples:* Students who

- will defend their ideas regardless of what others think,
- will set high goals of accomplishment and not be afraid of trying to reach them,
- will admit to a mistake,
- really want to try something new and hard, and
- prefer to take a chance or a dare.

MODIFICATIONS OF THE BASIC CURRICULUM

Content Modifications

The Williams model provides for three content modifications. Two of the strategies, organized random search and the skills of search, concentrate on methods used by professionals. In the first strategy, organized random search, students are taught to use a particular method or structure and to apply it to a different situation, thereby creating something new. In the second, skills of search, students learn various methods used by professionals and how to apply them. A third strategy—the study of creative people and creative processes—also is appropriate and important to show gifted students the more personal side of creativity.

Process Modifications

The Williams model includes some curriculum modifications appropriate for gifted students. The major changes are in the areas of process: open-endedness, a discovery approach, freedom of choice, and a variety of methods. Perhaps the most important modification is open-endedness. Williams's model incorporates open-ended, provocative questions and learning experiences. Several of the teaching strategies (e.g., discrepancies, provocative questions, and tolerance for ambiguity) directly address this aspect of teaching methods for the gifted. These strategies require that teachers develop and pose open-ended, stimulating, and challenging questions that easily interest gifted students.

Although not addressed as directly as the concept of open-endedness, a discovery approach is present in most of the teaching strategies in the model. Most of the ideas included place the teacher in the role of questioner and the student in the role of discoverer. The biggest difference between this and traditional discovery approaches is that in the Williams strategies the teacher usually encourages students to "discover" as many ideas (or solutions or principles) as possible rather than discovering a particular idea or principle. Williams also suggests freedom of choice, particularly for highly able students, by allowing students to choose an area of study and develop an original product based on that study. The final process modification is variety of methods. Because seven different strategies can be used in any content area to encourage different behaviors (re-sulting in a slightly different "twist" to each activity), the result is a great deal of variety in teaching strategies.

Product Modifications

Williams's model also provides for one product modification, which is not quite as clear-cut as the content modifications. In one section of the program, Williams suggests that highly able children be allowed to "go off on their own" to develop their creative products. He recommends that the teacher make certain that the final product of independent study "goes further" than a report that is turned in for a grade. The examples of acceptable products (e.g., an art piece, a research report for a journal, a film) are transformations rather than summaries. Although he does not address the aspects of audiences and problems, the recommended products are sophisticated.

Learning Environment Modifications

With respect to the learning environment, Williams recommends aspects of all the changes recommended for gifted learners. He provides for the development of a learner-centered, independent, open, accepting learning environment through a list of ways in which teachers can both directly and indirectly develop students' creativity. The indirect ways constitute most of those related to the environment, but some of the direct ways can be considered dimensions of the environment. The following recommendations are listed under the environmental dimensions to which they seem to relate most directly.

Learner Centered
- Maintain an attitude of learning with the students. Do not profess to know all the answers and be willing to explore student ideas.
- Treat students' questions and ideas with a great deal of respect and keep the emphasis on "rightness" or "correctness" to a minimum.

Independence
- Provide a period of time each day for working with a small group of students and encourage them to plan the use of this time.

- Have a suggestion box for students to propose classroom or playground improvements.
- Respect the students, and show that you are confident they will act appropriately and responsibly.
- Provide a safe psychological environment that is available to students when needed, but allow and encourage students to venture away from it.

Openness
- Be playful, and encourage fantasy and imagination, even when the task is a serious one.
- Allow students a free period of time each day to use as they please.
- Show that you believe each student is unique and capable of becoming or being a creative individual.
- Allow productive noise and messiness in the classroom. Provide a structure and boundaries that encourage fruitful nontraditional student activities.

Accepting
- When students have new ideas, talk and listen to them in a sensitive manner, sometimes encouraging them to go further with their ideas.
- Listen carefully to students, and attempt to see things through their eyes.
- Give students honest feedback when they produce a product or develop an idea.
- Challenge students by discussing reality, but stimulate them with fantasy.
- Recognize that each student's creative production may be new to him or her even though you may have seen it many times before.

The environmental dimensions of complexity and high mobility are discussed by Williams mainly in conjunction with his recommendations for the handling of gifted students who are developing independent projects. To assist students in independent study, Williams also recommends that the learning environment be as flexible as possible to allow movement within and outside the classroom. Suggestions include releasing students to work with students from other classrooms and releasing them for certain periods of time each week to work on their own in the library, in a resource room, or with an expert from outside the school. Students also should be allowed to search for and use media that will assist them in developing their products.

JUDGMENTS

Advantages

Williams's Teaching Strategies for Thinking and Feeling has several advantages. The first and perhaps most important is its unique combination of thinking and feeling behaviors. A second related advantage is that the model concentrates on a specific and well-defined set of behaviors. These are observable, measurable behaviors derived from research on the characteristics of creative, productive adults.

Another strength of this model is its emphasis on open-endedness of learning experiences and teacher questions. As discussed earlier, several of the strategies directly address this concept through both open-ended and provocative questions.

Williams also advocates an individualized approach, including assessment and observation of thinking and feeling behaviors, compilation of information, interpretation of profiles, and design of both individual and group learning experiences based on the students' needs.

Disadvantages

The Williams model also has several disadvantages. First, even though the strategies and the total approach have been field-tested in a variety of classrooms, no research has been reported on the effectiveness of the strategies. In effect, no research has indicated that if teachers do all 18 strategies and attempt to develop the eight behaviors in their students, they will increase the students' creative behaviors. Data on the effectiveness of the strategies should have been relatively easy to collect during the field-testing, but the only data available are on the elements necessary for effective inservice and the frequency of use of the strategies. Data on student gains are conspicuously absent.

A second disadvantage is the model's lack of empirical or logical power. The model itself was not derived from a particular theoretical position or set of theoretical principles. Even though the Williams model was derived from Guilford's Structure of Intellect model of human intelligence (Guilford, 1975, 1977), the only resemblance it bears to this theoretical base is that it is morphological, or integrated, rather than hierarchical. The thinking behaviors of fluency, flexibility, originality, and elaboration are concepts first developed by Guilford (1967) as part of his definition of divergent thinking but are not a major part of his model of intelligence. One could argue that the subject matter in Williams's model is comparable to the content of Guilford's, the teaching strategies compare to the processes, and the pupil behaviors parallel the products. However, the individual items included in these categories do not appear to be related to those in Guilford's model.

Another weakness of the model is its lack of comprehensiveness as a total approach. It was not developed for use in programs for gifted learners, but as a way to develop creativity in all students. Indeed, Williams (1971) advocates using his and other models popular in programs for the gifted to improve education for all children. Even though the emphasis on specific behaviors is an advantage, concentration on a limited range of behaviors is a disadvantage. The development of divergent thinking and feeling is not enough. Educators must help gifted children develop a whole range of thinking and feeling behaviors, including divergent ones. For this reason and the fact that only two of the content modifications and one of the product modifications appropriate for the gifted are addressed by the approach, the Williams model must be combined with other models to form a comprehensive program for gifted students.

A final disadvantage is that few materials developed for use in implementing the model are available. If they can be located, however, they are practical and easy to use.

CONCLUSION

Williams's model does not provide a comprehensive program for curriculum development for gifted students. It does, however, offer certain unique features that highly recommend its use in programs for gifted students. The process modifications, individualization, and concentration on the cognitive and affective behaviors necessary for creativity development are ample justification for its use as a component in such programs.

If readers decide to implement this model, they are urged to develop procedures for assessing the effectiveness of the strategies, because such data are not available. Use of the needs assessment instruments for evaluation of progress is strongly advised, as is comparison of this method with others to determine the most effective strategies for use with gifted students.

A PROMISING NEW MODEL: PRISM OF LEARNING

The Prism of Learning is a new model that shows great promise for the field, and it probably will be included in future volumes. It was developed and is being polished by Drs. C. June Maker and Usanee Anuruthwong. The model integrates content and process, includes problem solving as a component, and is philosophically in tune with the Theory of Multiple Intelligences and the DISCOVER (Chapter 5) and TASC (Chapter 11) principles. The information for this chapter is taken from Maker and Anuruthwong (2002), unless otherwise noted.

The model (prism) has three dimensions: (a) the environment, (b) competencies or outcomes for the learners, and (c) learning processes. In the center of the prism, or the axis, are human abilities. The teacher's responsibility is to create an environment that will enable each child to develop his or her spectrum of abilities—that is, to become "illuminated from within."

Maker and Anuruthwong see problem solving as the key construct in both creativity and intelligence and believe that not only is creativity not separate from intelligence, but it is an *essential part* of intelligence. Problem solving requires five general capacities and 10 types of human abilities.

The information on this model is not organized in the same way as the information on the other models because the Prism of Learning model is evolving and not yet complete. As noted before, however, it is an exciting model with great promise for the future.

ELEMENTS/PARTS

General Capacities

Remembering
Remembering information and experiences is the most basic of the general intellectual capacities. To recall a previous experience or information received previously, it must be encoded in a way that is accessible when one wants or needs to use it. It must be retrieved so it can be used in a meaningful, relevant way in a present situation (Maker & Anuruthwong, 2003).

Creativity
Creativity is seen as the ability to think of, develop, or implement unique and appropriate ideas or solutions. When students invent ideas that are new to them but known to others, this is merely a different level of creativity from that of someone who develops an idea or problem solution that is unique. Both of these levels require the same creative process.

Reasoning/Logic
Reasoning or logic is the capacity to think in systematic ways, a necessary element in all human abilities. Logic may vary from one area to another, but it has a clearly defined set of principles that can be used to explain a chain of connections in the reasoning process. Logic also is necessary in creativity; creative thinking may result in application of unusual principles of logic or from application of usual principles in unusual ways.

Metacognition
Metacognition is the ability to monitor one's own thinking and to be self-aware. It can take the form of images, words, or thoughts. However, the ability to choose words, draw diagrams, act out, or in some way communicate thoughts or concepts to others is necessary if one's ideas are to be shared.

Intuition
Intuition is the phenomenon of knowing without the use of identifiable processes. Maker and Anuruthwong consider intuition as the real *first language* of human beings, and the words, symbols, and sounds that humans learn as the *second language*. Intuition is the general capacity closest to spiritual ability and is important to the functioning of all human abilities.

Human Abilities

Social/Humanitarian

Social/humanitarian abilities are the skills needed to get along with other people. Other social abilities include communicating effectively, seeing another persons' point of view, being patient with others, recognizing others' needs, and reading body language. At their highest level these abilities are manifested by efforts to improve the human condition. Individuals with humanitarian abilities have empathy, concern for others, high ethical and moral standards, and a desire to make the world a better place.

Emotional

Emotional abilities are those needed to handle one's own emotions. People who have these abilities can identify and describe their own feelings, identify the causes of emotions, and see the effects of expressing emotions in various ways.

Mathematical/Symbolic

Mathematical/symbolic abilities involve the use of abstract models, numbers, mathematical figures, and objects that symbolize abstract ideas. These capabilities include the skills needed to create and understand models or figures that symbolize or represent abstract concepts and relationships. They are the essence of the ability to explain relationships among quantities and entities.

Scientific/Natural

Scientific/natural abilities include keen observational powers, especially of the environment or change; curiosity about the how and why of the environment; and the desire to "experiment" with objects at hand. Scientific/natural capabilities are those such as perseverance; precision in observations, monitoring, and recording; willingness to take intellectual risks; and flexibility in thinking when hypotheses must be modified or discarded.

Somatic/Bodily

Somatic/bodily abilities include large and small muscle movements, as well as taste, touch, and smell. They make it possible to use the body flexibly to express feelings, emotions, ideas, and relationships. Additionally, they can be avenues of learning and stimulate ideas that come from the use of the body or are more easily learned through body movement.

Visual/Spatial

Visual/spatial abilities enable people to see things accurately and clearly through their eyes (physically) as well as to see images in their minds. Artists and inventors with high visual/spatial abilities can create accurate representations of what they see with their eyes or in their minds. These abilities are important in science, math, and technology, as well as in the arts.

Auditory/Sonance

Auditory/sonance abilities include skills in hearing, producing, and manipulating sounds. Auditory abilities include (physically) hearing things accurately and clearly, as well as hearing sounds in one's mind. Sonance is sensitivity to sounds of all types, and includes musical ability. Auditory abilities extend to alliteration and rhythm in poetry and the use of one's voice to produce certain emotional reactions in others.

Verbal/Linguistic

Verbal/linguistic abilities are related to the skills required to use words effectively. These include understanding word meanings, putting together sequences of words, creating pictures or emotions using words, using words accurately, and using words to entertain or persuade others. Both oral and written language are included in verbal/linguistic abilities.

Mechanical/Technical

Mechanical/technical abilities are those necessary for understanding, creating, and repairing machines or other devices. People who have mechanical abilities can see how rigid parts work together to transfer energy, can think of ways to design devices to do everyday tasks or make these tasks easier, and love to work with their hands. Those who have technical abilities understand and can use computers and other technological devices easily and effectively.

Spiritual

Spiritual abilities are those necessary to see beyond the material world. These abilities allow a person to develop awareness and understanding of phenomena related to the human soul or spirit.

Learning Processes

Learning, thinking, and remembering do not occur only in the brain. Every cell of the body remembers, and all cells are connected through a complex nervous system. Learning processes are nonlinear and nonsequential. Every individual has his or her personal, unique sequence of processes for learning, and these processes can be different for different tasks or various types or contexts of learning.

Competencies

Competencies are the things adults want children to learn as a result of school or life experience. Traditional educational settings have imposed an artificial separation of content areas and thinking processes. In truth, knowledge is connected and interdependent, just as the human body and all natural systems are connected and interdependent. In the Prism of Learning model, key ideas that lend themselves to the integration of information and competencies from traditional academic disciplines are identified for age groups. These key ideas, which provide themes that can serve as a structure for learning experiences, are divided into four levels:

- Grades K to 2: individuality, change, patterns, relationships, cycles, and environment
- Grades 3 to 5: conflict, communication, cooperation, interaction, and structures
- Grades 6 to 8: culture, extinction, exploration, diversity, and systems
- Grades 9 to 12: ethics, beauty, harmony, invention, and interdependence

Each subsequent level needs to revisit previous key ideas, with an emphasis on competencies needed for life success.

LEARNING ENVIRONMENT

Humans have a wide range of adaptive abilities and are sensitive to environmental conditions. Maker and Anuruthwong believe that learning environments have two major components: physical and dynamic. The physical environment includes the campus, school buildings, classrooms, and natural and manmade objects—everything that can serve as a stimulus for learning. The dynamic environment includes the instructional strategies and the dynamics of the teacher's interactions with the students and the interactions among students. The physical and dynamic environments are complementary, and they must be compatible to be effective.

THE LEARNING CENTER

The learning center created to facilitate the Prism of Learning is larger and more comprehensive than learning centers created in individual classrooms. Such a center is designed to be used by an entire school. A significant amount of space is required, because each of the human abilities except social/humanitarian has its own "corner" or space. Each space contains individual and group activities that are challenging and engaging and materials that students can use independently. These materials must have the potential to be used in a variety of ways, to excite curious minds, and to challenge students of different ability levels. The space for each ability needs to be large enough to accommodate five or six students at a time, without being crowded. Students need places to work and talk with others, as well as places to work alone.

In the center of the room are general tools such as computers, video equipment, audio recorders/players, and printers. Additionally, space (preferably round, to encourage student interaction) is needed where students can gather for group activities and to talk about projects.

Around this periphery are placed containers with color-coded, reusable cards with activities for the students to do alone or within a team or group. The problem-solving activities on these cards are related to the competencies (key ideas) and the human abilities. Problems range from very structured to "fuzzy," ill-defined ones and are designed to develop students' general capacities and their competencies (see the DISCOVER Problem Continuum, Chapter 5; Problem Based Learning, Chapter 7; or the TASC problem-solving process, Chapter 11).

A particularly appealing and unique element of these learning centers is "shoe-box experiments." Each box contains all the materials and instructions (in the form of pictures, written instructions, or an audiotape) for conducting an interesting and engaging learning experiment. Students can check out these shoe-box experiments and take them home to share with family and friends. This element alone is potentially powerful enough to change students, families, schools, and communities into environments where learning is viewed as exciting and valued. A student sharing a provocative learning task with others is empowered beyond the moment; the potential is for life-altering experiences and mindsets.

At a learning center that serves an entire school, each class is scheduled to go with its teacher and spend time in the center. Usually, a group activity, which may involve social/humanitarian abilities, begins the class's session in the center. These activities also may be used to teach a concept, exercise a particular learning process, introduce new materials, and so on. Most beginning group activities last no more than 15 minutes.

Most of the students' time needs to be spent on self-selected activities. They need to be free to explore and discover in all the centers and to spend an extended amount of time in the problem-solving activities that interest them most.

Toward the end of their time in the center, the students reconvene for sharing special projects (a few each day) and to record and reflect on their experiences in the center. These records and reflections become part of a portfolio, along with special projects or products or pictures of such projects or products.

ASSESSMENT AND EVALUATION

Observations

Assessment is not accomplished with a test, but with observations by teachers, teaching assistants, and center teachers on specially designed checklists. These checklists include problem-solving behaviors and characteristics of the students' products. The observations stretch over a significant amount of time and include multiple procedures and observers. Teachers use a rotation system, making a special effort to observe a certain number of students each day. Teachers observe each student at least two times each term. Teachers also may note special performances or products made by any students, whether or not the student is one they are supposed to be observing on a given day.

Assessment Day

For one or two weeks each year, all students using the center participate in specially designed assessment activities. One interesting, engaging activity is in each corner, and an adult who has high abilities in that area and has practiced observing the activity is there as well. On assessment days students begin in the center of the space as usual, but instead of choosing activities, they are assigned to a group and they rotate through all the corners with that group. All activities take approximately the same amount of time, and observers watch, take notes, and take pictures of children's products.

Student Portfolios

Another element of assessment is examination of student portfolios, which include drawings, records of corners visited and activities engaged in, and students' reflections on their performances. A self-assessment in each area of human ability also is included, and students are asked to perform this self-evaluation at least once each term.

Compilation

Teachers compile the information gathered and confer to determine each student's greatest strengths and any areas of challenge that may interfere with the development or expression of their abilities. Additionally, they may brainstorm or discuss ways to challenge the most able and to engage and motivate the more reluctant learners.

TEACHERS FOR
THE LEARNING CENTERS

As in any educational endeavor, good teachers are critical to a successful learning center. Two or three teachers are needed, and their skills and backgrounds need to be complementary, with a balance of discipline knowledge, personality, and technical skills. Initially, teachers need 7 days of training. During this time, they learn the theory and structure of the Prism of Learning model, the central concept of problem-solving and how to develop a wide range of problem-solving abilities, the five general capacities, the abilities, the learning processes, and the competencies. These teachers need to learn ways to stimulate children's thinking, exploring, and discovering in an exciting and flexible way.

Follow-up staff development is needed for 2 years, with more assistance if necessary. Two days should be spent in the teacher's own learning center with expert advisers, and they need to participate in an annual summer workshop. These steps help teachers internalize the model, work through their own frustrations, and assist other teachers to solve problems that have arisen. This is a time of renewal, intellectual challenge, and fun; workshops serve as a reminder that learning, for the teachers and their students, is all of these.

PARENT AND COMMUNITY CONNECTIONS

Parents are the most influential people in children's lives; they set the course for their child's life through the decisions they make constantly. What parents say becomes the reality for their child; children's subconscious minds are like sponges—they readily absorb their parents' expectations, values, and belief systems.

Activities available for children, the actions of adults, and the safety of the environment all impact children's learning and behavior. Those in an at-risk environment are distracted from healthy learning and have poor behavior models. Neighborhoods with ample schools, libraries, parks, and clubs where healthy learning can occur enhance children's desire to learn and their ability to make good choices.

A learning center must be introduced to families and community members. Everyone needs to understand the importance of a healthy environment for children and how each person in a community can contribute to positive experiences for children. Alliances need to be formed between the learning center and individuals, businesses, and social organizations.

Perhaps at times youth groups (religious, Boy Scouts, Girl Scouts, etc.) might reserve the learning center for a particular activity or series of activities. Such opportunities would benefit the entire community.

EVALUATION OF THE LEARNING CENTER

Ongoing appraisal and modifications are critical to the success of any endeavor. For a learning center, the monitoring and assessment include self-evaluation of all activities and procedures and the systematic collection of the perceptions of others. Teachers, children, administrators, parents, families, and community members need to be surveyed at different times during a school year. They need to be asked what strengths they perceive and how they suggest improvements might be made.

Student assessment needs to be compiled and included in an evaluation of a learning center. Achievement, as measured by mandated assessments, needs to be included, as do student self-concept, independence, and engagement in learning. When fully implemented, a learning center will improve the community as well as develop children's potential to become all they can be.

Current activities in an international context and future research will no doubt provide evidence of the success of this promising model. As the model is implemented, it will be refined and modified. Even the first glimpse shows much promise. New curriculum ideas, new thinking and problem-solving models, and new research emphasize the importance of teaching the attitudes and strategies that enable all people to be lifelong learners.

CONCLUSION

The Prism of Learning is an exciting addition to the educational *zeitgeist*. It embodies principles from research on brain function, learning, educational strategies, and the nature of children who are successful students. As an emerging model, it has the raw potential to accomplish what dedicated educators have always sought to excite students about learning, to light up their eyes with wonder and discovery, to become all they can be.

CHAPTER SUMMARY AND CONCLUSION

Three models have been descried in this chapter. Each offers a different facet to the development of curriculum for gifted students. The Kohlberg Discussion of Moral Dilemmas model focuses on the moral development of youth. Changes in the social fabric, from family structure to economic reversals and political realities, demand that educators prepare future leaders and shakers for a different world, and hopefully for a different approach to solving problems. For leaders to habitually examine issues and situations from multiple perspectives, to always consider short- and long-term effects of actions, to have integrity, and to believe in certain universal values holds at least the promise of a brighter future.

The Williams Teaching Strategies for Thinking and Feeling model addresses two critical areas: developing creativity and the affective component of human nature. To be worked out effectively, new problems require flexible, creative thinkers in positions of power. Also, the affective dimension of every action, solution, and situation must not be forgotten, for it is what determines whether a solution solves the problem or merely creates a situation ripe for another, often worse, problem.

The Prism of Learning is the newest and most comprehensive of the models in this chapter. As a new model, it will undoubtedly experience growing pains and setbacks, and meet with enthusiastic reception by some and cold rejection by others. Its strengths, however, provide assurance that it can survive assessment, modification, evaluation, and polishing, to emerge as a jewel in the crown of education.

Overall, even given the problems facing education, these three approaches offer hope, each in its own way. As long as society has a core of people who are focused on developing moral strength, thinking and feeling processes, and educating the whole child, hope is on the horizon.

RESOURCES

Kohlberg: Background Information

Carpendale, J. (2000). Kohlberg and Piaget on stages and moral reasoning. *Developmental Review, 20*, 181–205.

Dabrowski, K., with Piechowski, M. M. (1977). *Theories of levels of emotional development.* Oceanside, NY: Dabor.

Fan-Willman, C., & Gutteridge, D. (1981). Creative thinking and moral reasoning of academically gifted secondary school adolescents. *Gifted Child Quarterly, 25*(4), 149–153.

Gilligan, C. (1982). *In a different voice: Psychological theory and women's development.* Cambridge, MA: Harvard University Press.

Kazemek, F. E. (1989, Spring). Feminine voice and power in moral education. *Educational Horizons*, pp. 76–81.

Power, F. C., Higgins, A., & Kohlberg, L. (1989). *Lawrence Kohlberg's approach to moral education.* New York: Columbia University Press.

Reiman, A. J., & Peace, S. D. (2002). Promoting teachers' moral reasoning and collaborative inquiry performance: A developmental role-taking and guided inquiry study. *Journal of Moral Education, 31*, 57–66.

Reimer, J., Paolitto, D. P., & Hersh, R. H. (1983). *Promoting moral growth from Piaget to Kohlberg* (2nd ed.). Prospect Heights, IL: Woodland Press.

Kohlberg: Instructional Materials and Resources

Dana, N. F., & Lynch-Brown, C. (1991). Moral development for the gifted: Making a case for children's literature. *Roeper Review, 14*(1), 13–16.

Edwards, C. P. (1986). *Promoting social and moral development in young children.* New York: Teachers College Press.

Fleisher, P. (1993). *Changing our world: A handbook for young activists.* Tucson, AZ: Zephyr Press.

Lindsey, B. (1988). A lamp for Diogenes: Leadership giftedness and moral education. *Roeper Review, 11*(1), 8–11.

Williams: Instructional Materials and Resources

Patton, S. J., & Maletis, M. (n.d.). *Inventors: A source guide for self-directed units.* Tucson, AZ: Zephyr Press.

Williams, F. E. (1986). *The second volume of classroom ideas for encouraging thinking and feeling.* East Aurora, NY: DOK.

Williams, F. J. (1990). *Curriculum units: Classroom ideas: Vol. 3 for encouraging thinking and feeling.* Buffalo, NY: DOK.

Prism of Learning: Background Information

Armstrong, T., (2002). *The multiple intelligences of reading and writing: Making the words come alive.* Alexandria, VA: Association for Supervision and Curriculum Development.

Armstrong, A. (1994). *Multiple intelligences in the classroom* (2nd ed.). Alexandria, VA: Association for Supervision and Curriculum Development.

Costa, A. L., & Kallik, B. (Eds.). (2002). *Assessing and reporting on habits of minds.* Alexandria, VA: Association for Supervision and Curriculum Development.

Given, B. K. (2002). *Teaching to the brain's natural learning systems.* Alexandria, VA: Association for Supervision and Curriculum Development.

Jacobs, H. H. (1997). *Mapping the big picture: Integrating curriculum and assessment K–12.* Alexandria, VA: Association for Supervision and Curriculum Development.

Prism of Learning: Instructional Materials and Resources

Borkman, R. (2001). *Science through multiple intelligences: Patterns that inspire inquiry.* Tucson, AZ: Zephyr Press.

Charette, R. J. (2003). *Circles rolling through time.* Tucson, AZ: Zephyr Press.

Diehn, G. (1999). *Making books that fly, fold, wrap, hide, pop up, twist, & turn.* New York: Sterling.

Glock, J., Wertz, S., & Meyer, M. (1998). *Discovering the naturalist intelligence.* Tucson, AZ: Zephyr Press.

Jones, R. S. (2000). *Tools for the geographer.* Tucson, AZ: Zephyr Press.

Margulies, M. A., with Maal, N. (2001). *Mapping inner space* (2nd ed.). Tucson, AZ: Zephyr Press.

Paris, R. (1992). *Journalism.* Tucson, AZ: Zephyr Press.

Selwyn, D. (1993). *Living history in the classroom.* Tucson, AZ: Zephyr Press.

A. W. Peller & Associates. (www.awpeller.com) also carries a wide variety of materials to support learning based on the Prism model. Titles such as the following are included: *Nine Muses, Mythology, Folk Tale Plays from Around the World, The Discover Series, Create a Culture,* and *Incredible Mysteries of Our Planet.*

CHAPTER 13

Developing a Comprehensive Curriculum

In the previous chapters, we have presented a thorough review of each of 12 teaching–learning models and shorter reviews of three that are currently used in or appropriate for use in developing a curriculum for gifted students. Several models are close to providing a comprehensive approach within themselves, but no model should stand alone, without incorporating selected elements of other models. The majority of the models reviewed were not developed for use in gifted programs. Most were developed for some specific, well-defined purpose, but educators have used them in a variety of ways, some appropriate and many inappropriate. Too many educators assume that by using one particular teaching–learning model as a structure for curriculum, the learning needs of the gifted students in that program will be met.

The Cognitive Taxonomy (Chapter 3), for example, was developed for the narrow purpose of classifying educational objectives, according to their complexity, as a way to facilitate communication among professionals about the objectives of instruction. It was never intended as a framework for developing a sequence of questions to guide a discussion, and it certainly was not intended to form the basis of curriculum development for gifted learners. Nevertheless, it has been used in too many instances as the only curricular modification provided for gifted students. The same is true of the Teaching Strategies for Thinking and Feeling (Chapter 12). Although these strategies were developed as ways to stimulate a narrow range of human behaviors (e.g., the thinking and feeling behaviors involved in creativity), this approach is used inappropriately by some educators as the primary curriculum development model for programs for the gifted.

Thus, it is important that readers and the authors of the models interpret the comments in this chapter as an honest attempt to show how a comprehensive curriculum can be developed. Rather than recommending that educators "start all over again" with new models or new approaches, curriculum developers and teachers can begin with existing models or approaches to education of gifted students and move toward an integrated program. Incorporation of a variety of models adapted to student needs, one or more complementary models, or the addition of components to the Cognitive Taxonomy will result in appropriate curriculum for gifted learners.

Any critical comments about specific models or approaches in this volume should be interpreted only as criticism of large-scale adoption of the model or approach by educators rather than as criticism of the authors of the models (unless, of course, they have advocated the use of their model as a sole approach to education of the gifted). Authors generally have been clear about the goals of their models and the reasons for their development. Unfortunately, many educators have ignored the underlying assumptions made by the developers and have used the models for many purposes not intended by the authors.

Not every teacher or program developer will develop a curriculum in which all the modifications recommended by Maker (1982b) and Maker and Nielson (1995) are incorporated. The number and range of curricular modifications needed in a program will depend on the characteristics of the students. All the recommended curricular changes were designed to build on and extend the present and potential future characteristics of gifted students. Thus, if the students in a particular program do not possess the characteristics that the curricular change was designed to address, this particular curriculum modification is unnecessary, unless it is seen as a way to develop a particular desirable characteristic that is not present. In addition, other curricular modifications not discussed in this volume may be necessary or desirable because of differing characteristics of the students in the program.

CURRICULUM DEVELOPMENT

Maker (1982b) and Maker and Nielson (1995) suggest a multifaceted process in development of a curriculum for the gifted that includes the following:

- involvement of key individuals who assess the situation and assist in the formulation of goals and programs
- development of a definition of giftedness
- assessment of the students' needs
- development of a philosophy
- development of program goals
- choice of teaching–learning models
- development of objectives and strategies
- development of evaluation procedures
- development of a plan for curriculum implementation

The process has been adequately described elsewhere. Our discussion here assumes that program goals include the provision of curricular modifications in all the aspects of content, process, product, and learning environment recommended by Maker (1982b) and Maker and Nielson (1995), as briefly outlined in Chapter 1 of this volume.

When choosing teaching–learning models for use in developing curriculum for gifted students, the first step is to assess the appropriateness of the existing models for the particular situation. A checklist and questions for this purpose, with models listed alphabetically, appear in Chapter 1 (see Figure 1.1). Each individual familiar with the situation and the models should evaluate the models and compare their ratings to determine those that may be appropriate for the program. A second assessment should then be made to determine the model's comprehensiveness for providing needed modifications of the curriculum. A worksheet designed for this purpose also was presented in Chapter 1 (see Figure 1.2).

ASSESSING THE MODELS

To assist the reader in assessing the comprehensiveness of the teaching–learning models presented in this volume, we have completed the worksheet presented in Figure 1.2 (see Figure 13.1). The assessment in this chapter provides a summary of material presented in the "Modification of the Basic Curriculum" section in each chapter that describes a model. Those readers who do not understand why a particular assessment was made

(*text continues on p. 457*)

WORKSHEET FOR ASSESSING MODELS' COMPREHENSIVENESS

Rate each model on each criterion by placing a ✔ in the column if the modification is made in the model. If modification is not made, leave the space blank.

Curricular Modifications	Affective Taxonomy (3)	ALM (2)	BSD (4)	Cognitive Taxonomy (3)	CPS (6)	DISCOVER (5)	DMD (12)	ETM and SEM (8)	Group Investigations (9)	HTTS (10)	PBL (7)	Prism (12)	TASC (11)	TSTF (12)	Comments
Content															
1. Abstractness		✔	✔	✔		✔	✔			✔	✔	✔			
2. Complexity		✔	✔	✔		✔	✔		✔	✔	✔	✔			
3. Variety	✔	✔	✔		✔	✔	✔	✔	✔	✔	✔	✔	✔	✔	
4. Organization for Learning Value			✔			✔				✔	✔	✔			

(continues)

FIGURE 13.1. Worksheet for Assessing Models' Appropriateness. *Note.* Numbers in parentheses refer to chapters in this book. ALM = Autonomous Learner Model; BSD = Basic Structure of a Discipline; CPS = Creative Problem Solving; DMD = Discussions of Moral Dilemmas; ETM = Enrichment Triad Model; SEM = Schoolwide Enrichment Model; HTTS = Hilda Taba Teaching Strategies; PBL = Problem Based Learning; Prism = Prism of Learning; TASC = Thinking Actively in a Social Context; TSTF = Teaching Strategies for Thinking and Feeling. Adapted from *Teaching Models in Education of the Gifted* (2nd ed., p. 14), by C. J. Maker and A. B. Nielson, 1995, Austin, TX: PRO-ED. Copyright 1995 by PRO-ED, Inc. Adapted with permission.

Rate each model on each criterion by placing a ✓ in the column if the modification is made in the model. If modification is not made, leave the space blank.

Curricular Modifications	Affective Taxonomy (3)	ALM (2)	BSD (4)	Cognitive Taxonomy (3)	CPS (6)	DISCOVER (5)	DMD (12)	ETM and SEM (8)	Group Investigations (9)	HTTS (10)	PBL (7)	Prism (12)	TASC (11)	TSTF (12)	Comments
Content (*continued*)															
5. Study of People		✓				✓						✓			
6. Study of Methods		✓	✓	✓	✓	✓		✓	✓		✓	✓	✓		
Process															
7. Higher Level Thought	✓	✓	✓	✓	✓	✓	✓	✓	✓	✓	✓	✓	✓	✓	
8. Open-endedness		✓	✓	✓	✓	✓	✓	✓	✓	✓	✓	✓	✓	✓	
9. Discovery		✓	✓			✓	✓	✓	✓	✓	✓	✓	✓	✓	
10. Evidence of Reasoning						✓				✓	✓				
11. Freedom of Choice	✓	✓				✓		✓	✓		✓	✓	✓		

(*continues*)

FIGURE 13.1. *Continued.*

Rate each model on each criterion by placing a ✓ in the column if the modification is made in the model. If modification is not made, leave the space blank.

Curricular Modifications	Affective Taxonomy (3)	ALM (2)	BSD (4)	Cognitive Taxonomy (3)	CPS (6)	DISCOVER (5)	DMD (12)	ETM and SEM (8)	Group Investigations (9)	HTTS (10)	PBL (7)	Prism (12)	TASC (11)	TSTF (12)	Comments
Process (*continued*)															
12. Group Interaction		✓				✓	✓	✓	✓	✓	✓	✓	✓	✓	
13. Pacing		✓				✓		✓	✓		✓	✓	✓		
14. Variety		✓			✓	✓		✓	✓	✓	✓	✓	✓	✓	
Product															
15. Result from Real Problems			✓		✓	✓		✓			✓	✓	✓	✓	
16. Addressed to Real Audiences					✓	✓		✓	✓			✓	✓		
17. Transformation		✓	✓	✓	✓	✓		✓	✓		✓	✓	✓	✓	
18. Variety		✓	✓		✓	✓		✓	✓		✓	✓	✓	✓	

(*continues*)

FIGURE 13.1. *Continued.*

Rate each model on each criterion by placing a ✓ in the column if the modification is made in the model. If modification is not made, leave the space blank.

Curricular Modifications	Affective Taxonomy (3)	ALM (2)	BSD (4)	Cognitive Taxonomy (3)	CPS (6)	DISCOVER (5)	DMD (12)	ETM and SEM (8)	Group Investigations (9)	HTTS (10)	PBL (7)	Prism (12)	TASC (11)	TSTF (12)	Comments
Product (*continued*)															
19. Self-Selected Format		✓			✓	✓		✓	✓		✓	✓	✓		
20. Appropriate Evaluation		✓			✓	✓		✓	✓		✓	✓	✓		
Learning Environment															
21. Learner Centered		✓			✓	✓	✓	✓	✓	✓	✓	✓	✓	✓	
22. Encourages independence		✓			✓	✓		✓	✓	✓	✓	✓	✓		
23. Openness		✓			✓	✓	✓	✓	✓	✓	✓	✓	✓	✓	
24. Accepting		✓				✓	✓	✓	✓	✓	✓	✓			
25. Complexity		✓				✓		✓	✓		✓	✓	✓		

(*continues*)

FIGURE 13.1. *Continued.*

Rate each model on each criterion by placing a ✓ in the column if the modification is made in the model. If modification is not made, leave the space blank.

Curricular Modifications	Affective Taxonomy (3)	ALM (2)	BSD (4)	Cognitive Taxonomy (3)	CPS (6)	DISCOVER (5)	DMD (12)	ETM and SEM (8)	Group Investigations (9)	HTTS (10)	PBL (7)	Prism (12)	TASC (11)	TSTF (12)	Comments
Learning Environment (*continued*)															
26. Varied Grouping		✓				✓		✓	✓		✓	✓	✓		
27. Flexibility		✓			✓	✓		✓			✓	✓	✓		
28. High Mobility		✓				✓		✓	✓		✓	✓	✓		
Totals	2	24	10	5	15	28	11	23	22	12	25	27	22	11	

FIGURE 13.1. *Continued.*

should review this section in the appropriate chapter. All evaluations are based on whether the model includes direct, specific suggestions regarding how to implement a particular curricular adaptation. Some models indirectly address an idea but do not include specific suggestions. In these cases the model is not listed as making that particular curriculum modification.

The column totals in Figure 13.1 provide a summary of the comprehensiveness of the models by giving the total number of modifications provided. The names of some of the models are represented by initials or abbreviations for brevity's sake. These include ALM for the Autonomous Learner Model, BSD for the Basic Structure of a Discipline, CPS for Creative Problem Solving, ETM for Enrichment Triad Model, SEM for Schoolwide Enrichment Model, HTTS for Hilda Taba Teaching Strategies, DMD for Discussion of Moral Dilemmas, PBL for Problem Based Learning, Prism for Prism of Learning, TASC for Thinking Actively in a Social Context, and TSTF for Teaching Strategies for Thinking and Feeling. As can be seen, the most comprehensive models overall are DISCOVER, ALM, Group Investigations, ETM and SEM, Prism, and TASC.

Only the DISCOVER model makes all recommended modifications, yet even this model can be enriched by using elements of other models, such as the HTTS, PBL, or TASC. The pattern of check marks also should be examined to determine areas of strength and weakness for each model. The BSD, for instance, although not one of the most comprehensive in overall ratings, provides most of the content changes needed. HTTS, although not the most comprehensive overall, provides more of the process changes than any other approach. This information is useful in making decisions about which models can be combined or used together.

The row totals in the worksheet are an additional source of information. These totals indicate the number of available models that provide a particular curricular modification. For example, few models provide for several of the content changes, whereas all of the models provide for the process modification of emphasis on higher level thought. This information can be helpful in suggesting the range of options available for making specific curricular adaptations.

CHOOSING MODELS

After the appropriateness and comprehensiveness of the models have been assessed, each educator (or development team) must decide whether to

(a) adopt one approach as the basis for curriculum development and incorporate elements to make it more comprehensive, (b) adopt two or more approaches that are complementary, or (c) adopt and adapt models. Any one of these three options is appropriate, depending on the situation. If, for example, an earlier assessment showed that only one approach was evaluated highly by those involved (based on its appropriateness, flexibility, adaptability, practicality, and validity), this approach should form the basis of the program. Modifications then can be made to increase its comprehensiveness. In most cases, however, several models would be acceptable, allowing a range of options for different purposes. Combining several models also ensures that variety will be included in the curriculum and that curricular modifications will be made in more ways than one.

Perhaps the most effective strategy is to employ a combination of options—that is, to adopt complementary models and to adapt each of them to form a comprehensive approach. With this strategy equal emphasis is placed on each curricular modification, and the possibility is increased that a well-integrated program will result.

In this chapter we provide tables that summarize for each model the curricular modifications that should be made, suggested changes, and other models that can be combined with the model to provide a particular change. In listing other models that can be used with the approach, we do not mean to imply that all these models be used, but rather that they are all possibilities.

Representative suggestions for changes have been listed in the tables as a quick summary to aid the reader. For example, learning environment modifications that have not been listed as recommendations are essentially the same in many cases, and listing them for each model would be repetitious. In considering the potential implementation of an approach or model, educators should review the specific chapter. (The models are presented in the order in which they appear in this book.)

Betts and Kercher: Autonomous Learner Model

The Autonomous Learner Model was developed specifically as a framework for a comprehensive program to facilitate social, emotional, and cognitive development for gifted students. The framework includes specific components and suggestions for implementation, but specific processes and strategies to develop creative thinking, problem solving, research skills, and self-regulation processes frequently are implicit. To use the ALM as a framework for comprehensive curriculum development, educators must make a variety of adaptations in process dimensions (see Table 13.1). A combination of this model with process models, such as CPS, PBL, HTTS, or TASC, will provide most of the modifications recommended for gifted students. For further information, see Chapter 2.

Bloom: Taxonomy of Cognitive Objectives

Bloom's Cognitive Taxonomy was not developed as a structure for curriculum development. It was intended as a system for classifying educational objectives to facilitate communication among educators. To use the taxonomy as a comprehensive approach to curriculum development, educators must make a variety of adaptations in content, process, and product dimensions of the curriculum (see Table 13.2). None of the learning environment changes have been addressed by the approach, so combination with other models or adaptation is necessary to incorporate this dimension. The major changes include teaching the taxonomy to students and beginning activities at the application level. The taxonomy can be combined or used in conjunction with most of the other models reviewed. For further information, refer to Chapter 3.

Krathwohl: Taxonomy of Affective Objectives

Like Bloom's Cognitive Taxonomy, Krathwohl's Affective Taxonomy was not created for curriculum development and certainly not for the gifted. It is a system designed for classifying objectives in the affective domain and was developed to facilitate communication between professionals. Of all the models reviewed, Krathwohl's Taxonomy makes the fewest curricular modifications for the gifted; however, it can be used in conjunction with other models or adapted to provide a framework for curricular development in the affective area (see Table 13.3). The Affective Taxonomy can be included easily with curriculum developed based on other models. Indeed, the authors recommend frequently incorporating affective elements into curriculum. For more information, see Chapter 3.

(*text continues on p. 469*)

TABLE 13.1

Modifying and Complementing Betts and Kercher's Autonomous Learner Model

Program Goals	Suggested Adaptation of Model	Complementary Models
To organize curricula around basic concepts and abstract generalizations.	Organize content at all levels of thinking and investigations around complex, abstract content. Encourage students to choose complex content for individual projects.	BSD HITTS DISCOVER Prism
To provide economical learning experiences.	Organize activities as above; strive for integrated themes or multiple-purpose activities. Begin activities at the application level of Bloom's Taxonomy (Chapter 3).	BSD HITTS CT
To provide opportunities for students to study creative people and the creative process.	Model includes this element.	TSTF Prism
To include content areas not in the mainstream curriculum.	Work with content area teachers to compact curriculum and develop in-depth study extensions that will provide opportunities for students to broaden and deepen their understanding of the discipline.	BSD GI CPS HITTS CT TSTF ETM & SEM
To provide open-ended activities and ask open-ended questions.	Ask open-ended, provocative questions. Design activities in all components of all dimensions that are open-ended.	BSD GI CPS HITTS ETM & SEM TSTF
To include discovery learning.	Model includes this element.	BSD GI CT HITTS ETM & SEM TSTF

(continues)

Objective	Description	Models
To require that students explain their reasoning and provide support for their answers.	Ask "why" questions at all appropriate times (except when rapid generation of ideas in divergent production is desired). Expect students to provide support for their inferences and conclusions in discussions and written work.	DMD HTTS
To encourage students to choose topics and methods of studying chosen topics.	Model includes this element.	CPS GI CT TSTF ETM & SEM
To provide structured simulations and other activities in which students can develop leadership and group participation skills.	Use group building and interpersonal development principles also to structure interaction of groups with complex content and real problems. Observe group interaction to evaluate individual progress in leadership and group process skills.	DISCOVER HTTS GI Prism
To pace the presentation of new material rapidly.	Move through presentation of new materials and strategies as quickly as possible. If a few students need more time, provide the information in context of group or individual activities.	ETM & SEM HTTS
To instruct students using a variety of methods.	Incorporate a wide variety of thinking and creative activities in all components of the model.	CPS GI DISCOVER Prism ETM & SEM TSTF
To encourage students to address real problems.	Encourage students to design individual projects that require creative thinking and problem solving. Model includes this element.	BSD PBL CPS TASC GI

(continues)

TABLE 13.1 *Continued.*
Modifying and Complementing Betts and Kercher's Autonomous Learner Model

Program Goals	Suggested Adaptation of Model	Complementary Models	
To assist students in directing their products to real audiences.	Model includes this element.	CPS DISCOVER	ETM & SEM GI
To assist students in locating venues in which their products can be appropriately evaluated and guide the development of self-evaluation skills.	Teach students the criteria for professional evaluation of products; encourage them to apply the criteria to their own work. Provide opportunities for students to present their work to practicing professionals for evaluation and feedback.	CPS DISCOVER	ETM & SEM GI
To require that student products are transformations rather than summaries of existing information.	Guide students as they develop criteria to include transformation.	CPS DISCOVER	Prism TASC

Note. ALM = Autonomous Learner Model; AT = Affective Taxonomy; BSD = Basic Structure of a Discipline; CPS = Creative Problem Solving; CT = Cognitive Taxonomy; DISCOVER = Discovering Intellectual Strengths and Capabilities while Observing Varied Ethnic Responses; DMD = Discussion of Moral Dilemmas; ETM & SEM = Enrichment Triad Model and Schoolwide Enrichment Model; GI = Group Investigations; HTTS = Hilda Taba Teaching Strategies; PBL = Problem Based Learning; TASC = Thinking Actively in a Social Context; TSTF = Teaching Strategies for Thinking and Feeling.

TABLE 13.2

Modifying and Complementing Bloom's Taxonomy of Cognitive Objectives

Program Goals	Suggested Adaptation of Model	Complementary Models		
To organize curricula around basic concepts and abstract generalizations.	Organize activities at all levels of the taxonomy around complex, abstract content.	BSD	HTTS	
		DISCOVER		
To provide economical learning experiences.	Organize activities around complex, abstract content; begin at the application level of the taxonomy.	BSD	HTTS	
		DISCOVER		
To provide opportunities for students to study creative people and the creative process.	Use the taxonomy as a structure to design activities for the study of eminent, creative, and productive people.	ALM	TASC	
		DISCOVER	TSTF	
		Prism		
To include content areas not in the mainstream curriculum.	Teach the taxonomy to students and encourage them to use it as a way to structure their own investigations.	ALM	GI	
		BSD	HTTS	
		CPS	TASC	
		DISCOVER	TSTF	
		ETM & SEM		
To provide open-ended activities and ask open-ended questions.	Ask open-ended, provocative questions.	ALM	DMD	
	Design open-ended activities at all levels of the taxonomy.	BSD	GI	
	Emphasize activities at or above the application level.	CPS	HTTS	
To include discovery learning.	Begin activities at, or above, the application level.	BSD	PBL	
	Teach students to use inquiry or scientific methods.	ETM	Prism	
	Provide activities that require inductive thinking.	DISCOVER	TASC	
		HTTS	TSTF	

(continues)

TABLE 13.2 *Continued.*

Modifying and Complementing Bloom's Taxonomy of Cognitive Objectives

Program Goals	Suggested Adaptation of Model	Complementary Models
To require that students explain their reasoning and provide support for their answers.	Ask "why" questions, when appropriate, at all levels above simple recall. Encourage students to support answers, inferences, and conclusions.	DMD HTTS
To encourage students to choose topics and methods of studying chosen topics.	Use the taxonomy to design a variety of types of activities from which students can choose. Design open-ended activities at all levels of the taxonomy from which students can choose.	ALM GI CPS TASC DISCOVER TSTF ETM & SEM
To provide structured simulations and other activities in which students can develop leadership and group participation skills.	Use the taxonomy as a tool for observing group interaction. Use the taxonomy to develop activities for group interaction and social involvement.	ALM PBL DISCOVER Prism GI TASC HTTS
To pace the presentation of new material rapidly.	Move through activities and questions at the two lowest levels very quickly.	ALM HTTS ETM & SEM
To instruct students using a variety of methods.	Design a variety of types of activities at each level of the taxonomy. Incorporate critical and creative thinking. Include activities in the multiple intelligences and the human abilities.	ALM ETM & SEM CPS Prism DISCOVER TSTF

(continues)

To encourage students to address real problems.	Use activities at the analysis level to help students identify and structure real problems for investigation.	ALM PBL DISCOVER TASC GI
To assist students in directing their products to real audiences.	Teach the taxonomy to students as a tool for the use of audiences to evaluate their products. Encourage students to elaborate on their product syntheses and share them with real audiences.	ALM GI DISCOVER TASC ETM & SEM
To assist students in locating venues in which their products can be appropriately evaluated and guide the development of self-evaluation skills.	Teach the taxonomy to students as a tool for self-evaluation of products.	DISCOVER PBL ETM & SEM Prism GI TASC
To require that student products are transformations rather than summaries of existing information.	Be sure that students understand that "synthesis" is transformation.	ETM TASC DISCOVER

Note. ALM = Autonomous Learner Model; AT = Affective Taxonomy; BSD = Basic Structure of a Discipline; CPS = Creative Problem Solving; CT = Cognitive Taxonomy; DISCOVER = Discovering Intellectual Strengths and Capabilities while Observing Varied Ethnic Responses; DMD = Discussion of Moral Dilemmas; ETM & SEM = Enrichment Triad Model and Schoolwide Enrichment Model; GI = Group Investigations; HTTS = Hilda Taba Teaching Strategies; PBL = Problem Based Learning; TASC = Thinking Actively in a Social Context; TSTF = Teaching Strategies for Thinking and Feeling.

TABLE 13.3

Modifying and Complementing Krathwohl's Taxonomy of Affective Objectives

Program Goals	Suggested Adaptation of Model	Complementary Models		
To organize curricula around basic concepts and abstract generalizations.	Develop abstract generalizations that relate to affective behaviors and values.	BSD DISCOVER HTTS	Prism TASC	
To provide economical learning experiences.	Develop complex generalizations that relate to affective behaviors and values.	BSD DMD	HTTS	
To provide opportunities for students to study creative people and the creative process.	Analyze the affective behaviors and values of eminent, creative, and productive people.	ALM ETM HTTS	Prism TSTF	
To include content areas not in the mainstream curriculum.	Teach the taxonomy to students to use as they conduct investigations. Teach the taxonomy as an educational classification system.	ALM BSD CPS	ETM HTTS TSTF	
To provide open-ended activities and ask open-ended questions.	Ask open-ended questions at all levels of the taxonomy. Design open-ended provocative activities at all levels.	ALM DMD ETM	GI PBL	
To include discovery learning.	Begin activities at the valuing level. Teach the taxonomy to students as a way to structure their own value inquiries.	BSD ETM GI	HTTS Prism TSTF	

(continues)

To require that students explain their reasoning and provide support for their answers.	Ask "why" questions when appropriate at all levels except Receiving.	DISCOVER, DMD, ETM, HTTS, PBL, TASC
To encourage students to choose topics and methods of studying chosen topics.	At each level of the taxonomy, provide a variety of learning activities from which students can choose.	ALM, CPS, DISCOVER, ETM, TASC, TSTF
To provide structured simulations and other activities in which students can develop leadership and group participation skills.	Use the taxonomy to design group interaction activities. Use the taxonomy as a structure to observe the interaction of a group.	ALM, HTTS, PBL, Prism, TASC
To pace the presentation of new material rapidly.	Move through the lower levels very rapidly.	BSD, ETM, HTTS
To instruct students using a variety of methods.	Design a variety of types of activities at each level of the taxonomy.	ALM, CPS, ETM, GI, PBL, Prism, TASC, TSTF
To encourage students to address real problems.	Teach the taxonomy as a way to identify problems to investigate, as a way to analyze underlying ideas or assumptions.	ALM, BSD, CPS, GI, PBL, TASC

(continues)

TABLE 13.3 *Continued.*
Modifying and Complementing Krathwohl's Taxonomy of Affective Objectives

Program Goals	Suggested Adaptation of Model	Complementary Models	
To assist students in locating venues in which their products can be appropriately evaluated and guide the development of self-evaluation skills.	Teach the taxonomy to students as a model they can give to real audiences as a format to evaluate their products.	ALM	GI
		CPS	PBL
	Encourage students to share the products of their activities at the characterization level with real audiences.	DISCOVER	TASC
		ETM	
To require that student products are transformations rather than summaries of existing information.	Guide students as they develop criteria to include transformation.	CPS	Prism
		DISCOVER	TASC

Note. ALM = Autonomous Learner Model; AT = Affective Taxonomy; BSD = Basic Structure of a Discipline; CPS = Creative Problem Solving; CT = Cognitive Taxonomy; DISCOVER = Discovering Intellectual Strengths and Capabilities while Observing Varied Ethnic Responses; DMD = Discussion of Moral Dilemmas; ETM & SEM = Enrichment Triad Model and Schoolwide Enrichment Model; GI = Group Investigations; HTTS = Hilda Taba Teaching Strategies; PBL = Problem Based Learning; TASC = Thinking Actively in a Social Context; TSTF = Teaching Strategies for Thinking and Feeling.

Bruner: Basic Structure of a Discipline

Although Bruner's approach was not designed specifically for use with gifted students, it *was* intended as a model for curriculum design. As such, it includes adaptations in many areas that are recommended for gifted students. The major modifications needed to make the Basic Structure of a Discipline more comprehensive for gifted students are in the areas of process, product, and learning environment (see Table 13.4). Although an environment similar to that recommended for gifted learners would be necessary for implementing the model, Bruner does not make specific recommendations for developing such a climate. His approach to content is highly appropriate for gifted students. Bruner's model is compatible with most other models but best for use with HTTS, ETM, and SEM. For further information, see Chapter 4.

Maker and Schiever: DISCOVER

Because the DISCOVER Curriculum Model was designed by experts in the field of gifted education to meet the learning needs of all students, it is not surprising that this model provides for all of the suggested modifications for gifted students. Those models suggested as complementary are those based on research and a similar philosophy, and they can be used to enhance the implementation of the model (see Table 13.5). For further information, see Chapter 5.

Parnes: Creative Problem Solving

Like most of the models reviewed, the Creative Problem Solving (CPS) process was not designed to be a curriculum for gifted students. It was designed as a process for developing creative solutions to problems. Because of the emphasis on creativity and the use of creativity in a problem-solving setting, however, CPS provides an important dimension needed in programs for gifted students. Without adaptations, the model provides for most product and learning environment modifications appropriate for gifted learners and for some of the content and process changes. When combined or used in conjunction with models such as ALM, HTTS, or the BSD, it becomes a comprehensive approach (see Table 13.6.). For more information, refer to Chapter 6.

(*text continues on p. 479*)

TABLE 13.4

Modifying and Complementing Bruner's Basic Structure of a Discipline

Program Goals	Suggested Adaptation of Model	Complementary Models	
To organize curricula around basic concepts and abstract generalizations.	Model includes this element.	DISCOVER	Prism
		HTTS	TASC
		PBL	
To provide economical learning experiences.	Use broad themes and interdisciplinary activities.	DISCOVER	HTTS
To provide opportunities for students to study creative people and the creative process.	Study people who have contributed significantly to basic concepts.	ALM	TSTF
	Emphasize people who contributed significantly to understanding of the concept.		
To include content areas not in the mainstream curriculum.	Analyze data taught in regular programs according to each key concept and generalization. Teach only information that students do not know already.	ALM	ETM
		AT	Prism
	Provide opportunities for students to deepen or broaden key ideas.	DISCOVER	TSTF
		DMD	
To provide open-ended activities and ask open-ended questions.	Emphasize an inductive approach or inquiry method, or structure activities for investigation with open-ended questions.	AT	GI
		DISCOVER	HTTS
	Ask provocative questions in all disciplines.	DMD	TSTF
To include discovery learning.	Model includes this element.	ALM	GI
		ETM & SEM	HTTS
To require that students explain their reasoning and provide support for their answers.	Ask questions to discover students' reasoning or support when they have "discovered" a conclusion.	DMD	Prism
		DISCOVER	TASC
		HTTS	

(continues)

Objective	Description	Models	
To encourage students to choose topics and methods of studying chosen topics.	Provide options for students to choose areas of study within a particular content and related to the key concepts and generalizations in the content.	ALM CPS ETM & SEM	GI TASC
To provide structured simulations and other activities in which students can develop leadership and group participation skills.	Use simulation and structured interaction activities. Use computer simulations as tools to help students develop methodological skills in a discipline. Use the methods of anthropologists, sociologists, psychologists, and others who study the behaviors of people as a tool to study group interaction.	ALM GI HITS	Prism TASC
To pace the presentation of new material rapidly.	Provide fewer examples of key concepts to be developed than would be required for mainstream students. Use a process strategy to discover what students already know.	ETM & SEM	HITS
To instruct students using a variety of methods.	Encourage the use of a variety of investigative techniques. Make field trips to observe scientists, poets, musicians, artists, and other professionals at work.	ALM CPS DISCOVER ETM & SEM	GI Prism TASC TSTF
To encourage students to address real problems.	Provide opportunities for students to replicate or conduct research in a discipline of their choice using the methodology in that discipline. Use the inquiry method to structure investigation of issues of concern.	ALM CPS DISCOVER	ETM GI TASC
To assist students in directing their products to real audiences.	Extend students' work by asking "What would the [professional] do with her or his work?" Encourage students to share the results of their work with a variety of real audiences, including classmates. Provide information about possible markets, contests, and presentation possibilities.	ALM CPS	EMT GI

(continues)

TABLE 13.4 *Continued.*
Modifying and Complementing Bruner's Basic Structure of a Discipline

Program Goals	Suggested Adaptation of Model	Complementary Models	
To assist students in locating venues in which their products can be appropriately evaluated and guide the development of self-evaluation skills.	Extend students' thinking by asking "How would a [professional]'s products be judged?"	CPS	GI
	Provide examples of criteria and standards in professions of interest to students.	DISCOVER	PBL
	Study superior products in a discipline to discover the elements that determine (or contribute to) high quality in that discipline.	ETM	TASC
To require that student products are transformations rather than summaries of existing information.	Guide students as they develop criteria to include transformations of information.	CPS	TASC

Note. ALM = Autonomous Learner Model; AT = Affective Taxonomy; BSD = Basic Structure of a Discipline; CPS = Creative Problem Solving; CT = Cognitive Taxonomy; DISCOVER = Discovering Intellectual Strengths and Capabilities while Observing Varied Ethnic Responses; DMD = Discussion of Moral Dilemmas; ETM & SEM = Enrichment Triad Model and Schoolwide Enrichment Model; GI = Group Investigations; HTTS = Hilda Taba Teaching Strategies; PBL = Problem Based Learning; TASC = Thinking Actively in a Social Context; TSTF = Teaching Strategies for Thinking and Feeling.

TABLE 13.5

Modifying and Complementing Maker and Schiever's DISCOVER Model

Program Goals	Suggested Adaptation of Model	Complementary Models
To organize curricula around basic concepts and abstract generalizations.	Model includes this element.	BSD Prism HTTS TASC
To provide economical learning experiences.	Model includes this element. Teach students metacognitive skills.	HTTS TASC
To provide opportunities for students to study creative people and the creative process.	Include the exploration of people in students' problem-solving process. Teach students the problem continuum as a tool for ascertaining creative thinking.	CPS TASC Prism
To include content areas not in the mainstream curriculum.	Model includes this element. Facilitate guided discussions of moral dilemmas related to topics investigated. Use worksheet suggested by Bruner (Chapter 4) to analyze curriculum to determine what needs to be taught.	BSD Prism HTTS
To provide open-ended activities and ask open-ended questions.	Model includes these elements.	HTTS Prism
To include discovery learning.	Model includes this element.	BSD HTTS GI Prism
To require that students explain their reasoning and provide support for their answers.	Model includes this element.	HTTS

(*continues*)

TABLE 13.5 *Continued.*

Modifying and Complementing Maker and Schiever's DISCOVER Model

Program Goals	Suggested Adaptation of Model	Complementary Models	
To encourage students to choose topics and methods of studying chosen topics.	Model includes this element.	ETM	PBL
		GI	TASC
To provide structured simulations and other activities in which students can develop leadership and group participation skills.	Model includes these elements.	GI	Prism
	Teach students the Hilda Taba Teaching Strategies (Chapter 10).	HTTS	TASC
	Be aware of group dynamics within entire class as well as in small groups.	PBL	
	Vary the composition of small groups and the role of individuals within groups.		
To pace the presentation of new material rapidly.	Model includes this element.	ETM	
To instruct students using a variety of methods.	Model includes this element.	CPS	PBL
		ETM	TASC
To encourage students to address real problems.	Model includes this element.	ETM	TASC
		GI	
To assist students in directing their products to real audiences.	Model includes this element.	ETM	TASC
		GI	

(continues)

To assist students in locating venues in which their products can be appropriately evaluated and guide the development of self-evaluation skills.	Teach students to use the problem continuum and the HTTS to develop criteria for products and to evaluate their own thinking and their products.	ETM GI	HTTS TASC
To require that student products are transformations rather than summaries of existing information.	Guide students as they develop criteria to include transformation of information.	ETM HTTS	Prism TASC

Note. ALM = Autonomous Learner Model; AT = Affective Taxonomy; BSD = Basic Structure of a Discipline; CPS = Creative Problem Solving; CT = Cognitive Taxonomy; DISCOVER = Discovering Intellectual Strengths and Capabilities while Observing Varied Ethnic Responses; DMD = Discussion of Moral Dilemmas; ETM & SEM = Enrichment Triad Model and Schoolwide Enrichment Model; GI = Group Investigations; HTTS = Hilda Taba Teaching Strategies; PBL = Problem Based Learning; TASC = Thinking Actively in a Social Context; TSTF = Teaching Strategies for Thinking and Feeling.

TABLE 13.6

Modifying and Complementing Parnes's Creative Problem Solving Model

Program Goals	Suggested Adaptation of Model	Complementary Models	
To organize curricula around basic concepts and abstract generalizations.	Organize content around abstract, complex ideas and select problem situations that relate to those ideas. Problem situations should include abstract concepts and ideas. Organize content around problem situations and use fact finding as a way to gather information.	BSD DISCOVER DMD HTTS	PBL Prism TASC
To provide economical learning experiences.	Choose problem situations that do not overlap with content already presented or developed in other ways. Fact finding should involve several content areas or disciplines.	BSD DISCOVER HTTS	PBL Prism TASC
To provide opportunities for students to study creative people and the creative process.	Identify problems faced by creative or productive people and use CPS to identify solutions. Compare own solutions to actual solution developed by the individual studied.	ALM ETM GI	PBL Prism TSTF
To include content areas not in the mainstream curriculum.	Identify issues or problems of personal concern in the classroom, school, community, or world. Fact finding activities should be conducted across disciplines.	ALM BSD ETM GI	HTTS PBL Prism TASC
To provide open-ended activities and ask open-ended questions.	Model includes this element.	ALM BSD DMD	ETM PBL TASC

(continues)

To include discovery learning.	Model includes this element.	BSD ETM GI	PBL Prism TASC
To require that students explain their reasoning and provide support for their answers.	Ask questions calling for support *only* when appropriate (e.g., selection of problem statements, selection of criteria for evaluation, development of action plans). Avoid "why" questions during divergent production phases.	HTTS	
To encourage students to choose topics and methods of studying chosen topics.	Teach CPS to students as a strategy for making choices.	ALM DISCOVER ETM	GI PBL TASC
To provide structured simulations and other activities in which students can develop leadership and group participation skills.	Tape a CPS session in a group session and analyze interaction of members of the group. Use CPS as a method to develop solutions to group interaction problems. Design simulations in which participants must solve complex problems in order to bring closure to the activity.	ALM DISCOVER ETM GI	HTTS PBL Prism
To pace the presentation of new material rapidly.	Follow guidelines in Taba model (Chapter 10).	GI HTTS	PBL TASC
To encourage students to address real problems.	Conflict situations are naturally occurring problems for which CPS is appropriate. CPS also is a powerful process for students to use to instigate social action on community problems (e.g., polluted areas, disaster relief, changes in rules or laws).	ALM BSD GI	PBL TASC

(continues)

TABLE 13.6 *Continued.*

Modifying and Complementing Parnes's Creative Problem Solving Model

Program Goals	Suggested Adaptation of Model	Complementary Models
To assist students in directing their products to real audiences.	An essential step of CPS is acceptance finding. Proposed solutions should be presented to appropriate audiences (e.g., policy-making boards, administrators, steering committees, parties to a conflict) who can accept, modify, or reject a proposed solution.	ALM GI DISCOVER PBL ETM TASC
To assist students in locating venues in which their products can be appropriately evaluated and guide the development of self-evaluation skills.	Model includes this element.	ETM PBL GI TASC
To require that student products are transformations rather than summaries of existing information.	Guide students as they develop criteria to include transformation of information.	ETM Prism PBL TASC

Note. ALM = Autonomous Learner Model; AT = Affective Taxonomy; BSD = Basic Structure of a Discipline; CPS = Creative Problem Solving; CT = Cognitive Taxonomy; DISCOVER = Discovering Intellectual Strengths and Capabilities while Observing Varied Ethnic Responses; DMD = Discussion of Moral Dilemmas; ETM & SEM = Enrichment Triad Model and Schoolwide Enrichment Model; GI = Group Investigations; HTTS = Hilda Taba Teaching Strategies; PBL = Problem Based Learning; TASC = Thinking Actively in a Social Context; TSTF = Teaching Strategies for Thinking and Feeling.

Problem Based Learning

Problem Based Learning, which originated in McMaster's School of Medicine, was designed to meet an educational need: medical school graduates seemed ill prepared for working as practicing physicians. The graduates could not easily apply their memorized knowledge. PBL was designed to model the real-life situations that practicing physicians meet virtually every day. The success of the model has made it appealing to educators across disciplines and grade levels. PBL is appropriate for gifted students because its basic structure is a good match for the characteristics of gifted students, and therefore meets their learning needs (see Table 13.7). The HTTS, which will enhance PBL's effectiveness, can be incorporated easily into the model. See Chapter 7 for more information.

Renzulli: Enrichment Triad Model
Renzulli and Reis: Schoolwide Enrichment Model

The Enrichment Triad Model was designed as a comprehensive framework for program and curriculum development for gifted students. As a framework, it was not intended to provide specific guidelines for curriculum development in all areas. Renzulli, for example, recommends that certain process models be used to develop the Type II activities. Depending on which process models are used, the facilitator makes different process modifications. As recommended by Renzulli, the ETM can be used with process models such as the Cognitive Taxonomy, CPS, the Affective Taxonomy, STF, HTTS, or DMD (see Table 13.8). The ETM also can be used with a content model, such as BSD. For more information, review Chapter 8.

The Schoolwide Enrichment Model evolved from the ETM as the ETM was applied widely and educators noticed that many students benefited from the approach. Given that it has all the components of the ETM and merely casts a wider net (to include the entire school), the SEM also can be used with process and content models as suggested for the ETM. For more information, review Chapter 8.

Sharan and Sharan: Group Investigations Model

The Group Investigations model was not developed for gifted students, but it has common roots with developmental theories. Most of the modifications
(*text continues on p. 486*)

TABLE 13.7

Modifying and Complementing Problem Based Learning

Program Goals	Suggested Adaptation of Model	Complementary Models
To organize curricula around basic concepts and abstract generalizations.	Organize content at all levels of thinking around complex, abstract content. Encourage students to choose complex content for individual projects.	ETM TASC HTTS
To provide economical learning experiences.	Organize activities using thematic approach or abstract generalization. Teach students metacognitive skills and a problem-solving structure. Guide reflection, to optimize transfer of knowledge and skills.	CPS HTTS DISCOVER TASC
To provide opportunities for students to study creative people and the creative process.	Include the exploration of people in students' problem-solving process. Facilitate group discussions of select creative people and cause—effect elements in their lives. Invite creative people as guest speakers and ask them to discuss the processes they use to solve problems.	CPS Prism HTTS TASC
To include content areas not in the mainstream curriculum.	Use worksheet suggested by Bruner (Chapter 4) to analyze curriculum to determine what is being taught and what needs to be taught. Include Kohlberg's Discussions of Moral Dilemmas (Chapter 12) related to curriculum content.	BSD ETM DMD Prism
To provide open-ended activities and ask open-ended questions.	Model includes these elements.	ETM HTTS
To include discovery learning.	Model includes this element.	BSD GI ETM HTTS

(*continues*)

Objective	Teaching Strategy	Models
To require that students explain their reasoning and provide support for their answers.	Ask for support of ideas individually, in small-group, and in entire class settings. Encourage students to interact with each other's ideas, asking for support.	HTTS
To encourage students to choose topics and methods of studying chosen topics.	Model includes this element.	ETM, GI, Prism, TASC
To provide structured simulations and other activities in which students can develop leadership and group partici-pation skills.	The model includes these elements. Teach students the Hilda Taba Teaching Strategies (Chapter 10). Be aware of group dynamics within entire class as well as in small groups. Vary the composition of small groups and the role of individuals within groups.	GI, HTTS, Prism, TASC
To pace the presentation of new material rapidly.	Model includes this element.	ETM
To instruct students using a variety of methods.	Model includes this element.	CPS, ETM, HTTS, Prism, TASC
To encourage students to address real problems.	Model includes this element.	ETM, GI, TASC
To assist students in directing their products to real audiences.	Model includes this element. Assist students to find "real" audiences.	ETM, GI, TASC

(continues)

TABLE 13.7 *Continued.*
Modifying and Complementing Problem Based Learning

Program Goals	Suggested Adaptation of Model	Complementary Models	
To assist students in locating venues in which their products can be appropriately evaluated and guide the development of self-evaluation skills.	Teach students to use the HTTS (Chapter 10) to develop criteria for products and to evaluate their own thinking and their products. Assist students as needed to find real audiences for their products.	ETM	HTTS
		GI	TASC
To require that student products are transformations rather than summaries of existing information.	Guide students as they develop criteria to include transformation of information.	ETM	Prism
		HTTS	TASC

Note. ALM = Autonomous Learner Model; AT = Affective Taxonomy; BSD = Basic Structure of a Discipline; CPS = Creative Problem Solving; CT = Cognitive Taxonomy; DISCOVER = Discovering Intellectual Strengths and Capabilities while Observing Varied Ethnic Responses; DMD = Discussion of Moral Dilemmas; ETM & SEM = Enrichment Triad Model and Schoolwide Enrichment Model; GI = Group Investigations; HTTS = Hilda Taba Teaching Strategies; PBL = Problem Based Learning; TASC = Thinking Actively in a Social Context; TSTF = Teaching Strategies for Thinking and Feeling.

TABLE 13.8

Modifying and Complementing Renzulli's Enrichment Triad Model and Renzulli and Reis's Schoolwide Enrichment Model

Program Goals	Suggested Adaptation of Model	Complementary Models	
To organize curricula around basic concepts and abstract generalizations.	Develop abstract, complex generalizations for each content area to be explored. Organize Type I and Type II activities around these generalizations.	BSD DISCOVER	GI HTTS
To provide economical learning experiences.	Model includes this element.	BSD HTTS	TASC
To provide opportunities for students to study creative people and the creative process.	Include, as Type I activities, exposure to biographies and autobiographies of famous individuals who have contributed to the key concepts to be studied. Compare methods of inquiry used by these people with methods now used in various disciplines.	ALM DISCOVER GI	PBL TASC
To include content areas not in the mainstream curriculum.	Model includes this element.	ALM BSD GI HTTS	PBL Prism TASC
To provide open-ended activities and ask open-ended questions.	Combine with other process models to meet this objective for Type II activities.	ALM CPS DISCOVER	GI TASC
To include discovery learning.	Model includes this element.	ALM BSD DISCOVER GI	HTTS PBL TASC

(continues)

TABLE 13.8 *Continued.*

Modifying and Complementing Renzulli's Enrichment Triad Model and Renzulli and Reis's Schoolwide Enrichment Model

Program Goals	Suggested Adaptation of Model	Complementary Models		
To require that students explain their reasoning and provide support for their answers.	Ask questions that call for support or reasoning whenever appropriate; however, avoid "why" questions during divergent thinking activities.	CPS DISCOVER	HTTS	
To encourage students to choose topics and methods of studying chosen topics.	Model includes this element.	ALM DISCOVER	GI TASC	
To provide structured simulations and other activities in which students can develop leadership and group partici-pation skills.	Provide a variety of activities to help students develop skills needed to work effectively in a small group. Tape the activities or have "live" observers give feedback and helpful tips to improve group interaction. Offer minilessons, as needed, on interpersonal skills to individuals or small groups in the context of Type III activities.	ALM DISCOVER GI	PBL Prism TASC	
To pace the presentation of new material rapidly.	Model includes this element.	DISCOVER GI HTTS	PBL TASC	
To instruct students using a variety of methods.	Teach a variety of process methods of inquiry so that students will have the tools to conduct Type III enrichment.	ALM CPS DISCOVER GI	HTTS PBL Prism TASC	

(continues)

To encourage students to address real problems.	Model includes this element.	ALM BSD DISCOVER GI	HTTS PBL Prism TASC
To assist students in directing their products to real audiences.	Model includes this element.	ALM GI	TASC
To assist students in locating venues in which their products can be appropriately evaluated and guide the development of self-evaluation skills.	Teach standards of evaluation for professionals in a field. Help students develop criteria for product evaluation that are similar to those used by professionals. Help students develop procedures for self-evaluation and reflection on their own creative processes.	CPS DISCOVER GI	Prism TASC
To require that student products are transformations rather than summaries of existing information.	Guide students as they develop criteria to include transformation of information.	CPS	TASC

Note. ALM = Autonomous Learner Model; AT = Affective Taxonomy; BSD = Basic Structure of a Discipline; CPS = Creative Problem Solving; CT = Cognitive Taxonomy; DISCOVER = Discovering Intellectual Strengths and Capabilities while Observing Varied Ethnic Responses; DMD = Discussion of Moral Dilemmas; ETM & SEM = Enrichment Triad Model and Schoolwide Enrichment Model; GI = Group Investigations; HTTS = Hilda Taba Teaching Strategies; PBL = Problem Based Learning; TASC = Thinking Actively in a Social Context; TSTF = Teaching Strategies for Thinking and Feeling.

recommended for gifted students are incorporated into the structure of the model. Creative thinking processes, so essential for gifted students, are not specifically included. Recommended changes could be made easily by combining this approach with CPS, DISCOVER, HTTS, PBL, or TASC (see Table 13.9). In addition, including the BSD principles for content modification would make this collaborative learning model even more appropriate for gifted learners. For further information, see Chapter 9.

Hilda Taba Teaching Strategies

The Hilda Taba Teaching Strategies and curriculum development theory were constructed as models for use with all children. Because of its focus on the development of abstract thinking, this model is highly appropriate for use in gifted programs. The HTTS incorporates many of the content, process, and learning environment changes recommended for gifted students, but does not provide suggestions for products. These can be added and integrated easily by adapting the model, particularly by using the strategies for different purposes in the development of products (see Table 13.10). The model provides critical process modifications and is easily combined with other models discussed in this volume. Additional information is contained in Chapter 10.

Wallace and Adams: Thinking Actively in a Social Context

The TASC model was conceived and developed because of the extremely poor quality of education and the scarcity of teachers for Black pupils in KwaZulu/Natal schools in South Africa. The problems and level of educational service available for these students were daunting, to say the least. Out of this huge, seemingly insurmountable need came a rich and promising teaching model. The model incorporates a strong theoretical framework and best teaching practices from around the world, yet is flexible enough to be applied to virtually any educational setting or situation. Although it was developed for all students, it provides many of the curricular modifications that meet the learning needs of gifted students (see Table 13.11). For further information, refer to Chapter 11.

(*text continues on p. 496*)

TABLE 13.9

Modifying and Complementing Sharan and Sharan's Group Investigations Model

Program Goals	Suggested Adaptation of Model	Complementary Models	
To organize curricula around basic concepts and abstract generalizations.	Broad themes or interdisciplinary topics are recommended. Identify abstract generalizations and key concepts for each topic or theme.	BSD DISCOVER	HTTS Prism
To provide economical learning experiences.	Ensure that broad themes or topics are developed with complex generalizations and interrelated subtopics for investigation.	BSD DISCOVER	HTTS Prism
To provide opportunities for students to study creative people and the creative process.	Identify and investigate creative or productive people who have contributed ideas or impetus to the development of the content to be investigated in a topic or theme study.	ALM DISCOVER	ETM Prism
To include content areas not in the mainstream curriculum.	Design guidelines for small-group investigations that stimulate students to go beyond the regular curriculum to broaden and deepen their understanding of key concepts, key players, and key ideas (generalizations, laws) in chosen subtopics. Use Bruner's approach (Chapter 4) to identify abstract, complex themes for investigation.	ALM AT BSD DISCOVER	ETM GI HTTS TSTF
To provide open-ended activities and ask open-ended questions.	Model includes this element.	ALM CPS DMD	ETM HTTS
To include discovery learning.	Model includes this element.	BSD DISCOVER ETM	HTTS PBL TASC

(continues)

TABLE 13.9 *Continued.*
Modifying and Complementing Sharan and Sharan's Group Investigations Model

Program Goals	Suggested Adaptation of Model	Complementary Models	
To require that students explain their reasoning and provide support for their answers.	Ask questions that call for support or reasoning whenever appropriate; however, avoid "why" questions during divergent thinking activities.	CPS	HTTS
To encourage students to choose topics and methods of studying chosen topics.	Model includes this element.	ALM CPS	ETM TASC
To provide structured simulations and other activities in which students can develop leadership and group participation skills.	Provide a variety of group building activities to help students develop skills needed to work effectively in a small group. Offer minilessons, as needed, on interpersonal skills to individuals or small groups in the context of an investigation.	ALM HTTS PBL	Prism TASC
To pace the presentation of new material rapidly.	Select nonbook media to ensure valuable experiences for students. Have a variety of books available on the theme or topic. Remind guest speakers to pace their presentations rapidly. During discussions and process development activities, move through those requiring "lower levels of thinking" rapidly.	DISCOVER ETM HTTS	PBL Prism TASC
To instruct students using a variety of methods.	Teach a variety of process models and methods of inquiry to students so they will have the tools to conduct small-group investigations.	ALM CPS ETM	HTTS Prism TSTF

(continues)

To encourage students to address real problems.	Encourage students to select subtopics of broad themes that have the potential for investigating real problems (e.g., theme = conflict; subtopics such as terrorism, civil disobedience, gangs, conservation vs. development).	ALM BSD DMD	HTTS TSTF
To assist students in directing their products to real audiences.	Invite guests to presentations. Facilitate presentations to adult groups away from school as well as to classmates and other students at school.	ALM CPS DISCOVER ETM	GI PBL TASC
To assist students in locating venues in which their products can be appropriately evaluated and guide the development of self-evaluation skills.	Teach standards of evaluation for professionals in a field. Help students develop criteria for product evaluation that are similar to those used by professionals. Guide students in the preparation of evaluation forms to be completed by members of their audiences. Allow time for tabulating results and reflecting on their presentations.	CPS DISCOVER	ETM PBL
To require that student products are transformations rather than summaries of existing information.	Guide students as they develop criteria to include transformation of information.	CPS DISCOVER	Prism TASC

Note. ALM = Autonomous Learner Model; AT = Affective Taxonomy; BSD = Basic Structure of a Discipline; CPS = Creative Problem Solving; CT = Cognitive Taxonomy; DISCOVER = Discovering Intellectual Strengths and Capabilities while Observing Varied Ethnic Responses; DMD = Discussion of Moral Dilemmas; ETM & SEM = Enrichment Triad Model and Schoolwide Enrichment Model; GI = Group Investigations; HTTS = Hilda Taba Teaching Strategies; PBL = Problem Based Learning; TASC = Thinking Actively in a Social Context; TSTF = Teaching Strategies for Thinking and Feeling.

TABLE 13.10

Modifying and Complementing Hilda Taba Teaching Strategies

Program Goals	Suggested Adaptation of Model	Complementary Models	
To organize curricula around basic concepts and abstract generalizations.	Model includes this element.	BSD DISCOVER	PBL Prism
To provide economical learning experiences.	Teach students to use the strategies to facilitate metacognition, transfer of learning, and understanding of key concepts and abstract generalizations.	BSD DISCOVER	DMD
To provide opportunities for students to study creative people and the creative process.	Use interpretation of data strategy to discuss characteristics of creative and productive people and the causes–effects of these characteristics.	ALM Prism	TSTF
To include content areas not in the mainstream curriculum.	Using worksheet suggested by Bruner (Chapter 4), analyze regular curriculum to determine what specific information is being taught and what else needs to be taught.	ALM AT BSD DMD	ETM GI Prism
To provide open-ended activities and ask open-ended questions.	Model includes this element.	ALM CPS	DMD ETM
To include discovery learning.	Model includes this element.	BSD DISCOVER	DMD ETM

(continues)

	Model includes this element.	AT	DMD
To require that students explain their reasoning and provide support for their answers.			
To encourage students to choose topics and methods of studying chosen topics.	Encourage students to choose general topic areas for discussion and plan lessons around those topics. For the resolution of conflict strategy, have students select conflict situations they would like to discuss.	ALM CPS ETM	GI TASC TSTF
To provide structured simulations and other activities in which students can develop leadership and group participation skills.	Use role play or simulations to dramatize conflict situations prior to resolution of conflict discussions. Develop discussion skills that will facilitate student interaction in small groups for portions of all strategies.	ALM DISCOVER GI	PBL Prism TASC
To pace the presentation of new material rapidly.	Focus on key concepts and generalizations; avoid needless repetition.	DISCOVER ETM	Prism
To instruct students using a variety of methods.	Teach the principles underlying each strategy as a means of understanding the steps in the scientific method and other inquiry processes.	ALM CPS	ETM GI
To encourage students to address real problems.	Teach students to use the concept development strategy for organization and reorganization of data, as an aid in selection of a problem or topic area for investigation, and as a tool for writing up results of a study.	ALM BSD	CPS GI

(continues)

TABLE 13.10 *Continued.*

Modifying and Complementing Hilda Taba Teaching Strategies

Program Goals	Suggested Adaptation of Model	Complementary Models	
To assist students in directing their products to real audiences.	Use the application of generalizations strategy to predict how different audiences might react to a specified product. Use the interpretation of data strategy, with audiences, to form conclusions about the causes and effects of experimental results or new technology.	ALM CPS	ETM GI
To assist students in locating venues in which their products can be appropriately evaluated and guide the development of self-evaluation skills.	Use all strategies (except resolution of conflict) to develop criteria and procedures for evaluation of products.	CPS DISCOVER ETM	GI PBL TASC
To require that student products are transformations rather than summaries of existing information.	Guide students as they develop criteria to include transformation of information.	CPS Prism	TASC

Note. ALM = Autonomous Learner Model; AT = Affective Taxonomy; BSD = Basic Structure of a Discipline; CPS = Creative Problem Solving; CT = Cognitive Taxonomy; DISCOVER = Discovering Intellectual Strengths and Capabilities while Observing Varied Ethnic Responses; DMD = Discussion of Moral Dilemmas; ETM & SEM = Enrichment Triad Model and Schoolwide Enrichment Model; GI = Group Investigations; HTTS = Hilda Taba Teaching Strategies; PBL = Problem Based Learning; TASC = Thinking Actively in a Social Context; TSTF = Teaching Strategies for Thinking and Feeling.

TABLE 13.11

Modifying and Complementing Wallace and Adams's TASC Model

Program Goals	Suggested Adaptation of Model	Complementary Models	
To organize curricula around basic concepts and abstract generalizations.	Select theme (abstract generalization) that is broad enough to include provocative problem situations. Guide students in choice of problem situations, ensuring that content includes basic concepts as well as abstract elements.	BSD DISCOVER	HTTS Prism
To provide economical learning experiences.	Organize activities within integrated themes; design multiple-purpose learning activities. Teach students TASC Problem-Solving Wheel. Teach students metacognitive skills.	BSD DISCOVER	HTTS Prism
To provide opportunities for students to study creative people and the creative process.	Include the exploration of people in students' problem-solving process. Facilitate guided discussions of creative people and the creative process.	HTTS Prism	
To include content areas not in the mainstream curriculum.	Use worksheet suggested by Bruner (Chapter 4) to analyze curriculum to determine what needs to be taught. Facilitate moral dilemma discussions related to topics of investigations.	BSD DMD	HTTS
To provide open-ended activities and ask open-ended questions.	The model includes these elements.	HTTS	
To include discovery learning.	The model includes this element.	BSD	HTTS

(continues)

TABLE 13.11 *Continued.*
Modifying and Complementing Wallace and Adams's TASC Model

Program Goals	Suggested Adaptation of Model	Complementary Models
To require that students explain their reasoning and provide support for their answers.	Ask for support of ideas individually, in small-group, and in entire-class settings. Encourage students to interact with each other's ideas, asking for support.	HITS
To encourage students to choose topics and methods of studying chosen topics.	The model includes this element.	ETM PBL GI
To provide structured simulations and other activities in which students can develop leadership and group participation skills.	The model includes group interaction elements. Provide relevant simulations for students. Teach students the Hilda Taba Teaching Strategies (Chapter 10). Be aware of group dynamics within entire class as well as in small groups. Vary the composition of small groups and the role of individuals within groups.	GI PBL HITS Prism
To pace the presentation of new material rapidly.	Move through presentation of new materials and strategies as quickly as possible. If a few students need more time, provide the information in the context of group and individual activities.	ETM
To instruct students using a variety of methods.	The model includes this element. Encourage students to design individual projects that require creative thinking and problem solving.	CPS PBL ETM Prism
To encourage students to address real problems.	The model includes this element.	ETM PBL GI

(continues)

Objective	Teaching Strategy	Model
To assist students in directing their products to real audiences.	The model includes this element.	ETM GI
	Assist students in finding "real" audiences.	
To assist students in locating venues in which their products can be appropriately evaluated and guide the development of self-evaluation skills.	The model includes this element.	ETM HTTS
	Teach students the criteria for professional evaluation of products; encourage them to apply the criteria to their own work.	GI
To require that student products are transformations rather than summaries of existing information.	Guide students as they develop criteria to include transformation of information.	ETM Prism
		HTTS

Note. ALM = Autonomous Learner Model; AT = Affective Taxonomy; BSD = Basic Structure of a Discipline; CPS = Creative Problem Solving; CT = Cognitive Taxonomy; DISCOVER = Discovering Intellectual Strengths and Capabilities while Observing Varied Ethnic Responses; DMD = Discussion of Moral Dilemmas; ETM & SEM = Enrichment Triad Model and Schoolwide Enrichment Model; GI = Group Investigations; HTTS = Hilda Taba Teaching Strategies; PBL = Problem Based Learning; TASC = Thinking Actively in a Social Context; TSTF = Teaching Strategies for Thinking and Feeling.

Kohlberg: Discussions of Moral Dilemmas

Kohlberg's theory of moral development and his strategies for Discussions of Moral Dilemmas were developed to explain moral and ethical development and to provide a structure for raising levels of ethical development. Due to its concentration on high levels of ethical behavior and on reasoning, many curricular modifications appropriate for gifted students are made in all areas except products. To provide a comprehensive curriculum, the DMD must be used in conjunction with other approaches (see Table 13.12). Product adaptations are easily included by encouraging students to develop products that include the moral issues inherent in or related to the issue or topic they explored. Kohlberg's approach is compatible with most models and provides much-needed opportunities for students to consider and discuss moral issues. For further information, refer to Chapter 12.

Williams: Teaching Strategies for Thinking and Feeling

Williams's strategies were developed as methods to enhance the cognitive and affective behaviors involved in creativity. They are part of a model for individualizing and humanizing education by concentrating on creativity development. Because of this focus on creativity, the strategies are highly appropriate for use in programs for gifted students. Many modifications appropriate for gifted students in the areas of learning environment and process are included, but the model needs to be supplemented or adapted to provide necessary content and product modifications (see Table 13.13). Williams's strategies can be used effectively with any of the models reviewed. The reader may refer to Chapter 12 for further information.

Maker and Anuruthwong: The Prism of Learning Model

The Prism of Learning Model was developed by two experts in mainstream education as well as education for gifted students. Philosophically, the model is inclusive and accepting of all students, and practically it includes elements for widely diverse student populations. The combination of strong curricular principles, the concept of multiple intelligences, exemplary teaching practices, and a holistic view of students provides a promising structure for education for all learners. Table 13.14 demonstrates the model's strengths and broad applicability.

(*text continues on p. 505*)

TABLE 13.12

Modifying and Complementing Kohlberg's Discussions of Moral Dilemmas

Program Goals	Suggested Adaptation of Model	Complementary Models	
To organize curricula around basic concepts and abstract generalizations.	Present dilemmas that involve abstract and complex ideas. Present dilemmas that involve issues from several different disciplines. Present dilemmas that illustrate the moral/ethical side of key concepts and generalizations that are being developed and studied.	BSD GI HITS	PBL Prism TASC
To provide economical learning experiences.	Select only dilemmas that are excellent illustrations of the themes to be developed.	BSD HITS	PBL TASC
To provide opportunities for students to study creative people and the creative process.	Present moral and ethical dilemmas faced by famous individuals. Compare student resolution of the conflict with the resolution made by the person studied.	ALM DISCOVER ETM	HITS PBL Prism
To include content areas not in the mainstream curriculum.	Model includes this element.	ALM AT	HITS TSTF
To provide open-ended activities and ask open-ended questions.	Ask questions that enable students to respond thoughtfully in discussions.	ALM AT CT	ETM HITS TSTF
To include discovery learning.	Present dilemmas faced by others. Compare student resolution of conflicts to resolutions of other people.	BSD DISCOVER ETM HITS	PBL Prism TASC

(continues)

TABLE 13.12 *Continued.*
Modifying and Complementing Kohlberg's Discussions of Moral Dilemmas

Program Goals	Suggested Adaptation of Model	Complementary Models
To require that students explain their reasoning and provide support for their answers.	Ask "why" questions whenever appropriate after Step 2.	HTTS
To encourage students to choose topics and methods of studying chosen topics.	Encourage students to choose moral issues or dilemmas they would like to discuss.	ALM PBL ETM Prism GI TSTF
To provide structured simulations and other activities in which students can develop leadership and group participation skills.	Provide opportunities for students to role-play famous characters involved in historical moral and ethical dilemmas. Videotape discussions as a basis for analyzing group interaction processes.	ALM PBL GI Prism
To pace the presentation of new material rapidly.	Move through Steps 1 and 2 rapidly; spend more time at later steps.	DISCOVER HTTS ETM
To instruct students using a variety of methods.	Broaden the bases of moral development by including methods suggested by other theorists (e.g., Gilligan, Dabrowski, Piaget).	ALM HTTS ETM Prism GI TSTF
To encourage students to address real problems.	Model includes this element.	ALM DISCOVER BSD ETM CPS

(continues)

Goal	Teacher Behaviors	Models	
To assist students in directing their products to real audiences.	Encourage students to develop products such as original essays about issues or results from original research (e.g., a survey of attitudes toward an ethical issue).	ALM	GI
	Encourage students to develop products that are transformations, then direct their products toward real audiences for presentation and publication.	DISCOVER	Prism
	Organize seminars that involve students and professionals in the discussion of moral and ethical dilemmas in a discipline or field.	ETM	TASC
To assist students in locating venues in which their products can be appropriately evaluated and guide the development of self-evaluation skills.	Encourage students to develop defensible criteria for evaluation of products.	CPS	GI
	Encourage students to self-evaluate their products.	DISCOVER	TASC
	Encourage students to have their products evaluated by peers and audiences.	ETM	
	Encourage students to be self-reflective and evaluate own moral development.		
To require that student products are transformations rather than summaries of existing information.	Guide students as they develop criteria to include transformation of information.	CPS	Prism
		ETM	TASC

Note. ALM = Autonomous Learner Model; AT = Affective Taxonomy; BSD = Basic Structure of a Discipline; CPS = Creative Problem Solving; CT = Cognitive Taxonomy; DISCOVER = Discovering Intellectual Strengths and Capabilities while Observing Varied Ethnic Responses; DMD = Discussion of Moral Dilemmas; ETM & SEM = Enrichment Triad Model and Schoolwide Enrichment Model; GI = Group Investigations; HTTS = Hilda Taba Teaching Strategies; PBL = Problem Based Learning; TASC = Thinking Actively in a Social Context; TSTF = Teaching Strategies for Thinking and Feeling.

TABLE 13.13

Modifying and Complementing Williams's Strategies for Thinking and Feeling

Program Goals	Suggested Adaptation of Model	Complementary Models
To organize curricula around basic concepts and abstract generalizations.	Develop abstract generalizations in each content area to be studied. Develop complex generalizations that integrate content from several disciplines. Organize strategies and development of creative behaviors around complex, abstract generalizations rather than the "general" discipline.	BSD DMD CT GI DISCOVER HTTS
To provide economical learning experiences.	Select broad themes or topics to organize interdisciplinary content.	BSD HTTS DISCOVER
To provide opportunities for students to study creative people and the creative process.	Encourage students to study biographies and autobiographies of people who contributed to the themes or topics to be studied. Ask how an individual might have felt or thought about his or her contribution to society.	ALM Prism ETM TSTF
To include content areas not in the mainstream curriculum.	Analyze regular curriculum according to each generalization and key concept. Teach in the special program only that information not taught in the regular curriculum. See worksheet in Chapter 4 for this purpose.	ALM HTTS DISCOVER Prism ETM
To provide open-ended activities and ask open-ended questions.	Use a variety of strategies that incorporate open-ended questions. Provide a variety of open-ended activities to encourage student exploration and thinking development.	ALM DMD CPS ETM DISCOVER GI

(continues)

Objective	Strategy		
To include discovery learning.	Follow guidelines suggested by Bruner to structure inquiry processes.	BSD DISCOVER ETM	HTTS Prism TASC
To require that students explain their reasoning and provide support for their answers.	Incorporate "why" questions into discussions whenever appropriate. Use strategy recommended by Taba's application of generalizations (make predictions in divergent mode, then go back and ask for reasons later) so creativity will not be inhibited (see Chapter 10).	DISCOVER	HTTS
To encourage students to choose topics and methods of studying chosen topics.	Encourage students to suggest topics and methods for discussion. Teach the strategies to students and encourage them to lead discussions.	ALM DISCOVER ETM	HTTS PBL TASC
To provide structured simulations and other activities in which students can develop leadership and group participation skills.	Model includes this element.	ALM DISCOVER GI	PBL Prism TASC
To pace the presentation of new material rapidly.	In individual activities, encourage students to pace themselves. In group discussions, follow the suggestions made by Taba (see Chapter 10).	ALM ETM	HTTS
To instruct students using a variety of methods.	Model includes this element.	ALM AT CT DMD	ETM GI HTTS Prism

(continues)

TABLE 13.13 *Continued.*

Modifying and Complementing Williams's Strategies for Thinking and Feeling

Program Goals	Suggested Adaptation of Model	Complementary Models	
To encourage students to address real problems.	Encourage students to pursue a topic of interest further and develop an investigation of a real problem.	ALM	ETM
		AT	GI
	Encourage students to express their feelings about areas of concern.	BSD	Prism
To assist students in directing their products to real audiences.	When students have completed an area of study, developed a product, or conducted an experiment, encourage them to refine the findings for presentation to a real audience.	ALM	GI
		DISCOVER	PBL
		ETM	TASC
To assist students in locating venues in which their products can be appropriately evaluated and guide the development of self-evaluation skills.	Encourage students to develop criteria and procedures for evaluation of their own products.	CPS	GI
		DISCOVER	TASC
	Using criteria designed by students as well as that provided by audiences, have all student products evaluated by the student, peers, audience, and the teacher.		
	Allow time for students to reflect on the results of evaluations.		
To require that student products are transformations rather than summaries of existing information.	Guide students as they develop criteria to include transformation of information.	CPS	Prism
		ETM	TASC

Note. ALM = Autonomous Learner Model; AT = Affective Taxonomy; BSD = Basic Structure of a Discipline; CPS = Creative Problem Solving; CT = Cognitive Taxonomy; DISCOVER = Discovering Intellectual Strengths and Capabilities while Observing Varied Ethnic Responses; DMD = Discussion of Moral Dilemmas; ETM & SEM = Enrichment Triad Model and Schoolwide Enrichment Model; GI = Group Investigations; HTTS = Hilda Taba Teaching Strategies; PBL = Problem Based Learning; TASC = Thinking Actively in a Social Context; TSTF = Teaching Strategies for Thinking and Feeling.

TABLE 13.14

Modifying and Complementing Prism Model

Program Goals	Suggested Adaptation of Model	Complementary Models	
To organize curricula around basic concepts and abstract generalizations.	Model includes these elements.	BSD DISCOVER	HTTS Prism
To provide economical learning experiences.	Model includes this element.	BSD	HTTS
To provide opportunities for students to study creative people and the creative process.	Include the exploration of creative people in learning centers. Facilitate group discussions of select creative people and cause–effect elements in their lives. Invite creative people as guest speakers and ask them to discuss the processes they use to solve problems.	CPS HTTS	Prism TASC
To include content areas not in the mainstream curriculum.	Use worksheet suggested by Bruner (Appendix 4.A in Chapter 4) to analyze curriculum to determine what is being taught and what needs to be taught. Include Kohlberg's Discussions of Moral Dilemmas related to curriculum content.	BSD DMD	HTTS Prism
To provide open-ended activities and ask open-ended questions.	The model includes these elements.	ETM	HTTS
To include discovery learning.	Model includes this element.	BSD ETM	GI HTTS
To require that students explain their reasoning and provide support for their answers.	Ask for support of ideas individually, in small groups, and in entire class settings. Encourage students to interact with each other's ideas, asking for support.	HTTS	
To encourage students to choose topics and methods of studying chosen topics.	Model includes this element.	ETM GI	TASC

(continues)

TABLE 13.14 *Continued.*

Modifying and Complementing Prism Model

Program Goals	Suggested Adaptation of Model	Complementary Models	
To provide structured simulations and other activities in which students can develop leadership and group participation skills.	Model includes these elements. Teach students the HTTS. Be aware of group dynamics within entire class as well as in small groups. Vary the composition of small groups and the role of individuals within groups.	GI HTTS	Prism TASC
To pace the presentation of new material rapidly.	Model includes this element.	ETM	
To instruct students using a variety of methods.	Model includes this element.	CPS ETM	HTTS TASC
To encourage students to address real problems.	Model includes this element.	DISCOVER ETM	GI TASC
To assist students in directing their products to real audiences.	Model includes this element. Assist students to find real audiences.	DISCOVER ETM	GI TASC
To assist students in locating venues in which their products can be appropriately evaluated and guide the development of self-evaluation skills.	Teach students to use the HTTS to develop criteria for products and to evaluate their own thinking and their products. Assist students as needed to find real audiences for their products.	ETM GI	HTTS TASC
To require that student products are transformations rather than summaries of existing information.	Guide students as they develop criteria to include transformation of information.	ETM	HTTS

Note. ALM = Autonomous Learner Model; AT = Affective Taxonomy; BSD = Basic Structure of a Discipline; CPS = Creative Problem Solving; CT = Cognitive Taxonomy; DISCOVER = Discovering Intellectual Strengths and Capabilities while Observing Varied Ethnic Responses; DMD = Discussion of Moral Dilemmas; ETM & SEM = Enrichment Triad Model and Schoolwide Enrichment Model; GI = Group Investigations; HTTS = Hilda Taba Teaching Strategies; PBL = Problem Based Learning; TASC = Thinking Actively in a Social Context; TSTF = Teaching Strategies for Thinking and Feeling.

INTEGRATED APPROACHES

After reviewing and selecting appropriate models and devising or listing necessary adaptations, educators must develop student objectives and learning activities. This process involves reviewing the student needs assessment, program goals, and purposes and provisions of the models. Each curriculum will be unique, even if the same models form the basis, because each developer and each situation are different. A brief example of an integrated approach, a summary of students' needs, units and activities, models, and academic areas, is presented in Table 13.15. The sample curriculum was designed for an elementary resource room program in a middle-class school. The emphasis was on developing the following strengths of the gifted students in the program: curiosity, critical thinking, leadership, independence, affective skills, self-expression, and creative thinking. The general approach was a combination of units, special projects, and sharing activities. A range of school subjects was integrated, with units developed to build on rather than duplicate the regular program. Evaluation results showed the curriculum to be highly effective in accomplishing its purposes.

CONCLUSION

In this volume, wide range of teaching–learning models that can be helpful in developing comprehensive curriculum for gifted students has been presented. All were designed for different purposes and have different strengths and weaknesses and different advantages and disadvantages. Few have been validated through research as effective models for programs, and even fewer as effective models for use with gifted students. No comparative research indicates which models are more appropriate than others, but many practitioners believe firmly in the superiority of one or more of the approaches. We trust that individuals, teams, or committees developing curriculum for programs that serve gifted students will find the combination that is right for the unique learning needs of their students. Our hope is that the information in this text will inform, enlighten, guide, and assist these individuals and teams so their product serves their students in the best way possible.

(*text continues on p. 509*)

TABLE 13.15

Summary of Child Characteristics, Activities, Models, and Content Areas

Learner Needs	Learning Activities	Models	Academic Areas
Cultivation of natural curiosity	*Units*—Introduction to diverse, abstract, and complex generalizations such as culture, architecture, genetics, bioengineering, and ecology	ALM BSD DISCOVER ETM GI HTTS PBL Prism TASC	Fine arts Humanities Language Mathematics Physical education Science Social studies
Development of critical thinking skills	*Units*—Abstract content and thinking skills designed to elicit higher levels of thinking *Activities*—Inductive thinking, formal logic, and scientific method taught and practiced in context of substantive content	ALM CPS ETM HTTS Prism TASC	Humanities Language Mathematics Philosophy Science Social studies
Development of creative thinking skills	*Units*—Content and thinking skills integrated and designed to elicit creative thinking and problem solving *Activities*—Creative Problem Solving, Synectics, productive thinking, guided imagery,	ALM CPS ETM	Fine arts Humanities Language

(continues)

	SCAMPER, Odyssey of the Mind, and figurative language, taught and practiced within context of substantive content	HTTS Prism TASC TSTF	Mathematics Physical education Science Social studies
Development of leadership skills	*Units*—Content units that integrate group processes and leadership skill techniques into small- and large-group learning *Activities*—Group investigations, seminars, role playing, creative problem solving, conflict resolution, group decision making, simulations, and student government, all within context of substantive content	ALM CPS DISCOVER ETM GI HTTS PBL Prism TASC	Academic clubs Fine arts Humanities Language Mathematics Physical education Science Social studies
Development of independence skills	*Units*—Integration of goal setting, research skills, scientific method; and evaluation of products *Activities*—Community surveys, database searches, opinion polls, and self-evaluation of processes, products, and research, all within substantive content	ALM CPS ETM GI HTTS Prism PBL TASC	Fine arts Humanities Language Mathematics Physical education Science Social studies

(continues)

TABLE 13.15 *Continued.*

Summary of Child Characteristics, Activities, Models, and Content Areas

Learner Needs	Learning Activities	Models	Academic Areas
Development of self-expression	*Units*—Methods and techniques of self-expression integrated with academic content, career exploration *Activities*—Drama, mime, creative writing, poetry, photography, graphic arts, sign language, dance, music, visual arts, body language, personal symbols, publication, clothing design, interior decoration, and crafts, within context of substantive content	ALM AT DISCOVER ETM GI HTTS TASC	Fine arts Humanities Language Mathematics Physical education Science Social studies Vocational arts
Development of affective skills	*Units*—Integration of affective objectives with content and process objectives *Activities*—Moral dilemma discussions, conflict resolution, reflective journal writing, volunteering and community service, and simulations	ALM AT DISCOVER GI HTTS Prism TASC	Fine arts Humanities Language Mathematics Physical education Science Social studies

Note. ALM = Autonomous Learner Model; AT = Affective Taxonomy; BSD = Basic Structure of a Discipline; CPS = Creative Problem Solving; CT = Cognitive Taxonomy; DISCOVER = Discovering Intellectual Strengths and Capabilities while Observing Varied Ethnic Responses; DMD = Discussion of Moral Dilemmas; ETM & SEM = Enrichment Triad Model and Schoolwide Enrichment Model; GI = Group Investigations; HTTS = Hilda Taba Teaching Strategies; PBL = Problem Based Learning; TASC = Thinking Actively in a Social Context; TSTF = Teaching Strategies for Thinking and Feeling.

The models in this book offer hope for achieving educational excellence. Reaching that goal, however, is hindered or blocked by many obstacles.

Educational governing boards, many of which do not include professional educators, want results (higher test scores), and they want them quickly. The learning of teachers implementing a new and quite different approach follows a gentle curve, with occasional dips. The students' learning may reflect the same gentle curves and dips. True learning probably cannot be measured accurately in less than a school year, not all learning can be measured by the same instrument, and two different types of measurements cannot be compared as if they measured the same phenomenon.

Many parents buy into the myth that test scores indicate the worth of the education being delivered in a particular school, and others want their children taught using the same methods that were used when they were in school. After the annual publishing of mandated state assessment scores, real estate agents carry clippings used as indicators of where the "best" schools (those with the highest scores) are located.

Any meaningful change in educational practices probably can only come about one class, one school, one school district at a time. This allows optimism about the future of education, because pockets of excellence *do* have the potential of spinning off and spreading, embracing more students, more schools, and perhaps more states and countries.

References

Adams, H. B. (1985). The teaching of general problem-solving strategies. In *Developing cognitive strategies in young children* (Southern African Association for Learning and Educational Difficulties Conference Proceedings, 24–25 October, 1985). Durban, South Africa: University of Durban-Westville.

Adams, H. B. (1986). Teaching general problem-solving strategies in the classroom. *Gifted Education International, 4,* 84–89.

Adams, H. B., & Wallace, B. (1988). The assessment and development of high school pupils in the third world context of Kwa-Zulu/Natal. *Gifted Education International, 5,* 132–137.

Adams, H. B., & Wallace, B. (1991). A model for curriculum development. *Gifted Education International, 7,* 105–113.

Al-Shwailan, F. A. (1997). *The influence of teaching questioning strategies on the high cognitive processes of gifted students in the regular classroom.* Unpublished master's thesis, Arabian Gulf University, Manama, Bahrain.

Andre, T. (1978, May). *The role of paraphrased and verbatim adjunct questions in facilitating learning by reading.* Paper presented at the annual meeting of the Midwestern Educational Research Association, Bloomington, IN.

Aronson, E., Blaney, N., Stephan, C., Sikes, J., & Snapp, M. (1978). *The Jigsaw classroom.* Beverly Hills, CA: Sage.

Ayers, J. D. (1966, February). *Justification of Bloom's Taxonomy by factor analysis.* Paper presented at the Annual American Educational Research Association Convention, Chicago.

Baird, K. K. (1985). Do grades and tests predict adult accomplishment? *Research in Higher Education, 23*(1), 3–85.

Bandura, A. (1971). *Social learning theory.* Englewood Cliffs, NJ: Prentice Hall.

Bandura, A. (1977). *Social learning theory* (2nd ed.). Englewood Cliffs, NJ: Prentice Hall.

Barell, J. (1995). *Teaching for thoughtfulness: Classroom strategies to enhance intellectual development* (2nd ed.). White Plains, NY: Longman.

Barrows, H. (1985). *How to design a Problem Based Learning curriculum in the pre-clinical years.* New York: Springer-Verlag.

Barrows, H. (1988). *The tutorial process.* Springfield: Southern Illinois University School of Medicine.

Barrows, H. (1994). *Practice-based learning.* Springfield: Southern Illinois University School of Medicine.

Barrows, H. S., & Kelson, A. C. (1995). *Problem Based Learning in secondary education and the Problem-Based Learning Institute* (Monograph 1). Springfield, IL: Problem-Based Learning Institute.

Baum, S., Owen, S., & Oreck, B. (1996). Talent beyond words: Identification of potential talent in dance and music in elementary students. *Gifted Child Quarterly, 40,* 93–101.

Baum, S., Owen, S. & Oreck, B. (1997). Transferring individual self-regulation processes from arts to academics. *Arts Education Policy Review, 98*(4), 32–39.

Begle, E., & Wilson, J. (1970). Evaluation of mathematics program. In The National Society for the Study of Education (Eds.), *Sixty-ninth yearbook* (Part I, pp. 367–404). Chicago: University of Chicago Press.

Bentley, R., & Johnstone, E. (2002). Getting the wheels turning: Putting TASC into action. In B. Wallace & R. Bentley (Eds.), *Teaching thinking skills across the middle years.* (pp. 25–46). London: David Fulton.

Betres, J., Zajano, M., & Gumieniak, P. (1984). Cognitive styles, teacher methods and concept attainment in the social studies. *Theory & Research in Social Education, 12*(2), 1–18.

Betts, G. (1985). *The Autonomous Learner Model for the gifted and talented.* Greeley, CO: Autonomous Learning Publications and Specialists.

Betts, G., & Kercher, J. (1999). *Autonomous Learner Model: Optimizing ability.* Greeley, CO: Autonomous Learner Publications and Specialists.

Betts, G., & Knapp, J. (1981). Autonomous learning and the gifted: A secondary model. In A. Arnold (Ed.), *Secondary programs for the gifted* (pp. 29–36). Ventura, CA: Ventura Superintendent of Schools Office.

Beyer, B. K. (1984). Improving thinking skills: Practical approaches. *Phi Delta Kappan, 65,* 556–560.

Beyer, B. K. (1987). *Practical strategies for the teaching of thinking.* Boston: Allyn & Bacon.

Bloom, B. S. (1956). *Taxonomy of Educational Objectives: The classification of educational goals. Handbook I: Cognitive domain.* New York: Longmans, Green.

Blumberg, P., & Michael, J. A. (1991). The development of self-directed learning behavior in a partially teacher-centered problem-based learning curriculum. *Teaching and Learning Medicine, 4,* 3–8.

Bodnar, J. (1974). *Creative problem solving model.* Unpublished manuscript. (Available from C. J. Maker, Department of Special Education, University of Arizona, P.O. Box 210069, Tucson, AZ 85721-0069).

Borkowski, J. F. (1985). Signs of intelligence: Strategy generalization and metacognition. In R. S. Yussen (Ed.), *The growth of reflective thought on children* (pp. 105–144). New York: Academic Press.

Boyce, L. N., VanTassel-Baska, J., Burruss, J. D., Sher, B. T., & Johnson, D. T. (1997). A problem-based curriculum: Parallel learning opportunities for students and teachers. *Journal for Education of the Gifted, 20,* 363–379.

Brief, J. C. (1983). *Beyond Piaget.* New York: Teachers College Press.

Brinkerhoff, J. D., & Glazewski, K. (2000). *Hypermedia-based problem-based learning in the upper elementary grades: A developmental study.* (ERIC Document Reproduction Service No. ED455760)

Brooks, J. A. (1988). Taba Teaching Strategies: Effects on higher level cognitive functioning of academically gifted students (Doctoral dissertation, North Carolina State University, 1987/1988). *Dissertation Abstracts International, 49*(10-A), 2908.

Bruner, J. S. (1960). *The process of education.* Cambridge, MA: Harvard University Press.

Bruner, J. S., Goodnow, J. R., & Austin, G. A. (1956). *A study of thinking.* New York: Wiley.

Bruner, J. S., Goodnow, J. R., & Austin, G. A. (1985, June/July). Models of the learner. *Educational Researcher,* pp. 5–9.

Buros, O. K. (Ed.). (1959). *The fifth mental measurements yearbook.* Highland Park, NJ: Gryphon Press.

Callahan, C. M., Covert, R., Aylesworth, M. S., & Vanco, P. (1981). *SEA Test norms and technical manual.* Charlottesville: University of Virginia.

Carr, M., & Borkowski, J. (1986). Metamemory in gifted children. *Gifted Child Quarterly, 31,* 40–44.

Carter, K. R., & Ormrod, J. E. (1982). Acquisition of formal operations by intellectually gifted children. *Gifted Child Quarterly, 26,* 110–115.

Carter, M., & Rickarby, D. (2002). Introducing the use of the TASC problem solving wheel in reception and key stage 1 literacy: Developing children's writing skills. In B. Wallace (Ed.), *Teaching thinking skills across the early years.* London: David Fulton.

Caterall, J. S. (1995). Different ways of knowing: 1991–1994 National Longitudinal Study final report. In *Schools, communities and the arts: A research compendium.* Tempe, AZ: Arizona State University, Morrison Institute for Public Policy, School of Public Affairs.

Center for Civic Education. (1994). *National standards for civics and government.* Calabasas, CA: Center for Civic Education.

Chausow, H. M. (1955). *The organization of learning experiences to achieve more effectively the objectives of critical thinking in the general social science course at the junior college level.* Unpublished doctoral dissertation, University of Chicago.

Clark, B. (1983). *Growing up gifted.* Columbus, OH: Merrill.

Cohen, P. A. (1984). College grades and adult achievement: A research synthesis. *Research in Higher Education, 20,* 281–294.

Coleman, M. R., & Gallagher, J. J. (1995). The successful blending of gifted education with cooperative learning: Two studies. *Journal for the Education of the Gifted, 18,* 362–384.

Dabrowski, K., & Piechowski, M. (1977). *Theories of emotional development.* Oceanside, NY: Dabor Science Publications.

Damon, W. (1984). Peer education: The untapped potential. *Journal of Applied Developmental Psychology, 5,* 331–343.

Dapra, R. A., & Felker, D. B. (1974, September). *Effects of comprehension and verbatim adjunct questions in problem-solving ability from prose material: Extension of mathemagenic hypothesis.* Paper presented at the annual convention of the American Psychological Association, New Orleans.

Davidson, J., & Sternberg, R. J. (1984). The role of insight in intellectual giftedness. *Gifted Child Quarterly, 28*(2), 58–64.

Dewey, J. (1938). *Experience and education.* New York: Collier Books.

Dewey, J. (1943). *The school and society* (rev. ed.). Chicago: University of Chicago Press. (Original work published 1902)

Dewey, J. (1944). *Democracy and education: An introduction to the philosophy of education.* New York: Free Press. (Original work published 1916)

DISCOVER. (2002). Retrieved May 5, 2002, from http://www.discover.arizona.edu

Dods, R. F. (1997). An action research study of the effectiveness of problem-based learning in promoting the acquisition and retention of knowledge. *Journal for the Education of the Gifted, 20,* 423–437.

Doise, W., & Mugny, G. (1984). *The social development of the intellect.* Oxford: Pergamon Press.

Dressel, P. L., & Mayhew, L. B. (1954). *General education: Explorations in evaluation.* Washington, DC: American Council on Education.

Dressel, P. L., & Nelson, C. H. (1956). *Questions and problems in science.* Princeton, NJ: Educational Testing Service.

Education Development Center. (1970). *Man: A course of study.* Washington, DC: Curriculum Development Associates.

Educational Testing Service. (1972). *Sequential Test of Educational Progress.* Princeton, NJ: Addison-Wesley.

Ellis, K., & Durkin, M. C. (1972). *Teacher's guide for people in communities (The Taba Program in Social Studies).* Menlo Park, CA: Addison-Wesley.

Elm, D. R., Kennedy, E. J., & Lawton, L. (2001). Determinants of moral reasoning: Sex role orientation, gender, and academic factors. *Business & Society, 40,* 241–265.

Ennis, R. H. (1985). Critical thinking and the curriculum. *National Forum: Phi Kappa Phi Journal, 65*(1), 28–31.

Feldhusen, J. F., & Moon, S. M. (1992). Grouping gifted children: Issues and concerns. *Gifted Child Quarterly, 36*(2), 63–67.

Feldhusen, J. F., & Treffinger, D. J. (1980). *Creative thinking and problem solving in gifted education.* Dubuque, IA: Kendall and Hunt.

Felker, D. P., & Dapra, R. A. (1975). Effects of question type and question placement on problem-solving ability from prose material. *Journal of Educational Psychology, 67,* 380–384.

Feuerstein, R. (1980). *Instrumental enrichment: An intervention programme for cognitive modifiability.* Baltimore: University Park Press.

Firestien, R. L. (1990). Effects of Creative Problem Solving training on communication behaviors in small groups. *Small Group Research, 21,* 507–521.

Foot, H., Morgan, M., & Shute, R. (Eds.). (1990). *Children helping children.* London: Wiley.

Freeman, W. (1995). *Societies of brains.* Hillsdale, NJ: Erlbaum.

French, J. N., & Rhoder, C. (1992). *Teaching thinking skills: Theory and practice.* New York: Garland.

Gabbert, B., Johnson, D. W., & Johnson, R. T. (1986). Cooperative learning, group-to-individual transfer, process gain, and the acquisition of cognitive processing strategies. *Journal of Psychology, 120,* 265–278.

Gallagher, J. J. (1966). *Research summary on gifted child education.* Springfield, IL: Office of the Superintendent of Public Instruction.

Gallagher, J. J. (1975). *Teaching the gifted child* (2nd ed.). Boston: Allyn & Bacon.

Gallagher, J. J. (1985). *Teaching the gifted child* (3rd ed.). Boston: Allyn & Bacon.

Gallagher, S. A. (1996, November). *The effect of Problem Based Learning on complex thought.* Presentation at the annual meeting of the National Association for Gifted Children, Indianapolis.

Gallagher, S. A. (1997). Problem Based Learning: Where did it come from, what does it do, and where is it going? *Journal for the Education of the Gifted, 20,* 332–362.

Gallagher, S. A., Sher, B. T., Stepien, W. J., & Workman, D. (1995). Integrating Problem Based Learning into the science classroom. *School Science and Mathematics, 95,* 135–146.

Gallagher, S. A., & Stepien, W. J. (1996). Content acquisition in Problem Based Learning: Depth versus breadth in American Studies. *Journal for the Education of the Gifted, 19,* 257–275.

Gallagher, S. A., Stepien, W. J., & Rosenthal, H. (1994). The effects of Problem Based Learning on problem-solving. *Gifted Child Quarterly, 36,* 195–200.

Gardner, H. (1983). *Frames of mind: The theory of multiple intelligences.* New York: Basic Books.

Gardner, H. (1999). *Intelligence reframed.* New York: Basic Books.

Garduno, E. L. H. (2001). The influence of cooperative problem solving on gender differences in achievement, self-efficacy, and attitudes toward mathematics in gifted students. *Gifted Child Quarterly, 45,* 268–282.

George, W. C. (1976). Accelerating mathematics instruction. *Gifted Child Quarterly, 20,* 246–261.

Gertzman, A. D., & Kolodner, J. L. (1996). A case study of Problem Based Learning in a middle school science classroom: Lessons learned. In D. C. Edelson & E. A. Domeshek (Eds.), *Proceedings of International Conference of the Learning Sciences 96* (pp. 91–98). Charlottesville, VA: Association for the Advancement of Computing in Education.

Getzels, J. W. (1975). Problem-finding and the inventiveness of solutions. *Journal of Creative Behavior, 9,* 12–18.

Getzels, J. W., & Csikszentmihalyi, M. (1967). Scientific creativity. *Science Journal, 3,* 80–84.

Getzels, J. W., & Csikszentmihalyi, M. (1976). *The creative vision: A longitudinal study of problem finding in art.* New York: Wiley.

Getzels, J. W., & Jackson, P. O. (1962). *Creativity and intelligence: Exploration with gifted students.* New York: Wiley.

Gilligan, C. (1982). *In a different voice: Psychological theory and women's development.* Cambridge, MA: Harvard University Press.

Gorman, M. E. (2001/2002). Turning students into ethical professionals. *IEEE Technology & Society Magazine, 20*(4), 21–27.

Graves, N., & Graves, T. (1990). *What is cooperative learning? Tips for teachers and trainers.* Santa Cruz: Cooperative College of California.

Grobman, H. (1962). Some comments on the evaluation program findings and their implications. *Biological Sciences Curriculum Study Newsletter, 19,* 25–29.

Guidance Associates. (1976a). *Values in American history: Conscience in conflict* [Sound filmstrip]. Mount Kisco, NY: Author.

Guidance Associates. (1976b). *Values in a democracy: Making ethical decisions.* Mount Kisco, NY: Author.

Guilford, J. P. (1967). *The nature of human intelligence.* New York: McGraw-Hill.

Guilford, J. P. (1975). Varieties of creative giftedness, their measurement and development. *The Gifted Child Quarterly, 19,* 107–121.

Guilford, J. P. (1977). *Way beyond the IQ.* Buffalo, NY: Creative Education Foundation.

Hanley, J. P., Whitla, D. K., Moo, E. W., & Walter, A. S. (1970). *Curiosity/Competence/Community: An Evaluation of Man—A course of study. An evaluation.* Cambridge, MA: Educational Development Center.

Hanninen, G. E. (1989). *The effects of the Hilda Taba Teaching Strategies on critical and creative thinking.* Unpublished doctoral dissertation, University of Idaho, Boise.

Harkow, R. M. (1996). *Increasing creative thinking skills in second and third grade gifted students using imagery, computers, and Creative Problem Solving.* Master's final report. Retrieved September 11, 2002, from http://80-web3.epnet.com.ezproxy.library.arizona.edu

Hartshorne, J., & May, M. (1930). A summary of the work of the character inquiry. *Religious Education, 25,* 607–619.

Heath, S. B. (1983). *Ways with words: Language, life, and work in communities and classrooms.* New York: Cambridge University Press.

Hebert, T. P. (1993). *Reflections at graduation: A comparative case study analysis.* Unpublished doctoral dissertation, University of Connecticut at Storrs.

Helmuth, L. (2001). Moral reasoning relies on emotion. *Science, 293,* 1071–1072.

Hertz-Lazarowitz, R., Sharan, S., & Steinberg, R. (1980). Classroom learning style and cooperative behavior of elementary school children. *Journal of Educational Psychology, 72,* 97–104.

Hetland, L. (2000). Learning to make music enhances spatial reasoning. *Journal of Aesthetic Education, 34,* 179–238.

High, M. H., & Udall, A. J. (1989). What are they thinking when we're teaching critical thinking? *Gifted Child Quarterly, 33,* 156–160.

Hmelo, C. E., & Coté, N. C. (1996). The development of self-directed learning strategies in Problem Based Learning. In D. C. Edelson & E. A. Domeshek (Eds.), *Proceedings of International Conference of the Learning Sciences 1996* (pp. 421–426). Charlottesville, VA: Association for the Advancement of Computing in Education.

Hmelo, C. E., & Ferrari, M. (1997). The Problem Based Learning tutorial: Cultivating higher order thinking skills. *Journal for the Education of the Gifted, 20,* 401–422.

Hmelo, C. E., & Guzdial, M. (1996). Of black and glass boxes: The development of self-directed learning strategies in Problem Based Learning. In D. C. Edelson & E. A. Domeshek (Eds.), *Proceedings of International Conference of the Learning Sciences 1996* (pp. 128–134). Charlottesville, VA: Association for the Advancement of Computing in Education.

Hmelo, C. E., Holton, D., & Gertzman, A. (1997, April). *Building artificial lungs: Design-based learning.* Paper presented at the annual meeting of the American Educational Research Association, Chicago.

Hmelo, C. E., Narayanan, N. H., Hubscher, R., Newstetter, W. C., & Kolodner, J. L. (1996). A multiple-case–based approach to generative environments for learning. *VIVEK: The Indian Quarterly of Artificial Intelligence, 9,* 2–18.

Holland, J. G. (1965). Response contingencies in teaching-machine programs. *Journal of Programmed Instruction, 5,* 474–482.

Hoomes, E. W. (1986). Future Problem Solving: Preparing students for a world community. *Gifted Education International, 4*(1), 16–20.

Howieson, H. (1982). A longitudinal study of creativity—1965–1975. *The Journal for Creative Behavior, 15,* 117–135.

Hoyt, D. P. (1965). *The relationship between college grades and adult achievement: A review of the literature* (Research Rep. No. 7). Iowa City, IA: American College Testing Program.

Hunt, D. E., Butler, L. F., Noy, J. E., & Rosser, M. E. (1978*). Assessing conceptual level by the paragraph completion method.* Toronto: Ontario Institute of Education.

Institute for Staff Development (Eds.). (1971a). *Hilda Taba Teaching Strategies program: Unit 1.* Miami: Author.

Institute for Staff Development (Eds.). (1971b). *Hilda Taba Teaching Strategies program: Unit 2.* Miami: Author.

Institute for Staff Development (Eds.). (1971c). *Hilda Taba Teaching Strategies program: Unit 3.* Miami: Author.

Institute for Staff Development (Eds.). (1971d). *Hilda Taba Teaching Strategies program: Unit 4.* Miami: Author.

Isaksen, S. G. (1992). *Creative Problem Solving: A process for creativity.* Unpublished training manual. Buffalo, NY: The Creative Problem Solving Group–Buffalo.

Isaksen, S. G., Dorval, K. B., & Treffinger, D. J. (1994). *Creative approaches to problem solving.* Dubuque, IA: Kendall/Hunt.

Isaksen, S. G., & Parnes, S. J. (1985). Curriculum planning for creative thinking and problem solving. *Journal of Creative Behavior, 19*(1), 1–29.

James, J. (1978). *Sidney Parnes: Creative Problem-Solving model.* Unpublished manuscript. (Available from C. J. Maker, Department of Special Education, University of Arizona, P.O. Box 210069, Tucson, AZ 85721-0069)

Jensen, E. (1998). *Teaching with the brain in mind.* Alexandria, VA: Association for Supervision and Curriculum Development.

Jensen, E. (2001). *Arts with the brain in mind.* Alexandria, VA: Association for Supervision and Curriculum Development.

Johnson, D., Johnson, R., & Maruyama, G. (1983). Interdependence and interpersonal attraction among heterogeneous and homogeneous individuals: A theoretical formulation and a meta-analysis of the research. *Review of Educational Research, 53*(5), 5–54.

Joyce, B., & Weil, M. (1986). *Models of teaching* (3rd ed.). Englewood Cliffs, NJ: Prentice Hall.

Jung, C. G. (1923). *Psychological types.* London: Routledge & Kegan Paul.

Kagan, S. (1985). Co-op Co-op: A flexible cooperative learning technique. In R. Slavin, S. Sharan, S. Kagan, R. Hertz-Lazarowitz, C. Webb, & R. Schmuck (Eds.), *Learning to cooperate: Cooperating to learn* (pp. 437–462). New York: Plenum Press.

Kant, I. (1965). *Critique of pure reason* (N. K. Smith, Trans.). New York: St. Martin's Press. (Original work published 1929)

Keefer, M., & Ashley, K. (2001). Case-based approaches to professional ethics: A systematic comparison of students' and ethicists' moral reasoning. *Journal of Moral Education, 30,* 377–398.

Kohlberg, L. (1966). Moral education in the schools: A developmental view. *The School Review, 74,* 1–29.

Kohlberg, L. (1971). Stages of moral development as the basis for moral education. In C. M. Beck, B. S. Crittenden, & E. V. Sullivan (Eds.), *Moral education: Interdisciplinary approaches* (pp. 23–92). New York: Newman Press.

Koschmann, T. D., Myers, A. C., Feltovich, P. J., & Barrows, H. S. (1994). Using technology to assist in realizing effective learning and instruction: A principled approach to the use of computers in collaborative learning. *Journal of the Learning Sciences, 3,* 225–262.

Krathwohl, D. R., Bloom, B. S., & Masia, B. B. (1964). *Taxonomy of Educational Objectives: The classification of educational goals. Handbook II: Affective domain.* New York: David McKay.

Lessinger, L. M. (1963). Test building and test banks through the use of the Taxonomy of Educational Objectives. *California Journal of Educational Research, 14,* 195–201.

Lewis, B. A. (1991). *The kid's guide to social action: How to solve the social problems you choose—and turn creative thinking into positive action.* Minneapolis, MN: Free Spirit Press.

Limburg, J. B. (1979). *The Taxonomy of Educational Objectives of the cognitive domain.* Unpublished manuscript. (Available from C. J. Maker, Department of Special Education, P.O. Box 210069, University of Arizona, Tucson, AZ 85721-0069)

Lori, A. A. (1999). *The effect of questioning strategies on the higher cognitive processes of Bahraini academically gifted students.* Unpublished doctoral dissertation, University of Arizona, Tucson.

Lowman, L. M. (1961). An experimental evaluation of two curriculum designs for teaching first year algebra in a ninth grade class. *Dissertation Abstracts International, 22,* 502. (University Microfilms No. 61–2864)

MacKinnon, D. W. (1965). Personality and the realization of creative potential. *American Psychologist, 20,* 273–281.

Maker, C. J. (1978). *Successful handicapped adults.* Unpublished doctoral dissertation, The University of Virginia, Charlottesville.

Maker, C. J. (1981). The gifted hearing-impaired student. *American Annals of the Deaf, 126,* 631–645.

Maker, C. J. (1982a). *Curriculum development for the gifted.* Austin, TX: PRO-ED.

Maker, C. J. (1982b) *Teaching models in education of the gifted.* Rockville, MD: Aspen Systems.

Maker, C. J. (1993). Creativity, intelligence, and problem solving: A definition and design for cross-cultural research and measurement related to giftedness. *Gifted Education International, 2,* 68–77.

Maker, C. J. (1997). DISCOVER Problem Solving Assessment, *Quest, 8*(1), 3, 5, 7, 9.

Maker, C. J. (2001). DISCOVER: Assessing and developing problem solving. *Gifted Education International, 15,* 232–251.

Maker, C. J., & Anuruthwong, U. (2002). *The miracle of learning: The Prism of Learning.* Manuscript in preparation.

Maker, C. J., & Anuruthwong, U. (2003, August). *The miracle of learning: The Prism Model.* Paper presented at the 15th Biennial World Conference of the World Council for Gifted & Talented Students, Adelaide, Australia.

Maker, C. J., & King, M. (1996). *Nurturing giftedness in young children.* Reston, VA: Council for Exceptional Children.

Maker, C. J., & Lane, R. A. (2001). DISCOVER: Changing the way we think about education. *Gifted Education Communicator, 32*(4), 24–26.

Maker, C. J., & Nielson, A. B. (1995). *Teaching models in education of the gifted* (2nd ed.). Austin, TX: PRO-ED.

Maker, C. J., & Nielson, A. B. (1996). *Curriculum development and teaching strategies for gifted learners* (2nd ed.). Austin, TX: PRO-ED.

Maker, C. J., Rogers, J. A., & Nielson, A. G. (1994). Giftedness, diversity, and problem-solving. *Teaching Exceptional Children, 27,* 4–19.

Maker, C. J., Rogers, J. A., Nielson, A. B., & Bauerle, P. (1996). Multiple intelligences, problem solving, and diversity in the general classroom. *Journal for the Education of the Gifted, 19,* 437–460.

Maltby, F. (1993). Teaching mathematics through thinking actively in a social context. *Gifted Education International, 9,* 45–47.

Maltby, F. (1995). The use of TASC to develop a selection of tools for effective thinking. *Gifted Education International, 7,* 18–23.

Maltby, F., & Beattie, J. (1996). A TASC for Telematics. *Gifted Educational International, 7,* 104–113.

Maltby, F., & Cowan, E. (1995). The use of TASC to develop a selection of tools for effective thinking. *Gifted Education International, 11,* 18–23.

Mansfield, R. S., Busse, F. V., & Krepelka, E. J. (1978). The effectiveness of creativity training. *Review of Educational Research, 48,* 517–536.

Martensen, D., Eriksson, H., & Ingleman-Sundberg, M. (1985). Medical chemistry: Evaluation of active and problem-oriented teaching methods. *Medical Education, 19,* 34–42.

Maslow, A. (1970). *Motivation and personality.* New York: Harper & Row.

Mayor, J. (1966). *The University of Maryland mathematics project* (Progress Report No. 11). College Park: University of Maryland, College of Education.

McCluskey, K. W., Baker, P. A., O'Hagan, S. C., & Treffinger, D. J. (1995). *Lost prizes: Talent development and problem solving among at-risk students*. Sarasota, FL: Center for Creative Learning.

McGuire, C. (1963). Research in the process approach to the construction and analysis of medical examinations. *National Council on Measurement in Education Yearbook, 20,* 7–16.

Meador, K. S. (1994). The effect of synectics training on gifted and nongifted kindergarten students. *Journal for the Education of the Gifted, 18,* 55–73.

Milholland, J. E. (1966, February). *An empirical examination of the categories of the Taxonomy of Educational Objectives*. Paper presented at the Annual American Educational Research Association Convention, Chicago.

Mills, C. J., & Durden, W. G. (1993). Cooperative learning and ability grouping: An issue of choice. *Gifted Child Quarterly, 36,* 11–16.

Morris, G. C. (1961). *Educational objectives of higher secondary school science*. Melbourne: Australian Council on Educational Research.

Muson, H. (1979, February). Moral thinking: Can it be taught? *Psychology Today,* pp. 48–58, 67–68, 92.

Myers, I. B., & Briggs, K. C. (1976). *The Myers–Briggs Type Indicator* (2nd ed.). Palo Alto, CA: Consulting Psychologists Press.

Myers, I. B., & Briggs, K. C. (1980). *Gifts differing*. Palo Alto, CA: Consulting Psychologists Press.

National Academy of Sciences. (1996). *National science education standards*. Washington, DC: National Academy Press.

National Council of Teachers of Mathematics. (2000). *Principles and standards for school mathematics: An overview*. Reston, VA: Author.

Nelson, A. M. (1975). *Undergraduate academic achievement as an indicator of success*. Washington, DC: Civil Service Commission.

Newman, D., Griffin, P., & Cole, M. (1989). *The construction zone: Working for cognitive change in schools*. New York: Cambridge University Press.

Noller, R. B., Parnes, S. J., & Biondi, A. M. (1976). *Creative action book*. New York: Charles Scribner's Sons.

Noller, R. B., Treffinger, D. J., & Houseman, E. D. (1979). *It's a gas to be gifted or CPS for the gifted and talented*. Buffalo, NY: DOK.

Norman, G. R., & Schmidt, H. G. (1992). The psychological basis of Problem Based Learning: A review of the evidence. *Academic Medicine, 66,* 380–389.

O'Leary, B. S. (1980). College grade point average as an indicator of occupational success: An update. *Personnel Research Report, 80,* 281–294.

Olenchak, F. R. (1988). The schoolwide enrichment model in the elementary schools: A study of implementation stages and effects on educational excellence. In J. S. Renzulli (Ed.), *Technical report on research studies relating to the revolving door identification model* (2nd ed., pp. 201–247). Storrs: University of Connecticut, Bureau of Educational Research.

Olenchak, F. R. (1990). School change through gifted education: Effects on elementary students' attitudes toward learning. *Journal for Education of the Gifted, 14*, 66–78.

Olenchak, F. R., & Renzulli, J. S. (1989). The effectiveness of the Schoolwide Enrichment Model on selected aspects of elementary school change. *Gifted Child Quarterly, 33*, 36–46.

Osborn, A. (1963). *Applied imagination.* New York: Scribners.

Osler, S. F., & Fivel, M. W. (1961). Concept attainment: I. The role of age and intelligence in concept attainment by induction. *Journal of Experimental Psychology, 62*, 1–8.

Osler, S. F., & Troutman, G. E. (1961). Concept attainment: II. The effect of stimulus upon concept attainment at two levels of intelligence. *Journal of Experimental Psychology, 62*, 9–13.

Parnes, S. J. (1966). *Programming creative behavior.* Buffalo: State University of New York at Buffalo.

Parnes, S. J. (1967). *Creative potential and the education experience* (Occasional Paper No. 2). Buffalo, NY: Creative Education Foundation.

Parnes, S. J. (1975). *Aha! Insights into creative behavior.* Buffalo, NY: DOK.

Parnes, S. J. (1981). The *magic of your mind.* Buffalo, NY: Bearly Limited.

Parnes, S. J. (1987). The creative studies project. In S. Isaksen (Ed.), *Frontiers in creativity research: Beyond the basics* (pp. 156–188). Buffalo, NY: Bearly Limited.

Parnes, S. J. (1988). *Visionizing: State of the art processes for encouraging innovative excellence.* East Aurora, NY: DOK.

Parnes, S. J., Noller, R., & Biondi, A. (1967). *Guide to creative action.* New York: Scribners.

Patel, V. K., Groen, G. J., & Norman, G. R. (1991). Effects of conventional and problem-based medical curricula on problem solving. *Academic Medicine, 66*, 380–389.

Paul, R. W. (1985, May). Bloom's Taxonomy and critical thinking instruction. *Educational Leadership,* pp. 36–39.

Phelps, E., & Damon, W. (1989). Problem solving with equals: Peer collaboration as a context for learning mathematics and spatial concepts. *Journal of Educational Psychology, 81*, 639–646.

Phenix, P. H. (1964). *Realms of meaning.* New York: McGraw-Hill.

Piaget, J. (1963). *The origins of intelligence in children.* New York: Norton. (Original work published 1952)

Piaget, J., & Inhelder, B. (1969). The *psychology of the child.* New York: Basic Books.

President's Committee of Advisors on Science and Technology Panel on Educational Technology. (1997). *Report to the President on the use of technology to strengthen K–12 education in the United States.* Washington, DC: Author.

Proviss, M. (1960). Ability grouping in arithmetic. *Elementary School Journal, 60*, 391–398.

Pryor, L. A. (1994). *Teaching strategies designed to meet the cognitive needs of the gifted and talented in the regular classroom.* Unpublished doctoral dissertation, Nova University, Miami, FL.

Puccio, G. J., & Avarello, L. L. (1995). Links between creativity education and intervention programs for at-risk students. In K. W. McCluskey, P. A. Baker, S. C. O'Hagan, &

D. J. Treffinger (Eds.), *Lost prizes: Talent development and problem solving with at-risk populations* (pp. 63–76). Sarasota, FL: Center for Creative Learning.

Puccio, G. J., & Gonzalez, D. W. (2004). The nature and nurture of creative thinking: Western approaches and emerging thoughts about issues in the East. In S. Lau, A. Hui, & G. Y. C. Ng (Eds.), *Creativity: When east meets west.* (pp. 393–428). Singapore: World Scientific.

Rash, P. K., & Miller, A. D. (2000). A survey of practices of teachers of the gifted. *Roeper Review, 22,* 94–94. (Abstract ERIC Document Reproduction Service No. EJ606615)

Raths, L. E. (1963). Clarifying values. In R. S. Fleming (Ed.), *Curriculum for today's boys and girls* (pp. 315–342). Columbus, OH: Merrill.

Raths, L. E., Harmin, M., & Simon, S. B. (1966). *Values and teaching.* Columbus, OH: Merrill.

Rawls, J. (1971). *A theory of justice.* Cambridge, MA: Harvard University Press.

Reilly, R. R., & Chao, G. R. (1982). Validity and fairness of some alternative employee selection procedures. *Personnel Psychology, 35,* 1–62.

Reis, S. M., & Renzulli, J. S. (1982). A research report on the Revolving Door Identification Model: A case for the broadened conception of giftedness. *Phi Delta Kappan, 63,* 619–620.

Reis, S. M., & Renzulli, J. S. (2003). Research related to the schoolwide enrichment model. *Gifted Education International, 18,* 15–39.

Reis, S. M., & Schack, G. D. (1993). Differentiating products for the gifted and talented: The encouragement of independent learning. In C. J. Maker & D. Orzechowski-Harland (Eds.), *Critical issues in gifted education: Vol. III. Programs for the gifted in regular classrooms* (pp. 161–186). Austin, TX: PRO-ED.

Reis, S. M., Westberg, K. L., Kulikowich, J. M., & Purcell, J. H. (1998). Curriculum compacting and achievement test scores: What does the research say? *Gifted Child Quarterly, 42,* 123–131.

Renzulli, J. S. (1977). *The Enrichment Triad Model: A guide for developing defensible programs for the gifted and talented.* Wethersfield, CT: Creative Learning Press.

Renzulli, J. S. (1978). What makes giftedness? *Phi Delta Kappan, 60,* 180–184, 261.

Renzulli, J. S. (1979). *Sample instruments for the evaluation of programs for the gifted and talented.* Storrs, CT: Bureau of Educational Research, University of Connecticut.

Renzulli, J. S. (1988). The multiple menu model for developing differentiated curriculum for the gifted and talented. *Gifted Child Quarterly, 32,* 298–309.

Renzulli, J. W. (1994). *Schools for talent development: A practical plan for total school improvement.* Mansfield Center, CT: Creative Learning Press.

Renzulli, J. S., & Gable, R. K. (1976). A factorial study of the attitudes of gifted students toward independent study. *The Gifted Child Quarterly, 20,* 91–99.

Renzulli, J. S., & Reis, S. M. (1985). *The Schoolwide Enrichment Model: A comprehensive plan for educational excellence.* Mansfield Center, CT: Creative Learning Press.

Renzulli, J. S., & Reis, S. M. (1994). Research related to the Schoolwide Enrichment Model. *Gifted Child Quarterly, 38,* 2–14.

Renzulli, J. S., & Reis, S. M. (2002). *The Schoolwide Enrichment Model: Executive summary.* Retrieved March 18, 2002, from: http://www.sp.uconn.edu

Renzulli, J. S., Reis, S. M., & Smith, L. H. (1981). *The Revolving Door Identification Model.* Mansfield, CT: Creative Learning Press.

Renzulli, J. S., Smith, L. H., White, A. J., Callahan, C. M., & Hartman, R. K. (1976). *Scales for Rating the Behavioral Characteristics of Superior Students.* Mansfield Center, CT: Creative Learning Press.

Risemberg, R., & Zimmerman, B. J. (1992). Self-regulated learning in gifted students. *Roeper Review, 15*(2), 98–101.

Roberts, C., Ingram, C., & Harris, C. (1992). The effects of special versus regular classroom programming on higher cognitive processes of intermediate elementary aged gifted and average ability students. *Journal for the Education of the Gifted, 15,* 332–343.

Robinson, A. (1991). *Cooperative learning and the academically talented student: Executive summary.* Storrs, CT: National Research Center on the Gifted and Talented.

Roe, A. (1952). *The making of a scientist.* New York: Dodd & Mead.

Rogers, J. A. (1993). *Understanding spatial intelligence through problem solving in art: An analysis of behavior, processes and products.* Unpublished doctoral dissertation, University of Arizona, Tucson.

Rogers, J. A. (1998). Refocusing the lens: Using observation to assess and identify gifted learners. *Gifted Education International, 12,* 129–144.

Rogoff, B. (1990). *Apprenticeship in thinking: Cognitive development in social context.* New York: Oxford University Press.

Rose, L. H., & Lin, H. (1984). A meta-analysis of long-term creativity training programs. *Journal of Creative Behavior, 11,* 124–130.

Ross B. (1991). Towards a framework for problem-based curricula. In D. Bud & G. Feletti (Eds.), *The challenge of problem-based learning* (pp. 34–41). New York: St. Martin's.

Ross, J. A., & Smyth, E. (1995). Differentiating cooperative learning to meet the needs of gifted learners: A case for transformational leadership. *Journal for Education of the Gifted, 19,* 63–82.

Ross, J. D., & Ross, C. M. (1976). *The Ross Test of Higher Cognitive Processes.* Novato, CA: Academic Therapy.

Salomon, G., & Perkins, D. N. (1989). Rocky roads to transfer: Rethinking mechanisms of a neglected phenomenon. *Educational Psychologist, 24,* 113–142.

Samson, G. R., Grave, M. E., Weinstein, T., & Walberg, H. J. (1984). Academic and occupational performance: A quantitative synthesis. *American Educational Research Journal, 21,* 311–322.

Schack, G. D. (1986, April). *Creative productivity and self-efficacy in gifted children.* An expanded version of a paper presented at the 70th Annual Meeting of the American Educational Research Association, San Francisco, CA. (ERIC Document Reproduction Service No. ED 307-732)

Schack, G. D. (1993). Effects of a Creative Problem Solving curriculum on students of varying ability levels. *Gifted Child Quarterly, 37,* 32–38.

Schiever, S. W. (1986). *The effects of two teaching/learning models on the higher cognitive processes of students in classes for the gifted.* Unpublished doctoral dissertation, University of Arizona, Tucson.

Schiever, S. W. (1991). *A comprehensive approach to teaching thinking.* Boston: Allyn & Bacon.

Schiever, S. W., & Maker, C. J. (1991). Enrichment and acceleration: An overview and new directions. In N. Colangelo & G. A. Davis (Eds.), *Handbook of gifted education* (pp. 97–110). Needham Heights, MA: Allyn & Bacon.

Schiever, S. W., & Maker, C. J. (1997). Enrichment and acceleration: An overview and new directions. In N. Colangelo & G. A. Davis (Eds.), *Handbook of gifted education* (2nd ed., pp. 113–125). Needham Heights, MA: Allyn & Bacon.

Schiever, S. W., & Maker, C. J. (2003). Enrichment and acceleration: An overview and new directions. In N. Colangelo & G. A. Davis (Eds.), *Handbook of gifted education* (3rd ed. pp. 163–173).

Schmidt, H. G., De Grave, W. S., De Volder, M. S., Moust, J. H. C., & Patel, V. L. (1989). Explanatory models in the processing of science tests: The role of prior knowledge activation through small-group discussion. *Journal of Educational Psychology, 81,* 610–619.

Schneider, B. H. (1987). *The gifted child in peer group perspective.* New York: Springer-Verlag.

Scruggs, T. E., & Mastropieri, M. A. (1988). Acquisition and transfer of learning strategies by gifted and nongifted students. *Journal of Special Education, 22,* 153, 166.

Scruggs, T. E., Mastropieri, M. A., Monson, J., & Jorgensen, S. (1985). Maximizing what gifted students can learn: Recent findings of learning strategy research. *Gifted Child Quarterly, 29,* 181–185.

Selman, R. (1971). The relation of the role-taking to the development of moral judgment in children. *Child Development, 42,* 79–91.

Sharan, S. (Ed.). (1990*). Cooperative learning: Theory and research.* New York: Praeger.

Sharan, S., Hertz-Lazarowitz, R., & Ackerman, Z. (1980). Academic achievement of elementary school children in small group versus whole class instruction. *Journal of Experimental Education, 48,* 125–129.

Sharan, S., Kussell, P., Hertz-Lazarowitz, R., Bejarano, Y., Raviv, S., & Sharan, Y. (1984*). Cooperative learning in the classroom: Research in desegregated schools.* Hillsdale, NJ: Erlbaum.

Sharan, S., & Shachar, H. (1988). *Language and learning in the cooperative classroom.* New York: Springer.

Sharan, S., & Sharan, Y. (1976). *Small-group teaching.* Englewood Cliffs, NJ: Educational Technology Publications.

Sharan, Y., & Sharan, S. (1992*). Expanding cooperative learning through Group Investigations.* New York: Teachers College Press.

Shore, B. M., & Dover, A. C. (1987). Metacognition, intelligence, and giftedness. *Gifted Child Quarterly, 31,* 37–44.

Short, K. G., & Pierce, K. M. (1990). *Talking about books: Creating literate communities.* Portsmouth, NH: Heinemann.

Simon, H. A. (1978). Information-processing theory of human problem solving. In W. K. Estes (Ed.), *Human information processing* (pp. 271–293). Hillsdale, NJ: Erlbaum.

Slavin, R. (1980). *Using student team learning*. Baltimore: Center for Social Organization of Schools, Johns Hopkins University.

Slavin, R. (1983). *Cooperative learning*. New York: Longman.

Solman, R., & Rosen, G. (1986). Bloom's six cognitive levels represent two levels of performance. *Educational Psychology, 6,* 243–263.

Stanford Achievement Test. (8th ed.). (1989). San Antonio, TX: Psychological Corp.

Stanley, J. C., & Bolton, D. T. (1957). Book reviews. *Psychological Measurement, 17,* 631–634.

Starko, A. J. (1988). Effects of the Revolving Door Identification Model on creative productivity and self-efficacy. *Gifted Child Quarterly, 32,* 291–297.

Stepien, W. J., & Gallagher, S. A. (1993). Problem based learning: As authentic as it gets. *Educational Leadership, 50*(7), 25–29.

Stepien, W. J., Gallagher, S. A., & Workman, D. (1993). Problem Based Learning for traditional and interdisciplinary classrooms. *Journal for the Education of the Gifted, 16,* 338–357.

Stepien, W. J., & Pyke, S. L. (1997). Designing Problem Based Learning units. *Journal of Education for the Gifted, 20,* 380–400.

Sternberg, R. J. (1988). *The triarchic mind: A new theory of human intelligence*. New York: Viking.

Sternberg, R. J., & Davidson, J. E. (1985). Cognitive development in the gifted and talented. In F. D. Horowitz & M. O'Brien (Eds.), *The gifted and talented: Developmental perspectives* (pp. 37–74). Washington, DC: American Psychological Association.

Sternberg, R. J., Ferrari, M., Clinkenbeard, P., & Grigorenko, E. L. (1996). Identification, instruction, and assessment of gifted children: A construct validation of a triarchic model. *Gifted Child Quarterly, 40,* 129–137.

Stoker, H. W., & Kropp, R. P. (1964). Measurement of cognitive processes. *Journal of Educational Measurement, 1,* 39–42.

Suchman, R. (1965). Inquiry and education. In J. Gallagher (Ed.), *Teaching gifted students: A book of readings* (pp. 193–209). Boston: Allyn & Bacon.

Sultana, Q. (2001, May). *Scholarly teaching: Application of Bloom's Taxonomy in Kentucky's classrooms*. Paper presented at the Third Annual Conference on Scholarship and Teaching, Bowling Green, KY. (ERIC Document Reproduction Service No. ED471982)

Suppes, P. (1969). *Sets and numbers: Teacher's handbook for book 1* (rev. ed.). New York: Random House.

Taba, H. (1962). *Curriculum development: Theory and practice*. New York: Harcourt, Brace & World.

Taba, H. (1964). *Thinking in elementary school children* (U.S.O.E. Cooperative Research Project, No. 1574). San Francisco: San Francisco State College. (ERIC Document Reproduction Service No. ED 003 285)

Taba, H. (1966). *Teaching strategies and cognitive functioning in elementary school children* (U.S.O.E. Cooperative Research Project No. 2404). San Francisco: San Francisco State College.

Taetle, L., & Maker, C. J. (2001). *The effects of the DISCOVER problem-solving arts-infused curriculum model on state-mandated standardized test scores*. Unpublished paper.

(Available from C. J. Maker, Department of Special Education, University of Arizona, P.O. Box 210069, Tucson, AZ 85721-0069).

Tallent, M. K. (1985). Effects of the Future Problem Solving program on gifted students' ability to solve futuristic problems (Doctoral dissertation, University of Texas). *Dissertation Abstracts International, 47,* 843A.

Tallent-Runnels, M. K., & Yarbrough, D. W. (1992). Effects of the Future Problem Solving program on children's concerns about the future. *Gifted Child Quarterly, 36*(4), 190–194.

Tatsuoka, M. M., & Easley, J. A., Jr. (1963). *Comparison of UICSM vs. traditional algebra classes on COOP algebra test scores* (Research Rep. No. 1). Urbana: University of Illinois Committee on School Mathematics.

Terman, L. M. (Ed.). (1959). *Genetic studies of genius: Vol. 1. Mental and physical traits of a thousand gifted children.* Palo Alto, CA: Stanford University Press.

Terman, L. M., & Oden, M. (1959). *Genetic studies of genius: Vol. 5. The gifted group at midlife.* Palo Alto, CA: Stanford University Press.

Torrance, E. P. (1977). Today's students' images of the future. In S. L. Carmean & B. L. Grover (Eds.), *Creative thinking* (pp. 5–21). Bellingham: Western Washington University.

Torrance, E. P. (1981). Predicting the creativity of elementary school children. *Gifted Child Quarterly, 25,* 55–62.

Torrance, E. P., Williams, S., & Torrance, J. P. (1977). *Handbook for training Future Problem Solving teams.* Athens: University of Georgia, Department of Educational Psychology.

Treffinger, D. J. (1978). Guidelines for encouraging independence and self direction among gifted students. *Journal of Creative Behavior, 12,* 14–21.

Tyler, L. L. (1966). The Taxonomy of Educational Objectives: Cognitive domain—Its use in evaluating programmed instruction. *California Journal of Educational Research, 17,* 26–32.

Uyeda, S., Madden, J., Brigham, L. A., Luft, J. A., & Washburne, J. (2002). Solving authentic science problems. *The Science Teacher, 1,* 24–29.

van der Horst, H. v. R. (2000). A problem solving strategy for gifted learners in South Africa. *Gifted Education International, 14,* 103–110.

Vygotsky, L. S. (1978). *Mind in society: The development of higher psychological processes.* Cambridge, MA: Harvard University Press.

Wallace, B. (2002a). Don't work harder! Work smarter! In B. Wallace & R. Bentley (Eds.), *Teaching thinking skills across the middle years: A practical approach for children aged 9–14* (pp. 1–24). London: David Fulton.

Wallace, B. (2002b). Teaching problem solving and thinking skills in the early years: Working across the curriculum. The earlier we start the better! In B. Wallace (Ed.), *Teaching thinking skills across the early years: A practical approach for children aged 4–7* (pp. 1–42). London: David Fulton.

Wallace, B. (2002c). Teaching problem solving and thinking skills through history; TASC: Thinking actively in a social context. In B. Wallace (Ed.), *Using history to develop thinking skills at key stage 2* (pp. 1–32). London: David Fulton.

Wallace, B. & Adams, H. B. (1987). Assessment and development of potential of high school pupils in the third world context of KwaZulu/Natal. *Gifted Education International (1)* 6–9; *(2)* 12–18.

Wallace, B., & Adams, H. B. (1988). Assessment and development of potential of high school students in the third world context of KwaZulu/Natal. *Gifted Education International, 5,* 72–78.

Wallace, B., & Adams, H. B. (with Maltby, F. B., & Mathfield, J.) (1993). *TASC: Thinking Actively in a Social Context.* London: AB Academic Publishers.

Wallace, B., & Bentley, R. (Eds.). (2002). *Teaching thinking skills across the middle years: A practical approach for children aged 9–14.* London: David Fulton.

Wallace, W. L. (1962). The BSCS 1961–62 evaluation program: A statistical report. *Biological Sciences Curriculum Study Newsletter, 19,* 22–24.

Wallach, M. A. (1976). Tests tell us little about talent. *American Scientist, 44,* 57–63.

Wallach, M. A., & Kogan, N. (1965). *Modes of thinking in young children.* New York: Holt, Rinehart and Winston.

Wallen, N. E., Durkin, M. C., Fraenkel, J. R., McNaughton, A. J., & Sawin, E. I. (1969). *The Taba curriculum development project in social studies.* Menlo Park, CA: Addison-Wesley.

Ward, V. S. (1961). *Educating the gifted: An axiomatic approach.* Columbus, OH: Merrill.

Watts, G. H., & Anderson, R. C. (1971). Effects of three types of inserted questions on learning from prose. *Journal of Educational Psychology, 62,* 387–394.

Whitmore, J. R., & Maker, C. J. (1985). *Intellectual giftedness in disabled persons.* Austin, TX: PRO-ED.

Williams, F. E. (1970). *Classroom ideas for encouraging thinking and feeling* (2nd ed.). Buffalo, NY: DOK.

Williams, F. E. (1971). Models for encouraging creativity in the classroom. In J. C. Gowan & E. P. Torrance (Eds.), *Educating the ablest: A book of readings on the education of gifted children.* Itasca, IL: Peacock.

Williams, F. E. (1972). *A total creativity program for individualizing and humanizing the learning process.* Englewood Cliffs, NJ: Educational Technology Publications.

Wilson, S. H., Greer, J. F., & Johnson, R. M. (1973). Synectics: A creative problem-solving technique for the gifted. *The Gifted Child Quarterly, 17,* 260–267.

Windsor, J. C., & Cappel, J. J. (1999). A comparative study of moral reasoning. *College Student Journal, 33,* 281–288.

Wolfe, P. (2001). *Brain matters: Translating research into classroom practice.* Alexandria, VA: Association for Supervision and Curriculum Development.

Yamada, H., & Tam, A. Y. (1996). A true test: Toward more authentic and equitable assessment. *Phi Delta Kappan, 70,* 703–713.

Zimmerman, B. J., & Martinez-Pons, M. (1990). Student differences in self-regulated learning: Relating grade, sex, and giftedness to self-efficacy and strategy use. *Journal of Educational Psychology, 82*(1), 51–59.

Zinn, K. L. (1966, February). *The use of the taxonomy and computer assistance in assembling sets of objectives, test items, and diagnostic test sequences.* Paper presented at the Annual American Educational Research Association Convention, Chicago.

Author Index

Ackerman, Z., 319
Adams, H. B., 375–408, 486, 493–495
Aicken, F., 164
Al-Shwailan, F. A., 368
Alvarado, A. E., 291
Anderson, R. C., 124
Andre, T., 124
Anuruthwong, U., 435–445, 496, 503–504
Armstrong, A., 447
Armstrong, T., 447
Aronson, E., 318
Ashley, K., 420
Austin, G. A., 134
Avarello, L. L., 224
Ayers, J. D., 123

Bagnall, J., 229
Baird, K. K., 169, 170
Baker, P. A., 224
Bandura, A., 402
Banks, J. A., 163, 164
Barell, J., 236
Barrows, H., 232, 234, 235, 236, 243, 244, 245, 246, 247, 250–251
Bauerle, P., 165, 406
Baum, S., 189, 190, 406
Beattie, J., 405, 407
Begle, E., 158
Bentley, R., 380, 389, 391, 393, 394, 395, 396, 402, 404, 405, 408
Berger, S., 229, 255
Betres, J., 367–368
Betts, G. T., 27–81, 458–462
Beyer, B. K., 84, 127
Biondi, A. M., 202, 206
Blaney, N., 318

Bloom, B. S., 2, 3, 62, 83, 112, 121–122, 123, 125, 127, 156, 207, 227, 368, 459, 463–465
Blumberg, P., 253
Bolton, D. T., 123
Booth, D., 325
Borkman, R., 447
Borkowski, J., 237–238, 402
Boyce, L. N., 237, 255
Brief, J. C., 134
Briggs, K. C., 160
Brigham, L. A., 244, 256
Brinkerhoff, J. D., 253
Brooks, J. A., 369, 370
Brown, A., 292
Bruner, J. S., 5, 20, 115, 116, 121, 129–164, 285, 327, 334, 371, 469, 470–472
Burke, C., 326
Buros, O. K., 123
Burruss, J. D., 237, 255
Bushuizen, 253
Busse, F. V., 221

Callahan, C. M., 6
Camm, 159
Cappel, J. J., 421
Carin, A. A., 164
Carpendale, J., 446
Carr, M., 237-238
Carter, K. R., 161
Carter, M., 403
Caterall, J. S., 190
Chao, G. R., 169
Charette, R. J., 447
Chausow, H. M., 123
Christianson, 104
Clark, B., 67
Clinkenbeard, P., 236

Cohen, P. A., 169
Cole, M., 293
Coleman, M. R., 321–322
College Entrance Examination Board, 191
Costa, A. L., 447
Coté, N. C., 246
Cowan, E., 403, 408
Crandell, L., 229
Csikszentmihalyi, M., 166, 167, 169

Dabrowski, K., 371, 446
Dalton, J., 68, 325
Damon, W., 296, 318
Dana, N. F., 446
Daniels, M. A., 68
Daniels, J. E., 128, 194
Dapra, R. A., 124
Davidson, J., 136
Davidson, J. E., 238
De Grave, W. S., 252
De Volder, M. S., 252
DeVore, I., 144
Dewey, J., 203, 293, 317, 327
Diehn, G., 447
Dods, R. F., 252
Doise, W., 296
Dorval, K. B., 201, 229, 256
Dover, A. C., 161
Dressel, P. L., 123
Durden, W. G., 293
Durkin, M. C., 327, 328, 356, 364, 365, 373

Easley, J. A., Jr., 158
Education Development Center, 129, 144, 148–150, 157
Educational Testing Service, 366

Edwards, C. P., 446
Ehrenberg, L., 365
Ehrenberg, S., 365
Ellis, K., 327, 356, 364, 365, 373
Elm, D. R., 421
Ennis, R. H., 84, 89
Eriksson, H., 252

Fan-Willman, C., 446
Featherstone, B., 68
Feldhusen, J. F., 27, 67, 293
Felker, D. B., 124
Feltovich, P. J., 247
Ferrari, M., 232, 236, 243–249, 255
Feuerstein, R., 402
Firestien, R. L., 224
Fivel, M. W., 160
Fleisher, P., 68, 325, 446
Foot, H., 293
Fraenkel, J. R., 328
Freeman, W., 104
French, J. N., 84

Gabbert, B., 123, 124
Gable, R. K., 27, 287
Galbraith, J., 68
Gallagher, J. J., 4, 129, 139, 159, 204, 321–322
Gallagher, S. A., 231, 233–243, 245, 251–253, 256
Gardner, H., 166, 177, 180, 188
Garduno, E. L. H., 296
Garvin, K., 68
George, W. C., 7
Gertzman, A. D., 248–249
Getzels, J. W., 166, 167, 169, 203–204, 225
Gilligan, C., 422, 446
Given, B. K., 447
Glazewski, K., 253
Glock, J., 447
Goldberg, 159
Gonzalez, D. W., 199
Goodall, J., 144
Goodnow, J. R., 134
Gorman, M. E., 421
Grave, M. E., 169
Green, T. D., 292

Greenwald, N. L., 256
Greer, J. F., 203
Griffin, P., 293
Grigorenko, E. L., 236
Grobman, H., 158, 159
Groen, G. J., 253
Guilford, J. P., 125, 223, 434
Gumieniak, P., 367–368
Gutteridge, D., 446
Guzdial, M., 245

Hanley, J. P., 148–150, 157–158
Hanninen, G. E., 368
Hare, P., 325
Harkow, R. M., 225
Harmin, M., 409
Harris, C., 125, 286
Hartman, R. K., 6
Hartshorne, J., 420
Heath, S. B., 293
Hebert, T. P., 287–288
Helmuth, L., 420
Herr, P. R., 291
Hersh, R. H., 446
Hertz-Lazarowitz, R., 319, 325
Hetland, L., 191
Higgins, A., 446
High, M. H., 369
Hmelo, C. E., 232, 243–249, 255
Holland, J. G., 124
Holton, D., 249
Hoomes, E. W., 217
Houseman, E. D., 209–210, 229
Howieson, H., 170
Hoyt, D. P., 169, 263
Hubscher, R., 245
Hyde, A. A., 164
Hyde, P. R., 164

Ingleman-Sundberg, M., 252
Ingram, C., 125, 286
Inhelder, B., 335
Institute for Staff Development, 334, 336–337, 339, 340, 342, 364, 373
Isaksen, S. G., 201, 204, 206, 221, 228, 229, 256

Jackson, J. B., 229
Jackson, P. O., 203, 225
Jacobs, H. H., 447
James, J., 221
Jensen, E., 104, 180
Jensen, R., 194
Johnson, D. T., 237, 255
Johnson, D. W., 123, 319
Johnson, R. M., 203
Johnson, R. T., 123, 319
Johnstone, E., 389, 394, 395, 396
Jones, R. S., 194, 448
Jorgensen, S., 161
Joyce, B., 1–2
Jung, C. G, 160

Kagan, S., 318, 325
Kallik, B., 447
Kant, I., 409
Kaufeldt, M., 194
Kazemek, F. E., 446
Keefer, M., 420
Kelson, A. C., 232, 245, 246
Kennedy, E. J., 421
Kercher, J. K., 27–81, 458–459, 460–462
Kettle, K. E., 292
King, M., 176, 194
Kiser, M. A., 128
Knapp, J., 28
Kobert, D., 229
Kogan, N., 225
Kohlberg, L., 2, 20, 283, 343, 371, 409–423, 445, 446, 496, 497–499
Kolodner, J. L., 245, 248–249
Kong, Y., 255
Koschmann, T. D., 247
Krathwohl, D., 2, 3, 83, 98, 116, 122, 127, 156, 227, 278, 459, 466–468
Krepelka, E. J., 221
Kropp, R. P., 123, 124
Kulikowich, J. M., 287

Lane, R. A., 175, 176
Lawton, L., 421
Lessinger, L. M., 123
Lewis, B. A., 228, 229
Limburg, J. B., 126

Lin, H., 224
Lindsey, B., 446
Lori, A. A., 368, 370
Lowman, L. M., 159
Luft, J. A., 244, 256
Lynch-Brown, C., 446

MacKinnon, D. W., 160, 263, 264
Madden, J., 244, 256
Maker, C. J., vii, viii, 14–19, 21–25, 51, 62, 112, 121, 147, 151, 165–194, 170n, 241, 242, 250, 278, 315, 316, 327–328, 359, 361, 362, 369, 372, 406, 435–445, 450–457, 469, 473–475, 496, 503–504
Maletis, M., 447
Maltby, F., 402, 403, 405, 407, 408
Mansfield, R. S., 221, 223–224
Margulies, M. A., 448
Martensen, D., 252
Martinez-Pons, M., 27
Maruyama, G., 319
Masia, B. B., 83
Maslow, A., 196
Mastropieri, M. A., 27, 161
Mathfield, J., 408
May, M., 420
Mayhew, L. B., 123
Mayor, J., 159
McCluskey, K. W., 224
McGuire, C., 123
McNaughton, A. J., 328
Meador, K. S., 226
Menhennett, L., 229
Meyer, M., 447
Michael, J. A., 253
Milholland, J. E., 124
Miller, A. D., 225
Mills, C. J., 293
Monson, J., 161
Moo, E. W., 148–150, 157–158
Moon, S. M., 293
Morgan, M., 293
Morris, G. C., 123
Moust, J. H. C., 252
Mugny, G., 296

Muson, H., 418
Myers, A. C., 247
Myers, I. B., 160

Narayanan, N. H., 245
NAS, 174
National Academy of Sciences, 174
National Council of Teachers of Mathematics (NCTM), 174
NCTM, 174
Neill, 159
Nelson, A. M., 169
Nelson, C. H., 123
Newman, D., 293
Newstetter, W. C., 245
Ngeow, K., 255
Nielson, A. B., vii, viii, 14–19, 21–25, 51, 62, 112, 121, 165, 170n, 176, 181, 185, 186–187, 241, 242, 250, 278, 315, 316, 359, 406, 450–457
Noller, R. B., 202, 206, 209–210, 229
Norman, G. R., 235, 251, 252, 253

Oden, M., 263
O'Hagan, S. C., 224
O'Leary, B. S., 169
Olenchak, F. R., 287, 289
Oreck, B., 189, 190, 406
Ormrod, J. E., 161
Osborn, A., 195, 198, 212, 221
Osler, S. F., 160–161
Owen, S., 189, 190, 406

Paolitto, D. P., 446
Paris, R., 448
Parnes, S. J., 143, 195–229, 284, 469, 476–478
Passow, 159
Patel, V., 252, 253
Patton, S. J., 447
Paul, R. W., 84, 87
PCAST-PET, 174
Peace, S. D., 446
Perkins, D. N., 246
Phelps, E., 296, 318

Phenix, P. H., 285
Piaget, J., 87, 134–135, 317–318, 327, 328–331, 335
Piechowski, M., 371, 446
Pierce, K., 302, 326
Pirto, J., 194
Power, F. C., 446
President's Committee of Advisors on Science and Technology Panel on Educational Technology, 174
Proviss, M., 159
Pryor, L. A., 368
Puccio, G. J., 199, 224
Purcell, J. H., 287
Pyke, S. L., 237, 255

Rash, P. K., 225
Raths, L. E., 409, 410
Rawls, J., 409
Reagan, R., 128
Reilly, J., 68
Reilly, R. R., 169
Reiman, A. J., 446
Reimer, J., 446
Reis, S. M., 139, 257–260, 262–268, 270, 276, 282, 285–289, 291, 316, 479, 483–485
Renzulli, J. S., 2, 4, 6, 7, 27, 65, 67, 130, 139, 154, 155, 257–292, 316, 479, 483–485
Rhoder, C., 84
Rickarby, D., 403
Risemberg, R., 27
Rizza, M. G., 292
Roberts, C., 125, 286
Robinson, A., 293, 323, 325
Roe, A., 263, 285
Rogers, J. A., 170n
Rogoff, B., 293
Rose, L. H., 224
Rosen, G., 123, 128
Rosenthal, H., 253
Ross, B., 237
Ross, C. M., 286
Ross, J. A., 293
Ross, J. D., 286

Sage, S., 255
Salomon, G., 246

Samson, G. R., 169
Sawin, E. I., 328
Schack, G. D., 225, 276, 286
Schiever, S. W., 165–194, 283,
    333, 369–370, 372, 373,
    469, 473–475
Schmidt, H. G., 235, 251, 252,
    253
Scruggs, T. E., 27, 161
Selman, R., 343
Selwyn, D., 194, 448
Senn, P. R., 256
Shachar, H., 320
Sharan, S., 152, 155, 293–326,
    319, 479, 486, 487–489
Sharan, Y., 152, 155, 293–326,
    479, 486, 487–489
Sher, B. T., 237, 245, 255, 256
Shore, B. M., 161
Short, K. G., 302, 326
Shute, R., 293
Sikes, J., 318
Simon, H. A., 237
Simon, S. B., 409
Slavin, R., 318, 319
Smith, L. H., 6, 258
Smyth, E., 293
Snapp, M., 318
Solman, R., 123, 128
Stanley, J. C., 123
Starko, A. J., 286
Stefanakis, E. H., 194
Steinberg, R., 319
Stephan, C., 318
Stepien, W. J., 237, 238, 243,
    245, 252, 253, 255, 256
Sternberg, R. J., 136, 236, 238,
    402
Stoker, H. W., 123, 124

Suchman, R., 98
Sultana, Q., 125
Sund, R. B., 164
Suppes, P., 159
Swartz, R., 128

Taba, H., 2, 3, 34, 62, 112, 116,
    129–130, 152, 153, 154,
    219, 273, 283, 284, 302,
    327–373, 422, 486, 490–492
Taetle, L., 190
Tallent, M. K., 226
Tallent-Runnels, M. K., 226
Tam, A. Y., 169–170
Tatsuoka, M. M., 158
Terman, L. M., 263, 264
Thornley-Hall, C., 325
Tinbergen, N., 144
Torp, L. T., 255
Torrance, E. P., 67, 169–170,
    217, 224, 226
Torrance, J. P., 217
Treffinger, D. J., 27, 67, 201,
    209–210, 224, 229, 256
Troutman, G. E., 160
Tyler, L. L., 123

Udall, A. J., 68, 128, 194, 369
Uyeda, S., 244, 256

Van der Horst, H. v.R., 388,
    407
VanTassel-Baska, J., 237, 255
Vygotsky, L. S., 293, 295, 327,
    402

Walberg, H. J., 169
Wallace, B., 375–408, 486,
    493–495

Wallace, W. L., 158, 159
Wallach, M. A., 169, 225, 263
Wallen, N., 328, 364, 365
Walter, A. S., 148–150,
    157–158
Ward, V. S., 139, 285, 334,
    411
Washburne, J., 244, 256
Watts, G. H., 124
Webb, C. D., 325
Weil, M., 1–2
Weinstein, T., 169
Wertz, S., 447
Westberg, K. L., 287
White, A. J., 6
Whitla, D. K., 148–150,
    157–158
Whitmore, J. R., 188
Williams, F. E., 278, 423–435,
    445, 447, 496, 500–502
Williams, S., 217
Wilson, J., 158
Wilson, S. H., 203
Windsor, J. C., 421
Wolfe, P., 104, 176, 194
Workman, D., 245, 253, 256

Yamada, H., 169–170
Yarbrough, D. W., 226

Zajano, M., 367–368
Zimmerman, B. J., 27
Zinn, K. L., 124

Subject Index

A. W. Peller publisher, 373, 448
Abstractness
  Affective Taxonomy (Krathwohl), 115–116
  Cognitive Taxonomy (Bloom), 112, 115–116
  of curricula for gifted students, 4
Acceptance
  Basic Structure of a Discipline (BSD), 155
  curricula for gifted students and, 9
  Hilda Taba Teaching Strategies, 358
  Teaching Strategies for Thinking and Feeling
    (Williams model), 432
Accommodation, 329–330
Acquiescence in responding, in Affective Taxon-
  omy (Krathwohl), 94
Adaptability of teaching–learning models, 13
Adventure trips, in Autonomous Learner Model
  (ALM), 43, 60
Affective Taxonomy (Krathwohl)
  advantages and disadvantages of, 126–127
  assumptions underlying, 84–86
  characterization by value or value complex
    level in, 95, 97, 103, 108
  complementary models for, 115, 116, 121,
    156, 273, 466–468
  conclusion on, 128
  content modifications, 115–117
  development of, 121–123
  effectiveness of, with gifted, 125
  effectiveness of, with nongifted, 123–125
  elements/parts of, 86–87, 89, 94–98, 102–109
  examples of thinking levels in, 102–103
  giftedness assumptions underlying, 86
  goals of, 466–468
  learning assumptions underlying, 84–85
  learning environment modifications, 114,
    120–121
  modifications of basic curriculum, 113–114,
    459, 466–468
  modifications of model, 114–121
  organization level in, 95, 97, 103, 107

overview of, 83–84
  process modifications, 113–114, 117–119
  product modifications, 114, 120
  purpose of, 459
  and real-life problem situations, 105–108
  receiving or attending level in, 89, 94, 96, 102,
    105
  research on effectiveness of, 123–125
  resources on, 128
  responding level in, 94, 96, 102, 105–106
  summary of student and teacher activities
    and roles, 96–97, 105–108
  teaching assumptions underlying, 85–86
  valuing level in, 94–97, 103, 106–107
  worksheets for assessment of, 14–19, 21–25,
    452–456
ALM. See Autonomous Learner Model (ALM)
ALPS. See Autonomous Learning Publications
  and Specialists (ALPS)
American Psychological Association (APA),
  121–122
Analysis
  Basic Structure of a Discipline (BSD),
    135–137
  Cognitive Taxonomy (Bloom), 88, 91, 100, 107
Anuruthwong, Usanee. See Prism of Learning
APA. See American Psychological Association
  (APA)
Application, in Cognitive Taxonomy (Bloom),
  88, 91, 99, 106–107
Application of Generalizations strategy (Hilda
  Taba Teaching Strategies), 340–342, 359,
  363
Applied Imagination (Osborn), 221
Apprenticeship, in Problem Based Learning
  (PBL), 237–238
Appropriateness of teaching–learning models
  to situation, 12, 14–19
Arts, in DISCOVER Curriculum Model, 180,
  189, 192

Arts with the Brain in Mind (Jensen), 180
Assessment. *See also* Evaluation
    of creativity, 169–170
    DISCOVER Assessment, 170–173, 192, 193
    in Prism of Learning, 441–442
    of teaching–learning models, 12–26, 451–509
Assimilation, 87, 329–330
Attending or receiving, in Affective Taxonomy
        (Krathwohl), 89, 94, 96, 102, 105
Autonomous Learner Model (ALM)
    advantages and disadvantages of, 65–67
    adventure trips, 43, 60
    assumptions underlying, 28–32
    college and career involvement, 38–39, 56–57
    complementary models for, 34, 62, 152, 153,
        155, 156, 359, 371, 460–462
    conclusion on, 67
    content modifications, 51, 62
    cultural activities, 41–42, 59
    definition of autonomous learner, 28
    development of, 63–64
    elements/parts of, 32–49
    Enrichment dimension, 33, 40–44, 50, 58–60,
        78–81
    exploration, 40–41, 58
    giftedness assumptions underlying, 31–32
    goals of, 460–462
    group-building activities, 34–35, 52–53
    implementation of, 49–51, 77–81
    In-depth Study dimension, 33, 44, 49, 50, 61,
        69–76, 78–81
    In-depth Study Forms, 69–76
    Individual Development dimension, 33,
        36–40, 50, 55–57, 78–81
    inter/intrapersonal area, 36–37, 55
    investigations, 41, 58–59
    learning assumptions underlying, 30–31
    learning environment modifications, 63
    learning skills, 37–38, 56
    modifications of, 51, 62–63, 458–462
    organizational skills, 39, 57
    Orientation dimension, 33–36, 50, 52–54,
        78–81
    overview of, 27–28
    Personal Educational Plan (PEP), 37, 66
    process modifications, 62
    product modifications, 62–63
    productivity, 39–40, 57
    program and school opportunities and re-
        sponsibilities, 36, 54
    research on effectiveness of, 64–65

    resources on, 67–68
    self/personal development in, 35–36, 53
    seminar criteria, 45–48
    Seminars dimension, 33, 43–48, 50, 60–61,
        78–81
    service, 42–43, 59
    summary of student and teacher activities
        and roles, 52–61
    teaching assumptions underlying, 29–30
    technology, 38, 56
    understanding giftedness, talent, intelligence,
        and creativity, 34, 52
    worksheets for assessment of, 14–19, 21–25,
        452–456
Autonomous Learning Publications and
        Specialists (ALPS), 68
Awareness, in Affective Taxonomy (Krath-
        wohl), 94

Basic Structure of a Discipline (BSD)
    advantages and disadvantages of, 161–163
    assumptions underlying, 130–138
    complementary models for, 115, 116, 121,
        129–130, 152–156, 156, 371, 469,
        470–472
    conclusion on, 163
    content modifications, 139–141, 147–148, 152
    development of, 156–157
    effectiveness of, with gifted, 159–160
    effectiveness of, with nongifted, 157–159
    elements/parts of, 138–139
    examples of teaching activities in, 144–150
    giftedness assumptions underlying, 137–138
    goals of, 470–472
    importance of structure and, 131–134
    intuitive and analytic thinking and, 135–137
    learning assumptions underlying, 130,
        134–135, 137
    learning environment modifications, 144
    Man: A Course of Study and, 129, 144, 147,
        148–150, 157–161
    modifications of basic curriculum, 139–147,
        469, 470–472
    modifications of model, 147–156
    motivation for learning and, 137
    overview of, 129–130
    process modifications, 141–143, 152–153
    product modifications, 143–144, 153–154
    readiness for learning and, 134–135
    research on effectiveness of, 157–161
    resources on, 163–164

summary of student and teacher activities and roles, 145–146

teaching assumptions underlying, 130

Worksheet for Curriculum Design, 151

worksheets for assessment of, 14–19, 21–25, 452–456

Behavior modification and cybernetic models, 2

Betts, George T. *See* Autonomous Learner Model (ALM)

Bloom's Taxonomy. *See* Cognitive Taxonomy (Bloom)

Bruner, Jerome. *See* Basic Structure of a Discipline (BSD)

BSD. *See* Basic Structure of a Discipline (BSD)

Career involvement, in Autonomous Learner Model (ALM), 38–39, 56–57

CATS. *See* Commonwealth Accountability Testing System (CATS)

Center for Gifted Education (CGE), 255

Center for Problem-Based Learning, 255

CGE. *See* Center for Gifted Education (CGE)

Choice. *See* Freedom of choice

Civics curriculum, 399, 400–401

Cognitive development theory (Piaget), 87, 134, 328–330, 335–336

Cognitive Taxonomy (Bloom)

advantages and disadvantages of, 126–127

analysis level in, 88, 91, 100, 107

application level in, 88, 91, 99, 106–107

assumptions underlying, 84–86

complementary models for, 62, 115, 121, 156, 273, 317, 368, 463–465

comprehension level in, 87–88, 90, 99, 105

conclusion on, 128

content modifications, 112, 115–117

development of, 121–123, 449, 459

effectiveness of, with gifted, 125

effectiveness of, with nongifted, 123–125

elements/parts of, 86–93, 98–101, 104–109

evaluation level in, 89, 93, 101, 108

examples of thinking levels in, 99–101

giftedness assumptions underlying, 86

goals of, 463–465

knowledge level in, 87, 90, 99, 105, 110–112

learning assumptions underlying, 84–85

learning environment modifications, 120–121

modifications of basic curriculum, 109–112, 459, 463–465

modifications of model, 114–121

overview of, 83–84

process modifications, 117, 117–119

product modifications, 120

purpose of, 449, 459

and real-life problem situations, 105–108

research on effectiveness of, 123–125

resources on, 128

summary of student and teacher activities and roles, 90–93, 105–108

synthesis level in, 88–89, 92, 100, 107

teaching assumptions underlying, 85–86

worksheets for assessment of, 14–19, 21–25, 452–456

Collaborative learning. *See* Cooperative learning; Group Investigations model

College involvement, in Autonomous Learner Model (ALM), 38–39, 56–57

Commitment, in Affective Taxonomy (Krathwohl), 95

Commonwealth Accountability Testing System (CATS), 190

Community connections

Autonomous Learner Model (ALM), 42–43, 59

Prism of Learning, 443–444

Complexity

Affective Taxonomy (Krathwohl), 115–116

Basic Structure of a Discipline (BSD), 156

Cognitive Taxonomy (Bloom), 112, 115–116

of curricula for gifted students, 4, 10

Hilda Taba Teaching Strategies, 363

Teaching Strategies for Thinking and Feeling (Williams model), 429

Comprehension, in Cognitive Taxonomy (Bloom), 87–88, 90, 99, 105

Comprehensive Approach to Teaching Thinking (Schiever), 372

Comprehensiveness of teaching–learning models, 12–13, 21–25, 451–457

Computer technology, in Autonomous Learner Model (ALM), 38, 56

Concept Development strategy (Hilda Taba Teaching Strategies), 336–339, 359, 362–363, 368, 369

Conceptualization of value, in Affective Taxonomy (Krathwohl), 95

Concrete operational stage, 134

Content modifications

Affective Taxonomy (Krathwohl), 115–117

Autonomous Learner Model (ALM), 51, 62

Basic Structure of a Discipline (BSD), 139–141, 147–148, 152

Cognitive Taxonomy (Bloom), 112, 115–117
Creative Problem Solving (CPS), 207,
  217–218
  in curricula for gifted students, 4
  DISCOVER Curriculum Model, 181, 185
  Discussions of Moral Dilemmas (DMD), 417
  Enrichment Triad Model (ETM), 267, 282
  Group Investigations model, 300
  Hilda Taba Teaching Strategies, 356–359
  Problem Based Learning (PBL), 241, 249
  Schoolwide Enrichment Model (SEM),
    267–268, 282
  Teaching Strategies for Thinking and Feeling
    (Williams model), 430
  Thinking Actively in a Social Context
    (TASC), 381–382, 398–401
Controlled or selective attention, in Affective
  Taxonomy (Krathwohl), 94
Convergent thinking, in Creative Problem
  Solving (CPS), 199, 201, 202
Cooperative learning, 293–294, 323. See also
  Group Investigations model
CPS. See Creative Problem Solving (CPS)
Creative Problem Solving (CPS)
  advantages and disadvantages of, 226–228
  assumptions underlying, 197–198
  complementary models for, 62, 219, 273, 284,
    317, 423, 469, 476–478
  conclusion on, 228
  content modifications, 207, 217–218
  definition of creativity, 196
  development of, 221
  effectiveness of, with gifted, 225–226
  effectiveness of, with nongifted, 221–225
  elements/parts of, 198–206
  examples of teaching activities in, 210–216
  giftedness assumptions underlying, 198
  goals of, 476–478
  learning assumptions underlying, 197
  learning environment modifications,
    209–210, 220
  modifications of basic curriculum, 206–216,
    469, 476–478
  modifications of model, 216–220
  overview of, 195–196
  process modifications, 207–208, 218–220
  product modifications, 208–209
  research on effectiveness of, 221–226
  resources on, 229
  steps in creative problem solving process,
    199, 200–202
  summary of student and teacher activities
    and roles, 214–216
  teaching assumptions underlying, 197–198
  worksheets for assessment of, 14–19, 21–25,
    452–456
Creative Studies Project, 222–223
Creativity
  assessment of, 169–170
  in Autonomous Learner Model (ALM), 34, 52
  definition of, 196, 264–265
  giftedness and, 264–265
  intelligence and, 225–226
  in Prism of Learning, 436
  steps in creative problem solving process,
    199, 200–202
Criteria rating grid, 212, 213
Cultural activities
  Autonomous Learner Model (ALM), 41–42, 59
  DISCOVER Curriculum Model, 180
Cultural heritage, DISCOVER Curriculum
  Model, 180–181
Curiosity, in Teaching Strategies for Thinking
  and Feeling (Williams model), 428–429
Curriculum development. See also specific
  teaching-learning models
  abstractness and, 4
  acceptance versus judgment and, 9
  complexity and, 4, 10
  comprehensiveness of teaching–learning
    models and, 12–13, 21–25, 451–457
  content modifications in, 4
  discovery and, 6
  evidence of reasoning and, 6
  flexibility versus rigidity and, 10
  freedom of choice and, 7
  group interaction and, 7
  high mobility and, 10–11
  higher levels of thinking and, 6
  independence and, 9
  integrated approaches for, 505–508
  learner-centered approach and, 9
  learning environment modifications in, 8–9
  multifaceted process of, 450–451
  open-endedness and, 6, 9
  organization for learning value, 5
  pacing and, 7–9
  process modifications in, 5–6
  product modifications in, 7–8
  qualitative differences in, 3–4
  study of methods and, 5–6
  study of people and, 5

varied groupings and, 10
variety and, 5, 7–9
worksheets on, 151, 360

Demonstrating preference for value, in Affective Taxonomy (Krathwohl), 95
Different Ways of Knowing, 190
DISCOVER Assessment
administration of, 170–171, 192
debriefing after, 171–172
disadvantages of, 192
scoring of, 172–173
teachers and, 193
DISCOVER Curriculum Model
active, hands-on learning in, 178
advantages and disadvantages of, 191–193
arts integrated into, 180, 189, 192
assumptions underlying, 173–176
complementary models for, 62, 156, 362, 371, 440, 473–475
conclusion on, 193–194
content modifications, 181, 185
cultures and languages of students integrated into, 180–181
development of, 188
DISCOVER Assessment, 170–173, 192, 193
DISCOVER Projects, 165–167, 188, 189–191
elements/parts of, 176–181
giftedness assumptions underlying, 175–176
goals of, 473–475
group activities and choice in, 177–178
interdisciplinary themes in, 179–180
learning assumptions underlying, 174–175
learning environment modifications, 187
modifications of basic curriculum, 181, 185–187, 469, 473–475
modifications of model, 187–188
multiple intelligence and, 166, 177, 178
overview of, 165–166, 173
problem solving and, 166–169, 176
process modifications, 185–186
product modifications, 186–187
research on creativity assessment and, 169–170
research on effectiveness of, 189–191
resources on, 194
summary of student and teacher activities and roles, 182–184
teaching assumptions underlying, 175
worksheets for assessment of, 14–19, 21–25, 452–456

Discovery learning. *See also* DISCOVER Curriculum Model
Affective Taxonomy (Krathwohl), 117–118
Basic Structure of a Discipline (BSD), 140–143
Cognitive Taxonomy (Bloom), 117–118
Creative Problem Solving (CPS), 219
and curricula for gifted students, 6
Enrichment Triad Model (ETM), 283
Schoolwide Enrichment Model (SEM), 283
Teaching Strategies for Thinking and Feeling (Williams model), 430–431
Discussions of Moral Dilemmas (DMD)
advantages and disadvantages of, 421–423
assumptions underlying, 410–412
complementary models for, 412, 423, 497–499
conclusion on, 423
content modifications, 417
development of, 419–420
effectiveness of, with gifted, 421
effectiveness of, with nongifted, 420–421
elements/parts of, 412–416
giftedness assumptions underlying, 411–412
goals of, 497–499
learning assumptions underlying, 410–411
learning environment modifications, 418–419
modifications of basic curriculum, 416–419, 496, 497–499
overview of, 409–410, 445
process modifications, 417–418
product modifications, 418
research on effectiveness of, 420–421
resources on, 446
teaching assumptions underlying, 411
worksheets for assessment of, 14–19, 21–25, 452–456
Divergent thinking, in Creative Problem Solving (CPS), 199, 201, 202
DMD. *See* Discussions of Moral Dilemmas (DMD)

Emotions. *See* Affective Taxonomy (Krathwohl); Teaching Strategies for Thinking and Feeling (Williams model)
Enrichment dimension (ALM), 33, 40–44, 50, 58–60, 78–81
Enrichment Triad Model (ETM)
advantages and disadvantages of, 288–290
assumptions underlying, 260–265

complementary models for, 152, 155, 156, 273, 283, 284, 371, 402, 479, 483–485
conclusion on, 290–291
content modifications, 267, 282
development of, 285
elements/parts of, 265–266
giftedness assumptions underlying, 262–265
goals of, 483–485
implementation of, 272–278
interest centers in, 272–273
Interest-A-Lyzer and, 272
learning assumptions underlying, 260–262
learning environment modifications, 270–271
modifications of basic curriculum, 267–271, 479, 483–485
modifications of model, 278, 282–285
overview of, 257–259
process modifications, 268–269, 282–284
product modifications, 269–270
program objectives of, 258–259
research on effectiveness of, 286–287
resource persons or guest speakers in, 272–273
resources on, 291–292
summary of student and teacher activities and roles, 276–281
teaching assumptions underlying, 260–262
Type I Enrichment Activities, 272–273, 276–277
Type II Enrichment Activities, 273–274, 277–278
Type III Enrichment Activities, 274–276, 278
visitations or field trips in, 272–273
worksheets for assessment of, 14–19, 21–25, 452–456
ETM. *See* Enrichment Triad Model (ETM)
Evaluation. *See also* Assessment
Autonomous Learner Model (ALM), 70
Cognitive Taxonomy (Bloom), 89, 93, 101, 108
Group Investigations model, 308–309
Prism of Learning, 441–442, 444
Program Evaluation and Review Technique (PERT), 221
Evaluation matrix, 205–206
Exploration, in Autonomous Learner Model (ALM), 40–41, 58
Extrapolation, in Cognitive Taxonomy (Bloom), 88

Facilitators, for Problem Based Learning (PBL), 234–235, 247, 248–249
Field trips, in Enrichment Triad Model (ETM), 272–273
Flexi-Think Program (TASC), 388
Flexibility
Basic Structure of a Discipline (BSD), 155
in curricula for gifted students, 10
of teaching–learning models, 13
FPS. *See* Future Problem Solving (FPS) program
Freedom of choice
Affective Taxonomy (Krathwohl), 118–119
Cognitive Taxonomy (Bloom), 118–119
Creative Problem Solving (CPS), 207–208
and curricula for gifted students, 7
DISCOVER Curriculum Model, 177–178
Enrichment Triad Model (ETM), 268
Hilda Taba Teaching Strategies, 359, 361
Future Problem Solving (FPS) program, 217, 226, 229

Gallagher, S. A. *See* Problem Based Learning (PBL)
Game development, 396–398
Giftedness
above average ability and, 263–264
Affective Taxonomy (Krathwohl), 86
Autonomous Learner Model (ALM), 31–32, 34
Basic Structure of a Discipline (BSD), 137–138
Cognitive Taxonomy (Bloom), 86
Creative Problem Solving (CPS), 198
creativity and, 264–265
definition and types of, 258, 260
DISCOVER Curriculum Model, 175–176
Discussions of Moral Dilemmas (DMD), 411–412
Enrichment Triad Model (ETM), 258, 262–265
Group Investigations model, 296
Hilda Taba Teaching Strategies, 334–336
Problem Based Learning (PBL), 235–236
Schoolwide Enrichment Model (SEM), 263–265
task commitment and, 264
Thinking Actively in a Social Context (TASC), 378–379
Group interaction
Affective Taxonomy (Krathwohl), 119
Autonomous Learner Model (ALM), 34–35, 52–53

Basic Structure of a Discipline (BSD), 153
Cognitive Taxonomy (Bloom), 119
Creative Problem Solving (CPS), 208, 220
in curricula for gifted students, 7
DISCOVER Curriculum Model, 177–178
Discussions of Moral Dilemmas (DMD), 417
Enrichment Triad Model (ETM), 283–284
Schoolwide Enrichment Model (SEM), 283–284
Group Investigations model
advantages and disadvantages of, 322–324
assumptions underlying, 294–296
carrying out the investigation in, 305
complementary models for, 153, 155, 156, 317, 359, 371, 486, 487–489
conclusion on, 324
content modifications, 300
development of, 293, 317–318
effectiveness of, with gifted, 320–322
effectiveness of, with nongifted, 319–320
elements/parts of, 297–299
evaluation in, 308–309
example of interdisciplinary study in elementary classroom, 309, 314–315
example of interdisciplinary study in secondary classroom, 315–316
giftedness assumptions underlying, 296
goals of, 294, 487–489
identifying a topic and organizing research groups in, 301–304
implementation of, 301–316
learning assumptions underlying, 295
learning environment modifications, 301
modifications of basic curriculum, 299–301, 479, 486, 487–489
modifications of model, 316–317
multifaceted tasks in, 298
multilateral communication and active learning processes in, 298
organization of classroom into "group of groups," 297–298
overview of, 293–294
planning learning tasks in, 304–305
preparing final product in, 306
presenting final product in, 307–308
process modifications, 300
product modifications, 300
research on effectiveness of, 319–322
resources on, 325–326
summary of student and teacher activities and roles, 309–316

teacher's role in guiding and communicating with groups, 298–299
teaching assumptions underlying, 295–296
worksheets for assessment of, 14–19, 21–25, 452–456
Grouping arrangements
Basic Structure of a Discipline (BSD), 156
curricula for gifted students and, 10
Guest speakers, in Enrichment Triad Model (ETM), 272–273

High mobility. *See* Mobility
Higher levels of thinking
Creative Problem Solving (CPS), 207
curricula for gifted students and, 6
Discussions of Moral Dilemmas (DMD), 417–418
Enrichment Triad Model (ETM), 268–269, 282–283
Schoolwide Enrichment Model (SEM), 282–283
Hilda Taba Teaching Strategies
advantages and disadvantages of, 370–372
Application of Generalizations strategy, 340–342, 359, 363
assumptions underlying, 328–336
complementary models for, 34, 62, 129–130, 152–156, 219, 273, 283, 284, 317, 359, 361, 362, 368, 371, 402, 423, 490–492
Concept Development strategy, 336–339, 359, 362–363, 368, 369
conclusion on, 372
content modifications, 356–357, 359
content samples in, 356–357
development of, 364–365
effectiveness of, with gifted, 368–370
effectiveness of, with nongifted, 367–368
elements/parts of, 336–348
giftedness assumptions underlying, 334–336
goals of, 490–492
Interpretation of Data strategy, 339–340, 349–352, 358–359, 363, 368
key concepts in, 356
learning assumptions underlying, 328–331
learning environment modifications, 357–358, 363–364
main, organizing, and contributing ideas, 356
modifications of basic curriculum, 348, 356–358, 486, 490–492
modifications of model, 358–364
overview of, 327–328

process modifications, 357, 359, 361
product modifications, 357, 361–363
questioning by teachers, 332–333, 343–345
research on effectiveness of, 365–370
Resolution of Conflict strategy, 342–343, 359, 363
resources on, 373
summary of student and teacher activities and roles, 353–355
supporting behaviors in, 343–348
teaching assumptions underlying, 332–334
training for teachers, 372
Worksheet for Overall Curriculum Design, 360
worksheets for assessment of, 14–19, 21–25, 452–456
Horizontal elaboration, 335–336

Imagination, in Teaching Strategies for Thinking and Feeling (Williams model), 429
In-depth Study dimension (ALM), 33, 44, 49, 50, 61, 69–76, 78–81
In-depth Study Forms (Autonomous Learner Model), 69–76
In-depth Study Personal Evaluation form (Autonomous Learner Model), 70
In-depth Study Project Rubric form (Autonomous Learner Model), 71–76
In-depth Study Proposal form (Autonomous Learner Model), 69
Independence. *See also* Autonomous Learner Model (ALM)
    Basic Structure of a Discipline (BSD), 155
    curricula for gifted students and, 9
    Hilda Taba Teaching Strategies, 358
    Teaching Strategies for Thinking and Feeling (Williams model), 431–432
Individual Development dimension (ALM), 33, 36–40, 50, 55–57, 78–81
Information-processing models, 1
Inquiry methods
    Affective Taxonomy (Krathwohl), 117
    Cognitive Taxonomy (Bloom), 112, 117
Intelligence
    in Autonomous Learner Model (ALM), 34, 52
    creativity and, 225–226
    definition of, 166
    Guilford's Structure of Intellect (SOI) model, 223, 434
    multiple intelligence, 166, 177, 178
Interact Simulations, 164
Interdisciplinary themes, in DISCOVER Curriculum Model, 179–180
Interest centers, in Enrichment Triad Model (ETM), 272–273
Interest-A-Lyzer, 272
Interpretation, in Cognitive Taxonomy (Bloom), 87–88
Interpretation of Data strategy (Hilda Taba Teaching Strategies), 339–340, 349–352, 358–359, 363, 368
Intuition
    Basic Structure of a Discipline (BSD), 135–137, 142–143
    Prism of Learning, 436
Investigations, in Autonomous Learner Model (ALM), 41, 58–59
Iowa Test of Basic Skills (ITBS), 287
ITBS (*Iowa Test of Basic Skills*), 287

Javits Gifted and Talented Education Program, 188
Jigsaw model, 318

Kentucky Instructional Results Information System (KIRIS), 190
Kercher, Jolene K. *See* Autonomous Learner Model (ALM)
KIRIS. *See Kentucky Instructional Results Information System* (KIRIS)
Knowledge, in Cognitive Taxonomy (Bloom), 87, 90, 99, 105, 110–112
Kohlberg, Lawrence. *See* Discussions of Moral Dilemmas (DMD)
Krathwohl's Taxonomy. *See* Affective Taxonomy (Krathwohl)

Learner-centered approach
    Basic Structure of a Discipline (BSD), 154–155
    in curricula for gifted students, 9
    Teaching Strategies for Thinking and Feeling (Williams model), 431
Learning assumptions
    Affective Taxonomy (Krathwohl), 84–85
    Autonomous Learner Model (ALM), 30–31
    Basic Structure of a Discipline (BSD), 130, 134–135, 137
    Cognitive Taxonomy (Bloom), 84–85
    Creative Problem Solving (CPS), 197
    DISCOVER Curriculum Model, 174–175
    Discussions of Moral Dilemmas (DMD), 410–411

Enrichment Triad Model (ETM), 260–262
Group Investigations model, 295
Hilda Taba Teaching Strategies, 328–331
Prism of Learning, 438–439
Problem Based Learning (PBL), 233–234
Schoolwide Enrichment Model (SEM), 262
Thinking Actively in a Social Context
    (TASC), 377–378, 401–402
Learning centers, in Prism of Learning,
    440–441, 442–444
Learning environment
    Affective Taxonomy (Krathwohl), 114,
        120–121
    Autonomous Learner Model (ALM), 63
    Basic Structure of a Discipline (BSD), 144
    Cognitive Taxonomy (Bloom), 120–121
    Creative Problem Solving (CPS), 209–210,
        220
    in curricula for gifted students, 8–9
    DISCOVER Curriculum Model, 187
    Discussions of Moral Dilemmas (DMD),
        418–419
    Enrichment Triad Model (ETM), 270–271
    Group Investigations model, 301
    Hilda Taba Teaching Strategies, 357–358,
        363–364
    Prism of Learning, 439–440
    Problem Based Learning (PBL), 242–243, 250
    Schoolwide Enrichment Model (SEM), 272
    Teaching Strategies for Thinking and Feeling
        (Williams model), 431–432
    Thinking Actively in a Social Context (TASC),
        386–387
Learning skills, in Autonomous Learner Model
    (ALM), 37–38, 56

MACOS. *See Man: A Course of Study* (MACOS)
Maker, C. June. *See* DISCOVER Curriculum
    Model; Prism of Learning
Man: A Course of Study (MACOS), 129, 144,
    147, 148–150, 157–161
Medical education, 231–233, 250–251. *See also*
    Problem Based Learning (PBL)
Metacognition
    Prism of Learning, 436
    Problem Based Learning (PBL), 234–235, 247
Mobility
    Basic Structure of a Discipline (BSD), 156
    curricula for gifted students and, 10–11
    Enrichment Triad Model (ETM), 271
    Hilda Taba Teaching Strategies, 363-364

Modifications. *See* Content modifications;
    Learning environment; Process modifi-
    cations; Product modifications
Moral development, 409–410, 419–420. *See also*
    Discussions of Moral Dilemmas (DMD)
Motivation for learning, 137
Multiple intelligence, 166, 177, 178. *See also*
    DISCOVER Curriculum Model
Myers-Briggs Type Indicator, 160

National Council for the Social Studies, 164
National Council of Teachers of English, 164
National Council of Teachers of Mathematics
    (NCTM), 164, 174
National Science Teachers Association, 164
NCTM. *See* National Council of Teachers of
    Mathematics (NCTM)

Observations, in Prism of Learning, 441
Odyssey of the Mind, 229
Office of Bilingual Education and Minority
    Language Affairs, 188
Open-endedness
    Affective Taxonomy (Krathwohl), 117
    Cognitive Taxonomy (Bloom), 117
    Creative Problem Solving (CPS), 207
    in curricula for gifted students, 6, 9
    Discussions of Moral Dilemmas (DMD), 417
    Enrichment Triad Model (ETM), 269, 283
    Schoolwide Enrichment Model (SEM), 283
    Teaching Strategies for Thinking and Feeling
        (Williams model), 430
Openness, in Teaching Strategies for Thinking
    and Feeling (Williams model), 423
Organization, in Affective Taxonomy (Krath-
    wohl), 95, 97, 103, 107
Organization for learning value
    Affective Taxonomy (Krathwohl), 115–116
    Basic Structure of a Discipline (BSD),
        140–141
    Cognitive Taxonomy (Bloom), 115–116
    in curricula for gifted students, 5
Organizational skills, Autonomous Learner
    Model (ALM), 39, 57
Orientation dimension (ALM), 33–36, 50,
    52–54, 78–81

Pacing
    Affective Taxonomy (Krathwohl), 119
    Basic Structure of a Discipline (BSD), 153
    Cognitive Taxonomy (Bloom), 119

in curricula for gifted students, 7–9
Enrichment Triad Model (ETM), 284
Schoolwide Enrichment Model (SEM), 284
Paired comparison analysis (PCA), 204–205
Parent connections, in Prism of Learning,
  443–444
Parnes, Sidney. *See* Creative Problem Solving
  (CPS)
PBL. *See* Problem Based Learning (PBL)
PCA. *See* Paired comparison analysis (PCA)
PCAST-PET, 174
Peller (A. W.) publisher, 373, 448
People. *See* Study of people
PEP. *See* Personal Educational Plan (PEP)
Personal Educational Plan (PEP; ALM), 37, 66
Personal models, 2
PERT charts, 221
Petter (A. W.) publisher, 373
Piaget's cognitive development theory, 87, 134,
  328–330, 335–336
Political systems curriculum, 399, 400–401
Portfolios, in Prism of Learning, 442
Practicality of teaching-learning models, 13
President's Committee of Advisors on Science
  and Technology Panel on Educational
  Technology (PCAST-PET), 174
Prism of Learning
  assessment and evaluation in, 441–442
  assessment day in, 442
  competencies and, 439
  complementary models for, 156, 423, 440,
    503–504
  conclusion on, 444–445
  elements/parts of, 436–439
  general capacities and, 436
  goals of, 503–504
  human abilities and, 437–438
  learning centers and, 440–441, 442–444
  learning environment and, 439–440
  learning processes and, 438–439
  modifications for, 496, 503–504
  observations in, 441
  overview of, 435
  parent and community connections in,
    443–444
  Problem Based Learning (PBL) and, 440
  resources on, 447–448
  student portfolios in, 442
  teachers for learning centers, 442–443
  worksheets for assessment of, 14–19, 21–25,
    452–456

Problem Based Learning (PBL)
  advantages and disadvantages of, 253–254
  assumptions underlying, 233–236
  collaborative learning in, 247–248
  complementary models for, 359, 371, 402,
    412, 423, 440, 479, 480–482
  conclusion on, 254
  content modifications, 241, 249
  content retention and, 252
  development of, 250–251
  effectiveness of, with gifted, 253
  effectiveness of, with nongifted, 252
  elements/parts of, 231–233, 236–238
  giftedness assumptions underlying, 235–236
  goals of, 232–233, 251, 480–482
  ill-structured problems and, 236–237
  implementation of, 243–249
  learning assumptions underlying, 233–234
  learning environment modifications,
    242–243, 250
  metacognitive coaching in, 234–235, 247
  modifications of basic curriculum, 238,
    241–243, 479, 480–482
  modifications of model, 249–250
  overview of, 231–233
  performance presentation in, 246
  post-problem reflection in, 246
  problem follow-up in, 245–246
  procedural coaching in, 235
  process modifications, 241–242, 250
  product modifications, 242, 250
  reflection in, 248
  research on effectiveness of, 252–253
  resources on, 255–256
  role of facilitator in, 247, 248–249
  role of problem in, 246–247
  self-directed learning and, 238
  starting new group in, 243
  starting new problem in, 244–245
  student apprenticeship and, 237–238
  substantive content and, 237
  summary of student and teacher activities
    and roles, 239–240
  teachers' challenges in, 248–249
  teaching assumptions underlying, 234–235
  worksheets for assessment of, 14–19, 21–25,
    452–456
Problem solving. *See also* Creative Problem
    Solving (CPS); DISCOVER Curriculum
    Model; Prism of Learning; Problem
    Based Learning (PBL)

characteristics of good problem, 246–247
DISCOVER Curriculum Model and,
    166–169, 177
ill-structured problems and, 236–237
steps in creative problem solving process,
    199, 200–202
Thinking Actively in a Social Context
    (TASC), 390–395, 403–405
Problem-Solving Wheel (TASC), 390–395,
    403–405
Procedural coaching, in Problem Based Learn-
    ing (PBL), 235
Process modifications
Affective Taxonomy (Krathwohl), 113–114,
    117–119
Autonomous Learner Model (ALM), 62
Basic Structure of a Discipline (BSD),
    141–143, 152–153
Cognitive Taxonomy (Bloom), 117–119
Creative Problem Solving (CPS), 207–208,
    218–220
in curricula for gifted students, 5–6
DISCOVER Curriculum Model, 185–186
Enrichment Triad Model (ETM), 268–269,
    282–284
Group Investigations model, 300
Hilda Taba Teaching Strategies, 357, 359, 361
Problem Based Learning (PBL), 241–242, 250
Schoolwide Enrichment Model (SEM), 269,
    282–284
Teaching Strategies for Thinking and Feeling
    (Williams model), 430–431
Thinking Actively in a Social Context
    (TASC), 386, 399
Process of Education, 130
Product modifications
Affective Taxonomy (Krathwohl), 114, 120
Autonomous Learner Model (ALM), 62–63
Basic Structure of a Discipline (BSD),
    143–144, 153–154
Cognitive Taxonomy (Bloom), 120
Creative Problem Solving (CPS), 208–209
in curricula for gifted students, 7–8
DISCOVER Curriculum Model, 186–187
Discussions of Moral Dilemmas (DMD), 418
Enrichment Triad Model (ETM), 269–270
Group Investigations model, 300
Hilda Taba Teaching Strategies, 357, 361–363
Problem Based Learning (PBL), 242, 250
Schoolwide Enrichment Model (SEM), 270
Teaching Strategies for Thinking and Feeling

(Williams model), 431
Thinking Actively in a Social Context
    (TASC), 386, 399
Productivity, in Autonomous Learner Model
    (ALM), 39–40, 57
Program Evaluation and Review Technique
    (PERT), 221
Prufrock Press, 373

Questions, in Hilda Taba Teaching Strategies,
    332–333, 343–345

Readiness for learning, 134–135
Reasoning
Affective Taxonomy (Krathwohl), 117
Cognitive Taxonomy (Bloom), 117
Creative Problem Solving (CPS), 219
in curricula for gifted students, 6
Discussions of Moral Dilemmas (DMD), 417
Enrichment Triad Model (ETM), 283
Prism of Learning, 436
Schoolwide Enrichment Model (SEM), 283
Receiving or attending, in Affective Taxonomy
    (Krathwohl), 89, 94, 96, 102, 105
Reflection, in Problem Based Learning (PBL),
    248
Reis, Sally M. *See* Schoolwide Enrichment
    Model (SEM)
Remembering, in Prism of Learning, 436
Renzulli, Joseph S. *See* Enrichment Triad Model
    (ETM)
Resolution of Conflict strategy (Hilda Taba
    Teaching Strategies), 342–343, 359, 363
Resource persons, in Enrichment Triad Model
    (ETM), 272–273
Resources
Affective Taxonomy (Krathwohl), 128
Autonomous Learner Model (ALM), 67–68
Basic Structure of a Discipline (BSD),
    163–164
Cognitive Taxonomy (Bloom), 128
Creative Problem Solving (CPS), 229
DISCOVER Curriculum Model, 194
Discussions of Moral Dilemmas (DMD), 446
Enrichment Triad Model (ETM), 291–292
Group Investigations model, 325–326
Hilda Taba Teaching Strategies, 373
Prism of Learning, 447–448
Problem Based Learning (PBL), 255–256
Schoolwide Enrichment Model (SEM),
    291–292

Teaching Strategies for Thinking and Feeling (Williams model), 447

Thinking Actively in a Social Context (TASC), 407–408

Responding, in Affective Taxonomy (Krathwohl), 94, 96, 102, 105–106

Risk-taking, in Teaching Strategies for Thinking and Feeling (Williams model), 429

Ross Test of Higher Cognitive Processes, 286

Rotation of learning experiences, 333–334

Satisfaction in response, in Affective Taxonomy (Krathwohl), 94

Schiever, Shirley W. *See* DISCOVER Curriculum Model

School Mathematics Study Group (SMSG), 159

School opportunities and responsibilities, in Autonomous Learner Model (ALM), 36, 54

Schoolwide Enrichment Model (SEM)

  advantages and disadvantages of, 289, 290

  assumptions underlying, 262–265

  complementary models for, 156, 371, 402, 483–485

  conclusion on, 291

  content modifications, 267–268, 282

  development of, 285–286

  elements/parts of, 266–267

  Enrichment Clusters in, 262

  giftedness assumptions underlying, 263–265

  goals of, 259–260, 483–485

  implementation of, 272–278

  learning assumptions underlying, 262

  learning environment modifications, 272

  modifications of basic curriculum, 267–272, 479, 483–485

  modifications of model, 278, 282–285

  overview of, 257, 259–260

  process modifications, 269, 282–284

  product modifications, 270

  research on effectiveness of, 287–288

  resources on, 291–292

  summary of student and teacher activities and roles, 276–281

  teaching assumptions underlying, 262

  worksheets for assessment of, 14–19, 21–25, 452–456

Science education. *See* Basic Structure of a Discipline (BSD); Woods Hole Conference

Selective or controlled attention, in Affective Taxonomy (Krathwohl), 94

Self-directed learning. *See also* Autonomous Learner Model (ALM)

  in Problem Based Learning (PBL), 238

Self/personal development, in Autonomous Learner Model (ALM), 35–36, 53

SEM. *See* Schoolwide Enrichment Model (SEM)

Seminars dimension (ALM), 33, 43–44, 45–48, 50, 60–61, 78–81

Sensing, in DISCOVER Curriculum Model, 178

Sequence and cognitive development, 329

Sequential Tests of Educational Progress (STEP), 365–366

Service. *See* Community connections

Sharan, Shlomo, and Yael. *See* Group Investigations model

SMSG. *See* School Mathematics Study Group (SMSG)

Social interaction models, 1

Social studies curriculum, 327, 364–365, 371. *See also* Hilda Taba Teaching Strategies

Social Studies Inference Test, 366

SOI. *See* Structure of Intellect (SOI) model

STAD. *See* Student Teams Academic Divisions (STAD) model

Stanford Achievement Test, 189, 190

STEP (*Sequential Tests of Educational Progress*), 365–366

Structure of disciplines. *See* Basic Structure of a Discipline (BSD)

Structure of Intellect (SOI) model, 223, 434

Student apprenticeship, in Problem Based Learning (PBL), 237–238

Student portfolios, in Prism of Learning, 442

Student Teams Academic Divisions (STAD) model, 318

Study of people

  Affective Taxonomy (Krathwohl), 116

  Basic Structure of a Discipline (BSD), 148, 152

  Cognitive Taxonomy (Bloom), 116

  in curricula for gifted students, 5

  Hilda Taba Teaching Strategies, 358–359

Synectics, 203

Synthesis, in Cognitive Taxonomy (Bloom), 88–89, 92, 100, 107

Taba Proram in Social Science, 327, 364–365, 371

Taba Teaching Strategies. *See* Hilda Taba Teaching Strategies

TASC. *See* Thinking Actively in a Social Context (TASC)

Taxonomy of Educational Objectives. *See* Affective Taxonomy (Krathwohl); Cognitive Taxonomy (Bloom)

Taylor Multiple Talent Model, 315-316

Teachers and teaching. *See also* Hilda Taba Teaching Strategies; Learning environment; Prism of Learning; Teaching Strategies for Thinking and Feeling (Williams model)
  Affective Taxonomy (Krathwohl), 85–86, 96–97, 105–108
  Autonomous Learner Model (ALM), 29–30, 52–61
  Basic Structure of a Discipline (BSD), 130, 145–146
  Cognitive Taxonomy (Bloom), 85–86, 90–93, 105–108
  Creative Problem Solving (CPS), 197–198, 214–216
  DISCOVER Assessment, 193
  DISCOVER Curriculum Model, 175
  Discussions of Moral Dilemmas (DMD), 411
  Enrichment Triad Model (ETM), 260–262, 272–281
  Group Investigations model, 295–296, 298–299, 310–313
  Hilda Taba Teaching Strategies, 332–334, 353–355
  importance of specific strategies for, 332
  learning centers and, 442–444
  Prism of Learning, 443–444
  Problem Based Learning (PBL), 234–235, 239–240, 248–249
  questioning by teachers, 332–333, 343–345
  rotating learning experiences and, 333–334
  Schoolwide Enrichment Model (SEM), 262
  selection of teaching–learning model and, 12
  Thinking Actively in a Social Context (TASC), 378, 383–385, 387–388

Teaching–learning models
  adapting and selecting models, 11–26
  appropriateness of, to situation, 12, 14–19
  assessment of, 12–26, 451–509
  assessment of situation for selecting, 11–12
  choosing models, 457–458
  combining models, 20, 26
  comprehensiveness of, 12–13, 21–25, 451–457
  conclusion on, 505, 509

  and curricula for gifted students, 3–11
  definition of, 1
  flexibility or adaptability of, 13
  integrated approaches for, 505–508
  nature of, 1–3
  practicality of, 13
  validity of, 13
  Worksheet for Assessing Models' Appropriateness, 14–19
  Worksheet for Assessment of Models' Comprehensiveness, 21–25, 452–456

Teaching Strategies for Thinking and Feeling (Williams model)
  advantages and disadvantages of, 433–434
  affective (feeling) behaviors in, 428–429
  cognitive (intellectual) behaviors in, 427–428
  complementary models for, 500–502
  conclusion on, 434–435, 445
  content modifications, 430
  curriculum dimension of, 424
  dimensions of, 424–427
  elements/parts of, 424–429
  goals of, 500–502
  learning environment modifications, 431–432
  modifications of basic curriculum, 430–433, 496, 500–502
  overview of, 423–424
  process modifications, 430–431
  product modifications, 431
  pupil behaviors and, 425, 427–429
  resources on, 447
  strategies dimension of, 424, 426–427
  worksheets for assessment of, 14–19, 21–25, 452–456

Technology, in Autonomous Learner Model (ALM), 38, 56

Thinking Actively in a Social Context (TASC)
  advantages and disadvantages of, 406–407
  assumptions underlying, 377–379
  complementary models for, 361, 371, 402, 423, 440, 493–495
  conclusion on, 407
  content modifications, 381–382, 389–401
  development of, 402–403, 449
  effectiveness of, with gifted, 405–406
  effectiveness of, with nongifted, 403–405
  elements/parts of, 379–382
  Flexi-Think Program, 388
  giftedness assumptions underlying, 378–379
  goals of, 376, 493–495

implementation of, 388–398
learning assumptions underlying, 377–378
learning environment modifications,
386–387, 401–402
modifications of basic curriculum, 381–382,
386–388, 486, 493–495
modifications of model, 398–402
overview of, 375–377
Problem-Solving Wheel, 390–395, 403–405
process modifications, 386, 399
product modifications, 386, 399
purpose of, 449
research on effectiveness of, 403–406
resources on, 407–408
summary of student and teacher activities
and roles, 383–385, 387–388
teaching assumptions underlying, 378
teaching principles and guidelines of,
375–376, 387
worksheets for assessment of, 14–19, 21–25,
452–456
Torrance Tests of Creative Thinking (TTCT),
169–170
Translation, in Cognitive Taxonomy (Bloom), 87
TTCT (*Torrance Tests of Creative Thinking*),
169–170
Tutors, for Problem Based Learning (PBL),
234–235, 247
Types I–VI problems, 167–169

UICSM. *See* University of Illinois Committee
on School Mathematics (UICSM)
University of Illinois Committee on School
Mathematics (UICSM), 158, 159

Validity of teaching-learning models, 13
Values clarification, 410
Values in a Democracy, 415–416
Values in American History, 415–416

Valuing, in Affective Taxonomy (Krathwohl),
94–97, 103, 106–107
Variety
Affective Taxonomy (Krathwohl), 116, 119
Basic Structure of a Discipline (BSD), 147,
153
Cognitive Taxonomy (Bloom), 112, 116, 119
Creative Problem Solving (CPS), 208
in curricula for gifted students, 5, 7–9
Discussions of Moral Dilemmas (DMD), 418
Enrichment Triad Model (ETM), 269
Hilda Taba Teaching Strategies, 359, 361
Visitations, in Enrichment Triad Model (ETM),
272–273

Web sites
Autonomous Learner Model (ALM), 68
Basic Structure of a Discipline (BSD), 164
DISCOVER Curriculum Model, 194
Enrichment Triad Model (ETM), 292
Group Investigations model, 326
Hilda Taba Teaching Strategies, 373
Schoolwide Enrichment Model (SEM), 292
Williams, Frank E. *See* Teaching Strategies for
Thinking and Feeling (Williams model)
Willingness to receive, in Affective Taxonomy
(Krathwohl), 94
Willingness to respond, in Affective Taxonomy
(Krathwohl), 94
Woods Hole Conference, 130, 137–138,
156–157
Worksheet for Assessing Models' Appropriate-
ness, 14–19
Worksheet for Assessment of Models' Compre-
hensiveness, 21–25, 452–456
Worksheet for Curriculum Design, 151
Worksheet for Overall Curriculum Design, 360

Zephyr Press, 373